STORMING CAESARS PALACE

STORMING CAESARS PALACE

How Black Mothers Fought Their Own War on Poverty

ANNELISE ORLECK

BEACON PRESS
BOSTON

Beacon Press
25 Beacon Street
Boston, Massachusetts 02108-2892
www.beacon.org

Beacon Press books
are published under the auspices of
the Unitarian Universalist Association of Congregations.

09 08 07 06   8 7 6 5 4 3 2 1

This book is printed on acid-free paper that meets the uncoated paper
ANSI/NISO specifications for permanence as revised in 1992.

Text design by Bob Kosturko
Composition by Wilsted & Taylor Publishing Services

Library of Congress Cataloging-in-Publication Data

Orleck, Annelise.
  Storming Caesars Palace : how black mothers fought their own war on poverty / Annelise Orleck.
     p. cm.
  Includes bibliographical references and index.
  ISBN 0-8070-5031-8 (pbk. : acid-free paper)
1. Duncan, Ruby. 2. Welfare rights movement—Nevada—Las Vegas. 3. Poor women—Nevada—
Las Vegas—Political activity. 4. Welfare recipients—Nevada—Las Vegas—Political activity.
5. Women social reformers—Nevada—Las Vegas. 6. Women in community development—
Nevada—Las Vegas. 7. Poor—Services for—Nevada—Las Vegas. I. Title.
  HV99.L37O75 2005
  362.5'09793'135—dc22   2005000652

This book is dedicated to the memory of the Operation Life women who did not live to see it completed: Aldine Weems, Mary Southern, Roma Jean Hunt, Betty Jean Clary, Dorothy Jean Poole

And to the women and men of the Operation Life coalition, who continued to work toward the ideal of a beloved interracial community long after most others had stopped trying.

CONTENTS

INTRODUCTION

Even in jaded Las Vegas, no one had ever seen anything like it. On a glorious spring Saturday in 1971, tourists gaped and gamblers dropped their chips as 1,500 protestors streamed past the equestrian statue of Julius Caesar on the Las Vegas Strip and entered the fabled Caesars Palace. Ruby Duncan, a cotton picker turned hotel maid and mother of seven, led the procession of singing and chanting welfare mothers and children. Actress Jane Fonda and civil rights leader Reverend Ralph Abernathy were at her side. "Nevada Gambles with Human Lives" their signs declared; "Nevada Starves Children." The ragtag army had come to protest Nevada's decision to throw one in three welfare families off the rolls and slash benefits for another third.

"We stopped the gambling for over an hour," Ruby Duncan recalls, still giddy thirty years later with the power of that moment. "No one had ever done anything like this before." Assisted by the National Welfare Rights Organization—which named the action Operation Nevada—Duncan, a thirty-seven-year-old with a ninth grade education, assembled a coalition of welfare mothers, Legal Services lawyers, radical priests and nuns, civil rights leaders, movie stars, and housewives in an unprecedented act of civil disobedience.

The next weekend they did it again, this time sitting down in the middle of the Strip itself. "We backed up traffic all the way to Los Angeles," Duncan boasts. The demonstrations went on for weeks. Tourism to Las Vegas was cut in half. By shutting down gambling on the world's best-known stretch of desert highway, the march cost the casino hotels and the state of Nevada untold sums of money. When a federal judge reversed the cutbacks two weeks later, slamming Nevada for running "roughshod over the constitutional rights of the poor," welfare rights advocates across the nation celebrated. America was embroiled in a pitched battle over poverty and welfare. President Richard Nixon was proposing to end the War on Poverty. California governor Ronald Reagan had declared war on welfare itself. It was the beginning of the end for the welfare state.

Operation Nevada was a success, but only for a short while. There would be more cuts and restorations in the years to come. So when the cameras and celebrities left Las Vegas, Ruby Duncan and her band of welfare mothers set their sights on a more ambitious and, they hoped, more lasting goal: upgrading life on the black Westside of Las Vegas, a Jim Crow shantytown that lacked paved streets, telephones, even indoor plumbing into the 1950s and 1960s. In

1972, the mothers of West Las Vegas formed a nonprofit community development corporation called Operation Life. Declaring "we can do it, and do it better," these welfare mothers brought the Westside its first library, medical clinic, daycare center, job training office, and senior citizen housing complex. Headquartered in an abandoned hotel, Operation Life became an anchor in a community neglected by federal, state, and city officials ever since black migrants flooded into Las Vegas to work in defense plants during World War II.

At the center of the action, any hour of the day or night, was Ruby Duncan—milk chocolate skin glistening, high-pitched voice ringing out through Operation Life's long hallways. Generating new ideas like a popcorn popper left on high, she was the engine of this poor people's movement. By turns inspiring, maddening, unflappable, and belligerent, she took no prisoners and brooked no dissent. But her style—and her vision—worked.

For nearly twenty-five years, the women of Operation Life brought fresh hope and energy to an economically devastated community languishing in the neon shadow of America's easy-money fantasy-land. Led by Duncan and assisted by an extraordinary coalition—a casino pit boss turned Legal Services lawyer, a politically savvy Franciscan priest, an oil heiress committed to fighting poverty, and a loyal cadre of activists inspired by the women's spirit and tenacity—these welfare mothers demanded a share of political power and a slice of American prosperity.

This book tells their story. It was a wild ride full of huge gambles and unexpected twists. To bring basic services to the Westside, the women of Operation Life staged eat-ins at the casinos and read-ins at "whites only" public libraries. They occupied crumbling buildings and turned them into job training centers, clinics, and daycare centers. They lobbied state and federal legislatures, and cornered agency heads to ask for money. From the mid-1960s into the 1990s, they made mob bosses, casino owners, mayors, governors, and senators profoundly uncomfortable, and remarkably responsive. Operation Life won accolades from conservatives as well as liberals—and even made a president or two sit up and take notice.

Most importantly, Ruby Duncan and the women of Operation Life dragged Nevada kicking and screaming into the twentieth century, convincing politicians to accept federal poverty programs they had long resisted: the Food Stamp Program, the Women and Infant Children Nutrition Program, and free medical screenings for poor children. And they persuaded federal officials to let them administer the programs themselves. "Why not?" asked Mary Wesley, an Operation Life cofounder and mother of eight. "This was something I really knew about: poor people and kids."

By the mid-1970s, Operation Life was one of the few poor mothers' groups in the U.S. running a federally funded medical facility. The clinic was managed so effectively that Caspar Weinberger—President Ford's hard-nosed Secretary of Health, Education and Welfare, and later Reagan's defense chief—held it up as a national model. Operation Life was one of the first women-run community development corporations and the first group of poor women to run a Women and Infant Children (WIC) nutrition program.

Duncan and the Operation Life women had hit on a dynamic, common-sense formula: a management system simple enough for marginally educated women to administer, but efficient enough to handle millions in federal funds with astonishing accuracy. Its WIC office was accurate down to pennies. Hiring poor women to administer their programs not only provided meaningful jobs for impoverished mothers but also vastly improved the quality of services in their community, because these women knew how to reach and serve the people most in need. Driving a beat-up old station wagon with room for ten, Operation Life activists—welfare mothers all—scoured the Westside, picking up mothers and children who'd never had medical care and driving them to the clinic. In that way, Operation Life's clinic reached the highest percentage of eligible children of any federally funded disease-screening clinic in the country.

Through the 1970s, Ruby Duncan's star continued to rise. She advised President Jimmy Carter on welfare and jobs programs, consulted with Senator Ted Kennedy on healthcare reform, and shaped U.S. Women's Bureau initiatives for bringing women into male-dominated trades—including construction, plumbing, and highway repair. By the end of the Carter years, Duncan and the women of Operation Life were poster women for a new model of welfare reform—from the bottom up.

But Operation Life, while remarkable, was not anomalous. It is one of scores of untold stories about America's antipoverty crusade of the 1960s and 1970s. The War on Poverty fell out of favor with the media and politicians almost as soon as it began. For many Americans, a single, crude, apocryphal image—the profligate, promiscuous, Cadillac-driving welfare queen—is all that remains in our collective memory of federal efforts to fight poverty. That image has fueled backlash politics from Lyndon Johnson's day to the present. One of the most sweeping federal initiatives of the twentieth century has largely fallen out of public discourse except as a cautionary tale, dredged up each election season to remind us all that "big government" doesn't work. The fortieth anniversary of President Johnson's declaration of "unconditional war on poverty"—January 8, 2004—passed without a ripple of remembrance.

Lost in that amnesia is any sense of what worked, and what didn't, in the complex array of antipoverty programs created by the 1964 Economic Opportunity Act. Much of what has been written about the War on Poverty has focused on Washington, D.C., and the failures of what critics see as top-down social engineering. Certainly, huge problems dogged the mid-1960s antipoverty campaigns, not the least of which was the hemorrhage of funds, lives, and human spirit caused by the Vietnam War. The War on Poverty, Martin Luther King Jr. famously said, was shot down on the battlefields of Vietnam.

Johnson's vision had plenty of limitations: paltry resources, condescension toward the poor, and an obsession with "reclaiming" poor young men so single-minded that most federal poverty planners barely saw the problems of poor women at all. Still, Johnson's call to "end poverty in our time" galvanized a generation. Poor women and men registered to vote, ran for office, and demanded a voice in shaping policies on public housing, schools, and welfare. Though Congress passed a raft of new antipoverty bills in the 1960s and 1970s, federal administrators were loath to release funds, and state governments were slow to adopt the new programs. Every major War on Poverty initiative, from job training to school lunches and pediatric medical screening, sat stalled in Washington for years, until poor people protested and sued. Federal antipoverty funds also nurtured vital new community institutions that brought healthcare, childcare, housing, and new businesses into economically deprived areas across the country.[1]

As the lives of the women portrayed in this book illustrate, the War on Poverty—like all government aid—was a double-edged sword. From the first federal relief efforts, during the 1930s, to the last grant Operation Life received from President George H. W. Bush, poor mothers found that there were always strings attached. Accepting cash relief, food stamps, and program funds from government agencies inevitably meant accepting government supervision. For welfare mothers, that supervision came in the form of caseworkers who asked prying and humiliating questions, searched their homes and belongings in midnight raids, and sometimes threatened to take away their children. For community groups such as Operation Life, federal supervision meant giving up the right to decide whom they hired. All too often, that meant that they could not give paying jobs to the women who had created Operation Life, hoping to get themselves off welfare.[2]

The battle to keep funding for such community groups during the Reagan and Bush years—and the ultimate demise of such groups—illustrates how unfairly the odds are stacked against poor women who try to break out of the roles assigned to them in this culture. Some of Operation Life's fiercest critics came of age during the New Deal and worked for War on Poverty programs. They saw themselves as stewards, rather than enemies, of the welfare state. But 1960s-era liberals had the same blind spot that conservatives did: they couldn't see women. The Johnson administration's plan to lift Americans out of poverty by giving jobs to poor men could not succeed when most of the nation's poor were single mothers and their children.

That myopia would cripple legislative initiatives and grass-roots organizations, particularly those like Operation Life that wanted job training for women and support for poor women's entrepreneurship. By the mid-1970s, Ruby Duncan and other women activists would force legislators to address those issues in federal discussions about alleviating poverty. As a result, the Carter administration's initiatives in job training and creation were vastly more inclusive of poor women than the antipoverty programs that preceded them. These gains were, however, short-lived. When Ronald Reagan swept into office in 1980 on a groundswell of resentment toward "big government" and "welfare queens," many of those initiatives were abandoned. The model of Operation Life, too, was lost—until now.

Storming Caesars Palace is told, in large part, from the point of view of the welfare mothers who created Operation Life: Ruby Duncan, Mary Wesley, Alversa Beals, Essie Henderson, Emma Stampley, and Rosie Seals. On one level, this book is, quite simply, their story: the experiences of poor black women who moved from Louisiana, Arkansas, Texas, and Mississippi to Las Vegas in the 1950s and 1960s in search of a better life for their children. This book traces their early years in cotton country and their migration to Las Vegas as part of the great exodus that took millions from the South in the 1950s and 1960s. It follows the women through their years in the Hotel and Culinary Workers Union when Las Vegas was still a Jim Crow town, their slide onto welfare, their battles for welfare rights, and the two decades during which they ran a revolutionary experiment in welfare reform.

But the canvas of this story is broader than the Silver State and more complex than individual lives. *Storming Caesars Palace* is a chronicle of antipoverty policy in the U.S. and of poor people's political movements. The lives of Operation Life women span the era of federal aid to poor families—from the passage of the Social Security Act in 1935 to the abolition of permanent aid to poor mothers under Bill Clinton in 1996. Highlighting the voices and experiences of poor mothers during these six decades, this book draws links between larger historical forces—economic shifts, national political debates, migration, urbanization—and the lived experience of poverty. Treating a despised population as the subjects of serious political biography, I hope to shed new light on government efforts to eradicate poverty in the United States.[3]

Lyndon Johnson's War on Poverty became Ronald Reagan's war on the poor. Bill Clinton ended welfare as we knew it. George W. Bush has, behind the scenes of the war on terrorism, sought to finish the job begun by his predecessors: shredding the social safety net first put into place under Franklin Roosevelt seventy years ago. With all the discussion and debate about how to improve this nation's system of providing aid to the poor, few humane, creative, or genuinely new ideas have surfaced in decades. Instead, each Congress seems determined to prove that it can be tougher on welfare than its predecessors.

To that end, Congress began the twenty-first century as it spent much of the twentieth, debating punitive welfare legislation that promoted heterosexual marriage but not relief for victims of domestic violence, that required poor mothers to work but did not allow them to go back to school, that set a five-year lifetime limit on public assistance but did not provide real job training or quality childcare. As the rhetoric condemning poor mothers heats up yet again, it is worth taking a closer look at what the women of West Las Vegas did. They offer us an alternative model for fighting poverty that affirms and supports poor families instead of demeaning and humiliating them. The Operation Life model worked then, and it could work now, but only if we make the leap of listening to the real experts on poverty: poor mothers.

CHAPTER 1

FROM THE COTTON FIELDS TO THE DESERT SANDS: LIVING AND LEAVING THE DELTA LIFE

Q: "Tell me where you come from and why you left."
A: "Honey, you don't want to hear that because, oh God, it'll make you cry."

—Emma Stampley, Las Vegas

A sweet, slow-moving stream runs through the center of Tallulah, Louisiana. On its eastern bank stands the most pleasant of neighborhoods, a span of brick houses with neat green lawns, vibrant flowerbeds, and sturdy, wide-spreading shade trees. In the hours just after dawn, a few tanned, sleek joggers run alongside the water. As the town awakens, well-dressed citizens step from the doors of well-kept houses, start their car engines, and glide into the workday. Most, but not all, are white. Many drive or ride the bus across the nearby Mississippi River to Vicksburg, Mississippi, where Civil War tourism has been swept aside by a flood of gamblers bound for one of the neon-trimmed steamboat casinos docked along the famous waterway.

Facing east, toward Mississippi, Tallulah seems a very livable town. It is not immediately obvious why—for more than half a century—most of the town's black residents have chosen, as soon as they come of age, to leave Tallulah for the promise of a better life in the desert metropolis of Las Vegas, Nevada. Turn around and face west, however, and the mass migration begins to make sense. Main Street echoes so many other Southern small-town centers: a fading commercial strip with a handful of businesses—a pharmacy, a furniture store—withering in the hot sun among the boarded-up storefronts. There are no diners or restaurants downtown, no pedestrian bustle, few signs of a living town except for a battered Popeye's Chicken at one end and a newer McDonald's at the other.

East of Main Street, one crosses the inevitable railroad tracks separating the black side of town from the white. A few middle-class African Americans live on the shady side of town. But there are no whites west of the tracks. "The black curtain," Tallulan Joanne Klein calls it, the invisible but still palpable dividing line now marking class as well as race distinctions in this town. Today, more than 140 years after the end of slavery, elderly black men and women tend tidy little gardens in a neighborhood that hovers in time between the plantation past and the postindustrial present. On small side streets, set back from more substantial frame houses, stand rows of shotgun houses, some of which were moved from nearby plantations. Many Louisiana Delta sharecroppers bought their homes from the field foremen who turned them off their land in the 1950s. Planters were willing to sell their flimsy outbuildings for little, since they would otherwise have knocked them down. Sharecroppers hauled the houses into town.[1]

Tallulah resembles scores of other Delta towns—so much so that it might be the unnamed "Southerntown" of John Dollard's classic 1937 study, *Caste and Class in a Southern Town*. It's all there: the cheerful white residential quarter with a handful of middle-class black residents, the swampy stream, the quiet main street, the railroad tracks, the black side of town, the shotgun houses, the small morning tide of African American women crossing the tracks to work in the homes of more prosperous white families. All that is missing is the nightlife, the bustle, the crowded streets full of "walking, loitering and laughing" that Dollard found on the black side of "Southerntown." In the seventy years since the Yale psychologist came to study the Delta, this region has been transformed by three historic changes: the dissolution of the plantation system, the end of Jim Crow segregation, and a mass migration North and West that saw more than five million African Americans leave the South between 1940 and 1970. No town was hit harder or changed more by these epochal forces than Tallulah.[2]

Fifty years ago, there were lumber mills in Tallulah where strong men and women could earn a better living than the cotton fields provided. Blues clubs brought the likes of B. B. King and Muddy Waters to millhands with money to spend and carloads of town-hungry cotton-field workers anxious for a Saturday night diversion. That was before mass migration emptied what had been one of the most lively black business districts in the Delta. By the end of the twentieth century, the black side of Tallulah had a devastated feel, the shells of once-jumping businesses sore reminders of a livelier time. The old clubs—the Flamingo, the Sportsmen's Club—stood dark and boarded shut. The Club 44 was gone without a trace, the rough and wild men who made up its clientele now just a piece of blues history. So too the Hotel Watson, the grocery and dry goods stores, and just about every other black business in Tallulah.

From the late 1940s, when the plantations began to disappear and the lumber mills shut down, until the late 1980s, when catfish farming and casino gambling came to the Delta, there were precious few opportunities for young black men and women in Tallulah. And so, for decades, they have followed the path that generations of black Tallulans had blazed before them—seeking their fortunes in the hotels, defense plants, and nuclear test sites of the Nevada desert. It is a migration that continues to this day.

The women whose story this book tells were the poorest of the poor from their earliest days— even by the standards of African America. Their parents and grandparents were those left behind after the first wave of black migration north during and after World War I. They were the minority still picking cotton long after other African Americans had left farm life behind for industrial or service work in New York, Detroit, Chicago, Cleveland, and Pittsburgh. The sudden flood of defense jobs created during World War II, the dissolution of the sharecropping system after the war when mechanical cotton pickers came in, and a no-longer-repressible fury at the cruelties of Delta life moved millions of African Americans to leave the South during the 1940s, 1950s, and 1960s. The childhood years of Ruby Duncan, Alversa Beals, Mary Wesley, and thousands of others who left cotton country for the desert after World War II were shaped by an anachronistic cotton culture that had long since ceased to be viable but that, even in its death throes, continued to structure the social and economic relations of an entire region.

Other parts of the Delta sent their native sons and daughters to Las Vegas, as well. Called by some "the most Southern place on earth," the Delta region of Mississippi sits just across the river from Tallulah, and it too launched an emigration to the desert. Most of the Mississippians who made their way to Las Vegas were—like their Louisiana counterparts—sharecroppers struggling from year to year to eke out a subsistence. But there were also independent farmers, proud to be among the few Delta blacks who owned their own land.

To the northwest, the Arkansas lumber and railroad town of Fordyce also sent carload after carload of its black residents to Las Vegas. The Fordyce-Las Vegas migration was similar in size to the Tallulah exodus, although lumber and railroad work generated a somewhat more economically independent and better-educated black population than was found in plantation counties along the Mississippi. Fordyce migrants would help to create a black middle class in Las Vegas.

Ever since the Depression, Delta towns in all three states have sent a steady stream of hopeful migrants to the Nevada desert. Smaller numbers of black migrants came from other parts of cotton country—Alabama, Oklahoma, and Texas. All across the South, they lined up at bus stations: men carrying little more than a hat and a change of clothing; women juggling babies, baskets of food, and a few precious family possessions. Some drove with friends. Others rode with local entrepreneurs who traveled back and forth between the Delta and Las Vegas in battered station wagons. The route from cotton country to Nevada took migrants across the still Jim Crow South, where it was a tricky business for African Americans to find lodging and food. Seasoned guides could ease the passage, especially for women. Some parents preferred to send their daughters with these drivers rather than worry about them traveling alone across the South on a bus or train.

Almost all followed family members who wrote glowingly of the neon-lit wonders of Las Vegas. "You can find money in the streets outside of these casinos," one former Deltan wrote to his daughter, prompting her to pull up stakes and head west. "I'm still looking for that money," Alversa Beals says quietly, half a century later.[3]

The women who left Tallulah and other Delta towns for Las Vegas took a world with them. The poverty and violence of cotton country, their troubled but close-knit families, their religious convictions—even their food and music—would shape the women's adult lives and the antipoverty movement they would go on to forge. A stream of cotton-field memories bubbled just under the red clay hardpan of the desert city they would come to call home. Sometimes, says Alversa Beals, her children would ask her to tell them about the way she lived back in Tallulah. "Did it feel like slavery?" they would ask. "No it didn't feel like slavery," she would answer softly. "It was slavery."

COTTON-FIELD GIRLHOODS

On a stiflingly hot day in August 1945—while millions of other Americans were celebrating the end of World War II—thirteen-year-old Ruby Phillips (now Duncan) dropped her heavy cotton sack and sank to the ground. She could not pick one more piece of cotton. Her thin dress soaked through with sweat, the exhausted girl lay down on the black earth between the endless rows of cotton and fell asleep. Deeply religious, Ruby imagined that God was calling her to testify. "I had this dream that one day I would be somewhere in this world talking to literally thousands of people and explaining the world the way I thought it should be," Duncan recalls. When she awoke that afternoon, she looked around nervously to make sure that no one had caught her napping. She then gathered up her long, white cotton-picking sack and resumed her daily labor.[4]

Ruby Phillips's life on the Ivory Plantation near Tallulah, Louisiana, more closely resembled that of her enslaved great-grandmother than the lives of most thirteen-year-old American girls in 1945. Just eight when she began working full time, the little girl learned to chop and pick cotton, hoe and plant corn. Her workday lasted from sunup to sundown, her work year from mid-April through mid-December. Only in the remaining four months was she allowed to attend school. By the time she was a teenager, Ruby could pick a hundred pounds of cotton a day. But family members and plantation owners considered that harvest far too little. Other Tallulah-area children—such as Rosie Seals and Alversa Beals, women Ruby would later meet in Las Vegas—could pick well over two hundred to three hundred pounds of cotton in a day.

Duncan's parents, like so many Delta sharecroppers, both died young—"they say from overwork," she says. Her mother, Ida Crockett, a tiny, auburn-haired, freckled woman who smoked a corncob pipe as she stirred her pots, looked like an old woman by the time she died at thirty. Ruby's father, Joe Phillips, died soon afterwards. Ruby never knew them. "I guess I was too young to even know what a mother was," she says. "At that age, you really don't know who to love, or who loved you. But my relatives loved me the best way they could."[5]

Ruby was not yet three when she was taken in by her mother's father and sister. For the next four years, she was passed around among the members of her extended family. All but one of her three sisters and one brother died in their youth from accidents or illness. Ruby keenly felt the loneliness of an orphan, and feared that "the old folks" thought her a burden and just another mouth to feed. Her Aunt Mamie Lynn was loving, Duncan says, but her grandfather and uncle chastised her for not working hard enough. With families living on the barest subsistence, there was intense pressure on children to contribute economically—or face harsh punishment.

"I was always getting a beating because I couldn't pick enough cotton," Duncan recalls. "It made me mad. It still makes me mad." Ruby would never forget the harsh feel of raw cotton on the tender skin of her young fingers, how it tore and roughened them, and how her fingers bled. Telling stories of her childhood, more than half a century later, she rubs her thumb unconsciously across her fingertips, still feeling the hated prickling cotton.

The Ivory Plantation, five miles south of Tallulah, epitomized a strange twentieth-century mix: part agribusiness, part Old South mythology. Owned by John Oliver of Shreveport, the Ivory Plantation was home to more than fifty black sharecropping families—several hundred people in all. Tenants and

Ruby Phillips at seventeen at the Tallulah County Fair, 1949. This
was the first photograph ever taken of her, since no sharecropper
on the Ivory Plantation had a camera. (Courtesy of Ruby Duncan)

wage laborers lived alongside the vast white-tipped cotton fields in a collection
of shotgun houses and log cabins. "It kind of looked like a town," says Duncan's friend, Angie Coleman. "But it wasn't. It was a plantation." Growing up,
Ruby and Angie learned a language of class and race that had changed little
since the days of slavery. The field supervisor was called "the boss man." The
Olivers' plantation home, set back from the road by a wide lawn and shaded
by live oak trees, was "the big house." The owner was "Mr. Johnny." His son
was "Little Mr. Johnny."[6]

But Mr. Johnny was rarely at the Ivory Plantation. By the 1940s, most of
the plantations of the Louisiana Delta were run by absentee landlords who
spent the bulk of their time in fine city homes in Baton Rouge, Shreveport, or

New Orleans. In Mississippi, Arkansas, and Texas, too, the planter lifestyle had largely given way to the managerial. Face-to-face interactions between land-lord and tenant became less frequent, as old-fashioned planter paternalism was replaced by a "corporate cotton culture" in which tenants were seen as em-ployees. Daily management of the farm and its workers was left to a straw boss or overseer, who supervised seeding, hoeing, and picking of cotton as well as weighing the crop both for tenant farm families and day laborers. Yet scientific methods and systems of rational calculation counted for little when the time came to weigh and pay for a crop. Crop settlements were still heavily rigged against tenants.[7]

In these last years of the plantation system, owners would return to the farm to check in once or twice a month, bringing their wives and children for a few days of revisited antebellum splendor. John Oliver and his family prided themselves on knowing their tenants personally. But just beneath that pater-nalistic familiarity was hard financial calculation. "Old Man Oliver was good to his workers," Angie Coleman recalls. "He'd go someplace where they had oil, and it was real good oil, and he'd bring some back and everybody would bring a bucket." The pigs would be slaughtered then, and the sharecroppers' wives were invited to take home the "chitlins"—fried hog intestines—for their families. This act of benevolence was performed with ritualistic fanfare, but it soon became clear that the owners gave no gifts. "They had a blue book," Coleman says. "They'd write everything in the book. And when the men got their paychecks at the end of the year, it *all* came right out of what they owed us." Duncan would never forget the annual chitlins fest. She flashed back to it many years later, while waiting in the hot sun for county officials in Las Vegas to distribute surplus food to poor families. *Handouts always come at a price,* she concluded grimly.

Aside from the occasional gathering, Duncan says, interactions with whites were rare. "The only time I saw white people was when they was rid-ing up and down on horses in the cotton patch, screaming at us while we was chopping cotton," she says. White planters and politicians in the cotton-growing South had long complained about "the evil of female loaferism" among black workers. Since Emancipation, when black women withdrew from the fields to stay home with their children, editorials in Southern news-papers chastised them for "playing the lady" and accused them of making their husbands "support them in idleness." This notion—that black women resis-ted hard work—remained central to the ideology of the white South. In the early decades of the twentieth century, powerful Southern Democratic congressmen and senators brought that notion to Washington, D.C., where it shaped federal labor and welfare policies. During the Depression, when Southern Democrats had seniority in both houses, they made sure that New Deal relief policies did not infringe on the labor practices of Southern planters. Federal assistance to the poor was a racially segregated system from the beginning.[8]

Federal Aid to Dependent Children (ADC), popularly known as welfare, was created in 1935 to enable mothers without husbands to stay home with their young children. Throughout the U.S., the primary beneficiaries were white widows and orphans. In the South, there was particular resistance to giving ADC benefits to black women, who were expected to work—picking cotton, doing laundry, or cleaning the homes of white people. Some Southern states even made it illegal for them to refuse these jobs. And when black women retired or were laid off, they did not receive Social Security or unemployment benefits, because those new federal programs excluded agricultural and domestic workers. Few had any recourse other than public assistance.[9]

In work relief programs such as the Works Progress Administration (WPA), Southern officials gave black women lower salaries and more physically demanding jobs than white women, and refused to hire them at all during planting and picking seasons. Once on the job, they were treated little differently from prisoners. In Jackson, Mississippi, just forty miles east of Tallulah, black women WPA workers were "supervised" by white men carrying loaded guns—to ensure there was no loafing. Ruby Duncan grew up in the shadow of those guns.[10]

For Ruby and other girls growing up on the Ivory Plantation, there was bitter irony in being told that they were unwilling to work. All they ever did was work—and plot their escape from the cotton fields. "I've been dreaming all my life," Duncan now says, thinking back on that sweaty, exhausted thirteen-year-old who stole a forbidden nap between the cotton rows all those years ago. "Only in those days, dreaming was all I had."

Eighteen miles north of Tallulah, on a plantation in Sondheimer, Louisiana, Alversa Burrell (now Beals) was also hatching an escape plan. Conditions in Sondheimer could hardly have been more stark. "Our house was so old you could see through it," Alversa Beals recalls with a shy smile, her tone a mix of nostalgia and repulsion. "It had holes through it and it used to rain through the ceiling. We had a big old dishpan that would catch the rain as it dripped in."

Many of the sharecropper shacks on Southern plantations dated back to slave days. Families cooked, ate, bathed, and slept in just one or two rooms, without window glass or screens. Dust blew in through the windows and the cracks between the boards; mud caked the floors in rainy seasons. Ashes from wood fires hung in the humid air, making the cabin unpleasantly oppressive in summer. In winter, inadequate insulation, failing roofs, and broken chimneys let in snow and rain as well as biting winds.[11]

Cheerfully, Alversa's mother took on the nearly impossible task of trying to make a cozy home for her children. She nailed up pictures from newspapers and pieces of brightly colored cloth to make the rooms feel brighter during damp, cold winter nights. "Trying to keep warm," Beals recalls. "That's what we did a lot of." In 1942, when Alversa was nine, her father left the family. He went first to Lake Charles, Louisiana, to find work. In 1949 he ventured west, and later landed a job as a porter at the Sahara Hotel and Casino in Las Vegas. Meanwhile, Alversa's mother—and the eleven children she raised alone—were left to work the farm themselves.[12]

Alversa was six when she first started picking cotton with her siblings. Even as a young girl, "Versie" could pick an extraordinary amount of cotton, nearly 285 pounds a day. Her brothers picked three hundred. When the cotton was picked out, she and her siblings planted and harvested corn in its place, half of which they gave to the planter at season's end as rent. But the family couldn't get ahead, bedeviled by boll weevils, floods, falling cotton prices, and a sharecropping system that left them with half the corn they grew and little else. "It didn't matter what you did, or how hard you worked," Beals recalls. "At the end of the year, you didn't have no money. All that cotton you picked, they'd give you about $100 and tell you that you owe them money."

Beals and her siblings had to share what little clothing they had. "My shoes were so ragged, the sole would come off and they would take a nail and put a hole in it, then take a piece of wire and twist the soles back up near the leather," she recalls. One winter, she and her brother had only one pair of boots between them. "When he had them on I couldn't go out. He would put on the boots and go out and tote wood in. Then I'd put 'em on and tote water into the house. That's the way we did it."

Electricity and indoor plumbing did not come to most white middle-class homes in the Delta until the 1940s. Poor black sharecroppers didn't have such luxuries until decades later. Doing laundry required pumping and hauling fifty pounds of water for each load, another fifty pounds to rinse. Wood had to be cut and carried in not only to provide heat, but for cooking and for boiling water. Alversa prided herself on being able to do "boys' work" as well as girls'. "I could cut wood just like my brother," she says.[13]

In Alversa's home, as in the shacks of most Delta sharecroppers, only two things stood between the family and gnawing winter hunger: children's hunting and fishing abilities, and their mother's skill at vegetable gardening and preserving every scrap of food not consumed during the summer. Delta streams were alive with bream, white perch, grunters, and turtles. Pecans grew wild along the water's edge, there for the picking. And Mrs. Burrell canned all fall. "My mama would can up lots of jars of fruits and things so she would be sure there was something besides beans for us to eat in the winter," Beals remembers. "Peaches, pears, tomatoes. We'd raise the tomatoes and she would cook 'em in the jar. Okra. Green butterbeans. She would always make sure we'd have something to eat."[14]

Survival depended, too, on learning the strict racial etiquette of the region. Black mothers taught their daughters canny ways to sidestep the sexual advances of white male overseers and employers. They taught their sons to keep their eyes averted when they spoke to white people, and to answer even the harshest tones in quiet, unassuming voices.

But Beals and Duncan recall sweet as well as bitter tastes from their Delta childhoods. Alversa made dolls out of corn cobs, wrapped in corn husk dresses. As she got older, she sewed clothes for her dolls from cloth fragments that dropped to the floor when her mother was sewing for the family. Her mother, poor as she was, found ways to show her children love. Beals recalls vividly the day she got her first store-bought doll. "I was nine or ten and they bought me a doll, just so I would know what a real doll was." Both Duncan and Beals remember how hungrily they waited for the few special treats they might expect on Christmas morning. "My mama had to borrow money just to buy us a little something for Christmas," Beals says. "And it wasn't much—maybe an orange or an apple or some candy. But we couldn't wait."

It's the cooking smells they remember best: the steam and sweet smoke of the holiday meals cooked by women so weathered from sun and overwork that the children couldn't tell whether they were forty or seventy. "The aunties was beautiful cooks," says Duncan's cousin, Joanna Klein, sighing and closing her eyes. "We ate till we got sick. And they encouraged us to. 'Pass the pumpkins, pass the biscuits. Pass the meat.' We had fun." If holidays and Sundays, church singing, and family dinners glow in the migrants' retelling, perhaps it is because they represented rare respite from the relentless labor that never seemed to lift them even a hair's breadth above where they had been the year before. But the year she turned thirteen, Beals says, the family did finish a little bit ahead. "And I got to get a brand-new coat."

Mrs. Burrell picked out a sensible coat for her daughter. "At that time," Beals recalls, "people had a black coat, a grey coat, or navy blue. My mom and my grandmom wanted us to wear dark colors." Standing out, they knew, could be dangerous. But, to Alversa, standing out felt like one step closer to getting out—and at thirteen, she could think of little else. Besides, she had her eye on something flashier: a buttery soft, maroon coat she had spotted. She begged her mother to buy it, but Mrs. Burrell refused. Versie grew uncharacteristically defiant. "I couldn't let the maroon coat go," she says. "I was holding on to this coat, just rubbing on it you know. A man in the store said: 'She likes this coat. Why don't you get it for her?' " Beals laughs with girlish pleasure at the memory. "He bought me that coat," she says with satisfaction. "It was the first time I had a new coat, and it was a maroon color coat."

For Versie Beals, that small victory loomed large. She spent her childhood under the hot sun, picking cotton in a drab, hand-sewn smock. But at night, and on Sundays in church, she could make herself over into a modern young woman with her own sense of fashion and individuality. She could claim for herself a small piece of postwar consumer culture. When she wore that soft maroon coat, she was more than a cotton picker. Half a century later, she still favors maroon.[15]

By the time she entered her teens, Alversa Beals was heartily sick of the sharecropping life. She liked to imagine living somewhere else, anywhere else, but hopefully in a big city far away. "I'm not going to pick cotton all my life," she told her cousins as they dragged their heavy cotton sacks up and down the rows. "And my children ain't gonna pick no cotton ever." Her cousins laughed at her. "You're just saying that," they told her. "There ain't nothing else you can do." Beals pauses, and her eyes reflect a long-ago hurt. "That's what they'd say to me," she says.

There was little chance that education would offer a way out. Education was a rare luxury for blacks in the rural South in the 1930s and 1940s. For starters, children in black sharecropping families were able to attend school only after the cotton crop was picked. That meant, in effect, that school was open only during the winter months. Finishing elementary or middle school was the best that most black children could hope for. "We couldn't get a learning, because we had to pick all the cotton," Beals says. She never got beyond the sixth grade.[16]

Ruby Duncan remembers white children calling her "nigger" from their yellow school bus as she walked eight miles to the abandoned church that was the Ivory Plantation school. While paying taxes to support a public education system that offered nothing to their own children, adults on Ivory and surrounding plantations had to raise additional funds from their desperately small earnings to bring a woman teacher down from Tallulah. The young woman stayed with a different local family each week. There were no desks in that abandoned church, few books, and little time to learn. Ivory Plantation children were allowed to attend school only during winter. "I could never do better than four or five months a year," Ruby Duncan says now. She never made it past the ninth grade. Poor education was just one more Delta dead end for smart, ambitious black children like Duncan and Beals. But it's the one that, over the course of their lives, would most shame them, and most fire their desire for betterment.[17]

When Duncan and Beals were young, President Franklin Roosevelt and Louisiana senator Huey Long promised aid to the rural poor and an expansion of work opportunities. Federal aid did come to cotton country during the Depression in the forms of cash and work relief. But the New Deal, a beacon of hope for so many, was at best a mixed blessing for black sharecroppers. Federal crop-reduction policies, which benefited Delta planters immensely, forced untold numbers of poor farmers into destitution. Planters evicted sharecropping families by the hundreds of thousands across the cotton-growing South. Only federal aid to the needy kept them from starving. The rural South had a greater percentage of its citizens on relief than any other section of the country. Nearly two-thirds of whites and a little under half of all black families in cotton country received federal aid during the 1930s.[18]

Southern planters were torn about the advent of federal aid to the poor. On one level, they welcomed it, because federal relief grants meant that planters no longer had to provide loans to sharecropping families to enable them to purchase food and clothing during the winter. Some Delta planters saw federal relief as a hedge against emigration. They applied heavy pressure on local welfare administrators to provide enough relief to black farm families that they would not feel the need to migrate north. But planters also complained that federal work relief programs were unfair competition. Works Progress Administration (WPA) jobs in the Delta paid thirty cents an hour when planters were paying field workers seventy-five cents a day. New Deal officials acquiesced without a fight, agreeing to purge relief rolls—and stop hiring WPA workers—during planting and harvesting seasons. And they looked the other way when Delta police rounded up members of the tenant farmers' union on vagrancy charges, forcing them to work on plantations or do jail time. Provisions to throw relief recipients back into the labor force during harvest seasons were written into state welfare regulations in agricultural areas across the U.S. Similar rules took hold in cities built on seasonal tourism, among them Las Vegas, Nevada.

Cultural stereotypes about black migrants' predilection for dependency spread rapidly. Even as planters used federal relief payments to lower their own labor costs, they warned that African American farm families were becoming too fond of life on the dole. "Relief has demoralized the nigger," planters complained, charging that black farmers were now less inclined to work for low wages. Many federal officials agreed. "It requires no difficult psychological adjustment for 'Rastus' to get his groceries from Uncle Sam instead of 'Massa John,'" one Texas official said. The idea that African Americans had been psychologically prepared for a welfare lifestyle by slavery and sharecropping had taken root. When black Southerners migrated North and West in the decades following the Depression, that negative baggage came with them.[19]

THE VIOLENT TWILIGHT OF PLANTATION AGRICULTURE

Ruby Duncan was a teenager when mechanical cotton pickers rolled onto Delta cotton fields in the 1940s, the final stage in the region's evolution from the feudal world of plantation agriculture to modern agribusiness. "When planters decided to alter their mode of production fundamentally," historian Jack Temple Kirby has written, "much of the region was convulsed. Millions of people were dispersed to cities. Sharecropping, a system three-quarters of a century old in 1940, shrank rapidly to insignificance." The fate of entire black agrarian communities, no longer needed for their labor, became uncertain. Social flux sparked outbreaks of violence that were fueled by racism, class antagonism, sexual tension, and meanness.[20]

This period was marked by constant racial violence along the southern Mississippi River as some whites—wary about their own loss of socioeconomic status—tried to deflate the rising expectations that New Deal job programs, migration, and defense jobs were generating among the local black population. Between 1930 and 1950, Mississippi had thirty-three reported lynchings of black citizens—a number that is almost certainly an undercount. Many, if not most, acts of racial violence went unreported because survivors feared for their own lives. Some historians believe that the body tolls grew higher as black soldiers, instilled with new pride and hopes of equality from their years of war duty, returned to their homes in cotton country. Returning serviceman Amzie Moore estimated that, in the Mississippi Delta alone, one black man a week was murdered by whites in the months following the end of World War II.[21]

Times of change are always dangerous. In Tallulah, poor black girls had to be careful and canny to survive relatively unscathed into adulthood. "I was always either afraid or angry or both," says Rosie Seals, a tough-talking, tobacco-chewing, churchgoing ex-Tallulan. Even when "the bosses spoke soft and sweet," says Seals, "you knew you took your life in your hands to cross them." Black Delta teenagers like Duncan and Seals learned about romance, sex, class, and race in a climate of violence and repression. Their elders taught them to navigate the dangerous and ever-shifting lines across which interracial relations were possible. And they modeled patterns of dignity and resistance that shaped these young girls' identities.[22]

But fear also could undermine the dignity of older black Deltans, much to the dismay of younger relatives. Duncan recalls an incident at Ivory Plantation that painfully illustrates that anxiety. It was 1950, and the Olivers had arrived unannounced for a weekend visit. Ruby's Aunt Mamie, who was maid and cook in "the big house," was summoned to get everything ready for a dinner that John Oliver Jr. was hosting. Mamie asked Ruby, then seventeen, to set the table. "Little Mr. Johnny" walked in suddenly and began yelling at the startled young girl. "You're not doing it right," he shouted. Duncan stood her ground, and screamed right back. "If you don't like it, then you do it!" she retorted and stormed off.

Her aunt's raw fear called Duncan back. "My Aunt Mamie started to cry," Duncan recalls. "She grabbed me and I could feel she was shaking badly. And she started to talk in that high voice the old folks sometimes had back then: 'Oh Mr. Johnny. She didn't mean it. She didn't mean it.' She was terrified so much she was shaking." The white teenager looked at the quaking woman and laughed. "Let Ruby go," he said finally. "She was just telling it the way it is."[23]

Duncan says her penchant for—and delight in—talking back springs from the anger and hurt pride she carries with her from the Ivory Plantation. But she can still feel her aunt's terror that day. "It scared her to death when I talked back to him," she says. Black parents and grandparents agonized over how much to tell children about the racist violence that permeated and twisted Delta life. They wanted to keep their children safe, but they didn't want to cripple them emotionally, or leave them paralyzed by fear.

Alversa Beals remembers how carefully her elders chose their words when whispering about the newest atrocity.

> My mama and my grandmother would never say it was the Ku
> Klux Klan. They would say: "Some of the white folks killed such
> a one." That's the way I remember them talking. They would

say, "They found them dead on the side of the road. They found them dead at the edge of the woods." But at my age, they would never tell us who killed them.

Mostly, Beals says, adults made sure they held those conversations out of earshot. "We would see our parents talking," Beals recalls, "but they wouldn't tell us. They kept a lot hidden."

Parents trained their children in the cruel realities of Delta life. "My grandmama always told my brothers: 'Don't touch nothing. Don't bother nothing,'" Beals recalls. A poor black boy did not want to get himself in any kind of trouble. Poor girls, too, had to be sure not to antagonize white males. Mothers gave their daughters advice on how to sidestep sexual advances if they could. But they also warned them: Don't risk your life by putting up a fight. "Whatever they ask you to do, just do it," Beals's mother and grandmother told her. "Whatever they asked you to do, you *had* to do it. If they asked a young girl to go to bed, she had to do that. You couldn't fight against it. We were always afraid."

Every woman interviewed for this book has a relative or family friend who was assaulted, tortured, or killed by whites during those years. None of these incidents was recorded in any official document, nor have the psychological effects been adequately measured. Like the war refugees from Europe and Asia who would arrive in American cities in the 1950s, many black migrants of the postwar generation suffered from what would now be called post-traumatic stress disorder. Five decades later, Ruby Duncan still chokes up telling her children about her youth. "I'll be fine in a minute," she says, wiping away sudden tears.[24]

But the wounds inflicted by these women's Deep South childhoods were offset by intense pride in parents, aunts, and uncles who refused to be cowed by racist neighbors, employers, and police. Individual acts of courage by relatives who took fearsome risks—and sometimes paid a terrible price—were powerfully imprinted on the women's memories, and became models for their own later activism.[25]

"My family has always been kind of outspoken," says Ruby Duncan. "They'd always say what they know is right." One uncle, sharecropper Nathaniel Bolden, was a founding member of the Northern Louisiana NAACP in the early 1940s. As a child, Duncan remembers hiding from torch-bearing night riders who came to her door looking for him. "They was fixing to lynch him," she says. "But somebody ran and hid him."

Bolden was also the president of an interracial Louisiana farmers' cooperative. The communal farms—or "projects," as black sharecroppers called them—were established during the 1930s by the Farm Security Administration to promote land ownership and cooperation among tenant farmers and farmworkers. Black residents of these cooperatives, and sometimes their white supporters, experienced intense Klan harassment, especially on interracial farms. Duncan's uncle received a series of death threats and in 1941 was assaulted by a knife-wielding white man. A white coworker was killed. "They got clear away with it," says Bolden's daughter, Joanna Klein.[26]

The men who killed Mary Wesley's father were never brought to trial either. Fifty years after the gunshots rang out, Wesley's voice still cracks when she talks about her father. "The Ku Klux Klan killed him," she says quietly. "I was only three years and eleven months old."

Born in the eastern hill country of Quitman, Mississippi, in 1938, Mary Wesley was to have been one of the lucky ones. Her father, Alec Wesley, owned his own land, and his truck farm did well enough that he could afford to hire three drivers to carry his produce to market. People tell Wesley that she looks like him: tall, statuesque, and powerfully built, with mahogany skin and carved, high cheekbones that betray mixed African and Native American ancestry. "I got my mouth from him, too," she says with pride and a sly grin. "They wanted my father to say 'Yes Sir' and 'No Sir' to every white man. But my father felt that he was a man and an equal. He wouldn't do it." She sits up straighter as she remembers. "And he always taught us not to say it either. 'Just say Yes and No. That's all you have to say to them.'"[27]

But Alec Wesley's defiance made him vulnerable, as well. Mary's mother told her the story of her father's final week. He was planning to travel to Las Vegas right after Christmas, in 1941. His mother lived there, and together with his brother, Wesley hoped to get a job at the new defense plant the government was building, out in Henderson, Nevada. The plan was for him to set up a home in Las Vegas, and send for his family to begin a new life. But Alec Wesley never made it to the desert. A few days before Christmas, a group of eight white men in Quitman challenged him to meet them at the railroad crossing. Wesley, calling their bluff, showed up—alone, but with a gun. His would-be attackers slunk away, but they were waiting for him, a few days later, in the woods where he worked. When Wesley got out of his truck on Christmas Eve morning 1941, they opened fire.

"They shot him in the back," his daughter says. The other men who worked with him were afraid to drive him to the hospital. "He tried to drive himself to the hospital but he had a wreck and the truck turned over. He died from the bullet wound. But they pretended it was the accident that killed him." There was never any chance that Alec Wesley's attackers would be prosecuted. The sheriff who filed the accident report, Mary Wesley believes, was one of her father's ambushers.

Mrs. Wesley jumped when she heard the knock on her door late that night. It was Christmas Eve, and her husband had been inexplicably gone all day. She had long feared this moment. "I remember it just like it was yesterday," Mary says. "Me being always a mommy's child, I was holding her long dress and I went to the door with her. And my cousin came to the door and my mother looked at his face. And she said, 'Alec's dead.' And I was looking at her, trying to figure out why was she crying."

That night at the wake, Mary stood with her father's sister at the side of the coffin, picking shards of automobile glass from her father's hair. Friends have told her that she cannot possibly remember that moment. But Wesley insists that she can recall every detail, right down to the color of the dresses worn by the women mourners.

A week after Alec Wesley was killed, the wives of his murderers brought baskets of food and children's clothing to his widow. Wesley believes that it was their way of apologizing. "These guys' wives knew their husbands did it," says Wesley. "But everybody was afraid to say anything."

In the South, with rare exceptions, white women were silent about white men's violence. As maverick white Georgia writer Lillian Smith wrote in 1947, white women "shut their minds against knowledge of what existed.... [be-cause] one question asked aloud might, like a bulldozer, uproot their garden of fantasies and tear it out of time, leaving only naked bleeding reality." Instead, Smith wrote, Southern white women "turned away from the ugliness which they felt powerless to cope with and made for themselves and their families what they called a 'normal' life."[28]

In the twisted, strangely intimate world of small-town life under Jim Crow, Mary Wesley found "normalcy"—and a form of safety—in the homes of the men who killed her father. Their wives offered to pay little Mary and her sisters to do odd jobs. Mrs. Wesley needed the money to supplement her wages as a waitress at a nearby café. And so Mary worked for these women for years, cleaning, cooking, and caring for their children, many of whom were scarcely younger than she. Remarkably, she came to feel close to these women, and felt free to speak her mind. By the time she was a teenager, Wesley was able to do the unthinkable: break the silence about her father's murder.

"I knew the names of the men who killed my father and I wasn't afraid to say them," Wesley recalls. "Their wives were really nice. But I told their husbands I hated them. That's what my mother always feared about me. I would just tell them what I thought of them." Today, Wesley can admit what she would not back then: "I was terrified of these men."

> *I tried never to be in the same room with them unless their wives and children were there. There were just a few things the women had control over and the house was one of them. They wouldn't touch me there. And I made sure never to run into them anywhere else.*

Even in tiny Quitman—population 1,400—it was relatively easy to steer clear of the men, for middle-class white women in Quitman led almost completely separate social lives from their husbands. White men of standing belonged to the Klan. Their wives belonged to bridge clubs that rotated play from house to house. Wherever the bridge club met, Wesley cooked, served food, and organized activities for the children while the mothers played. The work kept her busy and helped to feed her family. But she grew tired of the subservience she was expected to display when she was with the entire group.

> *When I was alone with any of them they was just fine. Everybody was just like your family. But when their friends came round, they wanted me to call them Miss and Mr. and they wanted me to use the back door. And I couldn't use the bathroom. I had to go home to use the bathroom.*

It may have been teenage annoyance, she says, or just an inability to sit on her grief and anger any longer. But one evening, Wesley let her long-time employers have it:

> *I was in there serving them and I raised my hand as if I was in school. I was maybe thirteen, fourteen. It was the early '50s, before any civil rights movement came to my part of Mississippi. I said I wanted to ask them a question. They asked me what was it. I said: How come when everyone of them was together, I had to say Miss and Yes ma'am and No ma'am, and go in the back door. Couldn't use the bathroom or eat with them. But when it was just me at one of their houses, I was like equal to them.*

Wesley understood how shocking it was for a young black girl to talk to a group of Quitman white women that way. Somehow she didn't care. There was a long silence in the room, Wesley recalls. "First they looked at me real strange, then each one of them looked at the other and they just burst out laughing." Something genuinely changed in the women at that moment, Wesley believes. "From that day on, I ate with them, used the bathroom, did whatever I wanted. Wherever they went, they took me. I would even stay the summer in Pascagoula [a Gulf Coast summer retreat] with them on the water. And if a restaurant wouldn't serve me, they wouldn't eat. I don't care if they had ordered their food. They would just walk out."

Wesley was keenly aware that she was being treated differently than other young black people in Quitman. She was singled out for kindness while local white vigilantes, with the help of Quitman's Sheriff Faulkner, continued to murder and lynch. Two years after Alec Wesley's murder, two black Quitman boys—Charlie Lang and Ernest Green, both fourteen—were arrested for the alleged attempted rape of a thirteen-year-old white girl. Many in Quitman, both white and black, knew the three youngsters were friends who frequently played together. But when a passing motorist saw the girl run from beneath a town bridge, and the two boys chase after her, he reported the incident to Sheriff Faulkner. He arrested the boys and quickly announced that they had confessed.

On October 12, 1943, Charlie Lang and Ernest Green were taken from the town jail, tortured, and lynched. Their genitals were cut off and pieces of flesh were torn from their bodies, which were hung from the bridge where they had been playing hide and seek. A screwdriver had been rammed down one boy's throat and protruded from his neck. No Quitman resident could have missed the message: even children would not be spared.[29]

Mary felt that she and her siblings had been granted some protection by the guilt that her employers felt over her father's murder. Wesley's mother was far less sanguine about Mary's safety. A fearful woman, she didn't even want Mary to finish school, and an uncle's offer to put Mary through college went ignored. "When I got to be sixteen," says Wesley, "my mother got really afraid that I would get hurt. So we began to talk about my leaving there."

Essie Henderson had to get out of town, too. She grew up hundreds of miles away from either Tallulah or Quitman, on a plantation outside of Houston, Texas. But she was no stranger to the violence wielded by white landowners and overseers against black sharecroppers. In the early 1940s, Henderson witnessed a terrifying attack on her mother that she says was a common punishment for black "insolence" in her part of Texas. Henderson recalls:

> *My mother was drug for about a mile behind a wagon because she didn't let a white man whip my brother. She fought them when she saw them hit her son. And they got so angry with her, they just tied her behind a wagon and drug her, head down. I watched her head hit again and again in the dust.*

The torture of Elizabeth Henderson in the 1940s bears an eerie resemblance to the 1998 mutilation and murder of James Byrd, a black man from Jasper, Texas, who was dragged to death behind a pickup truck driven by white supremacists.

Fortunately, Henderson's mother survived. But Essie's father, enraged at his wife's ordeal, threatened to get even—a prospect that seemed sure to leave him dead. He had already been shot three times by whites for "talking back," Essie recalls.

> *And when my mama got drug, we all thought he was going to get himself killed. He wanted to go up there with his shotgun and drill the people who done it. We said: "Don't do it. There'll be a lynching." He said: "Well at least I'll have killed me four or five people before they get me. They can fry me after I get through killing. I don't care what they do to me."*

Within a few years, Henderson says, her father left the plantation under cover of darkness because "he was gonna soon get killed." He moved to Houston where Essie and her brother later joined him.[30]

Henderson's parents divorced and her mother remarried. But Henderson had inherited her father's temper, and her stepfather had to step in more than once to protect her from it. Essie was twelve years old in 1948 when she challenged a white overseer's attempt to "short-weight" her—a common practice by which planters cheated sharecroppers out of their rightful pay.

> *I was weighing up my cotton, and I had 79 pounds. The first weight the man had was 59 pounds. So I said: "Excuse me sir, I know how to weigh cotton." That man lifted me up from the ground. I said: "You're cheating me." By the time my stepdaddy came I was up in that man's collar. My stepdaddy was very educated. He was no one to step on. He said: "What's going on? You dressing up on my child? And you're a grown man!" The white man said: "No. Your daughter is dressing up on me."*

The stepfather insisted quietly but firmly that Essie was in the right, and pulled her away to safety.

But Essie wasn't long for the farm. One year later, Essie Henderson left the cotton fields forever. She went to live with her brother in Houston, where she began to attend school regularly for the first time. "They had to come back for their sister," Henderson laughs. "A sassy little black girl didn't have no respect. I wasn't gonna let nobody run over nobody and they knew that."

THE ROAD OUT

Mary Wesley first sensed that the world was larger and freer than Quitman during summer visits to Gulf Coast resort towns with her employers. Ruby Duncan, Alversa Beals, and Rosie Seals, raised on remote plantations far from even small-town life, found a similar sense of freedom in Delta towns like Tallulah and Vicksburg. Town life introduced them to young black men and women who'd been able to attend school, and never had to pick cotton. In town a black woman could work in mills, restaurants, and clubs. And she could meet young men who had spent time living out of the South, in Pittsburgh, Chicago, St. Louis, or—increasingly, by the 1940s—in a remote desert boomtown called Las Vegas. Those stories whetted the appetite of rural black girls for adventure—and escape.

Before they could leave the Delta, though, girls in sharecropping families had to get themselves off the farm. Marriage and a move to a nearby town seemed the quickest escape route. At fifteen, all Rosie Seals could think of was leaving the plantation where she had been raised. "You chopped cotton in the summer, and in the fall you picked it. Then they'd be hollering how you owed them," she sniffs, her feisty eyes narrowing. "How in the world are you ever gonna get a fair shake in the country? I decided I was moving to town!" Seals's first good chance came in the form of a young man who promised to take her away from everything she hated. She married Zobie Sanders before she turned sixteen. "I got married and got myself to town," Seals says. "That's what I did."[31]

Courting in postwar cotton country was fueled by fantasies of electricity and running water, and many married too young. Some women got lucky: their youthful lovers grew into responsible husbands and fathers. But for Seals, as for many of the women she would later meet in Las Vegas, whispered promises of a golden future of town life—with heat and clean water and regular schooling for the kids—quickly turned sour. Seals's marriage lasted only a year. Like many Delta black men, Zobie Sanders was constantly on the move, looking for a better job. "He took up with other women when he was on the road," Seals says. "He was just a whore. And I wasn't staying married to no whore."

Alversa Beals's first romance, like Rosie Seals's, was bound up with dreams of leaving the plantation. Tallulah was the biggest town in the region, with expensive dress stores and two movie theaters. One was for blacks. The other allowed blacks upstairs only. But Beals, who got to town only rarely, was too excited to care. "They had a movie there, and little dancing places with bands playing and singing the blues," she recalls. "That's where I first saw B. B. King. We would all pile in a car, set in each other's laps, so we could go down there and be out a little bit." On one of those outings, in 1951, she met Edward Beals, a young man who worked at Tallulah's largest lumber mill. He proposed and she accepted. Alversa imagined that she'd move to town, get a real job, and raise children who could attend school regularly. And maybe she, too, could finish school. She was, after all, only eighteen.

But marrying Ed Beals was not the escape Alversa had envisioned. Against her wishes, the couple became cash renters on a large cotton plantation near Tallulah, and quickly fell into debt. "I married to get out of the fields," she says. "I married Edward Beals because he wasn't working in the fields. But when I married him, he quit working in the mill and we ended up back on the farm doing the same thing. I thought I was getting away but I just got deeper in."

The marriage lasted four years and produced as many children. With each child, the marriage deteriorated further. "Me and my husband didn't get along good," Beals says sadly, but without bitterness. "He was alcoholic and I wasn't. I didn't like to drink. He tried to teach me to drink with him. But the whiskey would burn my throat. And so he would pour some Coke or Seven Up in and then I still didn't like it. So we would fight. I was having babies. We were fighting. Fighting and babies. And working too."

There are no statistics to indicate just how widespread alcoholism, philandering, and physical violence were among rural black families in the forties and fifties. But among the women whose story this book tells, abuse by the men they loved and married was all too common. These women ended up as single mothers on public assistance, so their general view of men may be less positive than those of women whose marriages lasted. Still, their stories shed light on a critical, and rarely discussed, factor that caused many black women to leave their childhood homes in the South: their need to escape battering, philandering, and sexual violence by black and white men.[32]

Ruby Duncan was eighteen when she fled the Ivory Plantation in 1951. She wasn't chasing romance. She was fleeing sexual assault. "I was seventeen when

I got raped," she says. Duncan had been walking through the cotton fields one evening to the "big house" to help her aunt serve dinner. "It wasn't quite dark," she remembers, "and the cotton was five, six feet tall." A young man who had wanted to date her—but had been rebuffed by her uncle—was hiding in the cotton. "I didn't know he'd wait for me. He wrestled me into this old house, and I passed out. When I came out of it, I ran away. I didn't tell anyone because I was afraid I'd be beaten."

But when the rape resulted in pregnancy, Ruby's aunt was warm. Mamie comforted her and promised to help Ruby support the baby. "I didn't know what it meant to have a baby," Ruby says. "I was pregnant one day, and I had to learn to be a mother. I didn't know anything about that."

Aunt Mamie arranged for Ruby to live in Tallulah with another aunt, out of range of the boy who'd assaulted her. Soon Ruby found a job at a Main Street pharmacy, making the fantastic sum of nine dollars a week. She gave birth to her first child in Tallulah, and named him for the plantation where she was raised: Ivory. Even as a young, single mother, Ruby enjoyed those first years of town living. Tallulah was hopping in those years, full of good food and young people, great music and dance clubs. Ruby worked steadily and began to date a handsome man who worked for a Tallulah oil firm. When Ruby became pregnant again, the pharmacist gave her a raise to $9.50. And so, although Tallulah was abuzz with enticing tales of a better life out in the desert, Ruby decided to stay for a while. Her second son, David, was born there in 1952.[33]

Emma Stampley, too, became a mother young. She was only fourteen when she married. "I decided I'd marry the first man who asked, anything to get off the farm." One of ten children born to poor, independent black farmers in the Delta town of Fayette, Mississippi, Emma knew her family was better off than many of their neighbors. They weren't sharecroppers. "We owned a little property and everything we raised was our own," says Stampley, a tawny woman with large eyes and a soft, disarming drawl. Even her experience of racism was mild compared to that of most other Delta blacks. The family's closest friends were poor white farmers who lived just up the road. "This was quite unusual," Stampley says, laughing softly. As children, the neighbors slept in each other's rooms, and took baths at each other's houses. The parents cared for each other's animals.

Still, Stampley's family was poor, the work was unending, and life in the country seemed to promise little. So, at fourteen, she accepted a marriage proposal from a sweet-talking boy named Lee who promised to take her to live in Vicksburg, then a logging and mill town. Marrying young, she soon realized, was a terrible mistake. Stampley's parents had been prepared to put her through high school, an opportunity afforded few black Mississippi women in the cotton counties. Her early marriage ended her education prematurely. She started having babies, one after the other. And her young husband soon turned violent. She was caught, a child mother with a battering man her only means of support.[34]

Stampley stayed with her husband for almost fourteen years and bore eight children. When she contemplated leaving, she would stop short, over-whelmed by the thought of supporting them all on her own. "I would have preferred to have fewer children," Stampley says. "But there wasn't any birth control on the market for black peoples like they had for white. There was no place to go. I asked my doctor to tie my tubes and he said no. My doctor was Catholic and he explained to me why the Catholics didn't believe in that. He was the father of eleven."

White Delta physicians routinely refused contraception to black women well into the 1960s, according to a 1966 Congressional investigation. (In 1966 the U.S. Supreme Court made birth control legal for married women across the country. The Delta and many other regions were slow to comply.) Black fe-male patients reported being told by physicians that "if you haven't been preg-nant for two years you can't expect to be healthy." In 1966, when Stampley was trying to get a Vicksburg doctor to tie her tubes, Congressional investigators found that white Delta doctors were prescribing regular sexual intercourse for twelve- and thirteen-year-old African American girls as a way of keeping fit. While the plantation system was still functioning, sharecroppers got health-care from plantation doctors. Such practitioners generally had the same line as the planters: black women should have lots of children to help in the fields. By the 1960s, most poor black women got no healthcare at all. Left to their own devices, women shared recipes for homemade contraceptives. But as often as not, these techniques failed.[35]

Emma Stampley wanted to leave her abusive husband, but she kept get-ting pregnant. She was twenty-eight when she finally walked out. Now a sin-gle mother of eight children, she got a job at a Tallulah lumber mill. It was backbreaking physical labor, and only a few women did it—mostly single mothers with many mouths to feed. But the pay was good. "I did whatever men did," Stampley says. "Stacked lumber. Hooked chains. Set blocks. Ran a rip saw, cut-off saw." The men were dubious about the women, at first. "But if they found out you could do the job, then they'd start to tease you. That's when you knew you were in." Rosie Seals, too, worked in a lumber mill after her mar-

Emma Stampley and coworkers at a Vicksburg lumber mill in the late 1960s.
Stampley and Rosie Seals were among a handful of pioneering women who
broke into a previously all-male trade. (Courtesy of Emma Stampley)

riage failed. "I worked at Chicago Mills in Tallulah," she says. "But I got awful tired. That's why I decided to move."

By the 1950s, Delta towns like Tallulah and Vicksburg had become, for many young black men and women, little more than gateways to the rest of the country. Thousands of people moved into town from plantations in those years. But they were just passing through, buying suitcases, lining up for tickets, negotiating rides. The idea of leaving the South began to take on an air of inevitability.

"YOU CAN PICK UP MONEY RIGHT OFF THE GROUND, AND THERE'S ALL THOSE PRETTY LIGHTS"

Of the boastful migrants who returned triumphantly to Tallulah, Fordyce, or Vicksburg, driving shiny new cars and flashing money, a growing number came with wild stories about a town that few black Southerners had heard much about—the desert gambling resort of Las Vegas, Nevada. Tales of black migrant life in Las Vegas offered stark contrast to those told by visitors from Chicago, Pittsburgh, or New York. Las Vegas's warmth and endless sunshine were alluring to Southerners who shivered at descriptions of frozen Midwestern winters by relatives who had experienced one or two icebound years and decided to return to the South. Even the music in Delta bars lured young people to Las Vegas. "I'm gonna travel to the desert, out in the western land," Bessie Smith sang in "The Lonesome Desert Blues." "I'm gonna end my troubles in the burnin' sand."[36]

The availability of federal defense work in Las Vegas was also a lure. Work on federal projects seemed more likely to advance black men than did jobs in privately owned industries such as steel and automobiles. Too many black Deltans knew friends and neighbors who were stuck in menial jobs while white coworkers with comparable skills advanced. And the fantasy of Las Vegas as a high-rolling, all-night entertainment paradise was intriguing to small-town Southerners—black and white. Indeed, Southern whites made up a majority of those who migrated to Las Vegas in those years. Desert blues swept the Delta, as young men and women carrying babies, straw baskets, and cardboard suitcases piled into trains, buses, and cars for the two-day journey west.[37]

Following a trickle of migrants who had left during the 1930s, a veritable flood of black families from the Delta headed west in the 1940s and 50s. Most of them were drawn to California by promises of lucrative defense work. But tens of thousands headed for the desert, where federal defense contractors, white Southern impresarios, and East Coast gangsters were building America's first gambler's paradise.

The first black Tallulans to leave for Nevada were a handful of men hired to help build Boulder Dam in the 1930s. As federal moneys poured into the West to harness the region's rivers for agriculture and inexpensive electricity, dam-building projects lured hundreds of thousands of workers from the Depression-ravaged East. Boulder Dam, which alone employed twenty thousand men, drew particularly from the South. With a construction budget of $19 million, Boulder Dam became a magnet for the wandering unemployed of all races and ethnicities. Convinced that they had a better chance of being hired on a publicly funded construction project than by a private developer, African American men joined white Southern farmers on the long trek to Nevada.

When they found that no black workers were being hired, disappointed Deltans and the NAACP protested to Las Vegas and Nevada state politicians. Together they persuaded the U.S. secretary of the interior to force Boulder

Dam contractors to hire black workers. By 1936, forty-four black men, some from Tallulah, had been hired at Boulder. When the U.S. entered World War II five years later, government recruiters hungry for able-bodied workers descended on Tallulah and nearby Delta towns.[38]

Ruby Duncan's uncle, Nathaniel Bolden, got a job at Boulder Dam in the second round of black hires. The death threats that he had received during his years as president of the Louisiana farmer's cooperative had convinced the family that he was a marked man. They urged him to leave. His brother Top, one of the first Tallulans to emigrate to Nevada, promised to find him work on the Boulder construction crew. But Top may not have told his brother that black workers on the dam were frequently assigned the most dangerous jobs, or that dam construction work was inherently risky. Of the twenty thousand men who built Boulder Dam, 177 died.[39]

By the 1940s, a steady stream of migrants poured into Nevada. Most of them came to work at Basic Magnesium Incorporated, a huge defense plant in Henderson. Intent on building an industrial base in Nevada, state politicians convinced Franklin Roosevelt's administration to subsidize construction of a massive factory with the capacity to produce ten times Germany's annual magnesium output. They would make magnesium ingots, which were shipped to Los Angeles manufacturing plants and made into tracer bullets, aerial flares, incendiary bombs, airplane fuselages, and other products vital to the war effort. Unable to find enough workers in sparsely populated Nevada, and facing a shortage of white workers as a result of the draft, Basic Magnesium supervisors approached leaders of the tiny Las Vegas black community, who told them there was a ready labor force waiting back home in the Delta. In 1942, BMI sent recruiters to cotton country to lure black labor to the plant.[40]

Word of those defense jobs spread quickly in Tallulah, and, during the first years of the war, mill workers and plantation hands streamed out like a Biblical exodus. So many Tallulans left so quickly that the mayor ordered the bus company to stop selling one-way tickets to Las Vegas. Whites were panicking because all their workers were leaving. "So the blacks started leaving after midnight, late, in the wee hours of the morning," recalls Tallulan Lucille Bryant. Those determined to leave turned to friends, neighbors, and family members —anyone who had a vehicle that could make it across the hilly back roads of Oklahoma and Texas.[41]

Soon local entrepreneurs built lucrative businesses hauling black migrants from the pine and swamp country of Fordyce and Tallulah to their new homes in the desert. Willis Minor first ferried friends and family from Tallulah. By the war's end he was hauling anyone who wished to make a new life in Las Vegas. "Red" Mitchell did the same for the town of Fordyce. One friend recalled that Mitchell would occasionally tow "an inoperable car, doubling the number of people he could transport per trip." Inexperienced migrants paid not only for the transportation but also for the expertise of their guides. They were traveling 1,500 miles through harsh, hot terrain and hostile, segregated Southern towns. The trip took at least three days. Drivers had to know where they could stop for food, water, or lodging--and where they couldn't. Sometimes the driver would barrel straight through, without sleep or rest. It was, many migrants recall, a scary way to begin a new life.[42]

After 1945, most black workers lost their jobs at Basic Magnesium, but new opportunities quickly opened up. Some African American workers were being hired at the Las Vegas nuclear test site. Those were prize jobs, paying well and offering respect and decent working conditions. Not until twenty or more years later did black Las Vegans begin to wonder whether high cancer rates in their community might have anything to do with radiation exposure or other hazards of test-site work. If a man had a federal job, or relatively well-paying construction work, and a woman got herself maid work in one of the hotels then rising on the "Strip," they could buy a car, maybe even a small house, and raise children in comfort. Sure, black workers were restricted to the lowest-paid work. But both the construction sites and the new hotels were unionized, and black workers were welcome to join. Even for menial work in Las Vegas, they received many times what they'd earned in the Delta cotton fields. If the streets anywhere were paved with gold and silver, Las Vegas sounded like the place. "Come on out here," Lucille Bryant wrote friends in Tallulah. "They're giving away money, eight dollars a day, and *working in the shade*."[43]

Alversa Beals's father had left for Vegas in 1949. When he returned in 1950 to attend his mother's funeral, Alversa was a young woman, married with children. She was wary of her father, who had abandoned the family. But his stories of life in the exotic desert oasis intrigued her. "Jobs was plentiful. He told me about the casinos and the hotels and the movie stars he had seen living in Vegas—Sammy Davis Jr. and Redd Foxx. Yeah. I wanted to see them." He painted a picture of natural beauty and streets of gold.

> *He said you could come outside a casino in the morning after work and pick up a dollar in quarters that they just throwed on the ground. And I thought, "I sure would like to be picking up all that money." He said, the lights were so pretty. And the*

mountains were so tall, you could look up and see snow all over
the top. I was living in the flat lands in Louisiana. I wanted to
see mountains.

As Alversa's marriage to Ed Beals deteriorated, the pull to Las Vegas grew stronger, particularly after her brother moved there in 1951. By 1955, she decided she couldn't wait any more. "I wrote my brother a letter because we didn't have no phone," she says. "Come get me or send me a ticket," she wrote. "Cause my husband and I are separating and I need to leave town."

Her brother and his wife came back to Tallulah to drive Beals and her children to Las Vegas. She spent the night hours stroking the heads of her children and peering through the darkness trying to make out the dark countryside. The first morning, she woke up and panicked. She says, "I could see mountains. And I thought, Oh Lord, We're lost. How in the world are we going to get over that big mountain? I woke up my brother. I touched him and I said: 'How are we going to get over that mountain when we get to it?' " Her sister-in-law calmed her down. Laughingly, she said, "The road goes through it."

Essie Henderson's decision to leave Texas was made with greater urgency. She too had married young and left a violent husband. Henderson took her four kids and moved in with her brother in Houston. But Henderson's husband refused to accept the separation. "We was legally separated," Henderson says, "but it was like I was still married till I left there." It was too easy for her husband to find her. And he was dangerous.

That man brought guns to the house, looked in the window and
started shooting. That man was crazy. He hauled off and shot
my brother right through the window. Now what am I going to
do? Get shot by my ex? And you know where the police was at?
Waiting for him to kill me. Then they'd have come on the scene.

Henderson called her sister Earlene, who had recently moved to Vegas. "There's plenty of work here," her sister said. "Come on out." Henderson drove through the desert night and woke to a new life.

There are infinite variations on these migration stories, but they all come down to the same thing: economic betterment, good jobs, a sure way to support their children. A friend of Rosie Seals said she was heading to Las Vegas. "Where in the hell is that?" Seals asked. "She told me and she just said we should go west where we could finally make real money. I was pregnant, I needed work and I found it that very day." Mary Wesley came at age seventeen, because her mother wanted to get her out of Mississippi. She sent her to live with her aunt in Las Vegas in 1955. Emma Stampley joined a friend who was already in Las Vegas and was sending home letters about how much money she was making. "She wrote me how we could do better," Stampley recalls, "how we could get good jobs in the hotels. And that they had better schools. So a whole group of us came out together."[44]

Ruby Duncan practically had to be thrown out of Tallulah. Relatives in Vegas thought she'd never make up her mind to go. She was skeptical of what awaited her in the strange-sounding city, but finally she had almost no kin left in Louisiana. Her aunts, uncles, and cousins had been leaving one by one. In 1952, Duncan left with her six-month-old baby, David. Her two-year-old son, Ivory, was already there, staying with Duncan's beloved Aunt Mamie, who'd moved to Las Vegas the year before. Uncertain but excited, Duncan boarded the train to Las Vegas. "David was just a baby so I had to carry him in my arms the whole way," she recalls. "We had a shoebox full of fried chicken, sweet potato pie and cake that friends made us." All across the Southwest, she looked out the compartment window and tried to imagine what was coming. "Coming from Louisiana, I thought I was ready for hot," she laughs. "Honey I had no idea."[45]

By 1960, parts of the South had lost a quarter of their African American population. Arkansas and Mississippi lost the greatest number of people. Nevada experienced greater growth during the 1940s and 1950s than any other state in the union. In just five years during the 1950s, the desert state's small population increased by 40 percent, as hopeful migrants from fading agricultural backwaters tried to cash in on the promise of postwar prosperity in a new kind of American city, built on service jobs and easy-money fantasies. A strange mix of rugged individualism, Mormon hierarchy, radioactive mushroom clouds, and gangster entrepreneurship would soon make the city famous worldwide as a glittering symbol of postwar American opulence.[46]

CHAPTER 2

"THE MISSISSIPPI OF THE WEST": JIM CROW IN SIN CITY

*When I first got to the Westside, I saw all these little shacks
made of cardboard and metal, in rows as far as you could see.
I thought they were chicken coops. That's how people was living.*

—Mary Wesley, Las Vegas

Ruby Duncan's bus arrived in Las Vegas early one morning during the summer of 1952. Clutching her baby son, the young mother stared out her window at what appeared to be a refugee camp. Hundreds of dazed new arrivals from the South wandered around clutching trunks and cardboard suitcases, with sleepy, scared children in tow. Outside the station, entire families were camped on old blankets, their luggage set up in makeshift partitions around them. It was the peak of Southern emigration, and wave after wave of black refugees from Louisiana, Arkansas, and Mississippi were then pouring into the dusty boomtown. In 1940, only 178 blacks lived in greater Las Vegas. By 1960, there were more than eleven thousand African Americans living there, nearly 9 percent of the city's population.[1]

But Las Vegas was used to explosive growth. From 1951 on, the U.S. military had been detonating nuclear weapons at the Mercury test site, just sixty miles out of town. Mushroom clouds adorned the horizon from time to time, as much a part of the western sky as the red-rock mountains ringing the city. The city of Las Vegas had made the atomic cloudburst its official emblem, adorning postcards and hotel brochures. The test site and Nellis Air Force Base generated thousands of well-paying jobs. So did the new hotels popping up on the Strip—El Rancho, the New Frontier, the Sands, the Stardust, the Desert Inn. Since Bugsy Siegel's flashy Flamingo hotel opened in 1947, gangster impresarios had been rapidly recreating the old mining town as a glittering gambling mecca. They needed men to do construction work and to haul the bags

During World War II, black Southern migrants flooded Nevada by the tens
of thousands, hoping to find work at a huge federal defense plant outside
Las Vegas. Thousands crowded into the Westside of Las Vegas, living in
tents, shacks, cars, and trailers, without running water, heat, or electricity.
(Courtesy of the Nevada State Museum and Historical Society)

in their new fantasy city. And they needed women to be maids, laundresses, and kitchen help.

Living conditions were exceedingly rough in the blazingly hot town, especially for black migrants. While air conditioning was widely used in hotels, casinos, restaurants, and gas stations on the white side of Las Vegas in the 1940s, many houses on the Westside lacked even so much as flush toilets into the 1960s. But the money flowed freely, jazz and blues clubs were open till dawn, gambling was legal—and there wasn't a boll of cotton in sight.[2]

Carrying her son and her meager possessions, Duncan stepped off the bus and was hit by a blast of hot air that nearly leveled her. "I never had felt anything so hot," she remembers. Slowly, she worked her way through the crowd to find a cab that would take her to the home her family had made, twenty miles from Las Vegas, in the ramshackle desert town of Whitney. Her aunt had written the address on a piece of notebook paper. As the cab rode out of town, Duncan crumpled the sweat-stained paper nervously in her hands. The cab took Duncan to an old abandoned motel where her family was living, far out in the desert. She was excited to see her older son, Ivory, who'd been living with Aunt Mamie for most of the past year. But Duncan's first glimpse of her new home left her speechless.

Big weeds surrounded the run-down building, whose doors were only half attached. The wind and the dust blew right through it. The cab driver turned around and said, "Well, you're here."

> *I was in shock. I said: "Is this it?" He said: "I'm afraid so." Then everybody came running out shouting "Ruby's here! Ruby's here!" I just stood there. I thought this was the worst place on earth. It had to be halfway to hell because it was so hot. I called it an oven but it was hotter than an oven. Crazy-making hot.*

In time, Duncan acclimated to the scorching desert heat, but she never got used to the taste and feel of sand in her mouth. Sand got into her hair, her food, her children's freshly washed clothes. It coated everything during the years they lived in that motel. Drinking water had to be trucked in. For relief, she bathed Ivory and David in the little river that ran behind their room. Men from the test site later came out to tell her that the water contained radioactive waste.[3]

Other women arriving from the Delta during the 1950s had similarly bleak —and sometimes comical—first impressions of Las Vegas. Mary Southern, whose husband had worked during the war at the Basic Magnesium plant, came with her two children to join him in 1951. From the moment she stepped off that Louisiana train, the twenty-one-year-old Southern vowed to leave Las Vegas on the next train out.

> *I got to this place on the 19th of July 1951 and when I stepped off the train, as soon as everybody had hugged and kissed, I told my husband, "Let's move back into the station because that steam from the train is burning me." He said: "That ain't steam from the train." I said: "What do you mean?" He said: "Wait until we leave the train station." So we walked outside. You talk about hot! It had to be about 115. I said: "Ben, Why is it so hot?" He said: "I forgot to tell you." I said: "Now you tell me, when I have 80 cents in my pocket. If I had any more I'd catch that train and move on to California."*

A night's sleep and a new dawn didn't help much, Southern says. "I wanted to go home the minute daylight came. I don't know if the sun was up but it was already hot." Southern told a neighbor, "My husband tricked me into coming out here and just as soon as I get enough money I'm leaving." Southern coughs as the dust of memory catches in her throat. "That was 40-something years ago," she says with a sigh. "I've been leaving Las Vegas in my mind ever since."

Rosie Seals pulled up in a car in 1951 with a girlfriend—and an attitude. "I was pregnant, hot and mad," she recalls. "And I had 60 cents in my pocket." As she got out of the car and looked around the Westside, her heart sank. "I cried when I saw this place," Seals says. "It was so hot and it looked so dead. They didn't even have no paved streets when I came here. I had to burrow through the dust and mud to get to the outhouse every morning. And they had water in the house but no bathtubs. You couldn't even wash off the dust."

Mary Wesley took one look at the Westside and felt homesick. "People was mostly living in tents," she noticed when she arrived in 1955. "The house they had me live in when I first came had no floor. Just rugs. And a carpet hanging for a wall. The desert wind blew in. All you could see was desert for miles around. I didn't see how anybody could live here for long. I knew I was gonna go home to Mississippi. I missed the green and all the gardens so much. I couldn't imagine staying here."[4]

If these Delta migrants' first impression of Nevada was of the desolation and poverty, their next realization was harsher. Las Vegas was a Jim Crow town —not as violent or oppressive as their Delta hometowns, but every bit as segregated. "You know," Rosie Seals recalls, "when I first got here I thought: 'At least it looks all right at night because of all the bright lights downtown.' But then I found out they wasn't allowing black people to go into those hotels. They wasn't allowing us to sit or eat in all those pretty restaurants. It was upsetting. I knew back there they didn't allow blacks to eat in restaurants. But I thought it would be different when I came here. I said to my friends: 'You mean to tell me I can't do this and I can't do that?' They said: 'That's right!' I got mad. I said: 'Well, hell I could've stayed where I was instead of coming all the way over here.'"

WELCOME TO THE JIM CROW WEST

Many black migrants to the Southwest shared Rosie Seals's acid disappointment. "At that time Las Vegas was called the Mississippi of the West," recalled Mississippi migrant and future state senator Woodrow Wilson. Las Vegas was hardly alone among Sunbelt cities in segregating its African American resi-

1305 F Street in 1962. As late as the 1960s, many homes on the Westside lacked indoor plumbing, insulation against desert winter nights, and air conditioning, despite summer temperatures that frequently broke 100 degrees Fahrenheit. (Special Collections, UNLV)

dents. Black migrants from cotton country encountered racial barriers across much of California, Arizona, and New Mexico during the 1940s, 1950s, and 1960s. In the Sunbelt—the region that saw the greatest economic and population growth of any part of the U.S. from World War II on—restrictive housing covenants and racial segregation of schools, restaurants, hotels, and other public facilities were the rule. Blacks weren't singled out for discrimination; Southwestern Jim Crow practices severely limited the social and economic mobility of Mexicans, Native Americans, and Asian immigrants as well. Few Southwestern cities had laws on the books excluding nonwhites from public or private facilities, but segregation was enforced by local custom—and, occasionally, by the Klan. The Southern California KKK mixed the antiblack prejudices of white migrants from the Southeast with Western hatred of Mexicans, Native Americans, and Asians.[5]

As in Las Vegas, African American migrants in most Southwestern cities found themselves restricted to ghettos on the outskirts of town, with unpaved streets, outhouses, and shacks made of packing crates, tin, and tarpaper.

Writer Arna Bontemps moved with his family to Watts, in Los Angeles, during the Depression. He called it "Mudtown"—comparing it acerbically to Middletown, the postwar suburban developments where millions of white World War II veterans were then settling their families. "Mudtown," he wrote in 1945, "is as uniform as Middletown."

> It is as real, as American. Mudtown is that embarrassing section of the . . . city in which the new people from the South erect those absurd little shacks to house themselves till they could move on —or perhaps do better. . . . "So this is where the colored folks live," a tired little man once remarked on reaching the neighborhood at night, following a long journey from Louisiana. Then he added sorrowfully, "I mighta known."[6]

Wartime and postwar émigrés to those cities had hoped for better, of course. Like so many migrants before them, they had viewed the West as a new world, free from old hatreds and barriers. In reality, the West had a long history of organized violence toward Mexicans, Native Americans, and Asian immigrants, of racist-populist politics, and of segregated housing and schools. But few black migrants knew this history before they arrived. Or if they had an inkling, perhaps they had discounted what they'd heard. For, as Arna Bontemps explained, these migrants had "dreamed too long of a complete break with the South" to temper their expectations of the West.[7]

African Americans had been in Las Vegas since the city's earliest days, when it was little more than a refueling stop on the Los Angeles-Salt Lake rail corridor. The first black residents of the city were male railroad workers. Their wives, sisters, and daughters generally found work as maids and cooks, either in private homes or in one of the few hotels or restaurants catering to the railroads. The small black community was concentrated downtown in the oldest part of Las Vegas, now known as Glitter Gulch. Although they were excluded both from the town's legal brothels and the local Methodist church, black Las Vegans otherwise mingled freely with their white, Mexican, and Chinese neighbors in Fremont Street taverns, restaurants, and gambling clubs. And no city father stopped blacks from opening their own licensed brothel in 1934, the Idle Hour Club.[8]

There were few recorded racial tensions until the 1930s, when the federal contract to build Boulder Dam went to the Six Companies, a construction consortium that had an unwritten whites-only policy. There were only forty-four African Americans among the twenty thousand white workers laboring on the dam. Many of these white workers had migrated from the South, lured by the prospect of well-paying federal jobs. Openly hostile to the idea of laboring alongside African Americans, they were even more militant about not wanting to eat or drink anyplace that catered to blacks. Well before the wartime influx of Southern black migrants, many bars, casinos, and restaurants along the Boulder Highway that catered to dam workers made it known that black patrons were not welcome.[9]

The few black dam workers lived wherever they could find lodging. Ruby Duncan's cousin Joanna Klein doesn't recall any systematic discrimination during those years. Klein, whose father helped build the dam, lived in the desert town of Whitney during the 1940s. Though she, her siblings, and her cousins were the only black children enrolled at Duck Creek Elementary School, Klein says they were treated with respect and made friends easily. "I was the only one of the black race in the bigger grades in the Whitney school," she says. "But everyone was nice to play with."

For children used to the wet, green flatlands of the Delta, the desert surrounding Las Vegas was a Wild West adventure. The barren landscape, wild animals, sandstorms, and quicksand kept the young Klein and her brothers awake at night.

> *They had coyotes. We would listen to them howl at night. And they had wild horses that ran across the desert where we were. The boys would go out bare-back and catch the horses and ride. That part was fun.*

The children had to walk to the Whitney school through storms so strong, Klein says, "the wind would blow the sand all over you and knock you down." Her mother was afraid that Joanna would fall into quicksand and disappear. So she trekked out into the desert with sticks, tied with red cloth, to mark the treacherous holes. The children worried that their mother, too, might fall in and "nobody would ever have found her again."[10]

Until 1941, blacks were barely visible in Las Vegas, and there certainly weren't enough to capture the attention of most whites. But that year, the sudden influx of black Deltans recruited to work at the Basic Magnesium plant in nearby Henderson increased the black population more than sixteenfold. Basic Magnesium, a mammoth facility that was two miles long and one mile high, employed thirteen thousand workers—one tenth of Nevada's population—and 60 percent of them were Southern blacks.[11]

Segregationist sentiments quickly intensified. Black homeowners in downtown Las Vegas were pressured to sell out to white buyers, and white home-owners began to add covenants to their property deeds restricting sales to "members of the Caucasian race." (The language was often less refined than that: "No Niggers, no Chinese, and no goats," read one typical deed from the period.) The city gradually forced black businesses to leave the downtown streets. No threats were necessary. Authorities simply refused to renew the licenses of any black business owner who tried to operate east of the railroad tracks. And there was no point in appealing to three-term mayor Ernie Cragin, perhaps the most racist of Las Vegas officials, who ran the city, on and off, from 1931 through 1951. Owner of the lavish El Portal movie theater, Cragin had been forcing black patrons to sit in a restricted area since 1928. His police force was still arresting defiant black theatergoers—who wanted to sit where they chose—into the late 1940s. And for decades, the Cragin administration refused to spend city dollars to upgrade the all-black neighborhood of Westside.

By 1943, the flash-flood plain west of Union Station had become Las Vegas's own "Mudtown." Thousands of black migrants from Louisiana, Arkansas, and Mississippi set up housekeeping in tents, cardboard shanties, and wooden shacks that stretched out to the western horizon. Few people had indoor plumbing. Fewer still had telephones; by 1955 there were only two or three in the neighborhood. With large extended families crowded into one- and two-room shacks, migrants spent much of their time outside, especially in the cooler evenings.

These newcomers tried to make West Las Vegas feel as much like home as they could. Alversa Beals coaxed flowers and vegetables from the cracked, red-grey earth. Mary Southern cooked outside, stirring soup seasoned with neckbones, and collard greens sizzling in lard. The familiar aromas of Delta cooking wafted through narrow streets, and rose from rickety barbeque stands where ribs smoked and pots of red beans simmered. The sharp metallic sound of Delta blues guitar filled the dry air. As in other Mudtowns, segregated living in Las Vegas created the beginnings of a new urban black community—drawn not just from the Mississippi Delta but from Texas, Oklahoma, Kansas, and Alabama. The Westside in the 1950s was, like Bontemps's Watts, "a tiny section of the deep south literally transplanted." That the Westside felt like a little piece of the Delta in the desert was both comforting and profoundly disappointing. "It looked smaller than Tallulah," says Southern. "And a whole lot hotter."[12]

Like the Westside, Basic Magnesium, the federal weapons factory that had

brought most black Southerners to Nevada in the 1940s, was completely segregated, and federal housing near the plant was segregated as well. The housing projects reinforced the Jim Crow mentality that Southern migrants, black
and white, had brought with them. White workers were placed in Victory
Village. Black workers with families were offered apartments across Boulder
Highway in Carver Park. Each project contained its own ballfield, recreation
center, and elementary school. Grammar schools were segregated. Only the
town high school served students of both races.[13]

At other nearby federal installations, black military men and defense
workers lived in segregated quarters on base and were restricted to the segregated Westside when they were off-duty. Several all-black units were assigned
to guard Boulder Dam (renamed Hoover Dam in 1947) against saboteurs. Nellis Air Force Base was also home to large numbers of black airmen. Many
of them were raised in the North, and grew angry when they were shut out of
Las Vegas's famed nightlife. But downtown was expressly off-limits to African
American servicemen. To fortify the impregnable color line in the city, Mayor
Cragin's police force even closed clubs that catered to a "mixed" crowd. So
black soldiers' money flowed to the Westside, where black-owned casinos,
clubs, and hotels quickly opened up. The Westside soon boasted a Harlem
Club and a Cotton Club of its own. Jackson Street was hopping. When lively
nightlife spilled out into the streets, there were clashes between black soldiers
and Las Vegas police. One soldier was killed and three wounded during one
melee, in which a policeman was slightly injured. Defense workers, too, felt the
crunch of police batons if they drank too much or got too loud.[14]

Still, a great many black servicemen decided to stay in Las Vegas after the
war, preferring the Westside to the plantation towns and Eastern ghettos
where they'd once lived. Many black veterans found jobs at the Mercury nuclear test site, where they were hired as electricians, ironworkers, heavy equipment operators, carpenters, and truck drivers. The promise of permanent,
skilled, high-wage labor at a federal installation also attracted former Basic
Magnesium workers, many of whom had returned to the Delta after being laid
off at war's end.[15]

Mary Wesley was working as a waitress at a Westside tavern when she met
her husband, a Mississippi migrant who worked at the test site. They married
and soon had three children; four more would follow. Wesley hoped that their
combined incomes would give the children a middle-class life—a home of
their own, decent education and medical care. With tips, Wesley made as
much as two hundred dollars in a good week at her waitressing job. "In those

years, that was a fortune," she says. And her husband took home the kingly sum of five hundred dollars a week—more if he worked overtime, or got snowed in at the test site and had to spend the night at the federal dormitories. For black workers fresh from the cotton fields and lumber mills of the Delta, Las Vegas seemed truly a gold mine.

Still, the incredibly long hours put in by test-site workers wore on their marriages. Wives felt excluded from large parts of their husbands' lives. "It was all a Big Secret," Tallulan Mary Southern says. "That was where the government let off those bombs. You had to have badges and all that security. They couldn't tell even the wives what they were doing. So it was strange sometimes. You could never sit down and have a husband-and-wife conversation. You know: 'How was your day honey?' "

Westside residents were keenly aware that nuclear bombs were being detonated near their homes. Many knew that fake "Doom Towns" were constructed just up the road in Mercury, stocked with J.C. Penney's mannequins and household goods, to illustrate how an average American family would cope with a nuclear attack. But, like most Las Vegans, Westsiders treated the aboveground tests as festive occasions. There was not yet public knowledge of the dangers of radioactive fallout or "downwinder" diseases. Cora Williams, a childhood neighbor of Alversa Beals in Sondheimer, recalled that, on days when tests were scheduled, black residents would gather outside their Westside shanties before dawn.[16]

> We would arise, I guess about 4 a.m. and … see the big mushroom come up after the blast.… Then they would bring all the mannequins back from the blast and they would have them on display in the [store] windows saying she or he was in the atomic blast. And mostly after the blast would come a dust storm.

No one, Westsiders say, ever warned them that those dust clouds raining down on their homes, backyard vegetable gardens, and chicken coops might be dangerous.[17]

Only once, Ruby Duncan recalls, did federal officials warn any black family she knew that nuclear testing might have caused contamination. She and her family were living in the abandoned motel out in Henderson. Suddenly, one morning, inspectors from the test site came to tell them they'd have to move. The stream running by their hotel was dangerously radioactive. The inspectors spoke to the family in urgent, serious tones, Duncan recalls. "By that time," she says, "all the kids had been playing in the water for I don't know how long." Decades later, Westsiders would count the suspiciously high numbers of cancer deaths and think back to those mushroom clouds at daybreak that they had watched with awe and wonder.[18]

Westside residents *were* aware of the dangers related to overcrowding, inadequate sewage, and living in mud. Nearly twenty thousand black migrants had settled in Las Vegas in just a few years. But city officials refused to build a real sewage system. The mud that filled Westside streets, that bubbled over doorsteps and swallowed shoes during flash floods, carried human and animal waste, insects, and disease. The community had not a single medical facility. Nearby private hospitals would not accept black patients, and the one public hospital had segregated wards. The Federal Housing Authority refused to allocate funds for public housing until a proper sewage system was in place. But city officials dragged their feet when it came to making improvements on the Westside. To make matters worse, private lenders redlined the area, refusing to lend middle-class black families money to construct more durable housing there.[19]

The dry, searing heat was particularly hard on children and the elderly. The desert, everyone agreed, was completely unlike the humid Louisiana bayou country. Las Vegas temperatures could hit 120 degrees during the summer. In the era before air conditioning, there was little relief. The only cooling systems on the Westside in the 1950s, Beals recalls, were "swamp coolers. These were little tanks of water on the roof with fans that blew air through water-soaked pads into the rooms below." But even these were luxuries. Few homes had bathtubs, so immersion was not an option. Enterprising young men carried around galvanized washtubs, renting them out for baths at twenty-five cents a pop. Others made their money hauling ice in buckets and selling cups of ice water to parched Westsiders for ten cents a drink.[20]

Westside leaders had been pressing city officials since the early 1940s to make municipal improvements that would transform the Westside into a modern urban neighborhood. They demanded that the city oil the unpaved streets to reduce dust and mud, and seek federal funds for construction of public housing, schools, and parks. But city officials said there was no need to upgrade the Westside. "These people are not going to . . . stay in Las Vegas," black leaders were told. "They'll be going back home."[21] Most black migrants had no desire to return to the Delta, but that didn't stop white leaders from trying to persuade them.

In 1944, and again in 1945, Mayor Cragin ordered the destruction of all

Westside dwellings that did not conform to city housing codes. As migrant families scurried about miserably, collecting their meager belongings, city bulldozers knocked down hundreds of homes. The mayor called it "slum clearance," but, since no new homes were built to replace those that had been destroyed, the intent of the city fathers was clear. Still, the migrants did not leave. Some moved in with family members or friends. Others camped in abandoned cars, rusting trailers, or tattered tents. By 1947, the neighborhood was more crowded than ever. Repeatedly, Westsiders petitioned the city to install fire hydrants, electric lines, and sewers. The mayor declined. Low property values meant that the city would not be able to recoup the cost of such investments, he explained.[22]

In 1949, black activists surveyed housing on the Westside. They found that 80 percent of homes there did not meet federal minimum standards for human habitation. NAACP activists delivered the grim statistics to the Federal Housing Authority. The result was the first federally funded, low-income housing in Las Vegas: the Marble Manor Housing Project, which opened in 1952. Marble Manor included one hundred units of barracks-like modular housing, and would soon become home to Ruby Duncan, Alversa Beals, Rosie Seals, and Mary Wesley. White middle-class residents of nearby Bonanza Village protested bitterly, insisting that the low-income housing development would destroy their land values. Already approved and under way, Marble Manor was completed. But white opposition buried proposals for similar projects in other parts of Las Vegas. Ensuring that there would be no casual contact between the two housing developments, the city's newest highway was soon built just outside Marble Manor.[23]

That was only the first of several highways that would virtually fence off the Westside from the rest of the city. In 1955, the city's new mayor, C. D. Baker, finally paved the streets of the Westside, constructed a functional sewer system, and installed electric streetlights. Las Vegas had won the funds for these improvements by agreeing to let the federal government build Interstate 15 through the middle of the Westside. The superhighway effectively cut off the city's black residents from commercial districts and white residential communities. Angry Westsiders began to call I-15 "the concrete curtain," a bitter allusion to the "Iron Curtain," the infamous symbol of Communist domination in Eastern Europe.

Using highways to fence off poor, inner-city black communities was federal policy nationwide in the 1950s. Eager to erect a gargantuan, cross-country highway system, the federal government was cutting a deal with ma-

jor cities: they could get desperately needed urban renewal and public housing funds, but only if the new interstates could pass through them. Invariably,
these massive highways bisected poor communities. Writes columnist Molly
Ivins: "In any number of towns they laid the interstate down right on the
Black/White line, Bam." Across the U.S., residents in areas targeted for free-
way construction were put in a painful bind: If they fought the freeways, they
would lose a chance at new housing and other infrastructure improvements.
But once the freeways went through, cities such as New York, Miami, Minneapolis, and Las Vegas became more segregated than ever. Even in states like
Nevada and Minnesota, where there were relatively few black communities,
the interstates invariably came through them. While the intrusion of I-15 further depressed property values on the Westside, it spurred a construction
boom on the city's outskirts, as middle-class subdivisions sprouted like weeds
in the red-rock desert.[24]

Years of protest by Westside leaders finally moved the city to build more
homes. New Southern migrants continued to arrive daily, intensifying the already overcrowded conditions. In 1959, Las Vegas opened the federally funded
Madison Houses project, which filled immediately. Families placed their
names on long waiting lists, and returned to their shacks and trailers until the
federal government built more low-income housing. By the early 1960s, most
Westsiders had indoor plumbing, reliable electricity, doors that closed, and
windows that kept out the wind and rain. Mudtown was slowly disappearing.
The Westside was becoming a modern inner-city ghetto.[25]

AT WORK IN THE FACTORY OF FANTASY:
RACE, SEX, AND THE RHYTHM OF THE DICE

Defense work first drew black Deltans to Las Vegas, but, by the 1950s, hotel
work had become their economic mainstay. A vast infusion of organized
crime moneys and diverted millions from Teamsters Union pension funds
watered the desert playland in the years after World War II, financing a wave
of new hotel construction. There were jobs aplenty at the Sands, the Desert
Inn, the Flamingo, and other booming casinos on the glittering new Strip, as
well as at smaller hotels and motels downtown in Glitter Gulch. Black women
could easily land jobs as chambermaids or kitchen aides; black men were
wanted as porters and custodians. And they could jump freely from one hotel
to the next, quitting one job in the morning and getting another, better one in
the afternoon.

"When I first got here, I worked in the Flamingo Hotel," recalls Alversa

Beals. She was flabbergasted to receive her first paycheck. "It was a hundred and some dollars. I couldn't believe all that money was for me." Beals asked her sister-in-law, who worked with her, if there had been some mistake. She replied: "That's what you're gonna make every two weeks." Beals smiled. "This is gonna be good."[26]

Very quickly, however, black women workers hit a low glass ceiling. Better-paying jobs were off-limits to them. Waitresses and desk clerks on the Strip were strictly white. Dealers, who held the highest-paying floor jobs in the casino industry, were white and male. Yet many black migrants felt as Alversa Beals did: "I wasn't upset that this town was segregated. I liked the money I was making. As long as I wasn't back there chopping cotton I was happy."[27]

African American migrants from the South became the hotels' menial workers. They prepared the food, cleaned the rooms, carried the bags. But the only black workers that most white customers saw were the porters. This was intentional. Las Vegas was to be a white man's paradise. Jewish and Italian gangsters, Texan and Oklahoman cowboy hucksters became the lords of these new gambling kingdoms, which were dependent on fantasies of luxury and indulgence. African Americans were pointedly excluded, except as invisible laborers. They could not eat a meal, watch a show, or drink a glass of water either in the old sawdust-on-the-floor saloons downtown in Glitter Gulch or in the "carpet establishments" on the ever-more-fabulous Strip.[28]

Given Las Vegas's location, one might imagine that hotel owners and managers would have drawn more heavily on Mexican and Mexican American labor for its workforce. But the coincidental timing of several historical phenomena—the recruitment of thousands of Delta blacks by federal defense contractors during the war and by union organizers afterward, the sudden and spectacular growth of gambling in Las Vegas after the war, and the utter collapse of plantation sharecropping in the Mississippi Delta region—ensured that the bulk of the casino labor force in the 1950s and 1960s would be made up of African American refugees from the cotton fields.

Many of the early tourists to Las Vegas also came from cotton country, and the casinos catered to their tastes and prejudices. "As people started coming in to gamble," recalls Sarah Ann Knight-Preddy, one of the city's earliest black residents, "a lot of tourists from the Deep South brought their prejudices with them. It became very prejudiced in this town after that. It was all about money." Mass migration by Southern whites to sunbelt cities like Los Angeles and Phoenix meant that the largest pool of weekend gamblers was white men and women accustomed to race segregation. The men who ran Las Vegas hotels did not want to offend their best customers. "The big rollers that spent the money were from the South," says local black entertainer Bob Bailey. "From Louisiana, Mississippi, Texas and Arkansas. . . . They wanted to keep it here the same way it was where the big spenders came from." And so, as late as 1960, black entertainers performing at Strip hotels—even headliners like Nat King Cole and Lena Horne—could not enter through the front door.[29]

Southern attitudes about race relations were only one strand in a tangle of political, economic, and cultural forces that molded Las Vegas as it grew. Organized crime syndicates, cowboy entrepreneurs, labor unions and their politician allies were equally influential in establishing patterns of power and patronage in "the silver state." At the heart of it all was Nevada's bid in the 1950s to become the nation's gambling mecca.

Without water, oil, or significant mineral resources, Nevada staked its future on gaming. In the 1950s, everything from legislation to union negotiations was tuned to the rhythm of the dice. Casino earnings filled the coffers of state government and lined the pockets of state politicians. Real estate values soared, and tens of millions of dollars were generated annually in new tax revenues. Between 1931 and 1945, gambling tax revenues in Nevada averaged just $30,000 a year. By 1962, the state was earning $15 million a year in gambling taxes and another $15 million in sales tax revenue from tourists. By the early 1960s, tourists contributed between 70 and 80 percent of Nevada's tax income.[30]

The state's success in promoting itself as a gambling destination bore fruit for casino owners and politicians. And in Nevada, power brokers were often both. Cliff "The Big Juice" Jones—the state's lieutenant governor from 1947 to 1954 and a protégé of powerful Senator Pat McCarran—was the principal stockholder in at least twenty-four casinos and owned shares in many more, including the Pioneer, the El Cortez, the Thunderbird, the Golden Nugget, the Algiers, the Westerner, and the Dunes. Other leading figures in Nevada politics in the 1950s and 1960s—including Democratic governor Grant Sawyer and Republican governor Paul Laxalt—profited from the largesse of casino owners. Although the Nevada Gaming Commission rode herd on mob investments, they bent over backwards to ensure the growth and profitability of the gaming industry. In those years, when the state's overall population was still small—fewer than three hundred thousand people lived in Nevada in 1960—the state's housing laws, labor union contracts, and social welfare policy were all designed to manipulate a pliable casino labor force.[31]

Gambling had been legal in Las Vegas since 1869, except for a brief period (1911–1931) when Progressive reformers succeeded in outlawing it. In 1931, most gaming operations in Las Vegas were located in small clubs and catered primarily to Boulder Dam workers. Typical of these was the Pair-O-Dice Club, bought in 1939 by Guy McAfee—a former Los Angeles police captain and vice-squad commander who was looking to invest the cash he'd skimmed from illegal California gambling casinos. The Pair-O-Dice Club was the first to open on a lonely stretch of desert highway outside the city. Paying homage to L.A.'s famous Sunset Strip, McAfee sarcastically called it "the Strip."[32]

Well into the 1960s, Nevada's most influential politicians had a relaxed attitude toward investors with ties to organized crime. This was particularly true of Nevada's power broker and Democratic machine boss, U.S. senator Pat McCarran. First elected on Franklin Roosevelt's coattails in 1932, McCarran carefully nurtured the development of legal gambling in Nevada. In 1950–1951, when Tennessee senator Estes Kefauver held televised hearings to publicize the role of organized crime in the gambling industry, McCarran flexed his political muscles in Congress. First he tried, unsuccessfully, to block contempt citations against racketeers and other friends in the casino business who refused to testify. Then he succeeded at stopping a proposed 10 percent federal tax on gambling wagers that threatened to cripple the gaming industry—and put Las Vegas out of business.

Paradoxically, the Kefauver hearings turned out to be a boon to the Strip hotels. As states across the country shut down illegal gambling, Las Vegas hotels were flooded by organized crime dollars from Los Angeles, New York, Miami, Cleveland, and Havana. Nevada "has let every syndicate in the country into Las Vegas," a maverick county commissioner complained in 1952. By 1958, thirteen sparkling new gambling resorts had been constructed on the Strip, almost all with money from organized crime. Each was more flamboyant than the last, more whimsical, and more intent on providing luxurious service.

Ben "Bugsy" Siegel's Flamingo hotel, completed in 1947, was the first and most famous icon of the new Las Vegas. Siegel, a psychotic child of New York City's mean streets, rose up through the mob ranks as a contract killer for powerful bootleggers. In Las Vegas, he ran a racing wire—an operation that takes bets on horse races—for the Al Capone–Lucky Luciano syndicate during the war. A brutal, hot-tempered, good-looking clotheshorse who liked to party with young starlets in Hollywood, Siegel bet that Las Vegas gambling resorts would be far more profitable if they spiffed up their image. Until Siegel's era, most Las Vegas hotels had a Wild West theme. He decided to build a hotel that set new standards for sumptuous luxury, with plush carpets and crystal chandeliers, imported marble, a three-story waterfall, a forty-horse stable, exotic gardens, huge, fanciful swimming pools, and the biggest names in entertainment. Even the janitors had to wear tuxedos.

As any guidebook will tell you, Siegel did not live to see his vision of a new Las Vegas fulfilled. He was murdered three months after the Flamingo's grand opening. But over the next decade, mob money poured into Las Vegas, financing a panoply of similarly extravagant neon oases: the Stardust, the Sands (Frank Sinatra's headquarters for a decade), the Sahara, the Riviera, the Dunes, the Showboat, the Desert Inn, and, in the early 1960s, the ultimate Strip resort—Caesars Palace.[33]

It was at the Flamingo that Alversa Beals found her first job in Las Vegas. She worked for two years, living in a trailer, until she had saved enough money to send back to Louisiana for her four children. She had left them with her mother until she got settled. Ruby Duncan, too, found work at the Flamingo. She had previously worked cooking and cleaning in the home of hotel comedian Hank Henry. But, with the arrival of her fourth child, she needed a job that would pay more. She worked for a while at the Stardust and a smaller motel before landing a good job at the Flamingo in 1956. Mary Wesley, who waitressed at night on the Westside, worked day jobs as a maid at the Showboat and later the Sands.

Everything in these chrome-and-marble palaces was to run flawlessly and seamlessly. No distractions, no unmade beds, no slipping on spilled drinks, no overflowing ashtrays. Mob-affiliated hotel bosses, says Duncan, could be "very charming, as long as you cut their morning grapefruit just right." Hotel workers knew what was expected of them, Duncan says, and, if they did their jobs right, they were treated well. After sharecropping, says Duncan, working for mob bosses was easy, even pleasant. Union organizer Rachel Coleman remembers that "the mob was the easiest employer in the world to work with." Syndicate bosses didn't object to the union; the Teamsters Union, in fact, would soon be among their best friends and financiers. The rules were clear: keep the cash flowing, and workers would receive a share.[34]

That imperative to keep the cash flowing dictated who was hired for what job in Las Vegas. Sex, as well as gambling, was for sale. Prostitution, legal for a time in Las Vegas and still legal in northern Nevada, became second only to gambling as a revenue producer for the state. In Las Vegas, brothels weren't the big lure (technically illegal by 1955, they were regulated with a wink, a nod, and an occasional payoff to the local sheriff). The real attraction was the elaborately constructed fantasy of sex readily available behind every roulette wheel, bar stool, and Keno counter.

Every job applicant's age and appearance, as well as her race and sex, were coolly calculated by casino managers to enhance this fantasy. Young white women—preferably blonde and leggy—were channeled into highly visible jobs where white male customers could ogle them: restaurant and cocktail waitresses, showgirls, and desk clerks. Black women were barred from these jobs. Jim Crow sensibilities required that there be no flirting between white male gamblers and black women workers, at least not publicly.

Mary Wesley was told to cut her hair, wipe off her makeup, and take off her earrings before she could be hired for a chambermaid job at the Sands. No manager could take the risk of hiring a pretty young black maid. "White men would flirt" with her and "their wives wouldn't stand for it," a house-keeping supervisor told Wesley. Hotel operators worried that women would drag their husbands out of the casinos if they saw them flirting with black women employees. Wesley wondered why that wouldn't also be the case if women saw their husbands flirting with white maids, but she didn't press the issue. The rough men who managed the Strip hotels were very clear. Nothing was to interrupt the cash flow from customers to the casinos. Managers had no problem if a white customer wanted sex with a black woman. Concierges, pit bosses, and bellboys were happy to provide gamblers with whatever they wanted—behind the scenes. But no public scenes or disruptions would be tolerated.[35]

These new Strip hotels competed fiercely for tourists, promising visitors excitement in all forms—including buses into the desert to view atomic bomb tests and more than enough sex, faux or real—to put them in the mood for some serious gambling. In an era when "silent" mob investors were always watching, Vegas hotel managers knew that they were playing against one another not only for customers but also for strong, docile, and inexpensive workers. To ensure a steady labor supply, and to keep them cooperative, managers worked hard to establish good relations with the city's powerful unions. Most important among the city's unions was the Hotel and Culinary Workers Union, Local 226.[36]

Chartered in 1938, Local 226 quickly came to represent almost everyone who worked in the new Las Vegas hotel casinos. Now one of the largest local unions in the country, the Hotel and Culinary Workers Union was led for years by Al Bramlet, a streetwise white bartender from Arkansas, and Sarah Hughes, a charismatic black woman from the Delta. During the 1950s, Bramlet personally recruited labor for the new Strip hotels, traveling to New York, Los Angeles, San Francisco, and Chicago. He also made repeated trips to small towns in rural Louisiana and Arkansas, where he promised cotton pickers and mill-hands wages beyond anything they could hope to make in the Delta. Hughes provided the personal touch, reaching out to new members and persuading them to become union activists.[37]

The union cultivated loyalty among its black members by providing a measure of job security, medical benefits, and the rudiments of a political education. Hughes and Bramlet came to the Westside at night to hold meetings with small groups of black working men and women. Duncan would drag herself out after a day of cleaning private homes to listen to them speak. Their rhetoric excited her. Some of the maids she met at those meetings would one day rise to top positions in the union. Duncan soaked up everything she could about the financial underpinnings of Las Vegas and Nevada politics—for the Culinary Workers Union was one of the savviest players in Vegas. By the time Duncan and Beals began working as maids on the Strip, Local 226 had struck an accord with the largest Las Vegas hoteliers. Job seekers had to join the union if they wanted to work on the Strip.

Sarah Hughes, who gave frequent pep talks to hotel maids about union solidarity, was something of a revelation to migrants fresh from the cotton fields: a powerful black woman who went head to head with the rough men who ran casino gambling in Las Vegas. "She always taught us that the members *were* the union, and if we stick together we would have a strong union," recalls Rachel Coleman, a Vicksburg, Mississippi, native and Vegas chambermaid who went on to become a business agent for the union. Shortly after Duncan, then twenty-three, got hired as a maid at the Flamingo in 1956, Hughes paid her a visit at work. "Right away she just made me feel so comfortable," Duncan recalls. "And she was so strong."[38]

> *"You don't take anything that you don't have to take," she told us. "Stay and do your work and do it right because I can't fight your battles if you haven't done everything the way it ought to be. But don't ever let them walk on you."*

Struck by Hughes's confidence and courage, Duncan often thought: "God, I wish I was her."[39]

Duncan had always spoken up for herself. But being a lone hothead had brought her only so far. How much better to be a member of a sophisticated political organization wielding the collective clout of a union, instead of working alone, cleaning private homes. Joining the union made her feel part of something bigger. And for Duncan, as for many black migrants, the union provided a first experience of cross-racial solidarity. When white waiters and waitresses found out that back-of-the-house employees were not getting free meals, they gave up one of their daily meals so that maids and porters would be fed.[40]

Alversa Beals says her early encounters with Sarah Hughes and the union helped her realize that even a marginally educated single mother was entitled to basic human and political rights. Beals was taken to the union hall by her sister-in-law, an avid union member. As soon as Beals got her union card, she was told she should register to vote. Then in her early twenties, Beals had never voted before. "They asked me whether I was a Democrat or a Republican," she recalls. "I asked my sister-in-law 'Which one is you?' She said, 'I'm a Democrat.' So I joined the Democrats."

Next, Hughes taught Alversa Beals the basics of trade unionism, Las Vegas style:

> *I saw how union people would go together and they would try to get a raise. And if the union didn't get the raise, they'd talk about going on a strike. We would all have to vote and see if we should strike. Sarah Hughes would come and talk to us and we'd have a little meeting and she'd explain things to us.*

Of course, Beals and Duncan laugh now—nobody dared to strike in Las Vegas until the late 1960s. But the union gave the women a sense of belonging, a solid wage, and their first exercise of citizenship rights that most Americans took for granted.[41]

Union membership did nothing, however, to ease their work. Even women raised in the cotton fields found the demands of maid work in the big hotels backbreaking. "Maid work was so, so hard," Duncan recalls. "I really don't understand how these women could do 16 and 17 and 18 and 20 rooms a day. Because I just could do five. Before long I had to tell them that." Mary Wesley, later one of the first women to work on a Las Vegas Sanitation Department truck, says that hauling garbage cans was a breeze compared to maid duties on the Strip. "When I came home at the end of a day on the truck, I was so relaxed," she laughs. "I took a shower, painted the house. When I came home at the end of a day of being a maid I was so tired I just fell across the bed. I couldn't move." Many maids worked to the limits of their physical endurance—a situation that over time resulted in a high rate of accidents and physical breakdowns.[42]

Tallulan migrant Leola Harris was at first thrilled to land a maid job at the Thunderbird hotel just hours after she stepped off the bus. The Thunderbird was headquarters for Senator Pat McCarran, the state's most powerful politician, and Lieutenant Governor Cliff Jones, who owned 11 percent of the hotel. (Meyer Lansky was also rumored to hold hidden shares.) The posh resort once hosted fifty state lawmakers for several days—a junket called "The Lost Weekend" by journalists—as local power brokers tried to convince them not to increase the state gaming tax. (It worked.) Maids at the Thunderbird were expected to hew to the highest possible standards. Each cleaned a minimum of fifteen rooms per day, sometimes within just one or two hours. Tourists (and politicians) partied all night then stayed in bed until eleven or twelve. The maids then had to work like demons to prepare rooms for incoming guests.[43]

Leola Harris recalls being chastised regularly by a white supervisor at the Thunderbird for not working fast enough. Finally, she says, "I didn't even try to do all the rooms." She was fired from the Thunderbird, she says, but it did not worry her. Harris stormed out of the Thunderbird, walked straight into the union hall, and was given a job for the very next day. Before the 1960s were out, says Harris, "I must have worked at every hotel on the Strip."[44]

Duncan, too, challenged her bosses without thinking twice. Her supervisor at the Flamingo was always ordering her, at the last minute, to extend her hours. Duncan told the woman that she had small children waiting for her at home, so she just couldn't work overtime. One night, she says, the housekeeper called over to the staff just as they were ready to go off shift and said:

> *"You ladies cannot leave because there are more beds that have got to be made up." And I said: "I'm not going to make any more beds." She said, "Well you have to." I said, "I'm going home to my kids."*

The next evening, Duncan was called into the executive housekeeper's office and told she was insubordinate. "Why didn't you stay and do those rooms like the housekeeper said to?" the supervisor asked. "I didn't stay because it's not slavery time anymore," Duncan replied. "I did my eight hours and I wasn't about to do any more. That woman thinks she is still in Florida. But I know I have left the South."[45]

Duncan knew she had the union behind her. When the Flamingo fired her, she marched over to Sarah Hughes's office and filed a complaint. She watched with great relish as Hughes explained to the executive housekeeper that a supervisor cannot require a worker to stay overtime, nor can she demand overtime work without paying the worker time and a half. Duncan was reinstated and promised an extra check for overtime.[46]

On such matters, the union had clout. The Culinary Workers Union had an arrangement: Al Bramlet kept things running smoothly in return for a steady increase in the workers' wage scale and benefits. The arrangement clearly worked for the casinos, and for Bramlet, who had financial interests in several companies that had private contracts with the casinos.[47]

But the union's cozy relationship with the casinos also meant that it refused to challenge the industry's ironclad color bar. The big hotels in Las Vegas, Essie Henderson says, were just shiny plantations. "Here we was colored people in the morning when they wanted us to work. But at night, it was: 'Get those niggers on home to bed on the Westside where they can get some rest so they can come on back and do more work tomorrow.' "[48]

BLOWS AGAINST THE CASINO EMPIRE: CIVIL RIGHTS LAS VEGAS STYLE

A movement to end racial segregation in Las Vegas began to pick up steam in the late 1950s. Black protestors in Montgomery, Alabama, had forced desegregation of the city's bus system. Black schoolchildren in Little Rock, Arkansas, had desegregated the city's high schools. As television images of these victories appeared on the nightly news, black Las Vegans became more restive about their situation. African Americans were barred, not only from staying, eating, or gambling in Strip hotels, but from nearly all public facilities outside of the Westside. Downtown restaurant owners posted signs saying that they would not serve black patrons. On the Strip, the only place where blacks could eat was Foxy's deli, where the owner reserved two booths for them. "You could go into stores, but if you tried on clothing you couldn't put it back on the rack; you had to buy it," recalls James McMillan, a black Westside dentist and chair of the local NAACP.

McMillan and other Westside leaders had been watching excitedly as civil rights protests heated up in the Southeast. Then McMillan received a letter from the national NAACP, calling on all local chapters to intensify civil rights protest in their own cities. In a series of community meetings around the Westside, black Las Vegans strategized about ways to increase pressure on business and political leaders to end segregation throughout the city.[49]

The city's new mayor, Oran Gragson, who had openly courted black votes during his campaign, met with Westside leaders and seemed sympathetic to their demands. So did Donal "Mike" O'Callaghan, a former Henderson schoolteacher and high-ranking Job Corps official in the Kennedy administration, who would become Nevada's governor in 1971. Several top gaming industry financiers expressed support, arguing that segregation was bad for tourism because it made Las Vegas look like a Southern backwater.

But progress on the civil rights front was slow. Nevada was an overwhelmingly white state with a long history of prickly resistance to government interference in the behavior of private citizens. A number of statewide civil rights bills died in committee, were filibustered, or were simply voted down. Despite their close ties to owners of the city's major hotels, men like Gragson, O'Callaghan, and liberal newspaper publisher Hank Greenspun were either unable or unwilling to force an end to segregation in Las Vegas.

Frustrated, McMillan and other Westside leaders started talking seriously about staging a massive protest on the Strip. A march that disrupted gambling, if even for one day, could drive home their message: desegregate the casinos or face huge losses in tourist dollars. The Strip was the key pressure point because the big hotels were loath to accept even brief disruptions of gambling. And if the "carpet palaces" on the Strip integrated, then the old downtown "sawdust joints" would have to follow suit.[50]

As in the Montgomery bus boycott and other high-profile civil rights struggles, maids had an important part to play in the Las Vegas civil rights movement. Daily acts of resistance by black maids, porters, and kitchen staff began to worry hotel managers. Mary Wesley protested against hotel policies that forced her to use the back-door service entrance. "I had this maid job at the Sands and they would never let me come in through the front doors. It really bugged me. I said to them, 'You mean I can make your beds, I can touch up your pillow but I can't walk in through the front door?' That made me mad." Although protests by black workers at Strip hotels were individual and spontaneous, hotel owners and city officials were well aware that this was a unionized workforce. The union had never openly challenged segregation in Las Vegas, but there was no guarantee that the workers would not.[51]

Because Las Vegas was fast becoming one of the world's premiere entertainment spots, the shock troops of the civil rights movement also included some of the biggest names in show business. Black musicians and singers had helped put Las Vegas on the map. Nat King Cole, Josephine Baker, Sammy Davis Jr., Harry Belafonte, Lena Horne, Pearl Bailey, the Ink Spots, the Mills Brothers, Duke Ellington, and Count Basie appeared regularly as star attractions on the Strip in the 1950s. But they were unwelcome to eat or sleep at the hotels that emblazoned their names in lights.

Just as galling for many of these stars, they looked out over the footlights onto all-white audiences. Black Las Vegans were banned from even entering the rooms where their favorites performed. Nor could black entertainers hire local black dancers or musicians to perform in their shows. Beyond their most essential personnel, black performers in Las Vegas were accompanied by white orchestras and chorus lines of white women. Blacks were not hired as stage-hands or lighting technicians, either. The big-money shows in the city's fanci-est theaters were set up and broken down by all-white crews.

Each night, after the stage curtains fell, black entertainers would have to drive down the Strip and cross the "concrete curtain" to the Westside, where they could eat, drink, gamble, and find lodging. In the late 1940s, black per-formers stayed in private homes or rooming houses. By the 1950s, black celeb-rities such as boxer Joe Louis had begun to open hotels on the Westside. Louis's Cove hotel, in which Sammy Davis Jr. also owned stock, became famous as a watering hole for African American stars. One of the few black-owned hotels in Las Vegas, the Cove boomed while Las Vegas remained a Jim Crow town.

Rigid race segregation on the Strip, ironically, was a boon to Westside ho-tels, restaurants, and clubs. Well-known black entertainers frequented the Westside's El Morocco, Town Tavern, Club Alabam, and other after-hours clubs. Eventually, white celebrities and tourists followed. Some consciously sought to transgress the city's color line. Others came for the music. Vegas stars such as Frank Sinatra and Dean Martin could be found at Westside clubs, along with Hollywood weekenders such as Gregory Peck and Dorothy La-mour. Even staid television host Ed Sullivan frequented the Westside, hunting for new talent for his variety show.[52]

The excitement and cash infusion that these black entertainers brought to the Westside had an electrifying effect, generating well-paying jobs for black cocktail waitresses, dealers, and casino managers. Black workers had no hope of getting such jobs on the Strip. Sarah Ann Knight-Preddy, whose parents had come to Las Vegas in the 1940s, found work on the Westside as one of the city's only female card dealers. Mary Wesley, a hotel maid by day, waited tables each night at the Westside's Town Tavern, which featured jam sessions, good food, gambling, and drinks. When Wesley's customers hit big in the tavern casino, they sometimes left tips that equaled—or surpassed—her week's wages as a hotel maid.[53]

Despite the ramshackle houses, the unpaved streets, the legendary mud puddles that could swallow ankles and knees, a surprising number of black Las Vegans look back on the segregation era with nostalgia. "The Westside had its own dignity at that time," Duncan remembers:

We had Jackson St. which was lit up and was just jumping every which way. There was action and fun in West Las Vegas. And people was more happy and more sound-minded I think at that time. When integration came through, we all lost that closeness. We all just started going someplace else to spend our money. And when that happened everything dried right up.[54]

Black Westsiders enjoyed a sense of community across class lines in those years, says Duncan. Rich and poor, famous and unknown, were thrown together in the same clubs and restaurants, in the same small, crowded neighborhood. That feeling of solidarity left performers like Sammy Davis Jr. with a lasting affection for the people of the Westside. A few years later, Davis would offer personal and financial support to Duncan and the poor mothers of the Westside in their struggle for welfare rights. Duncan believes that his support grew out of the years when Davis spent so many nights gambling, singing, and drumming in Westside clubs.[55]

By the late 1940s and early 1950s, African American entertainers had already raised money and acted as ambassadors for the civil rights movement in the South, in Los Angeles, and in New York. But there was no locale in the country where their activism was more central to the dismantling of Jim Crow than in Las Vegas. Lena Horne, known for her no-nonsense stance on bigotry, was one of the first to say no to segregation on the Strip. During World War II, she had refused to perform at a USO show for an audience in which Nazi prisoners of war were seated in front of black U.S. soldiers. In 1947, Bugsy Siegel, eager to cash in on Horne's glamour and popularity with white audiences, asked her to be one of the early acts at the Flamingo. He also booked her a room there. Siegel, who made his own rules and carried a gun at all times, quickly squelched anybody who objected—including white bandleader Xavier Cugat, who made the mistake of treating Horne rudely. But Siegel made Horne a virtual prisoner in her hotel room: forbidden to eat in the hotel dining room, use the pool, gamble in the casino, or drink in the lounge. For the next seven years, Horne demanded that the casinos change their policy. Finally, in 1955, the Sands hotel opened its front door to Horne and other black performers, inviting them to stay where they played.[56]

But other hotels were slow to follow suit. The Platters, a well-known a cappella group, were playing the Flamingo in 1955 while their mega-hit, "The Great Pretender," was flooding the radio airwaves. Moments after a performance that was greeted by wild applause and cheers, one band member realized that he had left his jacket on the stage. When he tried to reenter the nightclub to retrieve it, he was brusquely escorted out by two bouncers. Once off the stage, he had immediately become just another black man, and the rules for black men on the Las Vegas Strip were clear and firm: no entry into nightclubs. For black women, the rules were, if anything, even harsher. Singer Eartha Kitt couldn't get served at a burger-and-fries drive-in on the Strip, although her show at the El Rancho hotel was selling out nightly. Nat King Cole was bounced out of the Tropicana in 1957 while headlining at the Sands. When the Tropicana manager was told who Cole was, he retorted: "I don't care if he's Jesus. He's black and he has to get out of here."[57]

Little by little, both at the top of the marquee and in the back of the house, segregation began to crack. Sammy Davis Jr., whose name was practically synonymous with the Las Vegas Strip, announced that he would no longer play any hotel where he could not spend the night. By the late 1950s, most of the big hotels had given in: black performers could lodge on the Strip. But Davis pushed the boundaries further when he and his "Rat Pack" buddies Dean Martin, Joey Bishop, and Frank Sinatra decided to play poker in the Sands swimming pool. Davis slipped his thongs under a beach chair and dove in. A tense silence reigned over the usually boisterous swim area. An irate guest stormed off to speak to the management. Within minutes after the singer emerged from the water, a crew rushed in to drain, clean, and refill the entire pool. Black Las Vegans relate this story with humor, but it reflects the depth of white "Negrophobia" in this Southwestern desert town.[58]

New, more cosmopolitan winds were blowing into the city, however, and in 1955 a group of white investors from New York and Los Angeles opened Las Vegas's first explicitly interracial casino hotel. Located on the fringes of the Westside, the Moulin Rouge drew white customers as well as black by combining the very best in black entertainment with the illicit thrill of mixed-race socializing. The $3.5 million Moulin Rouge packed its dimly lit lavender showroom nightly for lavish spectaculars. Former heavyweight champion Joe Louis greeted guests at the door. Headline acts such as Lionel Hampton and His Orchestra, child dancers Gregory and Maurice Hines (billed as the Hines Kids), "Queen of the Blues" singer Dinah Washington, and the Mills Brothers were frequently joined by black stars from the Strip who dropped by after hours. Louis Armstrong made several surprise appearances. Harry Belafonte climbed onto the stage for late-night improvisations. Sammy Davis Jr. liked to sit in on the drums. And the jam sessions often wailed on through sunrise.[59]

The Moulin Rouge quickly acquired a reputation as the place in Las Vegas where big-name black and white entertainers could hobnob, play music, and perform on the same stage. Westside regulars Frank Sinatra and Dean Martin were followed there by Tallulah Bankhead, Bob Hope, Milton Berle, and jazz bandleaders Tommy and Jimmy Dorsey. The Moulin Rouge made the cover of *Life* magazine as the icon of a new, integrated pop culture scene. *Life*'s photo spread displayed the hotel's all-black Watusi chorus line, noting that the Moulin Rouge was the city's first hotel to hire black dancers such as "Boots" Wade and Dee Dee Jasmin. The white owners also hired black waitresses, dealers, and cooks: Ruby Duncan occasionally worked nights in the club's kitchen, making extra money to supplement her day job cleaning private homes.

Perhaps the most striking *Life* photos showed black and white customers rubbing shoulders happily at the blackjack table. That feeling of happiness was real, say Westsiders who remember fondly their nights out at the Moulin Rouge, which was an easy walk from their Westside homes. It wasn't just about the music, or a lucky streak. "There was never one fight, not one black and white incident," recalls Bailey, who was master of ceremonies at the hotel. "People knew the rest of the town was so wrong and everything at the Moulin Rouge was so right."[60]

The club's reputation extended well beyond Las Vegas. A national "Miss Moulin Rouge" contest, organized by bandleader Lionel Hampton, spread to Denver, Albuquerque, El Paso, Chicago, and New York. "This contest is the gateway to tomorrow," Hampton declared. "Besides offering a wonderful opportunity to talented youngsters, it calls attention to a real citadel of democracy." But in November 1955, just five months after it opened, the Moulin Rouge was dark and shuttered—a victim of financial mismanagement and, some suspect, strong-arming by Strip hoteliers who had seethed while the club drew away their after-hours clientele. No acts have played the purple-ceilinged showroom for half a century.[61]

In the decade that followed the rise and fall of the Moulin Rouge, racial barriers on the Strip began to crumble. Black performers were given rooms in the city's poshest hotels. Harry Belafonte broke the ban on black gamblers by sitting down at a 21 table in the elegant Sands casino. For a while, the dealer tried to ignore him, but Belafonte quietly refused to move. Finally, a floor manager came over to the table, no doubt having conferred with the top hotel authorities. He nodded to the dealer. Belafonte was dealt his cards. White patrons took seats next to him. Soon a crowd gathered round. You could almost hear the collective sigh of relief, says Nevada Historical Museum director Frank Wright. "They all saw that this wasn't so much of a threat."[62]

Flamboyant singer Josephine Baker opened the doors of Las Vegas showrooms to ordinary black Las Vegans, not just the stars who passed through to perform. When she saw only white faces at her first show at El Rancho Vegas, she announced that there would be no second show unless there were black patrons to watch it. "I'm not going to entertain," Baker said from on stage. "I'm going to sit right here until you make up your minds." Anxious to prevent a scene, hotel managers ran through the hotel and told several black maids and porters to go home, change their clothes, and come back dressed for the nightclub. "Every night thereafter," Bob Bailey recalls, "she had two tables and she insisted that there be Blacks at those tables. And she picked up the check. It was fantastic. She really . . . shook things up."[63]

The glitziest hotels were beginning to cater to the wishes of their stars. But, as late as 1960, most black Las Vegans still could not get served a cup of coffee downtown. That spring, moved by images of lunch counter sit-ins across the South, Westside leaders gave city officials an ultimatum: Begin desegregating public accommodations in thirty days, or black Las Vegans would march on the Strip, block traffic, enter the hotels, and boycott any business that discriminated against them.

Activists organized pep rallies in local churches, met with union officials, and went door to door to gather support for the proposed march. National media picked up the story, which got big play in newspapers, television stations, and radio broadcasts. City officials panicked, fearing that televised images of civil rights marchers on the Strip might link Las Vegas in the minds of potential visitors with Little Rock or Montgomery. Mayor Gragson asked Las Vegas NAACP president James McMillan to call off the demonstration, offering to hire more blacks for city jobs. But Gragson said he had no leverage over hotel owners or any other private business owners in the city. McMillan turned him down—despite bomb threats phoned in to his children, which prompted Westside men to stand vigil outside the dentist's house for ten days. McMillan told city officials to expect a massive protest.[64]

Just days before the march, however, several syndicate figures flew to Las Vegas, intent on blocking the demonstration. McMillan sent them a message, using as his courier a Westside club owner who had frequent dealings with the mob. "Tell these people that I'm not trying to cut into their business," McMillan said. "All I'm trying to do is make this a cosmopolitan city, and that will make more money for them." There are no records of the alleged mob summit, but McMillan received a phone call a few days later. Call the manager at the Desert Inn, he was told. Moe Dalitz, a longtime racketeer who owned the Desert Inn, had a message for him. The conversation, says McMillan, was very brief. "It's been settled," he was told. "We have accepted your terms."[65]

Fittingly, Westside activists chose the Moulin Rouge (closed for business but open for hire) as the site for their announcement that segregation of public facilities in Las Vegas was coming to an end. With Mayor Gragson, Governor Grant Sawyer, and other officials looking on, McMillan told a crowd of news reporters that the casino empire was lifting its color bar. Black customers would now be welcome anywhere in Las Vegas.[66]

The next morning, the NAACP sent out teams of African American men and women to test the waters. They walked through the front doors of Strip hotels with no interference. They were allowed to gamble, order food at the restaurants, and reserve tables in the nightclubs. Within days, the NAACP reported, 80 to 90 percent of hotels in Las Vegas were willingly serving black patrons. The major pockets of resistance came from the owners of older hotels. Texan émigré Benny Binion, owner of Binion's Horseshoe Club in Glitter Gulch, and a handful of other downtown hoteliers banned black patrons well into the 1960s. But the majority capitulated quietly. Jim Crow left Las Vegas without much of a fight. And the Moulin Rouge earned a spot on the National Register of Historic Places as a civil rights landmark.

Segregation of public facilities ended in Las Vegas for the same reason it had started twenty-five years earlier: profitability. If the tourist trade in the postwar years was dominated by white Southerners driving in for weekends from their new homes in Los Angeles, Phoenix, and Albuquerque, by 1960 the age of jet travel was in full swing and tourists came to Las Vegas from all over the world. Hotel owners could no longer assume that a majority of their customers supported segregation. "They knew that some southerners wouldn't want to gamble at an integrated casino," says James McMillan. "But they also ... needed to make sure the convention business stayed.... Money moves the world. When these fellows realized that they weren't going to lose any money, that they might even make more, they were suddenly color blind."[67]

AFTER INTEGRATION

Black Las Vegans celebrated the end of segregation in Strip casinos, hotels, and restaurants. Duncan remembers how excited she was the first time she got to see Nat King Cole on the Strip. She saw Sammy Davis Jr., Wayne Newton, and gyrating heartthrob Tom Jones. Duncan and Beals got tickets every time Jones came to town. Their daughters would later tease them about him. "Mama's palms got sweaty whenever he was around," laughs Beals's daughter Renia. When they could, Westsiders wrangled "comps"—free passes—from friends and relatives who worked in the hotels. But nightclub tickets were too expensive for them to buy often. Desegregation of public facilities was an important psychological breakthrough. Economic progress was harder to achieve.

Good jobs and decent housing were still out of reach for many Westsiders.

Years after the Moulin Rouge agreement, black workers were still relegated to "back of the house" positions. Blacks could spend their money at Strip hotels, says Essie Henderson, but they couldn't earn much money there. "You'd be amazed at what black people can do," Henderson says wryly. "We can park cars; we can serve food. But they weren't hiring nobody black for any of those jobs. And this was in the 60s."

Mary Wesley was waitressing at the Town Tavern on the Westside when she sensed that things might be changing. A skinny, mustachioed white customer came in day after day, sat at her station, and watched her. One day he called her over. "It was Al Bramlet," she says, president of the Culinary Workers Union. "He wanted me to be the first black food waitress on the Strip. He had been coming to my job for a month. He said, 'You have the personality and you have the skills.' "[68]

Wesley was thrilled at Bramlet's offer. But she reluctantly turned it down. With eight children—seven of her own, and another that she'd adopted—Wesley worried that she might not be the ideal candidate. What if one of her children got sick? "How would it look if I was the *first* and I messed up, or if I couldn't be there every day?" Four decades later, her voice still quivers. It still hurts, having passed up her chance to become a civil rights pioneer. And she might have been able to earn a better living for her children.

Bramlet's search for a pioneering black waitress was motivated, at least in part, by blistering criticism from Westside activists who said the union wasn't doing enough for its black members. Black workers had been the union's backbone since the late 1940s, but they were still excluded from all but the most menial jobs on the Strip. In 1960, James McMillan, Sarah Ann Knight-Preddy, and other NAACP leaders demanded that Al Bramlet begin placing black waiters, waitresses, and maître d's at unionized hotels. "We had a confrontation about hiring blacks," McMillan recalls. "I told Bramlet what a racist he was, and we really went to it." But little came of the encounter except mutual animosity. Job options for black workers on the Strip were severely limited throughout the 1960s, particularly for women. "We could be maids, or we could be in the kitchen or the laundry," says Henderson. "That was about it."[69]

Housing options were equally slim. Outside of the Westside, there were very few neighborhoods where banks would approve mortgages for black families to buy homes. And the Westside continued to receive far less than its share of municipal services. As late as 1970, there was no library on the Westside, no medical center, inadequate housing, and dilapidated and segregated schools.

The state Equal Rights Commission, created in 1961, investigated civil rights violations—including discrimination in employment, housing, and public services—but it was powerless to act on its findings. Bob Bailey sat on the commission in its first years. "I've signed more subpoenas for owners of hotels here than the Kefauver Committee did," Bailey later joked. But hotel executives denied that they discriminated in hiring. There simply weren't enough blacks qualified as waiters, waitresses, bellmen, or dealers, they insisted. Many recalcitrant owners didn't even show up when subpoenaed to testify at Commission hearings. State courts ruled that the hotel owners were within their rights to refuse.[70]

Many casino owners fiercely resisted civil rights legislation in Nevada. But none was more adamant, or freer with invective, than aviation and film mogul Howard Hughes. In the 1960s, he was buying hotels on the Strip as if they were pieces in a Monopoly game. Hughes's buying spree was welcomed by state officials, who hoped that he could wrest control of the Strip from unsavory organized crime figures and make Las Vegas tourism respectable. Hughes promised to give Nevada gambling "the kind of reputation that Lloyds of London has, so that Nevada on a note will be like Sterling on silver."

The deeply racist Hughes didn't believe African Americans were good for business. He even fought against improving housing conditions on the Westside, because that might encourage more black migrants to settle there. Flexing his muscles in the state capital, Carson City, Hughes blocked open housing and school integration bills during the late 1960s. As one of the largest employers in the state of Nevada, he fought fiercely against equal employment legislation. And he handed out staggering amounts of cash in the capitol to curry support for his views.[71]

Nevada did not outlaw race-based discrimination in either public accommodations or employment until 1965, after Congress passed the 1964 Civil Rights Act. And the only reason Nevada legislators were willing to pass a civil rights bill then, says Bailey, was that "otherwise the Feds would be in the state looking into their business." But Nevada offered only limited civil rights guarantees. Private home owners, for example, were free to discriminate by writing restrictive covenants that forbade the sale of their homes to African Americans or Mexicans.[72]

Much to the fury of Las Vegas NAACP activists, Bramlet and the Culinary Workers Union gave only anemic backing to civil rights laws. Through the late 1970s, Westside activists would lock horns with Bramlet over the union's tacit cooperation with hotel hiring policies. Still, Ruby Duncan, who met Bramlet in the early 1950s, says he played a key role in politicizing her and in galvanizing poor and uneducated black Las Vegans to take action on their own behalf.

Duncan remembers the small-framed, intense man who would meet late into the night with black workers on the Westside. He would spend long hours, says Duncan, patiently explaining to groups of fifteen or twenty black hotel workers how a union stood behind its members, what their rights were, how they no longer needed to put up with abuses by employers. Bramlet was the first white man Duncan had met who seemed to be sincerely on her side. Bramlet and Sara Hughes convinced her that it was possible to organize across racial lines toward a more just society. That vision, Duncan says, helped shape and direct her later career as an advocate for poor families and for the political empowerment of low-income women.

Duncan is not naive about racism in the Culinary Workers Union, or about the character of Al Bramlet. In 1977, he was found under a pile of rocks in the desert, executed for refusing to pay for two car bombs that hadn't gone off. (He had ordered them planted in front of nonunion restaurants.) But, during her early days in Las Vegas, Duncan says, Bramlet was a friend and mentor. Some black women union members affectionately (or maybe sarcastically) called him "The Great White Father." And the union, for all its flaws, did improve conditions for the city's black workers. "In the 50s," muses Duncan, "it was okay for black people in the union. Everybody felt the union was doing what it should—*at that time*." Over the next few years, the expectations of black migrant women in Las Vegas, like those of poor people across the country, would change. Duncan would no longer look to others to fight her battles. Poor women, she was realizing, were going to have to learn how to fight for themselves.

CHAPTER 3

"BAD LUCK AND LOUSY PEOPLE": BLACK SINGLE MOTHERS AND THE WAR ON POVERTY

I'm used to being broke. I'm used to being sad.
I'm used to lousy folks and I'm used to being mad.
Bad luck and lousy people, No, No they don't bother me.

—Words and music by Dinah Washington, headliner
 at the Moulin Rouge and "Queen of the Jukeboxes"
 in Westside bars and taverns in the 1950s and early 1960s

In 1959, Ruby Duncan wasn't sure whether she was heading for a stable, working-class life or a fast downhill slide. In truth, she stood at a crossroads. At twenty-seven, she was a striking young woman with a steady job and a host of suitors, including a Nellis Air Force Base airman who wanted to marry her. Duncan was also a single mother, supporting six children on her wages as a Flamingo hotel maid. That's not how she had envisioned her future when she left the Ivory Plantation. But trauma, romance, and limited access to contraception had left Duncan—like one in four black women of her generation—with a burgeoning family and no partner with whom to raise them.

Duncan's children were her worry and her joy. Ivory, her oldest son, was the gift that emerged from her sexual assault. David was fathered by an oil worker Duncan dated in Tallulah who said he loved her and had tried to stop her from leaving. One day, when Ruby was living in Whitney, Nevada, with her aunt and two young sons, the ex-boyfriend appeared at the plywood plank that passed for her front door. "When I looked up, he was there," she says. They rekindled their relationship, and after Ruby became pregnant for a third time, her boyfriend persuaded her to return to Tallulah with her sons. Ruby stayed there just long enough to give birth to a daughter, Georgia—and to find out that her lover was married. "And he had about a thousand children," she says, laughing ruefully.

Duncan wasn't about to give up her ambitions—or her children's future —for a philanderer who wanted to drag her back to the farm. In 1952, she and her children returned to Las Vegas for good. Duncan found a job cooking and cleaning in the home of comedian Hank Henry, a regular performer at the Silver Slipper casino. Henry and his wife treated Duncan well and paid her enough to support three children at Aunt Mamie's motel-turned-family-homestead in the desert.[1]

On Friday nights, Duncan was eager to get out of Whitney and meet other young Las Vegans, particularly the African American airmen then stationed at Nellis Air Force Base. "I had a thing for airmen," she admits. "I felt like they were more clean and more decent." Duncan doesn't apologize for playing the field. She was a beautiful young woman, with striking cheekbones that she attributes to her Cherokee heritage, electric eyes, and a sonorous laugh. "Naturally, as a young woman, I wanted to be loved," she says. Those relationships produced two more sons, Ronnie in 1955 and Kenneth in 1956, and her second daughter, Sondra, in 1959. Duncan says she was interested in settling down, but the children's fathers were not. "When I found out they were the type that wasn't interested in fathering," she says, "I pushed them on."

Having children out of wedlock didn't carry the stigma for Duncan, or for other black single mothers in that era, that it did for young white women. Several surveys from the late 1940s through the mid-1960s showed that African American women prioritized motherhood over marriage. In stark contrast to whites, most black unwed mothers surveyed said that a single mother could do just as good a job raising her children as could a married mother. And they preferred to remain single rather than enter into a bad marriage. "It's better to be an unwed mother than an unhappy bride," was one widespread view.[2]

But Duncan wanted to give her children a nice home, a good education, new clothes, and quality medical care, and she couldn't do that alone. For one brief period Duncan had to go on welfare to support them. Hank Henry first told Duncan about Aid to Dependent Children (ADC), federal assistance for single mothers. Duncan applied and was accepted but "couldn't stand being on welfare," she recalls. It was demeaning, and besides, it did not give her nearly enough money to support her children. So in 1956, Duncan went to work at the Flamingo hotel. It wasn't all drudgery: she regularly cleaned the suite of singer Pearl Bailey, with whom she struck up a lifelong friendship. At Christmastime, Bailey would cook meals for Duncan's children and send the food over to the house. But Duncan's wages couldn't keep food on the table the rest of the year. Even working full time at union scale, Duncan was among the one in four Americans who lived near or below the poverty line in the mid-1950s. And her children were among the one in three U.S. youngsters then classified as poor. The family moved into the Cadillac Arms, which, despite its lofty name, was a squalid public housing project on the Westside. Duncan knew that marriage could be her ticket out, but she hadn't yet met the right man.[3]

Until she met Roy Duncan. Tall, handsome, and powerfully built, the Nellis airman struck Ruby as responsible and solid. He told her he wanted to be a father to all of her six children. "Roy always wanted a big family," she says, and Ruby's brood provided one ready-made. The couple met at a dance at the airbase and were married in 1959. The family moved out of the projects and into a tidy, blue-and-pink house on the Westside. When Ruby again became pregnant, Roy convinced her to stop work and stay home with the children. They could afford it, he told her. After he mustered out of the Air Force, Duncan worked for a private sanitation company during the day, and as a high-school janitor at night. Ruby stopped working while her last two children were babies, but eventually went back to her maid job at the Flamingo. It was a large family and they needed the income.

"Roy was always a great provider," Ruby Duncan recalls. And the children adored him. "He took care of us through thick and thin," says Roy Jr. "Whether physically or in spirit, he was always there to help us." The children, particularly the boys, were awed by Roy Duncan's physical prowess. "I remember one time seeing him pull a tree out of the ground," Roy Jr. recalls. "He bear-hugged it and pulled it way out. I would say: 'That's my Hercules.'"[4]

A family photograph from the early 1960s captures Ruby and Roy's desire for middle-class normalcy. Decked out in their Sunday best—all the boys in suits and ties, the girls in white dresses—the Duncan clan exudes health, happiness, and all-American pride. Under the surface of all that good cheer and photogenic respectability, though, tensions were brewing.

Ruby did not want any more children, but she could not convince a doctor to help her. "The only way you could get birth control in that time was for your doctor to prescribe it," she says. "And all the doctors I knew were Catholic. They sure weren't going to give us any. And we ourselves didn't know too much about birth control. I was a healthy woman so I just kept on having babies."

The day after Roy Jr. was born in 1960, Ruby Duncan took matters into her own hands. "I'm not leaving the hospital until you do something to keep me from having babies," she told the obstetrician. But he told Duncan that no

Ruby and Roy Duncan in 1962 with Sondra, Georgia, Ivory, David, Ronnie and Kenneth Phillips, and Roy Duncan Jr. Roy Duncan was working two jobs, and the family had purchased a home of their own. (Courtesy of Ruby Duncan)

married woman could get her tubes tied unless her husband, who was back at work, gave permission. "I think you better call him," she said. "Because I'm not having any more children." She reached back, took hold of the bars at the head of the hospital bed, and tightened her fists around them. "They tied my tubes," she recalls with satisfaction. "They found Roy and he was agreeable because they told him I was very frustrated. I was grabbing the head of the bed and screaming, 'I'm not going to have another baby!'"

The Duncans stayed together—on and off—for four more years, but the marriage was troubled by Roy's temper and increasingly explosive outbursts. "He became abusive," says Duncan. "Verbally and physically. Every way and all the time. I couldn't take that." In 1962, she walked out. "He came after me," she says. "He wouldn't let me leave." Roy Duncan poured on the warmth and charm. He promised to be different. And the thought of supporting all of the children on her own was daunting. So Ruby went back. "He tried to be a good father," she says. "I guess that's why I stayed for so long. I was interested in keeping my children happy and clothed and fed. And he was a great provider." But in 1964, when the children saw Roy hit their mother one time too many, they grabbed brooms and mops and a kitchen knife and chased him out into the street. Roy Duncan never hit their mother again, but the marriage was definitely over. The children didn't see him again for years.[5]

After Roy Duncan left, Ruby took a deep breath and thought about how she was going to feed and clothe seven children. She didn't want to be a maid ever again. But there were plenty of good jobs on the Strip, she knew. She just had to figure out how to get one. Someone told her that the executive chef at the Sahara hotel had a reputation for kindness and for giving black women a chance to train for well-paying kitchen jobs. Duncan drove her decrepit station wagon to the Strip, parked in the Sahara lot, and talked her way into the kitchen, lying to security guards that she had an appointment to see the chef.

"Hi Chef," she greeted him in her piercing, deep-South soprano. "I'm here because I'm a single woman and I have seven children. I must work. You *have* to give me a job." The chef laughed and told Duncan to slow down and take a breath. He looked at her for a long time. Finally he smiled. "I do have a young lady off for a few weeks," he said. "Can you come in tomorrow?" Duncan rushed home to tell the children, and found a woman who could watch them after school. The next afternoon she happily set off for work at the flashy, camel-flanked Sahara, then the tallest building in Nevada.

Duncan loved her new job. She learned how to cook for thousands of people, and relished the camaraderie of the Sahara kitchen staff. Supervisors praised her thoroughness and style, bantered with her, and laughed at her sometimes bawdy jokes. "One supervisor would always call me 'punkin,'" she says. He also taught her how to prepare 1,200 salads a day. "I would get all my bowls and I was in there with both hands flying," Duncan says. Even the hotel boss took a liking to her, asking Duncan to personally prepare his grapefruit every morning. "I could have stayed and stayed," she says.

In late 1967, an accident in the Sahara kitchen changed her life. It was early morning, and the high-spirited Duncan was in a hurry. "The boss wanted his half a grapefruit," she recalls, and she had to restock the kitchen first. Duncan raced across the floor, carrying a heavy pot of vegetables—unaware that moments earlier, someone had spilled a large bucket of cooking oil. "Before I knew anything I had hit the floor and everything went everywhere," she says. Duncan landed hard on her backbone, damaging her spine so severely that she was in and out of the hospital for nearly a year. The injury was permanent, and the pain chronic.

For a while, Duncan held onto the hope that she could continue working. She took a less strenuous job at the New Frontier kitchen. But when a coworker found her passed out in the walk-in freezer, Duncan knew she could no longer do heavy labor. Even standing on her feet for too long was a strain. While the union and the hotel battled over giving her disability payments, Duncan was left with no way to support her children. A social worker came into her hospital room one day with an application for public assistance. Duncan was depressed at the thought of going on welfare, she says. She had tried it briefly and hated it. But she was flat on her back, and had no choice. Duncan grabbed a pencil and filled out the form, vowing that her stint on welfare would be short-lived.

Several months later, Duncan drove over to the state Welfare department to ask about job training. "I can't stand very long," she told caseworkers. "But there's nothing wrong with my hands, my eyes, or my ears." They expressed regret, but said her disability made her a poor candidate for a training program. Did they need a receptionist? Duncan asked hopefully. No, again. "So I decided I'd go back home and call the press," she says, a glimmer of mischief in her eyes. She reached Mary Manning, a sympathetic reporter at the *Las Vegas Sun,* and asked if the paper needed any office help. Manning didn't think so. "But do you want to talk about your situation?" Manning asked. "*Absolutely,*" Duncan said, buttering up the newswoman. "I need all the help I can get, Mary. I can't put things into words the way you can—and I can't reach people the way you can."[6]

A long article appeared in the *Sun* the next day, entitled "Welfare Mother Wants to Work," chronicling Duncan's futile attempts to get training and the "Catch-22" rules of the Welfare department that excluded mothers eager to enter the job force. Duncan's phone rang a few days later. "We think we can help you," said a chagrined Welfare staffer. There was an opening in a new program that trained welfare mothers to become seamstresses. The sewing class did not result in a job as a seamstress, but it proved to be Duncan's springboard into political action.

Duncan's moment in the media spotlight was enormously gratifying, giving her a rare sense of being somebody. And it clued her in to the state's hypersensitivity to unfavorable press attention, a lesson she would rely on later. But home alone with her children, it was hard for Duncan to escape the realization that her life had hit the skids. She was back on welfare, with no man, no job, and few prospects. And as she struggled to find her footing in the late 1960s, many other Westside women—among them Alversa Beals, Mary Wesley, Essie Henderson, and Rosie Seals—found themselves on the same downhill slide, falling from the relatively dignified position of union workers to the debased status of welfare mothers. The women's personal circumstances varied, but the same themes appeared again and again: too many children, too little access to birth control, and too many husbands and boyfriends addicted to gambling, alcohol, and violence.

Bad luck and lousy people. Dinah Washington's voice poured like raspy silk from Westside jukeboxes. One of the only black female recording artists then writing her own lyrics, Washington captured in her words and voice the bitter taste of fading hope. Marriages failed. Bodies weakened by long hours of heavy physical labor were more prone to accidents and injuries. And when children—and there were always so many children—got sick, their mothers arrived at work late, or not at all, and got fired. Sometimes the women blew their opportunities completely on their own, making bad decisions that came back to haunt them. They spent money they should have saved. Fell in love with irresponsible men. Stayed when they should have left. Or left when they should have stayed. And because they were poor, black, and female in a culture that devalued all three, those missteps cost them dearly.

Alversa Beals made the same mistake twice: she married one drunken batterer and moved in with another. In 1955, she had left Tallulah to escape Ed Beals, but within a year of arriving on the Westside, she was once again living with a violent alcoholic. Beals didn't marry the man she calls her common-law husband, in part because Ed Beals never granted her a divorce. But she was also deeply ambivalent about him. "I don't know why I always get somebody that drinks," she says, her voice tinged with regret. "I don't like to drink. It makes me sick."

Beals had intended to continue working as a hotel maid, but her rapidly expanding family made that impossible. "I lived with him five years," she says of her live-in boyfriend. "And I had five babies." Beals loved having a large family—she was one of eleven, herself—and she was a devoted mother. But her man wasn't much of a provider. He let drinking and depression get the better of him. "He wouldn't really work. He'd half work," she says. "He'd work enough to draw unemployment. Then when that run out, he'd go back and get another job as a porter." And he had too much in common with her first husband. "They would beat you up," she says quietly. "I had a black eye all the time, so I just stayed home with my babies. I had to get away from both of my husbands." With nine children to feed, the thought of leaving was, for a long time, more frightening than the thought of staying.

By 1961, however, Beals decided that she could do better for her children on her own. She applied for surplus food and emergency medical coverage from the county, and a federal cash grant for single mothers. She also qualified for a federally subsidized apartment at the Marble Manor projects. These programs, though paltry, gave Beals and her children a relatively new roof over their heads and (nearly enough) food on the table.

Many other women in the Westside projects had applied for public assistance to escape battering husbands and boyfriends who they feared might also hurt their children. Later studies would show that a majority of all women applying for welfare are fleeing batterers. Alversa Beals, Essie Henderson, and Emma Stampley dreaded becoming dependent on government support. But they were determined to make themselves independent of the men who were beating them—and they saw government aid as a lifeline.[7]

Beals never again lived with a man. Eventually she met Robert, with whom she had two more children and a satisfying twenty-year relationship. Robert indulged Beals's children, buying them shoes and dresses. (Just buying a trinket for all eleven was no small expenditure.) Still, Beals never let him move in with her family. She had made a conscious decision to raise her nine girls and two boys by herself.[8]

But eleven was enough. Beals tried for years to find a doctor who would provide her with birth control. "I was having a baby every year. I got a girl in 53, 54, 55, 56, 57, 58, and 59. That's the way they lined up. That's when I started asking them to help me stop." After her seventh child was born, twenty-seven-year-old Beals begged her doctor to tie her tubes. "These babies are killing me," she told him. The doctor refused to help. Frustrated, Beals asked a pharmacist at her local drugstore if there was something she could use. But it didn't work: "I still ended up with another baby," she says.[9]

In the early 1960s, there were strict limits on the contraceptives that women could buy over the counter, especially in Mormon-dominated Nevada. (Only in 1966 did the U.S. Supreme Court grant married women across the country unfettered access to contraceptives; unmarried women would have to wait until 1973.) And many cities and towns were prickly about giving birth control to women on welfare, even as they penalized single mothers for having too many children. In Chicago, single women who had babies while on AFDC were threatened with jail time, but caseworkers were prohibited from sending them to Planned Parenthood clinics that dispensed free contraceptives.[10]

At thirty, Alversa Beals was desperate to stop having children. Finally, she met a woman whose doctor had agreed to tie her tubes. "Girl, please give me your doctor's name and number," Beals said. The doctor was initially reluctant to help her. At her age, he said, Beals was unlikely to have many more children. She laughed. "My mother had babies till she was in her late forties," she said. "I'll have twenty-something babies by then." Finally, the doctor relented, writing on Beals's medical records that it would endanger her health to have more children.

But there was still one more hurdle. All married women in the 1960s needed their husbands' written permission to get their tubes tied. And a decade after leaving Tallulah, Alversa was still legally married to Ed Beals. She asked her welfare caseworker for help. "I actually had a nice welfare lady," Beals says. "She was white but she was nice." The caseworker knew just what to do.

> *She sent the papers down to Tallulah and got somebody to go out and find Ed. They told him I had to have the surgery, that it was a matter of life and death. So he signed it. But then he went and told my mama that I was sick. Mama said, "How come you haven't told me you're going in the hospital and going to have surgery? I've done packed my suitcase so I can come out there and keep the kids while you're sick." I said, "Mama. They just did that to make my husband sign. All I'm doing is having my tubes tied."*

When the papers arrived from Tallulah, Beals experienced a rare moment of bonding with a caseworker. "I screamed I was so happy," she recalls. "Me and her really laughed about it. I took the papers to my doctor and that was it." Beals handed her Medicaid card to the secretary, and walked into the doctor's office. It would have been simpler and less expensive to fit Beals with a diaphragm or prescribe birth-control pills. But many doctors were unwilling to give poor mothers control over their own bodies. Instead, both Beals and Duncan were sterilized. The women were happy—ecstatic, even—that they'd never again have to worry about becoming pregnant. Given their limited options, they felt that sterilization was a good choice.

One in five Americans thought single black mothers should have no choice: they should be forcibly sterilized. State legislatures in California, Illinois, Louisiana, Maryland, Mississippi, North Carolina, and Virginia debated forced sterilization bills in the mid-1960s. And across the country, unwed mothers were declared ineligible for public housing. The "no unwed mothers" policy was officially color-blind, but African American women were disproportionately targeted. In Carson City, state legislators pointed fingers at single mothers in Reno and Las Vegas, accusing them of burdening taxpayers. Lawmakers demanded that they either find husbands to support them or stop having sex.[11]

Some Westside women found ways to stop having babies. Leola Harris ended her marriage in 1967 because her husband spent his paychecks on gambling, alcohol, and other women. Harris walked out after only one child and told her incredulous husband: "If I have another baby by you, I tell you what I want you to do for me. Get someone to throw some gas on me, scratch a match and say 'Burn Baby Burn.' One child I could manage to raise myself. Any more and forget it." Once divorced, Harris did not get pregnant again.[12]

Gambling was a particularly vexing issue for Westside women who waited in vain for husbands to bring home paychecks. Poor parents knew they could not risk scarce resources on a game of chance. But the lure of easy money beckoned. This was Vegas, after all, where jackpot dreams always hovered, just out of reach—an itch that grew irresistible in moments of desperation. And desperation was a familiar phantom on the Westside in the late 1960s, as the economic base of the neighborhood shriveled and died. Rosie Seals's second husband, Milo Seals, turned to gambling to supplement his earnings. His habit devastated the family's finances. "Milo was a good man," Rosie says. "But you can't have nothing if you're a gambler. You can't have a pot to piss in or a bed to shove it under."

Mary Wesley's husband, too, squandered their money on cards and dice. By the mid-1960s, Wesley had borne nine children, including two sets of twins, a stillborn infant, and a baby who died in infancy, leaving her with seven. (She later adopted another because he "had no place to go," she says.) Wesley and her husband loved to talk about the house they wanted to build back in Mississippi. "I couldn't stand the desert," Wesley says. "I always wanted to go home." But after nine years in Las Vegas, they had not saved anything. Mary admits she spent freely, dressing up her children and buying beautiful cloth to sew her own clothing. The biggest problem, though, was that her husband gambled away his paychecks.

"Most of his money was gone before I ever saw it," Wesley sighs. "I had to pay all of the bills myself. I had to pay the babysitter and buy the food, buy the clothes and pay the rent." Wesley asked her husband if he would turn over his paycheck to her each week, but he refused. She ran out of patience when he spent the weekend—and all their money—at the craps tables, just one month after her youngest child was born. "If I had to take care of everything, I could do better by myself," she says. "I didn't have to take care of a man, too." Her mother, still stricken by her husband's murder, urged Mary not to take the children away from their father. "Why should I keep them with the father," Wesley retorted, "if he's not doing anything for them?"

One month after her youngest child was born, Wesley gathered the baby and her six other youngsters under the age of six—and walked out the door. "I just called a cab one day and took my kids and I moved. I rented a trailer and lived there with all my kids." Her husband provided some financial help, but Wesley had to work two jobs to make ends meet: cleaning rooms at the Showboat during the day, waiting tables on the Westside at night. "I was paying one check to the babysitter and the other for rent." For a while, Wesley was a supermom, supporting and raising eight children on her own—her seven and an adopted eighth. She was proud of her independence and her growing skill as a waitress. A white waitress named Lynn showed Wesley "how to carry nine cups of coffee at one time, and how to put seven plates on your arms." Lynn assured her that she could always find a good job waiting tables. "I got really excited about that," Wesley says. "I really thought I was going to be able to give my kids the best."[13]

After integration, though, as business at the Town Tavern began to dry up, so did Wesley's tips. And years of working two physically demanding jobs started to take their toll. Wesley fell ill several times, and in 1965 she lost both of her jobs. Too proud to ask for help, and not wanting to worry the children, Wesley maintained a sense of normalcy for as long as she could, carefully dressing the kids for school each day, painstakingly preparing meals for them to eat when they returned. Finally, there was nothing left. Swallowing her guilt and panic, Wesley bathed her children, dressed them in their finest clothes, and took them to Child Haven, a Las Vegas group home for destitute youngsters.

> *I told them I couldn't let my babies go hungry. And so they told me that they would keep the kids. I was so afraid that they were gonna take the kids from me for good. I said: "Just keep the babies till I get well enough to go back to work. That's all I need."*

Wesley's fear that her children might be taken away was not just a product of her guilt-plagued imagination. In the mid-1960s it was a very real threat. Caseworkers in Las Vegas and across the country, backed by state Welfare departments, frequently threatened to take away children from poor mothers whom they deemed unable to care for their offspring. None of Wesley's children was born out of wedlock, but she wasn't taking any chances. Even though she had agreed to leave her children at Child Haven until she found a new job, she couldn't stay away. Every morning when they opened up, she was there.

> *I would go in and volunteer so I could make sure my babies got fed. I would give them a bath, comb their hair, talk to them. Finally they said to me: "Miss, your kids don't belong here." So my sister came with her car. And they filled that car with all kinds of food. And they gave me a place to stay out in Henderson.*[14]

Wesley was determined not to linger on public assistance. After her father's murder, her mother had worked long hours as a waitress rather than allow the family to accept cash relief. During the brief periods when Wesley's mother had relied on aid, she "would keep it a secret that we were getting government help," Wesley says. "She didn't want to talk about it." Wesley felt the same shame when she was forced to accept AFDC. "I couldn't talk about how much trouble I was in. I was really confused about what to do."

Wesley did find another job waiting tables, but, lacking medical benefits, she put off seeking treatment for a raging gum infection until it landed her in the hospital. During the weeks that Wesley was out of commission, a hospital social worker restored the family's Medicaid insurance and cash relief. Wesley returned to work soon afterward, but her jobs never provided adequate health coverage. So she and her children moved on and off welfare for years.

Wesley's willingness to leave her gambling husband, and her attempts to care for her children on her own, might be seen as the laudable actions of a committed mother. But in 1965, leading U.S. social critics and policymakers saw such behavior on the part of black welfare mothers as "pathological." Daniel Patrick Moynihan, a close advisor to President Lyndon Johnson and author of the enormously influential 1965 report *The Negro Family: The Case for National Action,* blamed women like Wesley for the breakdown of the African American family and the persistence of black poverty. Such women were too aggressive and independent, Moynihan wrote, profoundly crippling and emasculating black men.

Such analyses conveniently ignored the political, legal, and governmental barriers that severely impaired the ability of black husbands and fathers, as well as black mothers, to provide for their families. The experience of Rosie Seals is sadly instructive in this regard. When Milo Seals died, leaving Rosie with seven children, she received virtually no pension or Social Security benefits. Milo had worked for years as a farmhand, but agricultural labor was excluded from the 1935 Social Security Act. His years as a nonunion construction worker in Las Vegas did not count toward a pension, either. Like many black construction workers, Seals went from project to project and was at times unemployed—making him, in the eyes of the Social Security Administration, an "intermittent worker" not covered under the act. In fact, most black workers, and 85 percent of employed black women, were excluded from old-age benefits under the Social Security Act. The social safety net constructed by the New Deal, said one NAACP official, was "a sieve with holes just big enough for the majority of Negroes to fall through."[15]

The exclusion of domestic workers from coverage hit black women especially hard. Working in private homes, they lacked old-age, disability, and unemployment insurance. By the 1960s, the Social Security Act was amended to include domestics—but only if they worked for a single employer. For most, working for wages too low to save, married to men who also lacked pensions, poverty in old age was nearly a certainty. Unless domestic workers were allowed to accrue Social Security in their own right, women labor reformers had warned Congress years earlier, they would be forced to turn to the charity of their communities.[16]

That warning was borne out many times on the Westside in the 1960s. Without widow's benefits or a pension to fall back on, Rosie Seals was forced to work two jobs to support her children. She cleaned private homes—by definition, not covered by Social Security—and worked at a Westside laundry, but that work was intermittent and so also uncovered by federal benefits. Then, at thirty-seven, Rosie Seals had a stroke. Seals's doctor sent her to the Welfare office with a note saying that continuing to work could kill her. The Welfare worker read the note silently, handed it back, and said, "application denied."

This kind of caseworker-client interaction—quick, impersonal, and hostile—was fast becoming the norm. By the mid-1960s, when Duncan, Beals, Wesley, and Seals walked into the Las Vegas Welfare office to apply for aid, it had become difficult for most caseworkers to see poor black mothers as individuals. They had merged, instead, into a nameless, featureless social problem: the unmarried black mother. The nation's newest bogeywoman was stigmatized no matter what she said or did: She was a bad mother if she worked outside the home and neglected her children, a parasite if she applied for aid so that she could stay home. She was promiscuous if she pursued relationships with men, a man-hater if she chose to bring up her children without one. In a national climate that was rapidly growing more antagonistic to single black mothers, their simple requests for food, medical care, and shelter were greeted not with sympathy but with suspicion.[17]

BLACK MOTHERS, THE CULTURE OF CONTEMPT, AND THE WAR ON POVERTY

From the late 1940s through the 1960s, American novelists, scholars, politicians, and movies blamed mothers for a host of cultural and familial ills, recasting a largely sacred icon into an increasingly sinister figure. From journalist Philip Wylie's *Generation of Vipers*, which went through twenty printings between 1942 and 1955, to novelist Phillip Roth's 1969 classic *Portnoy's Complaint*, white sons chastised their mothers for being simultaneously overprotective and distant, frigid and frenzied, acquisitive and penny-pinching. In 1947, *Modern Woman: The Lost Sex*, a popular-psychology bestseller by psychiatrist Marynia Farnham and sociologist Ferdinand Lundberg, warned women that if they worked outside the home they would destroy the American family. In the hugely popular film *Mildred Pierce* (1945), Joan Crawford starred as a career woman whose ambition twists her already nasty daughter into a promiscuous killer. Some even blamed domineering mothers for race prejudice. Sons manifested their insecurities, experts said, through racist words and deeds.[18]

Black mothers were blamed for all this and more. A growing chorus of sociologists and criminologists accused them of literally giving birth to the nation's postwar social problems. Poverty, criminality, promiscuity, drugs, juvenile delinquency, and gang violence were laid at their door. Their steadily rising birthrate was viewed with alarm by many social workers, police , judges, and physicians, who divided black single mothers into two categories: incompetent and dangerous. The black single mother, wrote a sympathetic obstetrician, Howard Osofsky, in 1965, was widely seen by physicians as a "savage who must be protected by more capable and learned members of society."[19]

State and federal legislators tended to view her the same way. As civil rights organizers educated poor Southern blacks about their legal rights and entitlements, welfare rolls grew. So did the percentage of African Americans on assistance, although the percentage of nonwhite unwed mothers on ADC was half that of whites. In 1959, thirty percent of unwed white mothers who kept their children received public assistance, compared to only 16 percent of black unwed mothers. By the 1960s, though, black and Latina mothers outnumbered whites on the welfare rolls.[20]

Politicians, especially in the South, vilified public assistance as nothing more than a reward for black women's immorality and licentiousness. Black welfare mothers were not citizens seeking their rights, legislators charged, but charlatans extorting state funds to which they were not entitled. What's more, they alleged, black women were having babies to increase their welfare checks. Across the country, lawmakers proposed criminal penalties for welfare recipients who had more than one child out of wedlock. Russell Long, the influential U.S. Senator from Louisiana, described welfare mothers as "brood mares" —an image plucked directly from the language of the slave masters. The many reasons why a woman might become a single parent were obscured by a popular image of amorality that embodied a century of stereotypes about black women's sexuality.[21]

Social workers in Nevada, and across the country, could not help being affected by the barrage of negative images about their clients. The fact that Mary Wesley, Rosie Seals, Alversa Beals, Essie Henderson, and Emma Stampley were married when they conceived some or all of their children mattered little. Most Las Vegas caseworkers and Welfare administrators saw what they had been trained to see: irresponsible single mothers whose carelessness had created problems that they, as employees of the state, were left to resolve.[22]

The race of the unwed mother affected how social workers saw her. White girls who got pregnant out of wedlock were, by the 1950s, largely seen as psychologically disturbed individuals. With help, they could salvage their lives, especially if they gave up their babies for adoption—a choice that could keep them off the welfare rolls. A white mother's decision to bear and relinquish a child was even seen—by adoption lawyers and infertile couples, at least—as socially useful. Black unwed mothers, by contrast, were seen not as individuals, but as products of a pathological culture, loading unwanted children onto an already burdened society. Single black mothers who wanted to keep their babies were incomprehensible to white caseworkers raised in a culture where illegitimacy equaled shame. Such women seemed to them unregenerate and unrepentant.[23]

That's not, of course, how the women saw themselves. It was an abundance of family values—not a lack of them—that moved single black women to keep their children, Mary Wesley says. "Give my kids to someone else to raise?" she asks incredulously. "Why would I do that? How could I do that?" Her comments were echoed by black single mothers in Florida who withdrew from welfare in the 1960s rather than give their children away to married relatives. "People give away puppies and kittens," one woman explained. "They don't give away their children."[24]

The sympathies of the American public, however, were not with these women. Massive migration from the South was bringing millions of refugees into American cities, where the urban middle classes had grown restive and anxious, unwilling to live alongside rapidly expanding inner-city ghettos and their poor, maladjusted residents. From the 1930s through the 1960s, social scientists, popular authors, and policymakers churned out volumes about this new urban crisis. Their writings were strongly influenced by the scholarship of two liberal social scientists: John Dollard, a white psychologist, and E. Franklin Frazier, a black sociologist and former director of the Atlanta University School of Social Work.

Dollard and Frazier had tried to move scholarly discourse beyond assertions of black racial inferiority by providing social explanations for black poverty and familial instability. Frazier's *Negro Family in the United States* (1939) was one of the first books to devote serious scholarly attention to the history of the black family, and the lingering effects of slavery on urban as well as rural black life. Dollard's *Caste and Class in a Southern Town* (1937) attempted to sketch and document the psychic damages wrought by the racist social structure of the Mississippi Delta. As is so often the case with groundbreaking scholarship, these complex studies came to be known mostly for the weakest and most simplistic parts of their analysis: their portrayal of poor black mothers.

The two men argued that centuries of adaptation to the ravages of slavery and then sharecropping had damaged gender norms among the black poor, creating a matriarchal society and eroding the legitimate authority of black men. Their widely read books strongly reinforced stereotypes of black women's voracious sexuality, suggesting that the bleakness of black women's lives led them to seek quick gratification through casual sexual liaisons. Downplaying the sexual coercion that shaped so many black women's coming of age in the Delta, Dollard suggested that black women sought out numerous sexual partners, white as well as black, in a desperate quest for intimacy and fulfillment. Frazier viewed rural life in a somewhat more positive light, arguing that matriarchal families were balanced there by patriarchal churches. Migration to the city shattered that equilibrium. Poor black mothers became unmoored in the city, Frazier wrote, pursuing casual sexual liaisons while their children yielded to their own temptations in the mean streets of the new migrant ghettos.[25]

The work of Dollard and Frazier launched a tidal wave of scholarship in the 1940s, 1950s, and 1960s that boiled their analyses down to a single primary cause for urban anomie: black migrant mothers so damaged by racism and poverty, and so unmoored by the move from farm to city, that they had become disturbed and unpredictable. Aggressive, domineering, and promiscuous, the newly citified black woman had a genius for fraud and no capacity for shame. This new bogeywoman was an extraordinarily complex, manipulative, and tormented figure. And she seemed to pass on her moral disease to everyone she touched, ruining husbands, daughters, and sons. The welfare queen, missing only her pink Cadillac, had already begun to ride through the feverish American political imagination.

Stereotypes of black women filled social work textbooks and caseworkers' manuals. Maurice Davie's *Negroes in American Society* (1949) and later Thomas Pettigrew's *A Profile of the Negro American* (1964) popularized Frazier's notion of a black matriarchy and linked it to generations of "Negro criminality." Davie's migrant black mother spent grocery money on movies and dance halls, where she met men with whom she could have easy sex. She produced legions of unwanted children, on whom she took out her frustrations. "Sharp-tongued, bitter and resentful," migrant mothers robbed husbands and sons of the masculine authority and drive that might improve their families' condition. Pettigrew's black matriarch drove away husbands and destroyed the self-esteem of sons. She taught her daughters to harbor anger at men and trained them to "assume male as well as female responsibilities." Meanwhile she smothered her fatherless sons, leaving them no space to develop normal masculine traits. These "mother-raised boys" turned to violence to prove their masculinity.[26]

This depiction of poor black women as deformed and deforming spanned the political spectrum. Segregationists argued against racial integration of schools, warning of the dangers of exposing white children to the unrestrained sexuality of black girls and women. Conservative critics of the welfare state warned that government aid only encouraged black women's abnormal and irresponsible sexual behavior by providing "pay for play," as California governor Ronald Reagan put it in 1966. Even civil rights leaders took aim at poor black mothers. Urban League director Whitney Young, James Farmer of the Congress of Racial Equality, and Bayard Rustin, pacifist mentor of Martin Luther King Jr., worried aloud that economically and socially independent black mothers were eroding black men's sense of self-worth. For that reason, they contended, the federal government should design poverty programs specifically to benefit black men and boys.[27]

Thirty years of scholarly literature blaming poor black mothers for the decline of black families culminated in the male-focused vision of Lyndon Johnson's War on Poverty. To the largely white—and exclusively male—urban policy planners in the White House, fighting poverty meant creating programs to restore the masculine dignity of poor men, so that they could assume their proper place as income providers and heads of their households. If the program did not accomplish that goal, Vice President Hubert Humphrey warned in his 1964 book, *War on Poverty*, "the man without a job, without any opportunity to care for himself and his family" will develop "a sense of bitterness and rejection."[28]

As American ghettos continued to burn, politicians grew increasingly frightened about the potential of such men to generate violence and social chaos. More than a hundred riots erupted during Lyndon Johnson's presidency, leaving 225 people dead, over 4,000 wounded, and $112 billion in property damage. National guard troops and army tanks patrolled the streets of American cities. Johnson desperately wanted to do more with his presidency than send troops and tanks to turn their guns on American citizens. He had to show angry and fearful white Americans that he could restore the fractious peace, while giving black Americans hope for immediate economic and political gains. And Johnson needed to move quickly. He was convinced—correctly, it turned out—that his mandate would be short-lived. Only a brilliant and swift balancing act, wrote one contemporary observer, could "redefine civil rights in a manner that secures the power positions of white public leaders and places them in control."[29]

In his January 1964 State of the Union address, Johnson unveiled that master stroke. He declared "unconditional war on poverty," promising "not only to relieve the symptoms of poverty but to cure it and, above all, to prevent it."

His use of military metaphor was carefully chosen, at a time when he was sending young Americans to fight in the jungles of Vietnam. This too was war, he told Congress. "Our objective: total victory. There are millions of Americans—one fifth of our people—who have not shared in the abundance which has been granted to most of us, and on whom the gates of opportunity have been closed." The War on Poverty would develop job training, community development, a national volunteer corps, and federal coordination. "This program is much more than a beginning," Johnson insisted. "It is a total commitment by this President, this Congress and this nation to pursue victory over the most ancient of mankind's enemies."[30]

Those were grand words for a program with a first-year budget that was less than 10 percent of the annual cost of the war in Vietnam. Still, Johnson was not just spouting rhetoric. Despite his penchant for hyperbole and political grandstanding, Johnson was an admirer of Franklin Roosevelt. He had long hoped to develop an activist federal domestic policy that would surpass the New Deal in expanding economic, educational, and medical opportunities for poor and middle-class Americans. Under the rubric of his Great Society program, Johnson secured passage of sixty path-breaking social initiatives, including Medicare (for the elderly), Medicaid (for the poor), the Voting Rights Act, Legal Services, Head Start, the Department of Housing and Urban Development, a new GI Bill, Social Security increases, a generous student loan and grant program that opened up college education to the poor and lower-middle class, urban mass transit, and the Manpower Development and Training Act. In March 1964, Johnson announced the most controversial component of the Great Society programs: the Economic Opportunity Act, which ushered in the Office of Economic Opportunity, the Job Corps, and Community Action Programs.[31]

Johnson was careful to provide a little something for every sector of the electorate: farmers, students, commuters, Native Americans, immigrants, retirees, consumers, business owners, organized labor—even nascent environmentalists. Welfare mothers, however, were not on his radar screen. White House policymakers saw only two options for them: marry them off to men who would take care of them, or enroll them in the welfare system as closely supervised wards of the state. Control, not empowerment, was the goal.[32]

HANDING OUT FOOD FROM THE COURTHOUSE STEPS: WELFARE, NEVADA STYLE
The first time Ruby Duncan waited for her monthly rations of surplus food at the base of the Las Vegas courthouse steps in 1967, she flashed back to the slaughter of hogs on the Ivory Plantation. She could see in her mind's eye the

field bosses gesturing toward women sharecroppers, calling them by name to retrieve the steaming hog innards. In much the same manner, Clark County relief supervisors stood at the top of the county courthouse stairs, high above the heads of the poor gathered below. When called by name, each mother would climb the steps to get her two bags of groceries. Often, she had children waiting below, hungry, cranky, and tired. The county provided neither bathrooms nor water to those forced to wait in the blazing heat.

The county's surplus cheese and peanut butter provided essential protein to families who could not afford to buy their children meat. Still, the manner of distribution brought Duncan right back to the chitlin handouts at the Ivory Plantation. "We always had to pay for those when the season ended," she remembered. "When I would stand there in the Vegas sun waiting for our bags of food, I kept thinking: This still costs more than it's worth."[33]

The federal Commodities Food program had been run by the U.S. Department of Agriculture for decades, funneling military surplus cheese, bread, dried milk, and peanut butter to local governments to give to the poor. The Food Stamp Act of 1964 was meant to replace the commodities program, and give poor mothers more freedom to choose the food they gave their children. Food stamps were also intended to spare poor mothers the humiliation of waiting in bread lines, enabling them to shop in grocery stores like everyone else. But many state governments resisted the food stamps program for years, leaving millions of Americans dependent on commodities rations into the early 1970s. In scenes reminiscent of the Great Depression, poor mothers and children continued to line up outside special food warehouses, or gather at the back of open trucks as bags of food were handed down to them.[34]

In Las Vegas, says League of Women Voters activist Maya Miller, distribution of commodities was an intricately staged ritual intended to make poor families feel that they owed county commissioners a debt. Use of relief funds to consolidate political power was common among city and county officials across the country, who had come to view relief moneys as their personal patronage funds. Poverty politics involved complex jockeying for position among county, state, and federal authorities over who should administer— and pay for—assistance for the poor, a political dance that had been going on ever since the federal government took on the task of providing poor relief in the 1930s.[35]

Aid to Dependent Children was created as part of the Social Security Act of 1935 and became Aid to Families with Dependent Children (AFDC) in 1962, when Congress extended aid to unemployed fathers. It was widely unpopular from the very beginning. For years, many states—including Nevada—refused to participate. To soften their resistance, federal authorities gave state Welfare departments tremendous authority in administering relief programs. The result was fifty different welfare systems. Grant levels varied from one state to another. So did the criteria for inclusion. State officials restricted eligibility by setting up morality and behavior codes designed both to cut state costs and to control the behavior of suspect women. State Welfare departments also enacted "employable mother" rules, enabling them to cut women from relief rolls whenever there were local labor shortages. Across the South, women with children as young as three were thrown off the rolls during planting or harvesting seasons.[36]

Nevada refused to accept federal welfare funds at all for twenty years after the passage of the Social Security Act. "Fear and loathing of the welfare bureaucracy was immediate," observes Nevada historian Diane Nassir. Welfare was anathema to the rugged individualist self-image that Nevada residents and politicians cherished. Especially in the rural northern counties, Nevadans saw poor relief as the province of the church or the family—not of government. Mormon beliefs heavily influenced these attitudes. One northern Nevada legislator declared: "The Mormon philosophy is live within your budget and everybody take care of their own; get off the public dole." That sentiment was echoed by non-Mormons as well, recalls former governor Donal "Mike" O'Callaghan. "Nevada politics is really very conservative and in a lot of areas it was very parochial," he says. "It's an independent mining, ranching thing: We'll take care of our own. Long before liberal became a dirty word nationally, it was a dirty word here."[37]

As migrants from across the country poured into the state during the 1950s and 1960s, old-time Nevadans began to question what was meant by "our own." A demographic and political gap was widening between the largely white rural population of northern Nevada and an increasingly diverse Las Vegas. Many northern Nevadans, O'Callaghan believes, "were not ready to accept a growing urban area with different needs and different kinds of people." Nor was there money for relief in state coffers. Nevada was the least-taxed state in the nation, lacking an income tax, a gift tax, or an inheritance tax. The light tax burden appealed to the wealthy and to other migrants as well, but meant that state spending on education, welfare, and pensions was paltry compared with that of other states.[38]

Nevada politicians were also allergic to giving the federal government any more power than it already had. In no state did federal agencies control more land, nor was any state as bristly about federal intervention. Carson City law-makers rejected federal programs almost reflexively, long blocking even such innocuous palliatives as Aid to the Blind or the Totally and Permanently Dis-abled. But little by little, the state's monolithic opposition to federal assistance began to crumble. In 1955, Nevada became the last state in the union to accept Aid to Dependent Children, falling into line after the territories of Alaska, Hawaii, Guam, and Puerto Rico.[39]

Virtually everything that moves in the Silver State has some connection to gambling, and this decision was no exception. Legislators recognized that fed-erally subsidized welfare might provide an economic advantage to hoteliers whose labor needs fluctuated dramatically. "Casino hotels are a seasonal in-dustry," says Maya Miller, a longtime Nevada welfare activist. "Like the crops of the South, they require a pool of cheap labor." By the mid-1950s, Las Vegas workers were drearily familiar with seasonal pink-slipping. May to September was the peak season for Las Vegas and Reno hotels. Fewer tourists came to gamble during Thanksgiving and Christmas, and desert cold snaps kept them away in January and February. Hotels closed their swimming pools and laid off a chunk of their workforce for much of the winter. Essie Henderson says the layoffs were inevitably announced on the eve of winter holidays.

Keeping those low-wage maids, porters, gardeners, and kitchen aides around for March, when the casinos would hum once again, was critical. Ca-sino owners, who handed out large amounts of cash to Carson City lawmak-ers, had to help their workers survive through the lean winter season. But that safety net couldn't be too cushy. Hotel managers needed workers to return as soon as the tourists reappeared. So Nevada Welfare officials crafted a Welfare program that kept grants low enough to ensure that recipients would rejoin the workforce as soon as there were jobs available.[40]

With Nevada public assistance grants among the lowest in the nation, many mothers needed to work while on welfare, a practice that was legal if income was reported. By the late 1960s, 47 percent of Nevada welfare moth-ers held jobs, the highest rate in the country. The hotels where these women worked had a cozy reciprocal relationship with the Welfare department. When Essie Henderson was laid off by the Dunes in 1966, the top housekeeper offered to help her get public assistance.[41]

But, if hotel owners in Las Vegas and Reno were happy to use welfare as a means to support their low-wage workers during seasonal layoffs, state Wel-fare administrators had begun to panic about rising costs. Las Vegas was the fastest-growing city in the nation. Nevada officials envisioned welfare costs spiraling out of sight, and they committed themselves to slowing the growth of state Welfare rolls. Mike O'Callaghan became the state's first Welfare director in 1963–64. He walked into an office that had two scuffed desks, two phones, and a typewriter.[42]

Stella Fleming, longtime director of Clark County General Assistance, was in charge of doling out aid to the poor in Las Vegas. Fleming had held her job for decades by the 1960s, first coming to Clark County as a Red Cross worker during the Depression, recruited to provide emergency services to the refugee army of men building Boulder Dam. She felt comfortable assisting displaced male workers, almost all of whom were white, hungry, and grateful. Single mothers, by contrast, did not evoke her sympathy.

A virtual czar of Las Vegas relief operations, Fleming saw herself as protector and moral guardian of the city's poor. Her staff—county caseworkers —assessed how much each eligible family needed. Then Fleming herself determined how those needs would be met—how much food each family would get, how much would be doled out for emergency rent or heating assistance. Her personal involvement in every case that came before Clark County into the late 1960s made Fleming a hated figure among Las Vegas welfare mothers.[43]

George Miller—who became Nevada Welfare director in 1968—was equally thorny, colorful, and opinionated. First a New Dealer, then a Kennedy Democrat, Miller eventually became a high-ranking social services appointee of President Ronald Reagan and a national crusader against welfare fraud. Miller's career—and his highly negative view of welfare mothers—shed light on the Democratic antipoverty programs that helped shape him, and on the Republican critiques of the welfare state—critiques that he would later help to frame. Obsessed with fighting fraud, Miller quickly turned the Nevada Welfare department into a detective agency—every caseworker charged with ferreting out cheaters.

Nevada's welfare mothers came to see Miller as their personal nemesis. He returned their undisguised hostility. "They flood in like vultures to the kill," he said of welfare recipients. "We're weeding them out."[44] Miller came out swinging in his early days as Nevada Welfare chief. "Well, well, Mr. Welfare Director," one legislator greeted him acidly on his first day, "Who do you bleed for today?" Miller didn't blink. "I looked him back as cold as I could and I said, 'Senator, I don't bleed for no son of a bitch in this world but me. I bleed for me.'" Miller's views about poverty and welfare were framed by his experiences as a homeless migrant during the Depression and as an administrator for Lyndon Johnson's War on Poverty during the early 1960s. A self-described "old

Missouri boy who came to California at 16 with the Grapes of Wrath movement," Miller slept on the streets of Los Angeles during the early 1930s and pretended to be saved so he could get a hot meal at Christian missions. His life turned around when he pushed his way through a crowd of three hundred hungry men to win himself a government job. He rose to the top of the cut working for the California Youth Authority, earning a reputation as someone who could set troubled boys on the path to law-abiding manhood.[45]

In 1964, that reputation earned him an appointment as regional director of the Job Corps—a War on Poverty program aimed at turning high-school dropouts—aged sixteen to twenty-one—into reliable breadwinners. Among the most male-focused of 1960s antipoverty programs, Job Corps targeted angry young men from the inner city. Under the supervision of Mike O'Callaghan, the strapping, one-legged Korean War veteran and amateur boxer who ran Job Corps camps across the country, Miller taught young men like boxer George Foreman to read in the morning and cut timber in the afternoons. Men like Miller and O'Callaghan fit perfectly with the masculinist vision of the War on Poverty.[46]

Like Sargent Shriver and Frank Carlucci, President Nixon's director of the Office of Economic Opportunity, Miller felt that men were more likely than women to achieve economic self-sufficiency. "Moreover," Carlucci argued, "training and employment will often be much more expensive for women if child care must be provided." To men like George Miller, providing government funds to train single mothers for jobs was a wasteful and irresponsible use of public funds. But so was public assistance.[47]

In the next few years, Miller would attack those he believed were bilking the system with missionary zeal, cutting tens of thousands of poor families off the rolls and urging legislators to reject federal medical, food aid, and job training programs for welfare mothers. In ruggedly individualist Nevada, Miller did not expect much opposition. He was wrong.[48]

One particularly fierce opponent of George Miller's policies lived on a ranch just down the road from Carson City. Maya Miller—an angular, Los Angeles-born, oilman's daughter with a passion for progressive politics—recoiled at the persistence of poverty in an affluent society and fought for more generous social programs with the same zeal that George Miller showed in cutting them. In 1968, the same year that George Miller was appointed Nevada Welfare director, Maya Miller became president of the Nevada League of Women Voters and director of poverty and race issues for the national League. A mother of two, Miller found it hypocritical that middle-class mothers felt social pressure to stay at home with their children rather than work, while poor mothers were expected to leave young children and enter the workforce. When Maya Miller became the key poverty analyst for the national League of Women Voters, she pushed the staid organization to a radical position on welfare: seeing AFDC as earned compensation for the economically valuable work of mothering.[49]

Maya Miller was quickly cast by the press as a perfect foil for tough-talking George Miller. Admirers likened Maya Miller's desert-weathered look to that of painter Georgia O'Keefe. Conservative columnist George Will called her the Marlboro Woman. One Nevada columnist blamed her for calling down a "Plague of Women Voters" on the Silver State.

When George Miller waxed passionate about danger, greed, and moral corruption, reporters could always turn to Maya Miller for a riposte. "When he was testifying in the state legislature, he would describe poor women as hordes of barbarians who were after *our* riches," Miller says. "It was *us* and *them* in George Miller's world. And *they* always wanted more."

With good reason. Welfare grants didn't pay enough to live on, in Nevada or anywhere else in the country, forcing mothers to violate regulations by working and lying about it. Recipients lost a dollar in benefits for every dollar they earned, if they reported their earnings. Critics charged that such rules penalized initiative. So in 1967, Congress voted to allow recipients to keep thirty dollars plus one-third of whatever wages they earned. Even under this new law, if they reported their earnings, working welfare mothers risked losing medical insurance for their children. So many chose to be paid under the table—to become, in other words, "welfare cheats."[50]

Promising a "zero percent error rate," George Miller vowed to search out and cut such cheaters from the welfare rolls. To save taxpayer dollars, he also changed the formula for state welfare benefits, cutting Nevada's monthly base grant from $213.50 per family to $25 per child. All but the largest families on aid lost income. Despite having one of the country's highest per capita incomes, Nevada's grant was the lowest outside the Deep South. Now Nevada battled with its Southern sister states to see whose welfare grant would hit bottom first. On the Westside, families slipped deeper into poverty.[51]

HITTING BOTTOM AND RISING UP

George Miller's crusade was felt in nearly every poor household in Nevada. Even in 1968, twenty-five dollars was hardly sufficient to feed and clothe a child for a month. Alversa Beals fed her children on beans, corn bread, and white flour biscuits that year. When she'd left Tallulah for Las Vegas in 1955, Beals had been determined to provide a middle-class life for her children. Yet here she was thirteen years later, ladling beans over biscuits. Her children rarely had fresh milk or orange juice. Red meat was a holiday treat. Beals tried to make the most of the days just after the family's check came. She would make her children something special like spaghetti and meatballs or chicken and rice. But during the rest of the month, meals had a sameness that left her children disappointed, if not actually hungry.

Clothing rapidly growing children was stressful too, particularly if there was no money to purchase new school clothes when September rolled around. Beals could only afford to buy each child one pair of sneakers to last an entire school year. "My little girl would say 'Mom I don't want to go to school 'cause my shoes is ragged . . . and the kids is laughin' at 'em.' " She felt worse when the children had vision or dental problems and she could not afford to take them to a doctor. Treatment for the teeth and eyes was cosmetic according to the Welfare department. Medicare would pay for a pair of glasses now and then, but not for treatment of infections or degenerative diseases. One of Beals's daughters suffered for years from an untreated eye infection that permanently damaged her vision.[52]

Long-smoldering anger at the way they and their children were treated by the Welfare department exploded sometimes. For Rosie Seals, that moment came when she was denied aid after her stroke. "Application denied" was all her caseworker said. There was no explanation. When Seals attempted to protest, the woman pointed silently to the door. "The way she turned me out of there pissed me off," Seals says. "She wouldn't even give me an application to fill out." Seals returned to her doctor, who insisted that she could not work in her current condition. He wrote a reprimanding letter to the caseworker. "When she opened that letter she turned red as a piece of beef," Seals laughs. The woman thrust an application at her.[53]

Duncan's close friend Eddie Jean Finks had no work, no food, five children, and another baby on the way when she applied for government aid in 1964. Still, it took a year of visits to the Welfare office before she was approved for benefits. Finks's sister, Betty Jean, was denied aid so many times that she put her baby daughter down on the caseworker's desk and declared: "If I have to come back here one more time, you're not gonna have to put me in jail cause I'll go there on my own. At least they'll feed us there. I've got nothing to feed my kids. I ain't got no rent paid. I've got nothing." The Welfare office, she said later, wore her into a breakdown.[54]

But stonewalling by eligibility workers was nothing compared to the round-the-clock surveillance of suspected welfare cheaters that Miller ordered. "Man in the house" rules—which cut off aid to women with husbands or steady boyfriends—justified predawn raids by state welfare workers. By coming at times when people are normally sleeping, caseworkers hoped to find an actual male body in the woman's bed. They also searched for evidence of a man's presence—men's clothing, razors, or after-shave. Nevada also had a "substitute father" rule that justified raids on welfare recipients' homes. Any man with whom a welfare mother shared her bed was considered a "substitute father" and expected by the state to provide for her children. If a woman had a boyfriend for more than a few weeks, the state would cut off her aid on this pretext. "They watched us all the time," says Eddie Jean Finks. "If your brother was there, you had to call down to say who he was, and why he was there. They would sit in cars. Men, women, white, black. Half the time you knew they were there. Half the time you didn't."

Midnight raids by caseworkers, routine in Nevada, were commonplace across the country as well. Welfare rights activist Tanya Sparer, who once trained to become an AFDC caseworker in New York, was taught to enter clients' apartments and to scrutinize them "for telltale razors in the bathroom, whiskers in the sink or ashes in the ashtray." The Fourth Amendment protection from unlawful searches and seizures did not seem to apply to welfare mothers.[55]

Las Vegas caseworkers also looked for signs that a family had more money than they were admitting. If anything in the house seemed too expensive for a family on welfare, the caseworker would ask the woman who bought it for her. "It was something that kept you devastated and stressed at all times," remembers Eddie Jean Finks.

> *If you put a decent bed in your house, you'd find a person in your house asking "Where did you get the money to get this?" If you had a little decent food in your refrigerator they cut you off. If your kids had decent clothes to put on, they said you got some other source of money coming in from some place and you're not reporting it. Whenever I could get off welfare I did, because it was so nerve wracking.*

The system that denied recipients any right to privacy, that ordered state workers to barge into homes at all hours, turned client and caseworker into bitter enemies. Alversa Beals's heart would stop when she was awakened before dawn by pounding on her door. Her first thought was that something had happened to one of her children. Most often, though, it was a caseworker who would barge in and pepper her with questions while searching through her closets and bedroom drawers. "He was looking to see if any man's clothes was in there," she says. "They never told you when they was coming. They'd walk in your kitchen, sit down and start talking at you."

The next day the women would find each other on the street, in church, in grocery stores. They'd grumble about how much they hated strangers rifling through their personal belongings. Someone, they agreed, would have to do something to stop it. Finally, one woman in Marble Manor did, and her small act of resistance became legend.

The way the women tell it, their neighbor Stella simply snapped one day, but it sounds as if she enjoyed it. It was the third or fourth time that a caseworker had appeared at her door just after dawn. The woman entered Stella's bedroom uninvited, then stepped into the closet to search for a man's clothing. Quietly Stella shut the door and locked it. Then she went into the kitchen and began cooking breakfast. Stella did not free her captive until more state Welfare workers came looking for the caseworker. They had checked the woman's daily calendar and tracked her to Stella's house.[56]

Far more often, though, welfare recipients were the ones who were bullied. In 1967, Congress gave Welfare departments power to remove children of AFDC mothers "with multiple instances of illegitimacy."[57] The Las Vegas Welfare department decided to take Alversa Beals's children away. A black caseworker was sent to persuade Beals to give them up voluntarily. "Let a family take them that's got money and can raise them and feed them and buy them clothes," he told her. "You should give them up." Beals was aghast. "What are you talking about?" she asked. "Where was you when they was all little babies? I raised them." Then the caseworker took the gloves off. He said:

> I'm going to take all of them from you, Miss Beals. All these girls. You can't take care of them. You don't know nothing. You can't teach them nothing. You can't send them to school. They will never be nothing if they stay in your house.

Beals was panic-stricken. "I ain't giving nobody my kids," she said between sobs. The man was unmoved. "Stop feeling sorry for yourself," he told her. Beals refused to say another word. She watched in silent turmoil as the man looked around her house, scribbled some notes in a folder, and left.

Beals' six-year-old son heard the entire exchange. He ran to the home of a minister his mother knew. "That man made my mama cry," the boy said. The minister asked Beals what had happened. "I'm gonna get a gun," Beals told him with agitation. "He try to come and take my kids, I'm gonna shoot him. Ain't nobody gonna take my kids." The minister promised to stand by her. The next time the caseworker came, the minister told him that Beals was a good mother. He also called the state Welfare department, which dropped its plans to try to take Beals's children from her.

That particular crisis was never revisited. But Beals was tired of being threatened and feeling powerless. Nearly losing her children changed something inside her. An infinitely patient woman, Alversa Beals had reached her limit. Soon after that day, she heard about the National Welfare Rights Organization, and she exulted in its credo: Welfare recipients were citizens, with political and human rights to which they were constitutionally entitled. Like the civil rights heroes she had heard about—Rosa Parks in Montgomery, the marchers in Selma, young Ruby Bridges integrating her grade school in New Orleans—Alversa Beals realized that she had rights she ought to fight for.

"IF IT WASN'T FOR YOU, I'D HAVE SHOES FOR MY CHILDREN": WELFARE RIGHTS COME TO LAS VEGAS

I was trying to wake up Las Vegas, to let people know that we had rights, like anybody else.

—Rosie Seals, founding president of the
  Clark County Welfare Rights Organization

By 1967, the mothers of the Westside had begun to sense that something was changing for poor people across the country. Alversa Beals remembers the day when Ethel Pearson, a respected church elder and community organizer, knocked on her door to tell her about a new movement created and led by welfare mothers: the National Welfare Rights Organization. Beals gazed at the pamphlet that Pearson placed in her hand. It was the first time she had seen the words "welfare" and "rights" put together. The new group wanted to raise benefits to a livable level, and eliminate punitive and humiliating welfare regulations. Even as they spoke, Pearson told her, welfare rights organizers were canvassing poor neighborhoods across the country to start local chapters.

"Mother" Pearson, as she was known on the Westside, told Beals that she should start a welfare rights group in Marble Manor. The diminutive, immaculately dressed old woman looked Beals in the eye. "You got all these little kids," Pearson said. "If you want to hold your head up as a mother, go out and fight for your children." Beals could hardly imagine finding time to attend a meeting, let alone join a political movement. But Pearson's visit left her both exhilarated and scared. Mothers in other cities had begun to fight for change. Why not her?[1]

Pearson had come to Versie Beals's door as a paid organizer for the West Las Vegas Economic Opportunity Board (EOB), the first Westside outpost of President Johnson's War on Poverty. Created by Pearson and a group of Las Vegas ministers in 1966, the EOB was one of more than a thousand Community Action Agencies receiving federal money to run job training, Head Start, economic development, and community organizing programs in poor neighborhoods. Pearson was looking for ways to get Westside mothers engaged politically, and the nascent welfare rights organization—which was working with community action agencies across the country—seemed like just the ticket. The NWRO encouraged mothers to go head to head with housing departments, schools, Welfare offices, and government officials to get better shelter, food, and medical care. So when Pearson received a letter from NWRO asking her to help start a welfare rights chapter in Las Vegas, she and fellow EOB organizer Reverend Al Dunn headed to the Marble Manor project to see if they could find potential leaders.

This was an extremely controversial tack for organizers like Pearson whose salaries were paid with federal antipoverty funds. As Jacqueline Pope, an AFDC recipient turned activist, would later observe, organizers like Pearson were teaching the poor to "bite the hand that feeds them." Still, the president had called for an "unconditional war on poverty." For the first time since the Depression, the White House was urging poor people to organize on their own behalf. They did. The call for "maximum feasible participation" by the poor was like a stone thrown into a pond. There are few better examples of the War on Poverty's ripple effect than the National Welfare Rights Organization, a loose federation of welfare mothers' groups galvanized into a national movement by George Wiley, an African American chemistry professor, and Johnnie Tillmon, a dynamic welfare mother and organizer.

Alversa Beals liked the idea of starting a welfare rights group but didn't feel that she could lead it. "I get very shy in public," she says. "I couldn't talk. Neither could a lot of the other women. We needed someone with a forward kind of personality." Get Rosie Seals involved, she told Pearson and Dunn. "Even then, she had a loud mouth and she knew what she wanted to say."[2]

Seals says she agreed to organize the Clark County Welfare Rights Organization when she realized that some white AFDC mothers were getting more than their black counterparts. "It was like someone gave me an electric shock," Seals says. She was working alongside a white woman at a Westside commercial laundry, where many welfare mothers worked to supplement their checks. "Rosie, how much of welfare do you get?" the woman asked Seals. When Seals told her, the woman guffawed. "Hell, I get more than you get and you got more children than I got." That, Seals says, "pissed me off enough that I finally did something."

Seals called Reverend Dunn and told him about what she'd found out.

"Come down to the house so we can talk," she told him. Dunn brought NWRO pamphlets that Seals pored over carefully. She was astonished that "anyone out there gave a damn about welfare mothers." Seals looked the Reverend up and down. "Albert Dunn," she declared, "I don't know anything about this but I'm willing to learn." She phoned Versie Beals and some other women from the Marble Manor Project and asked them to come to a meeting in her living room the next evening. Only a handful came, but they talked long into the night—about wanting food stamps, higher benefits, and a clinic on the Westside. "None of us had money but we agreed we'd pay a dollar a month to get our pencils and papers and stuff that we had to have. We called ourselves welfare mothers and we called our group the Clark County Welfare Rights Organization."[3]

Suddenly everyone on the Westside was talking welfare rights. The women knew that the government was giving money to groups like EOB "to help poor people, give them training, help them find a job, give them learning," says Emma Stampley. In 1967, Congress had passed new amendments to the Social Security Act, requiring all women on AFDC to enroll in job training programs. An EOB sewing class was the only state-approved job training program for welfare mothers available on the Westside. It was a serious course that met five days a week, eight hours a day. Mothers were paid twenty-five dollars a week to attend and, if they did well, they might be placed as seamstresses in one of the Strip hotels. But the stakes were high: a woman's benefits could be terminated if she dropped or failed the course.

Each desk had a sewing machine, and Ruby Duncan chose one near the front. The Welfare department enrolled her in the class after she fell in the Sahara kitchen and demanded that they train her for a sedentary job. Emma Stampley, Essie Henderson, Alversa Beals, Mary Wesley, and Eddie Jean Finks had also been sent there by their caseworkers. Even though the class was mandatory, the women were excited about it. They wanted to land jobs sewing curtains, table linen, or uniforms for the Strip hotels. But there was more than sewing going on in that class.[4]

Middle-class feminists called it consciousness raising. Across the country, women were meeting in kitchens and living rooms, in coffee shops, classrooms, and offices, talking to each other for the first time about concerns they had previously had to cope with alone: their children, their lovers, birth control, battering, rape, abortion. As the women in the sewing class started talking to each other openly, "it felt good," says Ruby Duncan. "All those things that had been locked up inside us for so long finally started to come out."

At first, says Eddie Jean Finks, the women were just stitching at their individual machines. No one talked much. But then something changed. Like garment workers from New York to Hong Kong, from the nineteenth century to the present, the women talked while they sewed. They traded family stories, tales of love gone wrong, and bitter complaints about the welfare system. They came to know and depend on one another. "That sewing class really was the beginning of Clark County Welfare Rights," says Finks. Soon they were meeting at nights. They started out in Rosie's living room, but then the group got too big, so they moved to the Marble Manor common room, and from there to Father Louis Vitale's church across the street.

They spent a lot of time in those early days—in the class and at night-time meetings of the new welfare rights group—talking about nasty stereotypes. "All that stuff hurts you," Beals said. "It makes you feel so down and little. Even when I went to the doctor they would ask how many kids you got. I would say 'Eleven.' And they'd get that nasty smile. 'Well ain't they cheaper by the dozen?'"

Seals reeled off the labels they'd all heard about themselves. "Welfare mothers are no good," she said. "They're rotten. They're lazy. That's the stigma that hung on us. But it's not like that. It never was. We work hard. A lot of people think that raising kids is not a job. But if you gonna raise three or four kids, you got to keep the place clean. You got to wash. You got to cook. Believe me that's a job any way you look at it."

The women wanted recognition of their work as mothers. They also wanted the state to stop punishing them when they worked outside the home. "People was always telling us 'Get a job,'" Essie Henderson says. The truth was that many of the Westside women often held an outside job because Nevada—like many states—gave poor families less money than they needed to live on. Nevada's monthly welfare grant of twenty-five dollars per person was less than one-third of the state's calculated standard of need, and the state's standard of need was significantly lower than the federal standard.

"They knew damn well that the money they was giving us was not going to pay your rent and then pay for food," says Mary Wesley. "But they was telling us we couldn't have jobs. You couldn't make it unless you did something illegal. You had to do something—some work on the side—because you couldn't pay your rent, your utilities and have enough to feed your kids. I guess that's what keeps the rich richer and the poor poorer. All that stuff finally started to dawn on me then. It finally started to dawn on all of us."

Wesley came up with ways to make a few extra dollars: sewing dresses for friends, baking pies and cakes that she sold to neighbors. But when the state found out about her earnings, her medical benefits were cut. She raised the issue at her next CCWRO meeting. "If you don't get Medicaid, what do you do if one of your kids get sick?" Wesley asked the other women. They all knew what it felt like when a child fell ill. There was no medical facility on the Westside. Taking a child to the hospital could take hours by bus, and few of the women had any other transportation. And those with cars were targeted by the Welfare department. "They was telling the welfare recipients they couldn't have a car that cost more than a few hundred dollars," Wesley recalls. "That kind of car breaks down every month. You don't have transportation but you got to try to keep a job. But if we managed to keep a job, the welfare people would say we were frauds, liars and cheats."

It was becoming increasingly clear to the women that the welfare policies made no sense except to keep them a little bit hungry and forever dependent on state largesse. "They say they want you off welfare, but they never, never let you get ahead even a little bit," Wesley said. "If you have a home, nice clothes, even though you worked all those years, you have to sell them. If you have any sort of savings for emergency, you have to spend every penny of that. You can't have nothing saved for your kids."

Essie Henderson told the women that "the squeaky wheel gets the grease." Back in Texas, she had fired off a letter to President John F. Kennedy, complaining about how the Texas Welfare department mistreated her sister. If Kennedy helped the Freedom Riders, Henderson figured, maybe he would help them, as well. "My sister's got five kids and she's living with me," she wrote the president in 1963. "She's got to get help." At a time when few Americans had much noticed the growing American involvement in Vietnam, Henderson added that she wanted her tax dollars spent on the poor, not on the war. She received a reply written on White House stationery. "Take this letter back to the welfare office," Henderson remembers it saying, "and if they don't help your sister, then tell them in Washington."[5]

By the mid-1960s, Henderson had her own welfare quandary. Divorced and living in Las Vegas with her four children, Henderson applied for AFDC after being laid off from her hotel job. She was rejected three times. "I asked what was I supposed to do and the welfare worker said, 'You can put your children in a shelter.'" Stunned, but determined not to cry, Henderson snapped back archly: "My children don't like oatmeal when you cook it too long. How you gonna fix it in a shelter?" The caseworker's reply was terse. "You haven't lived here long enough to go on welfare." Nevada had a strict residency requirement; applicants who had lived in the state for less than a year were automatically rejected.

Henderson refused to take no for an answer. The next morning, she was the first in line outside the office door. "They unlocked the door and I busted in," Henderson recalls. "Weren't you here yesterday?" the caseworker asked. "The thing about today is, I'm not leaving," Henderson said. She sat her kids down. The youngest was crying, and office workers asked Henderson to quiet him down. "I can't keep him quiet because he's sick and he's hungry," she said. When her application was rejected once again, Henderson bundled her children off to the county General Assistance office for emergency food aid. Stella Fleming, in her fourth decade as gatekeeper of the county's larder, told an astonished and infuriated Henderson that she wasn't eligible. "Every time you reject me," Henderson said, "I'm gonna have to come back here because I don't have no choice." Eventually, the county provided some help.

Henderson did not stay on public assistance for long. But her commitment to welfare rights was lifelong. "People ask me where did we get the willpower and the guts to start a welfare rights group? If you had been living in this neighborhood, you wouldn't have stood still neither if you had a heart! People had four kids and they would cut them off with no good reason. They knocked on doors begging a piece of bread. And those who had a little bit more would help the others. That's what welfare rights was really about."

Ruby Duncan was initially resistant to Rosie Seals's attempts to get her involved in the Clark County Welfare Rights group. She came to it later, out of concern for her friend, Eddie Jean Finks. It bothered Duncan that Finks and her children might lose their welfare benefits because she was doing so poorly in the class. "I was so unhappy trying to sew," Finks recalls. "I could never get it right. And if it wasn't done right the instructor would make you rip the whole thing out and start from scratch. I got so nervous and so flusterated, I had to get on nerve medication just to survive the class." Finks grew more anxiety-ridden with each passing day. "Finally, one day they had to stretch me out in the back of the room. But Ruby was so kind and she would work with me. She said, 'Just try. Just keep trying.' Finally she said, 'Baby you just can't do it.'"[6]

One evening, Duncan was visiting her old school friend, Olestine Walker, and they got to talking about the class and how unjust it was that Finks might lose her welfare benefits because she couldn't sew. Walker told Duncan that she ought to come to a meeting of the Clark County Welfare Rights group. "I don't know anything about welfare rights," Duncan told her. Walker pressed the issue. "We have a right to get clothing and shoes and more money for our children to go to school," she said. Duncan was flabbergasted. "You gotta be crazy," she told her friend. "We can't be going down there and asking those people for money." A few days later, Walker came to Duncan's house and took her by the arm. "Ruby, I've come to get you," she said. "You're going with me." Duncan went to the meeting, prepared to leave early and not return. But she liked what she heard. Then thirty-five years old, Ruby Duncan began to learn how state laws and welfare policies were made.

> We could have shoes for our children if it wasn't for Senator Lamb being the chairman of the Finance Committee in the legislature. We could have clothing if it wasn't for Senator Young and all of those in the Ways and Means. So I looked around. And then I asked: "What is a legislature?" I didn't know what a legislature was.

Duncan's children needed shoes and clothing. She needed to apply her untapped intelligence and fast-popping ideas to something more satisfying than stitching a curtain hem. And she was intrigued by this unseen world of powerful men who held such sway over her daily life. Gradually, Duncan began talking politics in the sewing class. "We all felt that the welfare department was just very mean and vicious," Duncan recalls. "And we were sick and tired of being on welfare. So we started organizing everybody we could." Soon Duncan was carrying a clipboard and pencil to class, systematically buttonholing each woman in the room. "How would you like for us to try to find out our rights about welfare? Because we have rights." Some people were afraid, says Finks. "But I wasn't afraid. I couldn't hurt more than I already did."

Emma Stampley, another member of the sewing class, was new to the Westside and didn't know her classmates. So she listened to the conversations going on around her. One day, Ruby asked her if she, too, would join. "What is it for?" Stampley asked. The others explained that it was for women's rights and children's rights. "I thought: 'What the heck? I got kids! I'm a woman! I need to go.' "

Stampley was working nights at a small hotel called the Castaway and, like many Westside mothers, doing extra shifts at the local commercial laundry, Arrowhead Linens. But she needed additional assistance. When she went to the county to ask for commodities, the caseworker instead offered her a ticket back to Mississippi. "*You* take the ticket and go back to Mississippi," Stampley retorted. "If I'd wanted to be there, I would be there." When she tried to apply for Medicaid, she ran up against the one-year residency rule. Stampley recounted her experiences to Duncan the next day in class. "We're trying to eliminate that one-year rule," Duncan told her. "That's part of welfare rights." Stampley didn't need to hear any more. "OK," she said. "I'll join you."

The Westside women soon learned that word of their movement had spread. Rosie Seals got a phone call one day from a priest she had never heard of. Father Louis Vitale had just started a Franciscan community on the Westside, where he and two nuns shared spartan living quarters and tended a community garden and small chapel. Vitale wanted to get to know the neighborhood, and calling Rosie Seals was high on his list. "Miss Seals?" he asked. "I'm Father Vitale. I heard you were trying to get something together to help the welfare mothers and I'd like to help." Seals was incredulous but intrigued. "That's exactly what I'm trying to do," she told Vitale. "All the input I can get, I appreciate it." Seals understood that a movement of poor women could not make it without allies, and she wasn't about to spurn offers of aid from people with resources. If some white priest wanted to help, that was great.[7]

Louis Vitale was new to the Westside when he attended his first welfare rights meeting at Marble Manor in 1968, but he was already a veteran activist. A slight, wiry man with a wispy goatee, Vitale had marched with Cesar Chavez and the United Farm Workers in California, and studied liberation theology in Mexico and Latin America. Formerly an Air Force lieutenant, Vitale left the military after disobeying orders from his superiors to shoot down an approaching Soviet bomber. "We asked them why, if it was a bomber, was there a little old lady waving at us from the window," Vitale recalled. It turned out to be a passenger plane. After that experience, Vitale became a committed peace activist and entered the seminary. The young priest demonstrated against the war in Vietnam and, with other radical Catholic clergy, burned draftee records to make it harder for the government to find young men to ship off to war.[8]

Vitale was a thirty-six-year-old doctoral student in sociology when a new bishop was appointed for Las Vegas, who thought the church ought to be doing more for the community. He urged Vitale to go to the Westside, study conditions there, and make recommendations for church action. Vitale was shocked by what he found. "It felt like being in the heart of the South," he recalls. "It was very, very impoverished. The streets were just dirt." The priest, who wore plaid shirts and jeans in those days, instead of Franciscan robes, was excited when he heard that welfare mothers were organizing in the projects across the street from his church. He and Sister Carole Hurray, a young resident of the Westside Franciscan house, went to a meeting. They were the only white people present.[9]

"So here were all of these welfare mothers crowded into this room, all mothers from the projects," Vitale recalls. "It was obvious that these people were not yet part of any real organization. But something about their spirit really impressed me." The priest offered the women a comfortable space to meet at his church. From 1968 on, the Clark County Welfare Rights Organization met at St. James Church every two weeks, more often when crises occurred.

For Father Vitale and Sisters Mary Litell and Carol Hurray, supporting a movement for welfare rights made sense. Like militant nuns and priests across the U.S., they took seriously Pope John XXIII's call in 1962 for Catholic clergy to become more involved in the lives of the poor. Catholic priests and nuns had helped galvanize welfare rights groups in New York City, Boston, and Minneapolis in the past few years. St. Francis had celebrated the spirit of the poor, and Franciscans took vows of poverty. It felt natural for them to help a group of poor mothers fight for food and school clothing for their children. As for the mothers, they figured that it couldn't hurt their image or pocketbook to have the Catholic church on their side.

At first, says Vitale, he would just hang back and listen to the mothers. "They would talk about the difficulties of getting the kids off to school, and finding clothes. They talked about Christmas. 'What do you do so your kids aren't too disappointed?' They said that the two most difficult days of a welfare mother's life were Christmas and the first day of school." Random street shootings and police brutality worried them also. But the worst form of violence, the women agreed, was watching children go without enough food.

People on the Westside were initially afraid to join a welfare rights group, says Rosie Seals, "because they didn't want their little benefits to get cut off." Some worried that the state might retaliate by taking their children. Those with jobs worried about getting fired. Rosie Seals and Versie Beals walked the neighborhood from the beginning to the end of 1968, dragging themselves to just about every household in the projects. "This is to help betterify life for our kids," Beals told her neighbors. "They're coming along, growing up. We need to learn how to raise 'em right, how to get more food for them. You don't want to be on welfare all your life." Getting involved made Beals feel less helpless. "I could finally start to do something for my children, my sister's children, my brother's children, all the kids in the black community."

Wary Westsiders were hard to convince. "Lord it was a headache," Seals remembers grumpily. She had to make her pitch quickly or get doors slammed in her face. Seals would go back at night.

> They would say: "There's that big-foot cow! Here she comes again!" I said: "I don't care what you call me. It's time for you to wake up and do something for yourself. Because can't no one or two people fight no battle. It's gonna take us all."

"I was trying to wake up Las Vegas," Seals says now, "and that's what I did. I was trying to prove to the mothers this was something worth doing, to get 'em up off their asses." And when there was nothing left that she could think of to say, she just handed them an NWRO pamphlet and invited them to attend the next welfare rights meeting. To her dismay, she found that a good many of her neighbors had never learned to read. "Them that couldn't read, I tried to explain to them to the best of my ability," she says.

Rosie Seals's phone began to ring off the hook as panicked single mothers called to ask for help. Some had been rejected for welfare. Others were warned that their benefits would be cut if investigators found evidence that they were working, or if their children brought home failing grades in school. The Las Vegas Welfare Department came to rely on Seals's familiarity with the community and asked her to check up on mothers suspected of neglecting their children. Hoping she could prevent the state from taking her neighbors' children, Seals agreed to do home visits.

She was stunned by the conditions she found on the Westside. "I went in some houses where, when you pushed the door, you pushed a curtain of rags. That's all they had to keep the wind out. It made your heart ache." Seals visited women who were so paralyzed by depression that they seemed almost catatonic, sitting and staring at the walls in filthy rooms, while their young children crawled around unwatched and untended. "I went in homes where the baby's diapers had been on four and five days," Seals says, shaking her head in disbelief. "They just wasn't taking care of their kids." Seals tried to both comfort the women and shock them into action. She warned them that they could lose their children, and assured them that women not so different from themselves had pulled their lives together. Come to the Clark County Welfare Rights meetings, Seals urged the women. Talk out your troubles there, and find solace among women who are equally poor but are doing something to improve their condition.

Armed with practical, how-to handbooks provided by the National Welfare Rights Organization, Seals, Beals, Duncan, and others in the group promised to help Westside mothers deal with caseworkers, utility companies, doctors, and school authorities. "After welfare rights started, no one had to go to the welfare office alone," recalls Eddie Jean Finks. "We represented each other. So whatever they would tell you, you would have a witness." Before they organized, Finks says, there was no limit to what state caseworkers could ask: "When did you get pregnant? Who got you pregnant? How many men did you go with before you got pregnant? And why did you go to bed with all these men?" Once they had a welfare rights group, says her sister, Betty Jean Clary, "the welfare people stopped asking all that dirty stuff, that nasty stuff that would make you feel so devastated."

Las Vegas welfare rights activists had not yet won a single change in state policy, but their movement had already begun to give Westside mothers a sense of control over their lives. They enjoyed advocacy. And they were inspired to move beyond narrow self-help by welfare mother activists around the nation who were calling for a complete overhaul of the welfare system. One woman, in particular, spoke directly to them. "Johnnie Tillmon," says Essie Henderson, "turned us on."

THE NATIONAL WELFARE RIGHTS MOVEMENT

Johnnie Tillmon's biography was strikingly similar to those of many Westside women. She was born to sharecropping parents in Arkansas and picked cotton alongside them as a child. At eighteen, she left for Little Rock, where she worked as a maid, a dishwasher, a short-order cook, and a bomb-fuse inspector at a defense plant. In 1960, when her marriage to James Tillmon failed, she moved to California with her six children. Tillmon, then thirty-five, hoped for greater opportunities in the Watts section of Los Angeles—the original "Mudtown" in Arna Bontemps's description. But black women had few options there besides domestic and laundry work. Tillmon was hired at a commercial laundry, where she pressed 150 shirts an hour as a shirt line operator, and became shop steward for the laundry union. In her off-hours, she helped residents of her public housing project beautify the grounds and resolve food and rent problems. But in 1963, chronic arthritis forced her to quit her job, and a month-long hospitalization left her with no recourse other than welfare.[10]

Tillmon, who had worked hard all her life, was shocked by the change in people's attitudes the moment she became a welfare mother: she lost all dignity, privacy, and sympathy. But she was an instinctive organizer with a gentle directness and a deep well of self-respect. In 1963, long before a national welfare rights movement coalesced, Tillmon rallied welfare mothers at her housing project in Watts to form ANC Mothers Anonymous (ANC was the California welfare program). The women added "Anonymous," Tillmon said, because "we got a dictionary and found that anonymous meant nameless. We understood that what people thought about welfare recipients . . . was that they had no rights, they didn't exist; they was a statistic and not a human being. So we thought that would fit us very well."[11]

Watts was just a few hours' drive from Las Vegas, and many Westside women had relatives there, so word of the smart, feisty group of ANC mothers quickly spread through Marble Manor. Tillmon's group called for livable welfare allotments, job training, and daycare to enable mothers of young children to work outside the home. Tillmon enlisted the aid of local school principals and public housing managers to sway public opinion about welfare recipients. From the outset, she was driven by an impulse toward participatory democracy that many in the 1960s talked about—but very few lived. Tillmon pushed welfare mothers to become politically active, and they did: ANC mothers met with their representatives, ran voter registration and voter education campaigns, and ran for office. In 1963, this was path-breaking organizing. There was not another political figure quite like Tillmon. She created a new model for poor women's mobilization that encouraged alliances with educated middle-class people—but insisted that leadership remain in the hands of poor women. Ruby Duncan would later study and adopt many of Tillmon's strategies. Most importantly, Duncan was impressed by Tillmon's emphasis on job training. Mothers on welfare, Tillmon insisted, wanted to work. "Everybody [is] dying for a job," she said. "Everybody is saying, yes, we want to be trained for something that pays decently."[12]

In April 1966, Tillmon was invited to Washington, D.C., for the national convention of the newly formed Citizens Crusade Against Poverty, created by labor leaders and former Office of Economic Opportunity (OEO) administrators who wanted to pressure the federal government to fulfill its promises to the poor. The Economic Opportunity Act of 1964 had called for "maximum feasible participation" by the poor in regenerating their own communities. This quickly became the most controversial piece of Johnson's War on Poverty, as community groups used federal dollars to register poor people to vote, and organize tenants' councils, welfare rights groups, food cooperatives, and parent-teacher associations. Many mayors, city councilors, senators, and congressmen complained that taxpayers were being asked to subsidize subversion. Why, local officials demanded to know, was the federal government pouring fuel on communities that were already poised to explode?[13]

Activists countercharged that poor people never saw most of the money. The federal government had promised that War on Poverty funds would flow directly to community organizations. But in many places it was controlled by local elites instead: Democratic party bosses and big-city mayors in the North, segregationists and even actual Klansmen who sat on community action boards in the South. At the Citizens' Crusade Against Poverty conference in 1966, angry community organizers interrupted Sargent Shriver's keynote address. "Tell us where the poor are being helped," they demanded of the man

Lyndon Johnson had chosen to be chief architect and administrator of the federal War on Poverty.[14]

Johnnie Tillmon was among those who challenged Shriver that day. "The poverty program is a laugh," she said. "When all the money is spent, the rich will get richer and I will still be receiving a welfare check." If Shriver was truly concerned about fighting poverty, why had OEO not created job training and placement programs for poor mothers? When Shriver tried to describe successes of the community action program, activists shouted him down. "Don't listen to him," they cried. "He's lying!"

The melee embarrassed conference organizer George Wiley, an African American chemistry professor who had left academia for the civil rights movement. But it also inspired him. He was particularly moved by Johnnie Tillmon's speech. "The poor are developing a voice," he told his wife after the conference. "And if they can get together, somebody is going to have to listen to them."[15]

Wiley had left the Congress of Racial Equality, a mainstream civil rights group, to work on issues of poverty. Although the civil rights struggle had successfully challenged most legal forms of race discrimination, millions of blacks continued to live without adequate food, clothing, and shelter. That, he had come to feel, was "the most basic problem of black people." Wiley lobbied in Congress for a minimum wage bill that would extend coverage to low-wage workers in laundries, restaurants, hospitals, and farms. But he knew that such efforts would have far greater impact if they were backed up by grass-roots protest. By 1966, Wiley had become interested in helping to build an interracial poor people's movement that would bring together African Americans, whites, Chicanos, Puerto Ricans, and Native Americans.[16]

Poverty was a hot-button issue in the United States by the mid-1960s. Wiley found that there were quite a few former civil rights activists who shared his concern for the poor, yet still no one seemed able to generate the momentum necessary to galvanize a poor people's movement. At a 1966 conference on poverty, Wiley talked about this with Richard Cloward, a white sociology professor from Columbia University. "Here was a meeting of poor people from across the country," Cloward told Wiley. "But there was not a single workshop on welfare, despite the fact that most of the people at the meeting . . . were having trouble with the welfare system." To build a movement you had to have an engine. Cloward and his wife, political scientist Frances Fox Piven, believed that welfare rights could become the new rallying cry of the poor.[17]

The two conceived a plan to organize welfare recipients to demand the full benefits to which they were legally entitled, and to educate other poor families about their rights to welfare. But they were unable to convince mainstream civil rights leaders to devote resources to organizing welfare recipients. Whitney Young and Bayard Rustin both rejected the idea. In 1966, they tried George Wiley. "George took our theory and immediately saw the possibilities," recalled Piven. " 'The time is right,' he said, 'for issues that affect people at the bottom.' "[18]

Wiley knew that Johnnie Tillmon had created a dynamic poor mothers' movement in Los Angeles. In New York, Beulah Sanders, a magnetic woman with strong ties to labor, tenants' organizations, and anti–Vietnam War groups, had—with significant funding from the Community Action Program and help from Piven and Cloward—built the largest welfare rights coalition in the nation. Still, these "efforts were isolated, one from another," Wiley said. He wanted to meld these disparate mothers' groups into a coherent movement and coordinate protests nationally to maximize their impact. His research as an organic chemist had shaped his model for social change. "George created reagents—chemicals that you throw into a chemical reaction to make some sort of change," said a former colleague at Syracuse University. "His reagents did things that were previously undoable." Working with Piven and Cloward, Sanders and Tillmon, Wiley now set out to accomplish the same thing in politics.[19]

Street protests by welfare mothers could revolutionize American society, Piven and Cloward argued, through a carefully orchestrated "politics of turmoil." Disruption, they wrote, is "the only resource, short of violence, available to low income people seeking to influence public policy." In the short term, such pressure could win higher welfare benefits. But Piven and Cloward weren't interested in tinkering with the public assistance system. They wanted to explode it, and replace it with something better. Educate people about their rights, they urged Wiley, get hundreds of thousands more to surge onto state welfare rolls, and skyrocketing costs could precipitate a fiscal crisis. "When New York [is] faced with welfare bankruptcy," Cloward liked to say, "Mayor Lindsay and Governor Rockefeller [will] become your lobbyists for change in Washington."[20]

By the summer of 1966, the new movement had a strategy in place. What was needed now was political pressure—and theater. Here Piven and Cloward's politics of turmoil met Tillmon's and Sanders's politics of empowerment. Welfare-mother-activists announced that June 30 would become an annual day of protest for welfare rights. On June 30, 1966, six thousand mothers and children in twenty-five cities rallied in front of city, state, and federal offices, calling for higher welfare payments, grants for school clothing, and food stamps. "This is bigger than civil rights," declared comedian and activist Dick Gregory, standing on the steps of the Ohio State House. "This is human rights." Beulah Sanders led 1,500 mothers and children on a march through the rain to New York's City Hall, where they met with the city welfare commissioner, who promised to provide clothing grants in time for the coming school year. In Boston, welfare mothers rallied on the Common, asking that they not be penalized for working—and that authorities stop referring to their children as "illegitimate." In Philadelphia 150 women, men, and children held a "sleep out" at state offices, demanding a benefits increase mandated ten years earlier.

Demonstrators also rallied in Chicago, Louisville, Baltimore, San Bernadino, and other cities. Poor mothers had not protested in such a coordinated national action since housewives' councils successfully boycotted meat, dairy products, and bread to lower food prices during the Depression. The 1966 welfare rights protests were modest in size, but they made the evening news on two of the three major television networks, focusing national media attention on this new mothers' movement.[21]

Later that summer, Wiley organized a gathering of welfare mothers, civil rights workers, student organizers, academics, and social workers in Chicago. Tillmon and the other mothers swapped stories and strategies, which emboldened them further. "In the past, most of us had been so ashamed that we were on welfare that we wouldn't even admit it to another welfare recipient," Tillmon said. "But as we talked to each other, we forgot about that shame. And as we listened to the horrible treatment and conditions all over the country, we could begin thinking . . . that maybe it wasn't us who should be ashamed." They spent the next year organizing furiously.[22]

In the summer of 1967, welfare recipients demonstrated in forty cities. Two thousand mothers and children marched with Beulah Sanders in New York, demanding to see Mayor John Lindsay. They wanted the clothing grants they'd been promised for years, and telephones in their apartments. (Caseworkers had told mothers they weren't entitled to phones.) Displaying the discomfort that many silk-stocking liberals felt for militant black women, Lindsay called a news conference to announce that he would not meet with them. "The one way not to meet with the Mayor," he declared, "is to demonstrate in front of City Hall."[23]

The mothers refused to be dismissed. Momentum, and media attention, were building. In August 1967, representatives of mothers' groups from across the nation gathered in Washington, D.C., to officially launch the National Welfare Rights Organization (NWRO). George Wiley was appointed executive director, Johnnie Tillmon was elected chair, and Beulah Sanders a vice-chair. Delegates selected an interracial board of six African American mothers, two whites, and one Puerto Rican, and chose as NWRO's symbol two linked circles, uniting the civil rights and antipoverty movements. Sanders and other labor activists within NWRO called their new organization a "union" for poor women and children, and, like bread-and-butter trade unionists of old, promised to focus on practical concerns: "How do you get the money to live next week? How do you get clothing to send your kids back to school? How do you get them into a school lunch program? . . . How do you get back on welfare if your check is cut off?"[24]

The women quickly realized how difficult their road would be. As the newly minted welfare coalition was meeting, Congress proposed freezing the number of people on AFDC and imposing new work requirements on recipients. A thousand NWRO members descended on the Capitol to lobby against the measures. Many of them had once toiled in Southern fields for two dollars a day. For these middle-aged mothers, the idea of being forced to work at less than minimum wage, without federal labor protections, evoked unhappy memories. Calling the proposal "a betrayal of the poor and a declaration of war on our families," Tillmon and Sanders urged the Senate Finance Committee to listen to the testimony of poor mothers before voting on the measure. The committee refused their request, although New York senator Jacob Javits helped the women secure a room where they organized their own "people's hearing" on welfare. They invited every member of Congress, but not a single senator came.[25]

NWRO kept the pressure on, and a month later Tillmon and other welfare mothers were invited to testify at Senate hearings on the new welfare proposals. Senator Russell Long of Louisiana interrupted Tillmon's testimony to complain that, because of welfare, he could no longer find anyone to iron his shirts. Tillmon replied that she had ironed shirts for eighteen years—and when she was too sick to work, she couldn't feed her children. She had no choice but to apply for public assistance. All but two members of the Senate Finance Committee walked out of the room while the welfare mothers spoke. Upset by the senators' behavior, the women staged an impromptu sit-in, refusing to leave the witness table until all seventeen members of the committee returned to hear their testimony.

Senator Long angrily called the women "brood mares" and added: "If they can find the time to march in the streets, picket, and sit all day in committee hearing rooms, they can find the time to do some useful work. They could be picking up litter in front of their houses or killing rats instead of impeding the work of Congress." Capitol police warned the women they would face six months in jail if they did not leave peacefully. As the women streamed out, they shouted, "We won't iron your shirts for you anymore, Senator Long." The following June, on NWRO's annual day of protest, Tillmon organized a series of actions she called "Brood Mare Stampedes."[26]

Across the country, activist welfare mothers watched these news stories with interest and amusement. Powerful politicians seemed actually afraid to meet face-to-face with welfare recipients. Photographs of fist-waving, chanting welfare mothers were splashed across the pages of the nation's largest newspapers, with pithy quotes from the women themselves. The coverage had negative as well as positive effects, playing into stereotypes of black single mothers as angry and insatiable, always demanding more from the taxpayer. But, after decades of scholarly analysis and politicians' pronouncements about poor black mothers, Americans were finally seeing their faces and hearing their voices. And some important people began to listen.

The social stigma attached to poor, single mothers had long made Martin Luther King Jr. and other middle-class black leaders uncomfortable about allying themselves with the welfare rights movement. For years, welfare mothers accepted their invisibility in the civil rights movement. But when King ignored welfare issues in developing his 1968 Poor People's Campaign, Sanders and Tillmon asked to meet with him. Sitting next to King with her grandchild on her lap, Tillmon "jumped on Martin like no one ever had before," recalls King's assistant Andrew Young. She and other NWRO mothers asked King his position on several key pieces of welfare legislation, about which he was clearly uninformed. Finally Tillmon said: "You know Dr. King, if you don't know about these questions, you should say you don't know, and then we could go on with the meeting." An awkward silence followed, until King, not known to welcome criticism by women, apologized. "You're right, Mrs. Tillmon," he said. "We don't know anything about welfare. We are here to learn."[27]

Organized labor, too, began to respond to overtures from welfare activists. Beulah Sanders negotiated with District Council 37, the largest public employees' union in New York City, to develop job training and placement programs for welfare mothers. Sanders also forged alliances with social workers' unions in the city to lobby for more generous welfare payments.[28]

Protest in the streets and negotiation in the suites were two arms of NWRO's strategy for reforming the welfare system. The final thrust was a litigation campaign they hoped would take them before the U.S. Supreme Court to argue for a guaranteed minimum income for all Americans. Edward Sparer was NWRO's legal advisor and the chief "guru" to a new generation of poverty lawyers. He challenged the assumption that a woman gave up her Constitutional rights to privacy and due process when she accepted a welfare check. First Amendment rights to freedom of association and Fourth Amendment protections against unlawful search and seizure, Sparer contended, were not contingent on a person's economic status. And he argued that the Fourteenth Amendment guarantee of equal treatment under the law entitled all Americans to a minimum standard of living.[29]

Sparer's ideas inspired the poverty law movement, which attracted thousands of law school graduates in the mid-1960s. (Some of them would go on to blaze new legal paths in the fields of domestic violence, immigration, women's rights, health and consumer care, and the rights of the elderly.) Many of these young advocates shared Sparer's desire to revamp the federal welfare system, but they recognized that a Constitutional right to a minimum income would be, at best, years in the making. To meet the immediate needs of poor families, young attorneys went to work at Legal Services offices across the country, created by the Office of Economic Opportunity to ensure legal help for the poor. Recipients were anxious to overturn the most hated AFDC policies—the "man in the house rule," residency requirements, and employable mother rules. Legal Services lawyers challenged these regulations all the way up to the Supreme Court in the late 1960s, and won some major victories.[30]

Among those inspired by the poverty law movement were Jack Anderson and B. Mahlon Brown III, young white Las Vegans then attending the historically black Howard Law School in Washington, D.C. The two men had chosen Howard because they wanted to become civil rights lawyers. Instead, they found themselves caught up in a new movement—poverty law. Anderson and Brown came from very different walks of life: one was a former casino pit boss, and the other the son of powerful Nevada politicians. Both men rejected the idea of working for gaming interests or elected officials when they returned home. They left Howard determined to work with the poor. Brown became director of Clark County Legal Services and began raising money to hire Anderson. A welfare crisis was brewing in Nevada, and the two men would soon be at the center of it.

POVERTY IN BLACK AND WHITE

As Rosie Seals traveled to welfare rights conferences across the country, she started to connect her own grievances to those of welfare mothers from other states. She also realized that the welfare rights struggle was not exclusively an African American movement. "For the first time ever, I talked to a whole lot of white folks," she recalls. "I learned that white people disagreed about welfare. There were those who was interested in helping and those in the government who wasn't."

In the winter of 1968, Seals and several other Westside women traveled to Reno to meet representatives from largely white welfare rights groups. They were stunned to find that poor white families in northern Nevada lived in conditions as bad as, or even worse than, their own. Eddie Jean Finks stayed with a mother in Carson whose home life made hers seem comfortable. The woman, who had a small son, had been cut from the welfare rolls because caseworkers "said her husband was coming to see her. They said they was finding his tracks around the house in the snow." When Finks arrived, the woman had been without heat for three months. "All the food she had was a box of oatmeal and it had worms in it," Finks recalls. "That's what she was feeding the kid. And it was so cold in her house she had to put a mattress up behind the door to keep the snow from coming in." The woman's pipes were frozen, so she had no running water to bathe her son or do laundry. Says Finks: "They was just too afraid to speak up to the welfare department."[31]

For the next two years, black and white Nevada welfare mothers worked together to eliminate state regulations they saw as cruel and capricious. In rallies at the state capitol and testimony before the legislature, they called for the repeal of residency requirements that denied aid to families who had lived in Nevada for less than a year. In a state where so many people were recent migrants, they argued, this left thousands of children hungry. George Miller told state legislators that, without residency rules, poor mothers from across the country would descend on Nevada. Why, the women countered, would anyone choose a state where AFDC grants were among the lowest in the country?

Point for point, the women challenged the logic of Nevada's punitive welfare policies. If Nevada wanted the mothers of small children to go to work, the women asked, why were state inspectors fining women for setting up unlicensed baby-sitting collectives? If the state wanted to cultivate the value of paid labor, why did it reduce a family's benefits for every dollar a working teenager earned? The women were particularly incensed by Nevada's policy of cutting aid to children who were truants or received poor grades. Instead of punishing children who were having trouble academically, the mothers asked, why didn't the state spend the same money on tutoring? Finally, the women expressed ire at a 1967 state law requiring county prosecutors to interrogate every Nevada woman who applied for assistance. "They treated me like a tramp," a Reno mother said about prosecutors who grilled her about her sex life. When state officials refused to stop the practice, Rosie Seals and her northern Nevada counterpart wrote to the Department of Health, Education, and Welfare (HEW), which ruled the practice illegal and ordered it discontinued.[32]

The women then threatened to sue in federal court to stop Nevada from forcing welfare applicants to undergo lie detector tests and blood tests to reveal the paternity of their children. The state gave in, allowing applicants to make a simple declaration of needs and income, a practice HEW was then urging all states to adopt. But it was a shaky victory. The declaration of need was anathema to Carson City conservatives, who did not want to award aid on a welfare mother's word alone. "Why should welfare recipients be any more honest than the public?" George Miller asked. "Everybody, if they can, cheats on their income tax. Why would these people on the lower rung be any more honest than the people in the middle class?" Miller vowed to find new ways to screen applicants, and to cut off cheaters.[33]

Nevada's new welfare director lost two legal rationales for cutting women from the public assistance rolls when the U.S. Supreme Court struck down "man in the house" and "substitute father" rules in *King v. Smith*. "Destitute children who are legally fatherless," wrote Justice Earl Warren, "cannot be flatly denied federally funded assistance on the transparent fiction that they have a substitute father."[34] Two more legal victories for welfare recipients quickly followed. The court struck down residency requirements and banned the state practice of excluding applicants who move from a state with lower AFDC benefits. "Surely," wrote the justices, "such a mother is no less deserving than a mother who moves into a particular state in order to take advantage of its better educational facilities." Such strong wording convinced welfare mothers that federal courts were on their side.[35]

THE POLITICAL BAPTISM OF RUBY DUNCAN

By early 1969, the mothers of the Westside had begun to feel that they were activists in a human rights movement of significance and substance. But Rosie Seals was simply too ill to continue as president of the Las Vegas mothers' group. "You had to travel all the time and the phone would ring 24 hours," she says. "I just couldn't handle it anymore." Beals had watched as her friend's health deteriorated. "Rosie had high blood pressure. She'd get nervous and shaking." The two friends agreed that Seals should step down. Ruby Duncan had become increasingly active in welfare rights over the past few months. She seemed the best choice to take over the two-year-old group.

Duncan had begun to make a name for herself in state political circles in 1969, when the Nevada legislature cut funding for the EOB sewing class and other job training programs for welfare mothers. Duncan found out that the Economic Opportunity Act had earmarked federal funds to train AFDC mothers for jobs. The Nevada legislature had turned down the money and then, pleading poverty, shut down the jobs programs. Duncan led women from the sewing class on a march through the Westside in the Spring of 1969 to the state Welfare office. The women told caseworkers they had come to ask Las Vegas Welfare director Vincent Fallon to reopen the sewing class. Fallon had no say in the decision, the office manager replied. If the mothers wanted the class restored, they should speak to their legislators.[36]

Westside community activists agreed to sponsor welfare mothers to lobby in Carson City. Duncan volunteered to go. Essie Henderson went too. The bus ride to Carson took nine hours. On the way, organizers of the trip explained to the Westside mothers how the Nevada legislature worked, that there was a senate and an assembly, and that the Senate Finance Committee and the Assembly Ways and Means Committee had to approve all welfare policies. They told the welfare mothers the names of the committee chairs and described the personalities of important lawmakers. By the time the bus arrived in Carson City, Duncan felt ready.

It was April 4, 1969, and, dressed for the Las Vegas heat, Duncan shivered in the cold of the Sierra Nevada foothills. Moments after she stepped off the bus, a volunteer pointed out Senator Floyd Lamb, the powerful head of the Senate Finance Committee. Duncan felt something click inside her. Las Vegas organizers had made signs for protestors to wear, challenging by name each member of the Senate who had voted to cut programs for poor families. "Which one you said is keeping us from getting shoes for our children?" Duncan asked. They pointed to Senator Lamb, who was standing on the sidelines, watching. "Well give me his," Duncan said. She put on the Lamb sign and began marching around the state house.

Duncan swallowed hard as she noticed Lamb striding purposefully toward her. "The Lambs of Nevada were powerful people," she says. (His brother Ralph was sheriff of Clark County for eighteen years.) As the welfare mother made eye contact with the senator, civil rights activist Alice Key took Duncan's arm. "I want you to meet Senator Lamb," she said. Duncan introduced herself politely then immediately began upbraiding the man. "You're the one that's keeping us from getting shoes for our children," she said, thrusting her finger at him. "You!" Lamb tried to deflect the attack: "You've got to understand—" he told her, but Duncan didn't let him finish. "No," she said. "You can't tell me *anything* that will make me understand." When the marchers rallied on the steps of the state house, Duncan was asked to speak. "I didn't want to," she recalls. "And I don't remember what I said. But when I was done I looked up and people were hanging out the windows of the state offices and, all around me, people were clapping."

That evening, Duncan testified before the Nevada Ways and Means Committee. She was nervous and emotional. "The water was coming down my face as I was telling them what we went through," she says. "Sweat and real tears. I looked over and I saw these well-dressed men and they were sitting there smirking. At the table was nothing but white men in silk suits, silk ties, silk socks, bright and beautiful shiny loafers and shoes. And I said 'You don't have the money for welfare?'" Duncan thought she heard one senator chuckle. "Did you laugh at me?" she asked. The Senator denied that he had. "I'm done now," Duncan said quietly, "but remember me, gentlemen, because I will be back. You just inspired me to come back." With as much dignity as she could muster, Duncan turned and walked slowly from the Senate chamber. The room was so silent, she says, that she could hear her footsteps echoing. Not long afterward, Duncan was elected president of Clark County Welfare Rights Organization. The Westside mothers movement would never be the same.[37]

Duncan felt almost giddy with excitement as she read the newspapers in the months that followed, and discussed with other Westside mothers the latest developments in welfare politics. Sondra Phillips, Duncan's youngest daughter, remembers her mother reading late into the night, poring over news of the welfare rights movement and trying to make sense of the landmark Supreme Court decisions. "I would see her laying across the bed with her glasses on, reading and reading," Phillips says. "Watching my mother work like that, it really impressed me." Duncan's transformation in just a few months was remarkable. She had first learned during the winter of 1969 what a legislature was. By the next summer, she was reading and interpreting welfare laws herself, and developing an analysis of what was wrong with the welfare system.[38]

Duncan's political insight grew sharper and more sophisticated after she was elected to the NWRO National Coordinating Committee in 1969. "Dr. Wiley was the strongest man I had ever known," she says, with a hint of a schoolgirl crush for the tall, handsome, well-spoken professor with the distinctive Rhode Island accent. (Wiley had been named an *Ebony* "Bachelor of the Year" in 1960, although by 1969 he was married with two children.) "I had never met a man who wanted women to be as strong as men," she says. Wiley would talk late into the night, explaining the latest welfare bills being debated in Congress. "Dr. Wiley would never let us go to sleep," Duncan recalls. "He would say to us: 'Wake up everybody. You are sleeping while they're sitting up there on the hill making laws to keep you welfare mothers down. They have welfare plans to control you. You need to have plans of your own.'"

Wiley was a gregarious chameleon who could move effortlessly from the Senate chambers to a fund-raising dinner with wealthy backers, then to a street protest of angry welfare recipients. Duncan watched him and came to understand that, to be an effective advocate for the poor, she would need to navigate these very different worlds. Tillmon and Sanders, pragmatic field strategists, advised Duncan to use the tension between state and federal authorities to gain leverage for welfare mothers' demands—to play politicians off against one another. Most immediately, they taught her that recipients had the right to a fair hearing before their benefits could be reduced or terminated.[39]

That coaching was timely. Duncan returned home to find that half of Nevada's welfare recipients stood to lose benefits. The federal government now required welfare mothers to enroll in job training programs, and Nevada had just eliminated them. On June 30, 1969, NWRO's annual day of protest, thirty women marched to the office of city Welfare director Vince Fallon. Like his boss, George Miller, Fallon had come to his post from a War on Poverty job. A former social worker, he had been a Head Start administrator in Washington, D.C., and before that he'd worked for Catholic Charities for fifteen years. Vince Fallon thought of himself as a friend of the poor—but that was not how the Westside women saw him.[40]

Duncan told Fallon that hundreds of Las Vegas families had received notices that their benefits were about to be cut. These families, she said, had the right to hearings and, by law, there had to be welfare recipients on the hearing boards. Duncan, who towered over the slightly-built Fallon, handed him a list of caseworkers whom welfare families thought were rude and ought to be fired. In their place, she suggested, Fallon should train and hire welfare mothers. No one knew the system better than they did, she noted. Finally, Duncan asked Fallon to approve special grants for school clothing, furniture, emergency housing, and food. She had just learned about these at an NWRO meeting. Fallon said he'd have to get back to her.[41]

One week later, Duncan received a letter from Miller, rejecting her requests. In response, she called reporters at the largest northern Nevada daily, the *Reno Evening Gazette*—which was sure to be on George Miller's breakfast table—and blasted him. Nevada was in violation of the 1967 amendments to the Social Security Act, she charged. A federal judge had just ruled that attempts by nine states to cut AFDC benefits were unconstitutional. "Federal regulations say the states must raise welfare grants to keep up with the cost-of-living increases," Duncan said, "but Nevada has cut the grants instead." Indeed, Nevada had not increased benefits since 1957.[42]

Learning to navigate the layers of government, as Tillmon had taught her, Duncan next turned to the state Welfare board, a citizen's advisory board that helped set state policy. Duncan and two other Westside mothers traveled to Carson City to attend a board meeting, where they were joined by fifty activists from Reno. The women asked that Nevada allocate moneys for job training and cost of living increases in AFDC benefits. But board members, who backed Miller, voted down their requests. Frustrated, the women stood up and shouted at the commissioners, who hastily adjourned the meeting. When she returned home, Duncan demanded that the state Welfare board convene a session in Las Vegas, where a majority of the state's AFDC recipients lived. When a hearing was scheduled, Duncan wrote Miller and Governor Paul Laxalt and asked them to attend. Neither did. Scores of Westside mothers testified, but only Westside legislators heard them.[43]

Determined to gain a larger forum for their views, Duncan and the welfare rights group printed petitions calling for a special session of the state legislature, and collected hundreds of signatures from Westside voters. They also petitioned Stella Fleming to open a new food distribution center on the Westside to serve the thousands who had been affected by the most recent round of welfare cuts. They received no reply to either petition.[44]

Stymied, Duncan scrambled to come up with new tactics. Her daughter Sondra, ten, ran back and forth between the kitchen and the living room, serving food and drinks as Duncan, Essie Henderson, Rosie Seals, Alversa Beals, and other CCWRO activists sat and mulled over their options. "We knew we wanted to do something," Duncan recalls, "but we weren't sure what. So we read the materials from welfare rights and read the newspapers and watched the news to see what other welfare mothers were doing then."

What other welfare mothers were doing then was fairly dramatic. In February of 1969, Nixon's Secretary of Health, Education, and Welfare, Robert Finch, met with Tillmon, Sanders, Wiley, and the entire NWRO executive board. The group was elated; no member of Lyndon Johnson's cabinet had ever met with them. Finch called welfare mothers "an important constituency of HEW" and told them that the president was considering an overhaul of welfare that would establish a federal standard of payments. Shortly thereafter, Wiley was awarded a $430,000 contract by the Department of Labor to get welfare recipients to take leadership roles in promoting the federal Work Incentive (WIN) Program, created in 1967 to promote state-based job training programs for welfare mothers.[45]

But if Richard Nixon's administration seemed to be more receptive, state legislatures were growing more hostile. In New York, with the largest welfare caseload in the country, the legislature had slashed the benefits of more than 750,000 mothers and children in New York City alone. Poverty lawyers filed suit, while recipients took to the streets. This two-pronged strategy was becoming the hallmark of the National Welfare Rights Organization. George Wiley pretended to throw up his hands. If street demonstrations turned violent, he warned anxious New Yorkers, politicians had only themselves to blame. Speaking to a rally of five thousand welfare mothers and their supporters, Beulah Sanders said, "We will not let the children starve in this city. You'll have to take to the streets. You'll have to make this city hot. That's the only way to stop the war on the poor. . . . I'm ready to take the first step to jail. Are you with me?"[46]

Duncan pored over coverage of the New York protests, riveted by the dangerous chess game that NWRO seemed to be playing. The group made its rashest move to date in May 1969, when—in a move that took Wiley by surprise—Sanders and forty welfare mothers bolted the doors at a National Social Welfare Conference at the New York Hilton, effectively taking the 3,500 delegates hostage. As former HEW secretary Arthur Flemming struggled to maintain order from the dais, the welfare mothers took control of the microphones, demanding that the nation's largest social work organization support NWRO's adequate income proposals and donate thirty-five thousand from conference registration fees to their group. The welfare mothers marched up the aisles with plastic ice buckets, hitting up delegates for cash. "We're not all fat cats," one social worker cried out. Everyone seemed relieved when the police quickly reopened the hotel exits, ending the standoff. Delegates condemned the demonstrators' tactics, and the *New York Times* warned that the activists were hurting their own cause. But, remarkably, the attendees did vote to give thirty-five thousand dollars to sponsor NWRO summer internships that would enable social work students to work for local welfare rights groups. Duncan, reading newspaper accounts of the action, couldn't help feeling a sense of satisfaction at knowing that welfare recipients would finally get a chance to teach future social workers to see the welfare system from recipients' point of view.[47]

Duncan was downright gleeful about NWRO's credit card crusade. In Philadelphia, New York, Chicago, and other cities in 1969, hundreds of welfare mothers streamed into department stores, and requested credit cards. The campaign had several goals. Credit would enable poor mothers to shop where middle-class Americans did, instead of at overpriced ghetto stores that took only cash. Cash was something that welfare mothers were chronically short on, and since other Americans could buy on credit and pay over time, welfare mothers wanted the same right. And finally, public assistance didn't give people enough money to live on. Buying on credit amounted to an enhancement of low monthly grants.[48]

During the summer of 1969, three hundred New York welfare mothers walked into Sears Roebuck, played record albums, and tested their skill on electric sewing machines, while Wiley and Sanders asked that Sears grant them credit. When Sears managers refused, Sanders borrowed a tactic from the antiwar movement, calling on supporters to burn their Sears credit cards in front of the store. "Sears has got to learn one thing," Sanders shouted. "They have to deal with the poor." Organizers didn't ignore the specter of credit card debt. "We weren't stupid in what we asked for," said Roxanne Jones, a former dancer and waitress who led NWRO efforts in Philadelphia. The group requested only fifty dollars in credit, and each cardholder could increase her debt limit only by paying off that initial sum. By the end of 1969, NWRO members had credit at E.J. Korvette's, Gimbels, Abraham and Strauss, and Marshall Field.[49]

For Beulah Sanders, all of these public campaigns had a common purpose: establishing visibility, independence, and control for poor women. In the midst of the credit card campaign, she testified before President Nixon's Commission on Income Maintenance, a blue-ribbon committee exploring options for fundamental welfare reform. "Everybody from President Nixon on down is talking about us," she said. "Everyone has their own plan on what to do with welfare recipients. Well the only thing you can really do is get up off your 17th-century attitudes, give poor people enough money to live decently, and let us decide how to live our lives." She noted that the powerful U.S. senator from Mississippi, James Eastland, had received hundreds of thousands of dollars from the U.S. Department of Agriculture that year alone, to enhance profits on his cotton crop. Compared to cotton subsidies and other forms of corporate welfare, she said, AFDC amounted to peanuts.[50]

Richard Nixon thought he could please both sides. On August 9, 1969, he announced his plan for a minimum guaranteed income for all Americans. The Family Assistance Plan called for uniform national grants and eligibility criteria, and expanded the number of Americans eligible for government aid to include the working poor and unemployed fathers. Applicants could apply by making simple "declarations of need," putting an end to demeaning personal and financial investigations. All recipients would be required to enroll in job training programs and to accept "suitable" employment when caseworkers found it for them. Nixon even proposed expanding federal support for daycare centers. Anticipating protest from state officials, the president promised that the federal government would cover the increased costs. The catch: a family of four would receive only $1,600 a year. While this would constitute a significant increase for most welfare recipients in the South, it would be a dramatic decrease for welfare families in the North and West. The plan also called for deep cuts in food stamps and an end to commodity food distribution.[51]

The Family Assistance Plan (FAP) generated immediate and passionate resistance from every sector it was supposed to please. Organized labor, worried about downward drag on union wages, opposed requirements that recipients take jobs paying less than the federal minimum wage. Southern politicians opposed any plan that would shrink the labor pool for low-wage jobs in domestic and field work. "There's not going to be anybody left to roll these wheelbarrows and press these shirts," said Georgia congressman Richard Landrum.[52]

Johnnie Tillmon had a more nuanced response than most. She praised Nixon for taking the initiative in proposing a national guaranteed income, but warned that $1,600 was not enough for a family to live on. The National Welfare Rights Organization considered $5,500 (the average annual ADC benefit in New York) the bare minimum income for an American family. Other black leaders were not as gentle in their criticism. Coupled with the proposed food stamp reduction, the Family Assistance Plan would be "the greatest welfare cutback in recent times," charged Michigan representative John Conyers. Stung by attacks from Democrats and Republicans alike, Nixon began backing away from his proposal even before Congress held hearings.[53]

Nixon now told the American public that there was as much dignity in washing floors as in being president of the United States. Welfare mothers should work for their keep, he said, no matter what they did and how much they were paid. NWRO women found the president's remarks flippant and offensive. At Ruby Duncan's first welfare rights convention in late August, 1969, nearly everyone was talking about how to "zap FAP." "Many of the women here have been domestics at wages considerably lower than a welfare stipend," wrote a *New York Times* reporter. "Many have done farm work in the South, and still have the muscles to show it." They saw nothing inherently liberating about such demeaning and low-wage work.[54]

But how to make politicians sit up and listen? Tillmon urged the delegates to embark on a national campaign of economic boycotts and civil disobedience. "Hit them in the pocketbook," she told them. "Disrupt business as usual. Public officials leave the room when we try to speak calmly. The power structure understands us better when we boycott, jump up and down, pound the desk, break windows and things like that. We have not outgrown demonstrations yet." Duncan watched and listened. "I learned so much from Johnnie Tillmon and Beulah Sanders," she says. "I heard those ladies talking. I thought about what they said. And all of a certain, I began to understand."[55]

BACK HOME AND ON THE FRONT LINES

Less than two weeks later, nine Westside mothers climbed the stairs of the state Welfare department near the Westside and, without asking permission, strolled into the director's office and sat down in a circle around his desk. Vince Fallon looked up and asked brightly: "What can I do for you all? We're closing now." "That's okay," Ruby Duncan replied. "We came to spend the weekend with you because we need clothing. We need shoes for our children. Our checks need raising because you just can't live off this little bit of money."

Fallon told the women they had to leave. "We're not going," they answered together. The women had made arrangements for someone to watch their children. "We're prepared to keep you company all night," Emma Stampley said sweetly. Outside, forty other women and children were picketing, singing, and circling the building. "You should have seen the signs we had," Stampley says. "There was one I particularly liked. It was a buzzard sitting up on the limb. The big fat buzzard was eating the little buzzard on the ground." Rosie Seals stayed on the street, near a pay phone, ready to contact Legal Services lawyers if the women needed to be bailed out.

Fallon dialed the police. When several officers arrived, the director asked them to take the women down the back staircase. "Oh no," Duncan replied. "We are going down the front way, the way we came in." It was one of the first sit-ins in Las Vegas history, and the pure joy of it was energizing. "It was so much fun to demand," Duncan says. "To know that we were demanding from this big entity, this institution, the state. Knowing how ruthless they were to poor people. And especially a group of us so-called uneducated. I think they were caught by surprise as much as we were."[56]

As the Westside women were led from the Welfare department office in handcuffs, Duncan recalls, "people were coming out of stores looking at us, as they piled us into the police wagon. Then they took us downtown, fingerprinted us and put us in a cell." The women were singing civil rights songs in their cells at the Clark County jail when the bailiff came to tell them they were free to go. "I was peeved to be bailed out so soon," Duncan laughs. She was looking forward to a night's sleep and having someone else do the cooking.. "Yeah," says Mary Wesley. "They didn't let us get our rest." In January 1970, Duncan, Beals, Wesley, Stampley, and several other CCWRO women were convicted of disorderly conduct and sentenced to perform community service at local Boys' Clubs. "That just meant," says Duncan, "that we had to go on doing what we were doing anyway."[57]

A few weeks after the Welfare office sit-in, the Westside exploded after years of anger over police brutality. The Las Vegas police department was known across the nation for having one of the worst records of violence toward civilians of any urban police force. And black policemen were just as reviled as white. On October 5, 1969, two black officers stopped a black cab driver and pulled him out of his car. A crowd gathered to watch. Police warned them to back off. Young men threw rocks, and the crowd tried to roll the police car. Afterwards, roving bands of boys fanned through the neighborhood breaking windows and throwing homemade Molotov cocktails. They vented their rage on crumbling school buildings and the state Welfare office, where rioters broke windows, ransacked files, and covered the walls with angry graffiti. The violence lasted for three days. Two people were killed; fifty were injured. Two hundred were arrested, most for violating the 7:00 p.m. curfew ordered by the mayor after the violence began.[58]

It wasn't hard to understand what fueled the rage of the rioters. "Las Vegas Glitter Heightens Frustrating Life of Negroes," opined headline writers for the *Nevada State Journal*. The Westside was a festering mix of wounds and insults as old as the neighborhood's shoddy housing, and as new as George Miller. Unemployment for black men was chronically high in Las Vegas. A recent report by the state Equal Rights Commission had noted that racial discrimination in hiring in Nevada remained "so severe as to endanger the entire economy of our state." Housing in the city was as segregated as ever. And the 1969 legislature had just defeated an open housing bill.

As street fires burned down, a young man in handcuffs tried to explain his actions to reporters. He had just been mustered out of the Marines after a tour in Vietnam and had not been able to find work. "We're like dogs," he said. "You push one long enough and sooner or later he's going to turn on you. He knows he can't beat you, but still he turns on you. It's the frustration of it all, man. Well, now we're turning too. We are going to be beat, we know that. But we still got to turn." Another man arrested for violating the curfew, a low-wage metalworker with five children, said: "It's just this simple. We're tired. We're tired of being pushed; we're tired of struggling; we're tired of not having anything."[59]

Two weeks later, Beulah Sanders warned the U.S. House Ways and Means Committee that the poor would "disrupt this state, this country, this capitol" if they were not given a share of the nation's wealth. The only way to stop the violence was to create jobs for poor people, and give them a voice in the political process. "We are saying that we want to participate," Sanders said. "Are you prepared to let us sit down and help make some laws?" Recalling Senator Long's outburst two years earlier, she scolded the speechless congressmen. "The last time we tried to present our views to Congress, some people told us that we were wasting our time, that we should go home and kill the rats and roaches we were complaining about or, instead of coming here, we should take jobs even if it was just picking up dead dogs off the streets." Democrats as well as Republicans rose from their seats to condemn Sanders for threatening the committee with violence. She cut them off. "The poor have brains. They're not all dumb like you think they are. This country has failed to provide the jobs. That's the trouble."[60]

Ruby Duncan was making the same case in Nevada, the only state that didn't have a WIN job training program for welfare mothers. Pressing state legislators to allocate matching funds for the program, she told them that training the poor and placing them in jobs was the only way to stave off further street violence. George Miller had branded the WIN program a "hoax" and a nationwide failure. Duncan looked for help in what might have seemed an unlikely place. In a letter to President Nixon, Duncan refuted George Miller's contention that only fifty Nevada welfare mothers qualified for job training under WIN regulations. There were thousands who qualified, she insisted, and Miller was violating federal law by not enrolling them in job training. Nixon had campaigned on a law and order platform, Duncan reminded the president. He was honor-bound, she said, to punish state officials who flouted federal law.[61]

Nixon did not reply to Duncan, but an HEW commissioner did, warning Miller that Nevada was violating federal regulations by refusing to provide the

WIN jobs program. Senator Floyd Lamb, who had assured Ruby Duncan only months before that he would never block her children from getting school shoes, now gave a fiery speech on the floor of the Nevada legislature, urging his colleagues not to cave in to federal pressure. Senate Democratic majority leader Mahlon Brown Jr. of Las Vegas—the poverty lawyer's father—warned the legislature against taking a stand that would cost the state millions in federal dollars and create needless friction with Washington. But resisting federal power was a reflex in Carson City. Nevada legislators rejected WIN, federal dollars be damned. Only when HEW threatened to withdraw millions of dollars of federal funds did the legislature buckle. In 1970 Nevada became the last state in the union to institute a WIN program.[62]

A new states' rights rebellion was brewing in the West, with Nevada and California leading the way. In the early 1960s, the Southeast had been the crucible of states' rights, and Jim Crow segregation the flashpoint. By the late 1960s the battle had shifted to the Southwest, and welfare fraud was its rallying cry. Ranchers, oilmen, and energy companies resented the federal government's restrictions on the use of exploitable resources, and these wealthy players provided powerful financial support for the new fight against federal power. That battle dovetailed with the campaign by Western governors and administrators to trim welfare costs. These public officials appealed to the racism of working- and middle-class white voters, using coded language about a welfare system that rewarded immorality while ripping off honest taxpayers. California governor Ronald Reagan had sounded the battle cry back in 1966. "From now on," Reagan vowed, "the able-bodied will work for their keep." Reagan hit a nerve; his poll numbers soared.[63]

Battle lines were drawn between welfare rights activists, who looked to the federal government for support, and an enthusiastic insurgency in both major parties that stirred growing voter resentment against the "welfare state." The federal courts were the battleground where poverty lawyers tried to force state Welfare departments to comply with more generous federal welfare regulations. Nevada Legal Services took the state to federal court in 1969 for its failure to grant cost-of-living increases mandated by federal law. The Legal Services attorneys won: federal judges ordered Nevada to increase AFDC benefits immediately.[64]

Ruby Duncan, having literally made a federal case out of it, was one of the first women in Nevada employed through WIN. She was hired as an outreach worker, through George Wiley's Labor Department contract, to draw welfare mothers into the new job training program. When she got word of her new job, Duncan came home thrilled, says her daughter Sondra, then eleven. She burst in the front door and shouted to the children: "We're getting off welfare. It's time for us to move off." Suddenly, Duncan, thirty-eight, had an office, a respectable job, and a phone number where her children could call her. At night, Duncan studied for her high-school equivalency degree. "I was truly happy to see her with a pad and a notebook, running out to go to school," recalls Sondra. "When my mother told us we were moving off welfare, that made a big difference in our lives. And when she started making a salary, that proved to me that you could get off welfare, that there is life after welfare."[65]

But the WIN Program was seriously flawed. The job training was there— but there were scant federal funds for childcare and no chances that any more would be forthcoming. In the U.S. Senate, opponents derided daycare subsidies as "federalized babysitting." Some states did establish limited daycare for welfare mothers in the late 1960s, but Nevada was not among them. That left welfare mothers, once again, on the other side of the job divide. "Every time I went out for a WIN job, they would tell me I had too many kids," Mary Wesley said. "I wanted to work but they would always say 'No.' If they trained me for a job, I was gonna have to take off because one of the kids would get sick. They really got me thinking that I wasn't good material to go out to work because I had all these kids."[66]

Poor mothers across the country reported similar experiences when they applied at WIN offices. The program was touted as putting welfare recipients to work, but only twenty-four thousand of two million eligible welfare mothers were placed in jobs between 1968 and 1971. More than eight of ten women screened by WIN placement officers were rejected on the grounds that they were "inappropriate" for training—code for too many young children. WIN officials were more comfortable training and placing unemployed men. By 1972, men made up nearly half of those accepted to the program, although the vast majority of adult AFDC recipients were women.[67]

Ruby Duncan and Essie Henderson issued a statement in the fall of 1970, calling on state officials to provide real job training for women on welfare. They also condemned state regulations that denied welfare benefits to children attending college. "Here is a chance for children of the poor to become teachers, doctors, lawyers, businessmen," the women wrote. "Instead the welfare policies . . . keep families poor and on welfare and insure that many of the children will remain in the same drastic predicament." The state made no reply to Duncan's charges. But she received a letter from the State Employment Security Department warning her that, unless she stopped her political activities, she would lose her WIN job. She refused and was fired.[68]

Duncan had already lost a job that year as an outreach worker for the EOB when a controversy erupted over her receiving federal funds to attend a welfare rights conference in New Orleans. "We're using our own money to fight ourselves," state Welfare Board director Keith Macdonald complained. George Miller saw the bright side: "It might be worth $500 to have her out of the state for two days," he cracked. "Because if she is back there she can't harass me."[69]

Miller may well have wanted Duncan out of the way. By the spring of 1970, he had quietly begun a campaign to achieve "a zero-percent welfare error rate" in Nevada. Using random audits of recipients, Miller set out to prove that a sizable percentage had lied about their level of need or their income. He began the audit in Las Vegas, he said, because that was where most of the state's AFDC recipients, and welfare rights activists, lived. Rosie Seals didn't buy his explanation. "This whole damn thing," she charged, "is about that no-good sucker's prejudice for white over black."[70]

Miller insisted that he had nothing against black people or welfare recipients. The problem was that new applications for aid were being accepted without proper investigation. "You walk in there and they accept the form, process you and you're in," Miller said. "So I pulled out auditors and I had them go to Las Vegas and pick a hundred cases." His chief auditor called him soon after the investigation began, reporting an astonishing 50 percent error rate. Miller decided to audit every recipient in the state. That summer and fall, Miller began cutting recipients from the rolls and reducing the checks of others. Because the cuts were phased in gradually, it took a while for the women of the Clark County Welfare Rights Organization to appreciate the magnitude of what Miller was doing.[71]

Alversa Beals was among those whose checks were suddenly reduced. When she opened her July check, she found far less money than she was expecting. Beals started to cry. She called her caseworker, who told her that state investigators had determined she was collecting aid fraudulently. The mistake was the state's, but it was termed "fraud," even so. "I had a kid who used my maiden name," Beals says. "She was a Burrell instead of a Beals. So they said she wasn't my kid." Beals didn't see another check for that child for over a year. Emma Stampley was cut off entirely.

As neighbor after neighbor told Duncan of sudden decreases or terminations in their monthly benefits, she began to realize that something systematic was happening. In the fall of 1970, Duncan says, she decided to investigate what was going on. "I ran to Legal Services," she said, "and told Mahlon Brown that he's got to do something to help us."

CHAPTER 5

STORMING CAESARS PALACE: POVERTY AND POWER IN LAS VEGAS

Johnnie Tillmon said the way to make them pay attention is to hit them in the pocketbook. So I took Dr. Wiley for a drive down the Strip. And I said, "This is the main vein of Nevada. This is the pocket book."

—Ruby Duncan

B. Mahlon Brown III had just been made director of Clark County Legal Services when an agitated Ruby Duncan came pounding on his office door in the fall of 1970. Brown, then in his mid-twenties, was the sole attorney in the office. "I came out of law school and I was going to save the world," Brown recalls. "And within fifteen days of passing the bar I was made director of the county Legal Services program. That's not because I was wonderful. It's because everybody quit. In those days law clerks who hadn't even passed the bar were making more than the director of Clark County Legal Services." Brown's first act as director was to move Legal Services to the heart of the Westside, where the bulk of his clients lived.

Duncan was one of the first people he met on the job, Brown says, and the two clicked immediately—even though she admits she "nearly drove him nuts" with her frequent, frantic visits. Brown promised to represent every family that George Miller had thrown off the welfare rolls earlier that year. Within days, his office was packed with women and children holding termination letters. Realizing he needed help, Brown called his friend Jack Anderson, and convinced him to come back to Las Vegas to do battle with the state of Nevada. Anderson, the careful, detail-oriented former card dealer who had just graduated from Howard, was happy to come on board. "I was the schmoozer, the politician, the one who went out and glad-handed," Brown says. "Jack was the brains behind it."[1]

Brown and Anderson were typical of the young, shaggy-haired, green attorneys who staffed Legal Services offices in the early 1970s. The program drew talented law school graduates who went into the low-paying field of poverty law because they loved to take test cases that could yield new interpretations of law. Mandated by the Economic Opportunity Act, the Legal Services program operated 850 law offices across the country by 1969, providing legal representation to the nation's poorest citizens. But, from the beginning, Legal Services attorneys did more than try individual cases. "Equal justice cannot be accomplished by solving the problems of the poor on a case-by-case basis," Sargent Shriver said shortly after the program began in 1966. "There are too many problems, too few attorneys and too many cases in which there is no solution given the present structure of the law." Transforming federal poverty law would be a major goal of the Legal Services program.[2]

With that aim in mind, some of the top people in each law school class during the late 1960s took jobs with Legal Services, rather than with Wall Street law firms. Donald Rumsfeld, who directed the Office of Equal Opportunity under Nixon, joked that Legal Services was grooming the future leaders of the Democratic party. This relatively small group of attorneys transformed the American legal system, changing the way police, the courts, and the welfare system were allowed to treat the poor. Between 1965 and 1974, the U.S. Supreme Court heard arguments in 119 Legal Services cases—and several, such as *King v. Smith* (which ended the "man in the house" rule) and *Shapiro v. Thompson* (which ended welfare residency requirements) became landmark cases in poverty law.[3]

So when Ruby Duncan came into Mahlon Brown's office to tell him about the mass cut-offs, he immediately began thinking about how to frame the legal case in broader terms. But first Brown would have to navigate the politics of his home state. It was a world that Brown, a smooth-talking, debonair young man, moved in comfortably. Brown's grandparents were Las Vegas pioneers and pillars of the city's sagebrush aristocracy. His grandfather was one of the city's first doctors; his grandmother founded the Las Vegas Women's Democratic Club. Brown's father, Mahlon Brown Jr., was a liberal Democrat and majority leader of the state Senate. A veteran of the Pacific theater in World War Two, Senator Brown was also an "atomic veteran" who had been exposed to radioactive fallout during nuclear weapons tests. The senator passed on to his son a healthy suspicion of blindly following orders.[4]

Mahlon Brown III was disgusted, if sometimes amused, at the attitudes expressed by the state Welfare department. Nevada was the last state in the union to accept Aid to the Permanently and Totally Disabled. Even then, Brown said, bureaucrats interpreted that label so narrowly that few people qualified. One of Brown's clients claimed disability because he was dying of cancer. By the time the hearing examiner at the Welfare department ruled on the case, the old man had died. "We've determined that he's not permanently and totally disabled," the hearing examiner said. Brown paused in disbelief. "You're right," he said finally. "He's not disabled. He's dead." The department's treatment of welfare recipients was no better, Brown says. "The welfare system in Nevada in those days was maybe the most neanderthal organization in the whole country. We used to compare it with our southern sister states in terms of their compassion for human beings, particularly black human beings."[5]

The two attorneys found themselves, quite suddenly, in the national limelight. George Miller had fired a salvo earlier that year when he began conducting random audits of Las Vegas and Reno welfare recipients and then summarily cut or reduced the checks of thousands of poor Nevada women and children. From New York to California, people were watching Nevada to see if the cuts held. Mahlon Brown and Jack Anderson took their first action that fall, as the gubernatorial election approached.

In September 1970, an anxious Cleveland Woods wheeled his chair into the offices of Clark County Legal Services. Woods's wife had qualified for federal aid because Woods, a paraplegic in his late forties, was unable to work. The family of eight had been living solely on their AFDC grant of $252 per month. Then the state sent Mrs. Woods a letter terminating those benefits because her "husband's incapacity cannot be established." Mrs. Woods had asked the Welfare department for a fair hearing, but had heard nothing back—and no further checks arrived at the house.

Anderson called the family's caseworker, who said that the department wasn't convinced that Cleveland Woods couldn't work. In a state where a dying man had been ruled not permanently disabled, Anderson figured that it was a waste of time to argue the extent of Mr. Woods's disability. Instead, he told the caseworker about a recent Supreme Court decision that guaranteed welfare recipients a fair hearing before their benefits could be cut. In *Goldberg v. Kelley* (1970), the Court had ruled that welfare benefits were "not a gratuity" but an entitlement. AFDC recipients not only had a constitutional right to a fair hearing, the justices said, they had the right to be represented by a lawyer at that hearing, to be told why their benefits were being cut, and to call witnesses on their behalf. Ronnie Pollack, who argued the Goldberg case, urged the judges to see these as "elementary rights of individuals" in a democracy that could not be denied simply because a citizen received public assistance. A majority of the justices agreed.

Since AFDC benefits provided poor families "the very means by which to live," Justice William Brennan wrote, a recipient's right to welfare outweighed a state government's concern over rising expenditures. Further, since poverty was the result not of individual failings but of "impersonal forces," each state was legally bound to "bring within the reach of the poor the same opportunities that are available to others." This was as close as the High Court ever came to affirming Edward Sparer's contention that the Fourteenth Amendment guaranteed a minimum standard of living to all.[6]

Back in Las Vegas, that reasoning didn't wash. Jack Anderson tried in vain to explain to the Woods's caseworker that the family was entitled to a fair hearing. "I don't take my orders from the Supreme Court," the caseworker replied tartly. "I've got my state welfare manual right here." Anderson asked to speak to her supervisor, who told Anderson much the same thing. This was how the department operated, Anderson was told. There was nothing special about the Woods case. "Having a keen sense for the obvious," Anderson recalls dryly, "I said to myself: 'This is a class action.'" Anderson swallowed hard and realized that, for the first time in his fledgling career, he was going to court. He didn't even know what papers to file.[7]

Learning fast, Brown and Anderson filed a class action suit in federal court on October 1, 1970. By terminating so many poor mothers' benefits without prior hearings, they argued in *Woods v. Miller,* Nevada had violated both federal law and their clients' due process rights. Mrs. Woods, of course, was more concerned about whether her family was going to eat that month. So Anderson filed for a temporary restraining order to force the Welfare department to restore people's benefits until the case was resolved. The restraining order was granted. Judge Roger Foley, a former Nevada attorney general and civil rights stalwart, ordered the state to restore welfare benefits to all families who had not yet had a fair hearing. If, after a hearing, the welfare department cut any family's benefits, it would have to provide a clear, written explanation of the reasons. A wave of excitement swept through the Westside when Foley's decision was announced. The Woods and Beals families, and many others, waited hopefully for their checks to come.[8]

A LONG, LONG WAIT

Ruby Duncan and the mothers of CCWRO relished their transformation from defendants who had to justify their every move to caseworkers, to plaintiffs seeking justice from the courts. Duncan told reporters that George Miller would find himself in contempt of court unless he restored benefits and scheduled fair hearings. "We can win if we stick together," she concluded exuberantly, then invited anyone whose check had been cut off to give their names to Clark County Welfare Rights Organization, who would pass them on to Brown and Anderson.[9]

Months passed, but, despite Judge Foley's order, not a single family saw their benefits restored. The Woods family was getting eviction warnings. Anderson and Brown asked the court to cite Miller for contempt. Again Judge Foley ordered the Welfare department to resume benefits to anyone who had not yet had a fair hearing. Many families had gone without income for months. And food—available only from the county—was reaching only a fraction of the county's poor. "There were times we didn't have food and my mother would make cornbread with a dressing, onions and peppers," recalls Sondra Phillips. "Whatever she could find, she would throw in and bake it. She was very creative."[10]

Duncan and the women of CCWRO urged county relief czar Stella Fleming to declare a food emergency and open up county stockpiles to everyone who needed food. But she refused. Each application would be carefully screened to ensure that no one got food who didn't deserve it. Fleming's investigations slowed food distribution to a crawl. Of thirty thousand eligible Clark County residents, only two thousand were fed by the county in 1970. "We are spending thousands of dollars to keep out a few phonies," Reverend Jerry Furr, chairman of the Nevada Equal Rights Commission, told county commissioners. Furr, a white Methodist minister, had conducted a study of the commodities program and found that Fleming's fraud investigations were costly. Clark County's food program cost four times that of Washoe County, which fed the same number of people.[11]

With Ruby Duncan in the lead, a long line of Westside welfare mothers strolled into County Commission meetings in October 1970. At first they sat and listened. Then they asked permission to speak, telling commissioners that thousands of children in Las Vegas were hungry. The women wanted immediate expansion of food distribution and an end to Stella Fleming's one-woman food blockade. Their suggestion was echoed by the League of Women Voters, the Reverend Jerry Furr, and Sister Mary Litell of the Franciscans. In a vote that surprised everyone, the county commissioners sided with the welfare mothers and took food distribution out of Fleming's hands.

After four decades, the humiliating Las Vegas tradition of handing out food from the courthouse steps would end. Instead, as the mothers had requested, government surplus food would be arrayed on shelves, as in a grocery store. Families could shop for whatever they needed. Anyone who met federal income requirements would now be eligible. There would be no more costly investigations of who was truly hungry. The new commodities "market," which opened its doors in December 1970, was a huge victory for CCWRO. In just a few weeks, the new Clark County Food Distribution Service quadrupled the number of families in the county who were receiving food aid.[12]

The women won more than food, Father Vitale believes. The action strengthened their alliance with the League of Women Voters and established welfare mothers as a presence in city and county government. "Politicians couldn't act in the dark anymore," Vitale says.

> The commissioners had to look the women in the face while they said "I vote to take away this little grant that's going to give a kid a lunch." And that makes an enormous difference for anyone who is not totally hard-hearted or politically stupid. Before Clark County Welfare Rights, they could say anything they wanted—"oh they're just all a bunch of lazy people, they should just get out there and work, therefore I vote against it." Politicians did things like that in private, but when the women marched in there, the whole thing became public. [13]

As the November 1970 election drew near, the women—emboldened by their success with the County Commission—tried to influence the Democratic candidate for governor. Mike O'Callaghan, the former schoolteacher, juvenile delinquency counselor, and Job Corps official, had been attacked by conservative opponents. "They said that I was going to give the state away," O'Callaghan recalls, "that I was nothing but a social worker." O'Callaghan was behind in the polls as election day approached. Duncan knew that he would need votes from the Westside to win.[14]

Knowing that O'Callaghan was a devout Catholic, Duncan asked Father Vitale to invite the candidate to her house. "Mike, I want you to meet some of the welfare mothers," Vitale said. Duncan wanted to give O'Callaghan a taste of the welfare life in Nevada. "Everyone's benefits had been cut, so all we had to serve was Kool-Aid and some county cheese," Duncan recalls. "So we sliced it up kind of cute and pretty. And he sat there with us. He didn't look too much like he liked it but he did sit. We asked him what he would do for the welfare mothers. He promised he was going to help us."

Duncan and the CCWRO women created a disciplined political organization for O'Callaghan on the Westside. Beals and Mary Southern became

Democratic party precinct captains. Each had a crew of women who leafleted, registered voters, and offered to transport the elderly to the polls. "We walked the projects night and day," Duncan recalls. "We must have talked to literally hundreds and hundreds of people. These were all people we knew from organizing for welfare rights. We made sure they got out and voted for Mike O' Callaghan because he was going to help the welfare mothers." Westsiders understood the basic rules of patronage politics: newly elected officials reward those who helped them win. Maybe this time, the women hoped, they could make politics as usual work on their behalf.

O'Callaghan squeaked to victory with less than half of the total votes cast, but he had a strong showing on the Westside. "We helped get him elected," Duncan says. "He carried the Westside 100 per cent." His victory cheered liberal Democrats in the state, who felt they had elected a champion of their beliefs. "We all felt great about Mike O'Callaghan getting elected," says Vitale. "O'Callaghan had worked for Sargent Shriver with the Job Corps. He was a liberal Democrat connected to the Kennedys."

But disillusionment with the new governor came within days of his election. First, O'Callaghan asked George Miller—whom he had quietly consulted on welfare issues during the campaign—to stay on as Welfare director. Just four days after the election, Miller announced that the welfare rolls had skyrocketed and the state was facing a financial crisis. Four weeks before Christmas, he dispatched his entire, two-hundred-person staff to perform a door-to-door check and audit of every recipient in the state. Caseworkers went through the school attendance records of children, requisitioned bank statements and Social Security records, and talked to neighbors, ministers, and local employers. It seemed as though an invading army had descended on the Westside.

The week before Christmas, 1970, Miller went public with the results of his so-called "cheaters' report." Nearly one-quarter of Nevada welfare mothers, he charged, had lied about outside income and the presence of employable men in the home. "We found a 55 percent error rate," he said, "with 22 percent completely ineligible. We found a lot of under-the-table payments that weren't reported. People working at restaurants and that sort of thing." Most of the false reporting was in Las Vegas and Reno, Miller told reporters. "It's hard to cheat in the rural areas because everyone knows everyone and what their facts of life are." But urban cheaters "have been gypping Nevada out of about $1 million a year."[15]

In early January, 1971, Miller announced the largest welfare cut in Nevada

history—and one of the most sweeping actions ever taken against welfare recipients in the U.S. Over 3,500 families were cut from the rolls entirely, and
4,500 more had their benefits reduced. Over half of the state's AFDC recipients were affected, most of them in Las Vegas. To publicize his coup, Miller sent
a letter to every Welfare administrator, governor, and congressman in the nation, boasting about the cuts and urging them to follow suit. He condemned
the new federal policy of allowing AFDC applicants to get aid merely by saying they needed it. That policy, he said, had opened up the doors to widespread
cheating. "The other states are in much worse boats," Miller asserted. "They
just haven't found out about it yet."[16]

Mike O'Callaghan, the people's candidate, cheered his Welfare director
on. Many who had supported his candidacy were stunned. Thirty northern
Nevada welfare mothers swarmed O'Callaghan during a press conference demanding to know why he supported the cuts. They claimed—accurately—
that Nevada spent more on Seeing Eye dogs for the blind than on food for
AFDC children. Even those who had not been cut off said they could not make
ends meet on the meager cash allotment they received. The maximum amount
for a mother and three children was $144 a month—$160 below the official
poverty level. One welfare mother who got $135 a month had to spend $125 of
it for a two-bedroom apartment for herself and her three children. She told
O'Callaghan that she couldn't afford to heat the place, and the winter wind
blew through it, making her children shiver. "Why don't you stuff a rug under
the door like I used to do when I was a kid?" O'Callaghan replied.[17]

League of Women Voters' activist Maya Miller saw O'Callaghan's actions
as "a flouting of trust"—but she wasn't surprised. The new governor was a
savvy and ambitious politician, Miller says, who understood that the tide of
national politics was turning against the poor. "The word had come that the
governors of New York and California were thinking of doing something drastic about welfare because their rolls were expanding so dramatically," Miller
recalls. Nelson Rockefeller had set up a new office of Inspector General in New
York to investigate welfare fraud, and Ronald Reagan was calling for radical
cuts in the California welfare caseload. "So O'Callaghan set up Nevada as a
trial run, a little cameo for welfare reform"[18]

Maya Miller's contention is borne out by O'Callaghan's own words.
Speaking to reporters after a national governors' conference in early 1971,
where he met with Rockefeller and Reagan, O'Callaghan boasted that Nevada's
welfare cuts had something to teach the larger states. "Nevada is still small
enough that we can look at the individual cases and see what we have," he said.
"Other governors were surprised at what we could show them."[19]

Emma Stampley says she suspected O'Callaghan would betray welfare mothers from the first time she met him in Ruby Duncan's living room. "You're just telling us good lies," she had said to the candidate. "You ain't even gonna think about us when you get up there to Carson City." Another Westside mother had chastised Stampley for talking to O'Callaghan that way. "He's always been good to the people," she said. "Maybe so," Stampley answered drily. "But he ain't gonna be good to us."[20]

OPERATION NEVADA: TAKING A STAND AGAINST WELFARE CUTS

Between Christmas and New Year's, a stream of anxious women poured into the Legal Services office, carrying letters of termination or reduction. Many had received no warning—just notices in their mailboxes where their monthly checks should have been. Crowds descended on the state Welfare office as well. "It was just loaded with crying women," says Duncan. On New Year's Day, 1971, Duncan's telephone rang until 2:30 a.m. with calls from distraught mothers, some of whom were being evicted. Finally, she says, "I was so tired I took it off the hook and put it under my pillow so I could get some sleep."[21]

Duncan called Washington, D.C., and asked George Wiley for help. Now was the time and Las Vegas was the place, she argued, to force a showdown about welfare cuts. Wiley conferred with Tillmon, Ed Sparer, and the NWRO board. They all agreed "that we would use Nevada as a place to say, 'We're not gonna take this any more,'" recalls organizer Gatha Hesselden.[22]

Wiley's willingness to gamble his organization's resources and credibility in Nevada, Louis Vitale believes, partly reflected the confidence that NWRO leaders had in Ruby Duncan. "Ruby was then becoming recognized by National Welfare Rights, as much for her own personal power as for what she was doing in Nevada," Vitale says. "She was sharp, articulate, self-possessed, and gutsy." NWRO leaders also admired the coalition Duncan had assembled: talented lawyers like Brown and Anderson, radical priests like Vitale, Democratic party activists like Harriet Trudell, and iconoclastic Carson City philanthropist Maya Miller. "They commented on how much support there was," says Vitale. "They also liked how visible this city was, and how the jugular vein, as Ruby called it, was so exposed."[23]

Tillmon, Wiley, and Ed Sparer thought Las Vegas would be the perfect stage set for a poor people's march, spectacular enough to capture the attention of an otherwise protest-weary nation and to blunt the appeal of anti-welfare populists like Ronald Reagan and George Miller. Marching against a backdrop of roulette wheels and craps tables, Duncan hoped to recast Nevada's campaign against "welfare cheats" as a battle between mothers trying to feed their children and a state that based its economy on gambling and prostitution. Sparer loved the symbolic power of mounting a poor mothers' protest in Sin City. Given its dependence on tourism, Nevada would be sensitive to any negative press coverage. Most crucially, Sparer thought the tourist industry could not long withstand a disruption without suffering disastrous losses— although he was unsure whether this would trigger victory or backlash. It was a gamble NWRO was willing to make. The organization's progress nationally had slowed, and it badly needed a new model for mass action. Wiley called Duncan to tell her that she had NWRO's full support and that Johnnie Tillmon was on her way to Las Vegas.[24]

In preparation for Tillmon's visit, Westside welfare activists gathered in Duncan's living room. Duncan told the women what she'd heard at NWRO meetings: Poor women could dramatically enhance their political influence if they applied economic pressure on their state. Threatening a march on the Strip a decade earlier had brought down the color line in Las Vegas. This time, the women agreed, they would do more than threaten. By the time Johnnie Tillmon's plane landed at McCarran Airport, Duncan and the women had worked out their plan.[25]

Duncan picked up her friend and took her for a drive down the Strip. As they passed through the canyon of glittering neon signs—past the Sands, the Stardust, the Flamingo, and Caesars Palace—Duncan gestured broadly toward the lights flashing through the dashboard. "If we could get bundles of people in the street, right here," Duncan told Tillmon, "we could hit the heart of the power." Wouldn't it be fun, the two women mused, to cut off the roaring river of cash that flowed each day from the Strip into state coffers and into the pockets of legislators who liked to wax indignant about welfare fraud? The two women talked all the way to the Westside, where they spent a long evening over Versie Beals's chicken, cornbread, and greens, laying plans to shut down the Strip. "We were ready for war," Duncan says quietly. "But I would be lying if I said we weren't scared."[26]

When George Wiley came to town a few weeks later, Duncan made sure that she was the one who picked him up at the airport. She waited until they were driving along the Strip before broaching her idea. "This is the main vein of Nevada," she said to Wiley, as they watched the neon lights flashing on the faces of tourists who seemed to float from casino to casino. "This is *the* pocketbook."[27]

Wiley's decision to pour resources into Las Vegas could not have come at a better time for Jack Anderson and Mahlon Brown. "We had hundreds of people coming into the office with requests for their checks," Anderson recalls. "We were overwhelmed. So we did what we had to. We cried 'Help!'" Fortunately, says Anderson, "our cry for help was heard." The result was Operation Nevada: a legal assault on Nevada in the courts, combined with a series of carefully targeted mass protests designed to bring the state's economy and government to its knees.[28]

An emergency "lawyers' brigade" of forty attorneys and seventy law students, led by Edward Sparer, flew, hitchhiked and drove their battered Volkswagen beetles into town. Clark County Legal Services had a problem, and they were there to help. Judge Foley, at the request of the Welfare department, had sequestered the records of everyone who'd been cut off. "It was a class action, and we didn't know who our clients were," says Mahlon Brown. "We needed lawyers to come and help us find our clients. They walked through the poverty sections of Las Vegas, knocking on doors and asking people: 'Were you cut off welfare? And, if you were, would you like to be part of this suit?'"

Scores of welfare rights activists headed to Las Vegas as well, where they camped out in the living rooms of Henderson, Beals, Seals, Stampley, Duncan, and other Westside families. The CCWRO women divided the poor neighborhoods of Las Vegas into "door-knocking routes." Armed with "Points for Door-knockers" and a nine-page list of questions put together by Legal Services, the volunteers recorded information about employment, benefits, health status, marital status, family size, and lodging for every family affected by Nevada's welfare cuts. At the end of each day, the women filed "door-knock" reports with the young lawyers jammed into the Westside Legal Services office.[29]

Armed with the names and information of recipients who'd been cut, Legal Services attorneys requested hundreds of fair hearings. A state that had held only a handful of fair hearings the previous year now scheduled three hundred at once, assigning three Welfare officers to hold seventy-two hearings a day. They allocated a total of fifteen minutes to each, says Jack Anderson, creating a logjam of cases that left scores of women and children sitting day after day in a fifteen-by-fifteen-foot waiting room, where Ruby Duncan talked to them about the welfare rights movement. Judge Foley ordered the state to restore recipients' benefits until fair hearings were held for everyone. Anderson and Brown filed motion after motion, stretching out each hearing as long as they could.[30]

Infuriated by this strategy, which had Welfare officials pulling out their hair, Nevada charged Brown and Anderson with "solicitation." Most of the people named in the suit had not sought out representation, state attorneys argued; Anderson and Brown had gone fishing for clients. The state filed a formal complaint that could have gotten the two men disbarred, and demanded that the class action suit be dismissed. "We were looking for facts," counters Mahlon Brown. "They called that solicitation, one of the words that lawyers use to pick on other lawyers." Ultimately, all the charges were dismissed, but a clear message had been sent. If Legal Services pursued its lawsuit, Nevada would fight fire with fire.[31]

NWRO fought back, sending top-flight help to Brown and Anderson in the form of Ronnie Pollack. The tough-talking New Yorker had just successfully argued *Goldberg v. Kelley*—"that infamous new case that was creating all these rights that people didn't know they had," says Brown. Pollack quickly signed on as co-counsel in *Woods v. Miller*, much to the relief of the two inexperienced lawyers. "Ronnie Pollack took us by the hand and walked us through the courtroom," Anderson said.[32]

The legal playing field was now slanted in favor of welfare rights. But Operation Nevada still needed community support. Wiley and his top deputies were, as their detractors rightly labeled them, outsiders. They needed someone who understood Nevada politics and the personalities of the state's political elites. Wiley turned to Maya Miller. She had guided the National League of Women Voters to radical positions on welfare that had surprised and pleased the NWRO leadership. Tillmon in particular appreciated Miller's unapologetic feminism and her trenchant replies to the casually racist language that permeated Capitol Hill discussions of welfare policy. Wiley, too, admired Miller's moral clarity. He also knew that Miller had the means to support Operation Nevada.

Wiley cornered Miller at a D.C. conference on civil rights. "I certainly knew who George Wiley was," Miller recalls. In a city full of white shirts, suits, and ties, she says, "a tall, commanding-looking professor in a dashiki" stood out. Spotting Miller across the room, Wiley strode toward her. "He pinioned me and asked if I knew that they were thinking about starting up a major action in Nevada, and told me they hoped to engage not only the League but, specifically me." Miller promised to do what she could.

At the time, Maya Miller was zigzagging between Washington and Carson City, lobbying Congress for more generous food and cash assistance for the poor, and chastising northern Nevada "cow county" legislators for their miserly attitudes toward the disadvantaged. The Birkenstock-clad activist had a very precise goal: placing welfare mothers in decent jobs with government-subsidized childcare. But she also had a more lofty ambition: to convince male politicians that the unpaid labor of mothers deserved both recognition and economic compensation. And she rejected the stereotype of welfare mothers as bloated loafers. "I hated the expression *on welfare*," Miller says, "as though it were a marvelous train that you were on and had to be wrenched off."

Like Wiley, Miller had been a college professor—at both Stanford and the University of Nevada—and had patience for slow learners. But her patience with political elites was wearing thin. She was ready for more direct action. "I was isolated in wonderful forests and desert and wanted to be part of the civil rights movement," Miller said. "And so this one way I was able to."[33]

Ruby Duncan, too, was growing restive. It was time, she decided, to get the federal government involved in the Nevada welfare dispute. Firing off a letter to HEW secretary Elliot Richardson, Duncan charged that George Miller was violating welfare recipients' Fourth Amendment rights to protection from unlawful searches. Richardson's response was swift. State welfare agencies had a right to request whatever information they needed to determine eligibility, he wrote. But he promised to send investigators to Nevada, as Duncan had requested, to see if welfare workers had violated federal law or abrogated citizens' rights.[34] Despite his pointed criticisms of the War on Poverty, Nixon was still willing to do battle with states that were not in compliance with federal welfare regulations.

Duncan contacted U.S. senator Howard Cannon, pressing him for a copy of Miller's welfare audit. Recipients have a right to know why they were cut off, she argued. Cannon sent her a copy of the report. But he reminded her that every welfare applicant in Nevada signed a form granting the welfare department blanket permission to investigate their finances and living arrangements. Duncan asked Brown, Anderson, and NWRO attorneys if it was legal for Nevada to ask welfare applicants to sign away basic rights. They all thought it wasn't.

Duncan read every page of George Miller's "cheater's report." It listed five reasons for the mass terminations: a man living in the home, failure to report earnings adequately, unemployment benefits, changes in childcare costs, and changes in rent. But the report offered no documentation for the state's contention that two-thirds of Nevada welfare recipients were cheating. Duncan wrote HEW, asking that it conduct an investigation to independently verify Miller's findings. The agency agreed.[35]

But George Miller wasn't waiting around to be proven wrong. "I'm up for contempt of court and my rear end may be sitting in jail," he told legislators in late February. Miller requested permission to divert money that the governor had allocated for a five-dollar increase in AFDC grants, and use it instead to hire a lawyer to defend him against contempt charges in the Woods lawsuit. Miller had been offered a lawyer from the Attorney General's office but told legislators he wanted a private attorney. Referring to the top-flight legal talent that NWRO had brought into Nevada, Miller said: "I've got to go up against a machine gun with a pop gun. . . . I'm fighting the moochers. It would be a great saving to the state and the country if Nevada wins this case." Legislators approved Miller's request, offering him three times the amount he had asked for.[36]

Hoping to offset the hostility building in Carson City, Maya Miller held strategy sessions at her remote ranch in the Sierra Nevada foothills, inviting welfare rights leaders from Washington, Black Panther women from Oakland, welfare mothers from Reno and Las Vegas, and League of Women Voters activists from across the state. Over Miller's fresh-baked sourdough rye and hearty stews, an unlikely political coalition began to gel.

Miller's Washoe Pines ranch had been a spawning ground for radical politics ever since she and her husband, ichthyologist Richard Miller, bought it in 1945. Built in the 1920s as the writing retreat of Western novelist and silent film writer Will James, Washoe Pines became a divorce ranch in the 1930s, where dissatisfied wives awaited quick Nevada divorce decrees. In the early 1960s, the Millers opened an environmentalist summer camp at Washoe Pines that brought inner-city children from Oakland and Las Vegas to appreciate the fragile beauty of the Sierra foothills. Many Westside children got their first experience of mountain wilderness at the Miller ranch. Ruby Duncan's sons and daughters spent summers at Washoe Pines; Alversa Beals's daughter Renia remembers learning to ride a horse there. It was the first interracial summer camp in northern Nevada, and many whites who sent their children there would later find themselves drawn into the welfare rights struggle.[37]

So would counselors. Marty Makower, a thoughtful, long-haired twenty-one-year-old from Oakland, California, admired the spectacular views and Sierra sunsets at the ranch, but she was most taken by the politics that swirled around the place. When Maya Miller told her about plans for Operation Nevada, she offered to help. The young Californian drove hundreds of miles through the Nevada desert in her battered old pickup, gathering donated bedsteads and mattresses, delivering them—and activists who'd flown and bused into Nevada—to the homes of sympathetic locals who'd agreed to put them up.

On a trip to Las Vegas in February 1971, Makower met Ruby Duncan for the first time. Duncan was busy when Makower arrived, gathering emergency food supplies and fighting evictions. "One of the things that struck me about Ruby, who was the mother of seven children, was that any time a child appeared on the scene, she was completely taken with that child," Makower recalls. "That kind of warmth is irresistible." Makower rolled up her sleeves and offered to help Duncan. She set up housekeeping in a rusty old trailer on the Westside, amusing the mothers with her futile battle to grow vegetables in the hard desert clay.[38]

The situation was tense on the Westside, and there was a great deal for the activists to do. Hungry, nervous, and unable to concentrate, neighborhood children were falling behind in school. Johnnie Woods withdrew her five older children from school because the family had no money for food or clothing. The women of CCWRO surveyed the community to see how many others were in similar straits. "We found out there was a lot of homeless people on the Westside then," says Emma Stampley. And many mothers were keeping their hungry children home from school.[39]

Duncan went on television and radio to condemn the Welfare department for what she called its "violence" against poor children. She came across as a very angry black woman, an image she consciously cultivated. "Talking to the press, I was never nice," Duncan recalls. "I was always really mean. I always talked about George Miller. I always talked about Vince Fallon. I was always demanding to see the information that they had that we didn't have." But Duncan was not simply angry. What made her public persona so compelling, Makower says, was her mix of militancy and motherly concern. "Ruby could be enraged and it was all the more gripping because you knew what was underlying the rage. What she would want for her own kids, she would want for any kid. She was willing to fight for it and I found that terribly inspiring."[40]

In mid-February, George Wiley accepted Duncan's invitation to visit the Westside. Makower and the CCWRO women leafleted the projects to invite welfare mothers to meet with him. "Get it Together Welfare Moms," the fliers exhorted. "Don't be Cheated! Know Your Rights." Wiley spoke at Westside churches and visited families in their homes. Mary Wesley first heard him speak at the Zion Methodist church on February 8, 1971. "When I heard George Wiley talk about welfare," she says, "that's what made me know not to be ashamed.[41]

> *He said it was taxpayers' money. Now my father had died when*
> *I was three. He worked and his money was put into taxes and*
> *he never drew anything from it. And all of my friends and rel-*

*atives who had worked had taxes taken out of their checks,
whether they wanted it or not. Then I didn't feel ashamed no
more.*[42]

After the meeting, Duncan, Wiley, and Johnnie Tillmon led three hundred Westside residents on a march to the Las Vegas Welfare office. Standing outside Fallon's office door, Duncan called on him to schedule fair hearings for everyone who'd been cut, and restore their checks pending the outcome of those hearings. Mothers were being pressured by caseworkers to forego such appeals, Duncan charged. Betty Lou Wright, an out-of-work mother of three young children, had asked her caseworker what would happen if she appealed the state's decision to reduce her check. "He said I would probably lose and would be cut off without any money at all for four months," Wright stated in an affidavit. "He also said there was a chance I would be cut off permanently." Another woman said she'd been told that her benefits would be reduced, rather than terminated, if she waived her right to a hearing. Fallon insisted that no one had been coerced into signing away her rights.[43]

Unfazed, Duncan continued to read from her list of demands. Welfare recipients needed to see their personal files. CCWRO wanted a copy of the latest Nevada welfare manual detailing state eligibility rules. And the group wanted to set up a welfare rights information table in the lobby, as NWRO chapters had done in other cities. Fallon refused to grant any of these requests. "One week to comply," the women shouted, "or there will be hell to pay."

Vince Fallon saw faces he did not recognize that day, and concluded that NWRO organizers were driving the waves of unrest. "I don't think the local population would have done that without people coming from all over the country to get this going," Fallon says. "I think it was incited by people who had real experience in demonstrations." National organizers and Legal Services attorneys provided essential information about the women's constitutional rights, Duncan agrees. But they did not need outsiders to stir them up. "I always felt the greatest organizer we had was George Miller," says Jack Anderson. "Without his efforts none of this would have happened."[44]

On February 16, Wiley accompanied two hundred Westside mothers and children on a return visit to Fallon's office. The crowd stepped off four chartered buses, singing "It's Not Like It Used to Be" at the top of their lungs. A picket line of children circled in bouncy unison in front of the building, wearing sandwich boards that read "Mother Power." Wiley, Duncan, Beals, Seals, Stampley, Henderson, and Wesley walked upstairs to Fallon's office and reiterated their demands: no more evictions, fair hearings for every family whose benefits had been cut, and a copy of the latest Nevada welfare manual.

Fallon came down to the lobby where, surrounded by police officers, he spoke to the crowd with a bullhorn provided by Wiley. He denied that state workers were coercing welfare recipients, and said that he was arranging for local leaders to see copies of the Welfare manual. "We will process any requests made through normal channels," he said. Looking at Wiley, Fallon said he would never "bow down to persons from out of state." He would meet with no more than ten CCWRO mothers, he said, not "30 or 40 persons whose emotions are running high."[45]

Duncan understands why Fallon thought the Westside women were being manipulated by NWRO organizers. "They were caught by surprise," says Duncan. "They were surprised that we had the sense to know we had a right to a hearing. We had a right to see the state welfare manual. We had a right to a clothing allowance. We had a right to job training." Welfare authorities, she says, had long seen Las Vegas recipients as "lazy, uneducated, don't-know anything." These protests forced Welfare officials to deal directly with these women for the first time.

"I don't think we had any kind of dialogue prior to these demonstrations," says Fallon, "certainly not with Ruby Duncan's organization." Ultimately, he believes, protest "brought the welfare department into a lot closer relationship with the local welfare rights group. That was the seed of us working together for the benefit of everyone. When the main issues were settled, we had started a professional rapport. We may not have agreed on every point, but we were talking and discussing." Those were changes that came over time, however. In the late winter of 1971, Fallon was not yet ready to sit down and talk, and the welfare rights protestors seemed bent on confrontation.[46]

Empty-handed, a frustrated crowd of Westside women and children filed out of the Las Vegas Welfare office. A throng of reporters had gathered outside, including television crews from ABC and CBS national news. Entertainer Sammy Davis Jr. spoke to the crowd, calling himself "morally, spiritually and financially involved" with the welfare rights movement. Then Duncan spoke. "Over $600 million was spent on the Strip last year," she said. "Yet a mother with one child receives $1,008 a year on welfare. Black men and women are forced to do slave labor in the Strip hotels. When will we get our share of the pie?" Nevada earned tax revenues on every dollar tourists spent in Las Vegas. Surely the state had the money to feed hungry children.[47]

Duncan cleared her throat as reporters jostled around her. On March 6—

three weeks from that day—Nevada welfare families would do the unthinkable, Duncan announced. They would march on the Las Vegas Strip and shut down casino gambling. And they planned to do it again "on each successive weekend until injustices to poor people are ended in Nevada." Welfare mothers also planned to picket McCarran Airport every weekend to try to convince tourists to turn around and go home. "Things are going to be livelier than ever around here," one NWRO organizer commented.[48]

When Duncan stepped down from the microphone, Wiley stepped up. There would be "a long hot summer in Las Vegas," he warned, unless the state restored benefits. If violence erupted, there would be nothing he could do prevent it. Duncan listened nervously as Wiley spoke. She worried that threats of violence could backfire in Las Vegas, and she had opposed NWRO strategists who wanted the marchers to engage in civil disobedience and trigger mass arrests. "Oh no," Duncan had told the organizers. "What you do, you march the first time, make it solid 'n good. Then the next march on the next week, people will be ready to get arrested." Duncan told the organizers that their strategy "might work back East but it won't work here."[49]

Wiley had often played the reasonable statesman to NWRO women's angry militants, but now Duncan turned the tables. Breaking free of her role as Wiley's protégée, Duncan began backing away from Wiley's threat of chaos in the casinos. Three days later, she wrote the governor, asking that he meet with the Clark County Welfare Rights Organization for "meaningful dialogue."

Governor O'Callaghan claimed he did not get the letter until a reporter handed him a copy. Dismissing it as "typical press agent gimmickry," he asserted that the legality of the recent welfare cuts was a matter for the courts to decide. "Street demonstrations, running through welfare offices, and so on, really confuses the issue," he said. Echoing Fallon's words to Duncan only days earlier, O'Callaghan said that he would meet with Duncan and Brown but not with anyone from NWRO, whom he called "outside agitators."[50]

Appearing on the local television news, Duncan chastised the governor for holding himself aloof and for what she called his "lack of concern" for the 7,500 Nevadans affected by the welfare cuts. Her media persona repelled some white viewers, who thought her overly belligerent and did not take her seriously. "With Ruby, they're always 'stahving,'" said Robbins Cahill of the Nevada Resort Association, mimicking Duncan's high-pitched voice and Delta drawl. "They're stahving our children, and they're stahving our people." He and other white leaders—as well as some better-heeled blacks—dismissed her leadership abilities and vision. "Ruby lives in a Never-Never fairyland," Cahill said. "She envisions herself as the Messiah that's going to lead her people to a better land and a better living."[51]

But other Las Vegans, watching Duncan on television in early 1971, were mesmerized. No one could recall seeing a black woman so boldly taking on the white power structure. Harriet Trudell, a housewife and political maverick active in the Las Vegas Women's Democratic Club, recalls seeing Duncan on television and being "absolutely blown away. She was screaming about how the children were starving and the outrage of what the children had suffered. I wasn't turned off. My first view of her was that she was phenomenal."[52]

Duncan's children got a huge kick out of seeing their mother on TV. "You guys, I'm going to be on the news tonight," she'd announce during the buildup to the march. "What was really exciting about seeing her on the news was her expressions," recalls Sondra. "She was very dramatic, forceful. She always got your attention. And what always stood out were her eyes. When she was making a point, they would get bigger." Sondra says the Duncan clan never worried that their mother's adversaries would get in the last word. "They'd ask her a question and thought they could outsmart her. But she always came back with a response—very quick."[53]

If Duncan and the Westside mothers seemed surprisingly sure of their moral grounding, they were typical of mother activists throughout modern history. The welfare rights movement of the 1960s and 1970s fit into a long tradition of poor mothers' activism on behalf of hungry children—from rallies for "just price" during the American and French revolutions to black and Jewish women's meat boycotts, consumer picket lines, and rent strikes during the first half of the twentieth century. Mothers in many U.S. cities organized across lines of ethnic, racial, and cultural difference, engaging in marches, civil disobedience, and boycotts when they were unable to feed, clothe, and shelter their children. Claiming the moral authority of motherhood, they pushed the boundaries of acceptable behavior for poor women as they articulated a broader political vision: that all children were entitled to a decent quality of life. To claim those rights mothers lobbied legislatures, protested at executive mansions, and tried to disrupt business as usual. During the winter and spring of 1971, Nevada welfare mothers did all of those things.[54]

Duncan cast her request for a meeting with the governor as an issue of participatory democracy. "We consider your refusal to meet with us as a refusal by *our* government to meet our needs." She also spoke as president of the Clark County Welfare Rights Organization, which claimed to represent the 70 percent of Nevada welfare families who lived in and around Las Vegas. Poor Ne-

vadans "think it is only right for you, as our elected governor, to hear our grievances," she wrote. "We cannot wait. You leave us with no alternative other than
bringing our case to the people.... We ... must seek relief from the tragic cuts
through increased demonstrations."[55]

O'Callaghan attempted to defuse the situation by asking reporters genially
what all the fuss was about. "Ruby knows I'll meet with her. I said I would meet
with her or local people, but not with outsiders." Decades later, in an interview
in his office at the *Las Vegas Sun*, O'Callaghan insisted that he had to take that
stand. As a new governor caught between a militant welfare rights movement
and a fiercely conservative legislature, he needed to strike a compromise.

"When I came into office, there was definitely more need for AFDC,"
he admits. "I worked the budget around as best I could to at least put an extra
dollar in. I knew that wasn't enough. But I was sitting with what I had." The
governor says he warned Duncan and Mahlon Brown that mass protests, especially if they brought in non-Nevadans, would make legislators angrier than
they already were. "The welfare rights group became involved because they
wanted more money. And I don't blame them for that," O'Callaghan says.
"There should have been more money. There just wasn't." O'Callaghan had
found money for a five-dollar-per-month AFDC increase. "When outsiders
came in, it gave some people an excuse to eliminate even that amount. Because
of demonstrations, the legislature took the extra dollars away. So they got
nothing."[56]

THE BATTLE IS JOINED: WELFARE MOTHERS,
POPULIST POLITICIANS, AND OUTSIDE AGITATORS

While it seemed perfectly reasonable to a veteran campaigner such as O'Callaghan to argue that politics is the art of the possible, Nevada welfare mothers
found such advice patronizing. If they increased pressure on decision makers,
perhaps these men would think differently about what was possible. George
Miller made state policy, but he lived in Carson City, far beyond their reach.
Instead, the women targeted the man they knew and interacted with, city Welfare director Vincent Fallon.

On February 21, 1971, Fallon awoke to hear Ruby Duncan, Mary Wesley,
Leola Harris, Eddie Jean Finks, Essie Henderson, Rosie Seals, and about fifty
other Westside mothers and children singing "We Shall Overcome" in his
front yard. It was Sunday morning and Fallon at first thought the singing was
coming from his radio. Fallon's four children came into his room and told him
to look outside. He recalls:

There were several hundred people out in my front yard. We lived in a little neighborhood. That caused quite a stir. And that repeated itself about four or five times, that they would come out to our house. I like to think it wasn't my personality so much as it was that I was the manager. I was the focal point. Whether it was personal or not, they did demonstrate and we had police protection probably for six or seven months.

Two sets of curious children stared at each other during those demonstrations, from opposite sides of the Fallons' living room windows, from opposites sides of the class and racial divides. If they perhaps saw each other clearly, their parents could not. "What are you having for breakfast?" the women called to Fallon. "We hope it's good because we don't have anything to eat today." Fallon did not come out to speak to the protestors. Instead he called police, and soon afterwards drove away with his wife and children in a patrol car, watching the faces of the protestors through the window.

Only Fallon's inflation of the crowd's size suggests that he was afraid. There were fifty women and children outside his house, not several hundred. George Miller told reporters that Fallon feared for his family's life that day—an assertion that Fallon later dismissed. "I think for the people up in Carson City, a nice little town where nothing much happens, it had a greater impact than it did on me," he says. But that night, Fallon was rushed to the hospital with chest pains, convinced he was having a heart attack.[57]

Released later that night, he told reporters that he had not recognized many of the people who massed outside his home. He was convinced that "outsiders" had planned the protest. Fallon's statement that night reveals how small Las Vegas still was. The chief Welfare administrator for the city expected to recognize the face of every recipient in this jurisdiction. But he was also following a script written by Miller and O'Callaghan. Like Southern officials during the civil rights movement, Nevada authorities discredited welfare rights protests by blaming "outside agitators" for stirring up a local population that they insisted would have remained placid and compliant otherwise.

While Westside mothers acknowledge the important role played by George Wiley and Johnnie Tillmon, they say the march on Fallon's home was driven by their own frustration with the city's welfare chief—who kept insisting he could not help them. Why should Fallon have been able to retreat to his comfortable family life when he had deprived them of theirs? Fallon, in concert with Miller, had frightened their children repeatedly with midnight raids and threats to take them away from their mothers. The women felt no regrets about the way they challenged him now.[58]

But their actions provided grist for Nevada politicians, who warned that welfare rights protests threatened the peace and security of their state. Governor O'Callaghan, George Miller, and Nevada legislators played to Nevadans' traditional distrust of "outsiders," "professional agitators," "publicity hunters," and "power-hungry feds."[59] Miller called reporters to his office in late February and posed for photographs holding a copy of *People's World,* a Communist party newspaper with an article condemning the welfare cuts, headlined "Welfare Fightback in Nevada." Miller himself had thrust his welfare cuts into the national spotlight by announcing them to congressmen from the forty-nine other states. Now, he told reporters, his mail was running two hundred to one in favor of the cuts. In a flurry of anti–welfare rights activity, state legislators drafted a bill relieving Nevada of any financial responsibility for the poor and killed a proposal to put welfare mothers on the state welfare board. "Putting recipients on the welfare board," declared Miller's second in command, Dave Tomlinson, "would be like putting prisoners on the parole board." Finally the legislature petitioned Congress to give Nevada, and all other states, complete autonomy in matters of welfare.[60]

STORMING CAESARS PALACE

Back in Las Vegas, march organizers were worried about how the hotel owners might react to a protest on the Strip. "We were not too far from the Mafia days," says Father Vitale. "Many people in Las Vegas were afraid that forcing a shut-down of casino gambling, even briefly, might spark a violent response." On the eve of the march, Duncan called a meeting to discuss the issue. NWRO organizers, Westside families, and supporters among clergy, students, and faculty gathered at the university. A woman who had led many antiwar rallies in Las Vegas voiced her fears. "If we march down the Strip," she said, "someone could get hit in the head with a brick." The mood in the room was tense, and Duncan worried that people might back out of the plan. She slowly got to her feet. "When you're poor, and you have to send your children to school without food, or food money or decent clothes, that's a violence we live with every day. To get hit with a brick one day really wouldn't mean anything." Father Vitale scanned the crowd, trying to measure its response. If a middle-class person had used that language, he says, it might have fallen flat. "But Ruby said it straight from the heart: 'We experience violence every day. Getting hit with a brick? So what?' "[61]

Other Westside mothers were frightened. "I was scared," Versie Beals freely admits, "scared that somebody was gonna start shooting us." She felt worse, not better, when she heard that some black men on the Westside planned to buy guns to protect them. All that talk of guns had Maya Miller worried as well. "Since there'd been a move in the legislature to run these 'outside organizers' out on a rail," she said, "I envisioned some member of the local Sportsman's Club, who didn't have a legal way of getting at them, getting a gun."[62]

No one knew how the casino owners would respond, either. These men did not take kindly to anything that cost them money—which was, of course, the purpose of the march. "Our goal," Duncan had announced, is "to stop the gambling in its tracks, for at least one hour." Duncan, Mahlon Brown, and Jack Anderson met with Robbins Cahill of the Nevada Resort Association. They explained their plan to shut down gambling on the Strip. If the march cost hotel owners enough, Duncan said, maybe they would pressure legislators to rescind the welfare cuts. That was one risky strategy, Cahill warned. Strip hotel owners felt they were "being kidnapped and held hostage for something they had no power to prevent."[63]

Cahill's strong words worried Reverend Jerry Furr, chairman of the Nevada Equal Rights Commission. Furr, a white minister who moved to Las Vegas after he was driven out of Jackson, Mississippi, for civil rights activism, knew firsthand the kind of violence peaceful protests could spark. Las Vegas was not Mississippi, but Strip hotel owners had been associated with more than their share of violent killings. And their record on race was hardly sterling. Black hotel workers had charged seventeen major Strip hotels with hiring discrimination. That winter, the assistant U.S. attorney general had found the owners in violation of the 1964 Civil Rights Act and had given them until March 15 to come up with plans to hire women and minorities in nonmenial jobs. The feds were telling Strip owners whom to hire, and when—meddling in a world previously off-limits to government regulators. In early March, when Reverend Furr began meeting quietly with hotel owners to prepare them for the upcoming march, tensions were thick enough to cut with a knife.[64]

Furr had learned that Duncan and Wiley had a secret plan to divert the Strip march through the main casino at Caesars Palace. He quickly contacted the governor, Robbins Cahill, and William Weinberger, the hotel's president. Furr urged Weinberger to "disarm the guards at Caesars Palace against the possibility that some small, accidental untoward act happened that might result in a terrible tragedy." To Furr's great relief, Caesars's chief agreed to remove

On the eve of their first march on the Las Vegas Strip, March 6, 1971, Ruby Duncan posed with National Welfare Rights Organization chief George Wiley, actress Jane Fonda, Ralph Abernathy, president of the Southern Christian Leadership Conference, and NWRO organizer Tim Sampson. (Courtesy of Lee Winston)

all armed guards from the casino on the day of the march, and ordered employees not to disturb the marchers. In fact, the hotel owners association, in a precautionary move, voted on the eve of the march to allow demonstrators limited access to all hotels on the Strip. They did not want trouble.[65]

But there was no way to predict what would happen on the street. Donna Belle Ostrom, forty-seven, a working mother of six, announced plans for "a Taxpayers' Boston Tea Party" to free working people from paying for welfare fraud. The local John Birch Society planned to protest as well, calling the Strip march "a well-laid-out plan to further the Revolutionary Movement in this country." Even the state League of Women Voters broke with Maya Miller and refused to support the demonstration, fearing violence.[66]

Duncan assured everyone that the march would be peaceful. "There are a thousand ways to disrupt the gambling," she said. "Just having thousands of people walking by will keep people out." Three charter buses and more than twenty carloads of out-of-state welfare rights backers had arrived in previous days, swelling the ranks of expected marchers. "They came from every crack and corner of the United States," Duncan says, "from Canada to New York, from New York to Detroit, San Francisco, Seattle, Oregon. They came from Utah and Mississippi. They came from Louisiana, and every which way." One maverick Catholic priest from Milwaukee came with a group of welfare mothers with whom he'd recently staged a sit-in at the Wisconsin legislature. Several stayed at Duncan's house, where her children were accustomed to waking up to wall-to-wall strangers in sleeping bags.[67]

Duncan was buoyed by that outpouring of support, but she wasn't taking any chances: welfare mothers would not be marching alone. She and Wiley feverishly lined up celebrities to march alongside them. Jane Fonda and Donald Sutherland, who had just starred together in *Klute* and had formed a traveling antiwar troupe, agreed to march. So did civil rights leader Reverend Ralph Abernathy, United Farm Workers leader Cesar Chavez, famed pediatrician and pacifist Dr. Benjamin Spock, and antiwar activist Dave Dellinger. The presence of high-profile peace activists was key to Duncan's efforts to paint the upcoming march as a protest by peace-loving people against a vengeful state.[68]

Inviting celebrities to join their protests was a tactic that poor women in the U.S. had used before, often to great advantage. In turn-of-the-century Manhattan, wealthy society women had walked picket lines alongside young immigrant garment strikers. The presence of Belmonts and Morgans—dubbed the "Mink Brigade"—stopped police from beating the strikers, and transformed press coverage of the strike. During the 1930s, Cornelia Pinchot, wife of Pennsylvania governor Gifford Pinchot, marched with striking black laundry workers for the same reason. Duncan hoped that having the likes of Fonda and Abernathy at her side would ensure that no one got hurt.[69]

March 6 dawned chilly, with blustery desert winds kicking up and down the Strip. But by midmorning, a quarter-mile-long human column had formed, beginning in front of Circus Circus at the Strip's northern end. Linking arms at the head of the march, Duncan, Abernathy, Tillmon, Wiley, and Mary Wesley stepped onto the roadway, flanked by children. Behind them stood Jane Fonda, Dave Dellinger, Ronnie Pollack, a band of buckskin-wearing Ojibwa Indian welfare recipients from a North Dakota reservation, and sympathetic clergy from across the country. Above them, marchers could hear the steady drone of a police helicopter monitoring the protest. Sheriff's deputies on motorcycles drove alongside, keeping hecklers away from the marchers and allowing traffic to pass. Other officers were in plainclothes,

George Wiley and NWRO's chair, pioneering welfare rights organizer Johnnie Tillmon, addressed Westside welfare families and supporters who had come from across the country to support Operation Nevada. (Courtesy of Ruby Duncan)

or disguised as protestors. Only their occasional use of walkie-talkies gave them away.

Interspersed throughout the march were the mothers and children of the Westside—"long, long strips of people," says Duncan. "They were backed all the way downtown." In the moments before the march, Duncan introduced her children to some of the celebrities. Sondra says she didn't know who Fonda was, but she shyly shook the actress's hand and the two walked together for several blocks. "The Strip march felt good," Eddie Jean Finks remembers, "because all the tourist peoples took notice. Some even cheered."

Tourists gaped as the demonstration headed south down the famous strip of desert highway, past wedding chapels and multimillion-dollar hotels. Walking six to eight abreast, their arms linked as in Martin Luther King Jr.'s 1965 march on Selma, the marchers sang "We Shall Overcome" and carried signs that demanded "Give Us Back Our Checks." Children held up placards criticizing spending on the space program: "We Can't Eat Moon Rocks." (Apollo astronauts were visiting town that week.) Out-of-town marchers carried banners from their home organizations in Boston, New York, Los Angeles, and elsewhere. A photographer from *Life* magazine followed Jane Fonda's every move. Television cameramen walked backwards in front of the smiling, chanting marchers.[70]

But it wasn't all peace and harmony. Bystanders hurled angry comments from the curb. *Get off your fat asses. Stop having a kid a year for me to support. Hungry? Hock your mink!* Duncan's daughter Sondra, then twelve, remembers "people cursing us out, calling us poor and saying we need to work." Harriet Trudell, who had marched with Martin Luther King in Selma, brought her twelve-year-old son, Sonny, to the demonstration. "He was petrified," Trudell says. "The feeling of hatred was almost soul sickening."[71]

Her anxiety deepened when she saw Ruby Duncan nearly come to blows with a heckler. "Some guy kept walking in front of me," Duncan recalls, "saying 'Go to work. Go to work.' I wanted to push this man out of my face. But something in my mind said 'Don't touch!' so I didn't." Alversa Beals breathed a sigh of relief when the heckler gave up and walked away. Then Beals saw the marchers just ahead of her turn in at the entrance to Caesars Palace, and her heart started pounding all over again. "No, we ain't gonna march on Caesars Palace," she said under her breath. "I *know* we ain't doing this!" With its faux Roman statuary and spotlit fountains, Caesars was the pinnacle of Las Vegas excess, the nation's best-known symbol of conspicuous consumption. (The apostrophe in Caesar's was removed by founder Jay Sarnoff to show that the hotel belonged to every wannabe Caesar.)

The police, astride their motorcycles, had been a model of calm and restraint until the crowd veered into the hotel's grand driveway, lined with towering, imported Italian cypresses and eighteen enormous fountains. "When we made the turn into Caesars, one cop threw up his hands," Duncan recalls. "Oh my God," he said to Duncan. "Where do you think you're going?" Duncan just smiled. The march was going exactly where she had intended it to: straight into the gilt and red-velvet heart of the Strip.

The children cast curious looks at the replica of "The Rape of the Sabine Women" set amidst spraying fountains. Then the marchers entered the casino, with its Roman centurion guards and wisecracking, toga-clad cocktail waitresses. Essie Henderson looked back at the lines of people streaming into Caesars Palace and felt a rush of power. She and Harriet Trudell noticed "the fur salon was taking all the furs off and hiding them. They couldn't imagine that we weren't there to steal," Henderson says. Laughing, the women broke into song, creating their own version of the labor and civil rights anthem: "We Are into Caesars Palace, and We Shall Not Be Moved."

Gamblers dropped their chips and stared at the marchers in disbelief. At the craps tables, high rollers gripped dice in tightly rolled fists. Weinberger ordered all gambling stopped for one half-hour. "We stopped 'em," Duncan recalls with exultation. "We didn't even have to touch a table, just walk by and everybody was reaching for the covers and putting away the money." Children were photographed behind green-felt gaming tables, holding up signs with their skinny arms: "Don't Gamble With Human Lives," one read. "Nevada Starves Children," said another. The marchers circled the tables singing, "Amen, Hallelujah," and slowly filed through the lobby of the hotel. "We walked the periphery of the casino," notes Trudell. "They probably would have gone crazy if we'd entered the pit." Some denizens of the slot machines never did stop pulling their levers. "I'm too short to see what's going on," a New Jersey woman told reporters during the demonstration. "But I'm going to stay with this machine. I think it's ready for a jackpot."[72]

As the marchers walked through the casino, Reverend Abernathy paused before a huge statue of the Roman emperor. "Caesar," he said, "we come here in your name, because the poor are in need." Calling George Miller a "pharaoh" who should "let his people go," Abernathy told Caesar to render unto the poor what is rightfully theirs. "I can't obey the laws of the land when they conflict with the laws of God," he said. "Caesar, what are we going to do? Look at the way they treat our women." Duncan was "so tickled" that tears streamed from her eyes. Suddenly she felt a hand on her shoulder. "I looked around and it was the president of the hotel, and he says, 'Ms. Duncan, Don't worry. Nothing is going to happen to you.'" Duncan did not then know about Reverend Furr's meeting with Weinberger, and she was impressed that the executive had personally come out to reassure her. "Oh thank you!" she said. "I acted like I really was crying, because I didn't want this man to know that my tears were from laughing so hard." [73]

Weinberger had told sheriff Ralph Lamb that the marchers were welcome to stay at the hotel "until they get tired." For one day, black welfare mothers had the run of Caesars Palace. Tourists shook their heads as they watched them: tired, happy black women lounging on the steps chatting easily, carefree children running through the spray of the Roman fountains. "They're so young," a Caesars guard said, taking in the scene. "I'm glad they didn't get out of hand and get hurt."[74]

Duncan was elated with the march. "The greatest thing was we even stopped the gambling across the street at the Flamingo," she says. "They closed their doors. No hotel had ever closed its doors on the Strip. But they were worried about us. That day was the greatest satisfaction of my life." The children and their signs were beamed on the evening news from California to New York in the next few days. The mothers were quoted in the *Los Angeles Times,* the *New York Times,* the *Washington Post,* and an Associated Press article that appeared in local papers across the country.[75]

But tension replaced exultation the next night, as Duncan, Wiley, Brown, and a few other supporters gathered at the Moulin Rouge to plan a second Strip march. Wiley wanted to commit a large act of civil disobedience that would result in scores of arrests. Duncan fiercely resisted the idea. She was worried about what might happen if the women pushed too hard. As she was raising those concerns, Mahlon Brown recalls, the door burst open and several Las Vegas police officers rushed in, guns drawn. After scaring everyone thoroughly, the police apologized and said it had been a mistake. To this day Brown thinks otherwise. "They wanted us to know they were watching what we did," he says. "They clearly wanted to intimidate."[76]

The police raid had the opposite effect. The women had promised that they would march on the Strip every weekend until Nevada reinstated all the benefits that had been cut. The next march was the following weekend, March 13, 1971. And this time, marchers planned to sit down inside Howard Hughes's Sands hotel-casino and not leave until police arrested them. The celebrities and most out-of-towners had gone home. An estimated 250 people marched that second Saturday, mostly Westsiders and white welfare mothers from northern Nevada. Hughes ordered security guards "to lock all the doors as soon as they saw us coming," recalls Louis Vitale. "We had this guy go inside, pretending to be an ordinary tourist. He was going to let us in. Unfortunately he was playing the slots and, just when he was supposed to open the doors, he hit a jackpot and forgot about us." In Las Vegas, all plans bend before a gambler's lucky streaks.[77]

The marchers found the doors to the Sands barricaded by furniture and an unwavering cordon of security guards. Frustrated and excited, some protestors tried to break the glass doors down. The doors were twisted almost off their hinges. Cries of "Let's burn it," rose up from the crowd, which was crushing up against the doors. "If they say the hotel belongs to them, then we say the street belongs to the people," shouted George Wiley, directing protestors onto the Strip. "Let's take to the street." As infuriated motorists leaned on their horns, one hundred men, women, and children sat down across the Strip's six lanes of traffic, singing civil rights anthems. "We had decided it was time the world knew about our plight here," recalls Duncan's son David Phillips, then eighteen. "It was nice and peaceful, but we tied up the Strip and all of Glitter

Gulch." Traffic was backed up several miles, perhaps farther. "We tied up traffic all the way to Los Angeles," boasts Emma Stampley.[78]

Mary Wesley was working inside the Sands at the moment her friends sat down on the Strip. She told her supervisor that she needed to get off work early. "I knew that they were going to jail, and I didn't want them to go without me," she says. Wesley's supervisor warned her she would lose her job if she joined the marchers. "Lose my job?" she asked incredulously, "as a maid?" Wesley did not hesitate. "I quit right there, walked out, that was it." She walked out of the hotel and sat down on the hot blacktop. "I was one of the first ones they put on the truck to go to jail," Wesley recalls. "They had all these plastic handcuffs and I got everybody loose but my sister and one other person. When they came in to take us down, I handed the cop the handcuffs. I said: 'Save these for real criminals.' He was so angry."[79]

Wesley's moment of triumph was cut short by an embarrassing discovery. "When I sat down on the Strip I tore my pants." Wesley asked a prison matron to have the pants sewn before she was arraigned, but the matron didn't return with the pants in time. Wesley was the first person called before the judge that night. So she took off her shirt and tied it around her waist. "When the judge called me into court, they said 'everyone stand up,' " Wesley recalls, eyes twinkling. "I stood up and he freaked out, 'cause I didn't have any clothes covering me." Her case was dismissed.

The police arrested eighty-six marchers, most of them Westside mothers and their children. Ruby Duncan was handcuffed on one side to her ten-year-old son, Roy, and on the other to Lee Gates, a young man she knew from the Westside, who later became a judge. "They took us to the Convention Center and fingerprinted us," says Duncan. The justice of the peace, James Santini, would later become a Nevada congressman. Many of the arrested women, including Duncan and Harriet Trudell, had just worked to get him elected to his court post. "He wouldn't look at any of us," recalls Trudell with a merry laugh. "In a town like Las Vegas, we knew everybody. There wasn't anybody involved that we weren't connected to."

Finally it was Duncan's turn to stand before the judge. "Miss Duncan," Santini intoned, "What do you plead?" Duncan knew a media opportunity when she saw one. "Your honor," she replied, making sure her voice carried across the room. "I'm not guilty. I'm not guilty for trying to help the poor."[80]

It was Father Louis Vitale's first arrest. "I'd done a lot of things during the Vietnam War, even burning draft files," he says. "But this was the first time I was picked up by the police. And I worried that the Bishop would have me out of town the next day. I thought surely I was going to get fired." O'Callaghan later told Vitale that it was also the first time the Clark County sheriff's department had arrested a priest. He got a panicked phone call soon afterwards from the makeshift booking desk at the Convention Center. "We've got all these welfare mothers and we've got this priest," a deputy told the governor. "What do we do with the priest?" O'Callaghan, a devout Catholic, asked, "Well, what are you going to do with the others?" "We're putting them in jail," the officer responded. O'Callaghan chuckled. "Well you'd better put him in too," he said, "or he'll be very disappointed."

Sitting down on the Strip was "a master stroke in many ways," says Vitale. "This city was supposed to be an escape for people. They didn't want to come all the way here and be reminded of all the problems of the 60s and 70s. They didn't want to face the question of the poor, and blacks. And here it was right in their faces. Right on the Strip."

The judge ordered twenty-five-dollar bonds for each Clark County resident, one hundred dollars for other Nevadans, and five hundred dollars for people from out of state. Vitale had thought ahead about how he could raise money to bail everyone out. "We might get arrested," he told a fellow Franciscan priest. "If we do, come down to the jail with bail money. But, whatever you do, don't bail me out and leave all the welfare mothers in there." With eighty-six people in jail, Vitale's colleague had to come up with thousands of dollars. The good news, Vitale's fellow priest told him when he got him out of jail, was that everyone had been bailed out. "The bad news is I wrote a check on the Franciscan Center for bail money."

"We had $600 in our savings," says Vitale. "But he wrote a check for thousands." And, since the march was on a Saturday, there were no banks open to cash the check. Once again, Reverend Jerry Furr had paid a visit to William Weinberger of Caesars Palace. "You gotta know," Furr allegedly told Weinberger, "that if you don't cash this check, what you saw last week is nothing compared to what you're going to see next week." Caesars Palace covered the bail bonds.[81]

The focus of the welfare drama briefly shifted north to Reno. Johanna "Cookie" Bustamonte, a sharp-tongued, rail-thin blonde with a beehive hairdo, claimed that state welfare workers had suggested on three separate occasions that she take a job as a prostitute at the nearby Mustang Ranch brothel to "save taxpayers money and get off the welfare rolls." Several other Reno-area women came forward to say that they, too, had been pressured by caseworkers to become prostitutes. "Prostitution is considered more honorable in Nevada than welfare," Bustamonte wrote.[82]

George Wiley jumped on the issue. He had long been looking for a way to get white feminist leaders more actively involved in the welfare rights struggle. He called author and activist Gloria Steinem in New York City to tell her of Bustamonte's charges. Steinem and maverick black lawyer Florynce Kennedy were on the next flight to Reno. They announced plans for a March 19 candlelight procession across the Mustang Bridge, spanning the Truckee River, to the country's most famous legal brothel, the Mustang Ranch.[83]

The girls at the Mustang Ranch Brothel told reporters they resented the implication that they had ever been on welfare. "No one's forced into this work," one said, adding that she thought welfare mothers were foolish to "go to bed with all those men for nothing, when they could be paid for what they do." Ranch owner Joe Conforte said marchers were welcome at the Mustang as long as they didn't "interfere with business." But behind the scenes, he flexed some muscle. According to George Miller, Conforte warned police that he would bomb the bridge leading to his property if any marchers tried to cross. Unwilling to call his bluff, the march organizers called off the demonstration. But the issue of state-sponsored prostitution had been highlighted. Nevada officials were on the defensive.[84]

Wiley was called back to Las Vegas. He received an urgent message from NWRO organizers: Ruby Duncan and eleven other Westside welfare activists had been charged with assault and battery and were once again at the county jail. The women had attacked a welfare worker and taken welfare director Vince Fallon hostage. The fracas was sparked by the eviction of a Westside woman, Betty Lou Wright, who lost her job and then had her welfare benefits cut. City marshals came to move the family out on a cold March night. Wright's children stood on the street in their pajamas, while their mother wrapped the ten-month-old in blankets and newspaper.

Duncan, Wesley, Henderson, and a group of Westside women accompanied Betty Lou Wright to Vince Fallon's office and demanded he certify Wright for emergency aid. "All Fallon had to do was to sign a paper saying she had applied to welfare for housing aid, and they wouldn't evict her," Wesley recalls. The Welfare director told her there was nothing he could do. Without a word the women sat down. No one was going to move, Duncan announced, "until Betty Lou gets her money." Police arrested five of the women, including Wright. Her three children, who ranged in age from ten months to four years, were taken to Child Haven. This time the judge wasn't lenient. Bail was set at five hundred dollars each.[85]

Essie Henderson's mother was watching her grandchildren that day, as she always did when Henderson was working. When Essie did not come home on time, the children began to worry. To distract them, Henderson's mother let the children watch TV. Suddenly the children started shouting, "Mama's on TV. The welfare mothers done got locked up." Henderson's mother told the twelve-year-old to keep the TV off so the younger children wouldn't panic. "I don't want them to know your mama's downtown in the jailhouse for protesting," she said.[86]

Duncan was counting on the high bail to win her a night's sleep. "I figured we might finally get some rest because Mary and me, we were tired. We were ready for a good night's sleep. But the next thing we knew the rest of the ladies was marching around the jail singing." Rosie Seals was leading the fray. Seals had received a phone call early that evening from a caseworker who told her about the protest. She hurried through the alleyways of the Marble Manor project, breathlessly calling on neighbors to follow her to the Las Vegas police station.

"When we got to the jailhouse," a still-incredulous Seals says, "they had guns and dogs, I mean for five women trying to help some babies! They wouldn't let me in." Reporters were nearby and Seals didn't waste the moment. She knelt at the prison door and began to pray. Her children saw her on the news that night.

NWRO organizers bailed the women out and Seals found Wright a new, temporary home. Other women donated food, clothing, and cook pots. Betty Lou Wright had shelter again but it was a small victory. Many Westside families had been without income for months. More might soon find themselves homeless.[87]

The next morning, NWRO organizer Bruce Thomas—a former street tough whom Wiley had taken under his wing—accompanied Duncan and a throng of women back to the Welfare office. They were getting more and more stirred up as they walked, says Eddie Jean Finks. You could just tell that something was about to blow. Emma Stampley, Mary Wesley, and Ruby Duncan spoke to Wright's caseworker. Then they knocked on Vince Fallon's office door. "We asked him to have an interview with Betty Wright," says Wesley. "Just sign a form so she could get her check. He said he wouldn't do it with us all sitting there. So we told him we'd be back at noon."[88]

At noon they found the door to the Las Vegas Welfare office locked. They knocked. No one answered. They waited for three hours, growing more steamed with each passing minute. "We had told the welfare director that all we wanted to do was talk with him," says Mary Wesley. "After a while we realized that wasn't gonna happen. Those guys from the National wanted someone to go through the window. I volunteered." Stampley followed Wesley into Fallon's office. "The door was locked but he was there," Stampley recalls. "I kept that sucker in his office till everyone else came." On Fallon's desk, Stampley spotted the state welfare manual the women had been requesting for weeks. She picked it up and ran. "When I came out of Fallon's office there was so many police there I just went flying down the stairs," she recalls. "I got that manual they never wanted to give us. The one with all the rules, and the one with all the names."[89]

Thomas crashed through the front door and the crowd pressed in. Duncan, Wesley, Finks, Seals, and Henderson grabbed Vince Fallon, lifted him over their heads, and carried him down the stairs. Within minutes, police arrived and Westside mothers were fighting hand-to-hand with armed officers. "These guys came at me," Mary Wesley recalls. "And one cop punched me with his walkie-talkie." Wesley says she could hear her father's voice in her head as she fought. "Don't ever let anybody hit you," he'd always told her. "And always make your first lick count because you might not have a second chance." Wesley grabbed the policeman's walkie-talkie and smashed it over his head.

Frightened by the sight of Mary Wesley out of control, caseworkers hid behind their desks. Wesley was a tall, powerfully built woman who punched as fast as she talked, and she was not easily subdued. "I was so mad about being hit, about everything that was happening," she recalls. "It took eleven of them to handcuff me. When they finally had me, I told them: 'You don't know me. I am like General MacArthur. I shall return!'"

Fallon and Miller would both later insist that knives and guns had been taken from the women who stormed the welfare building that day, a charge the women denied. "We weren't trying to hurt anybody," Betty Jean Clary insists. "We was just trying to show them a point. Some of us there wasn't even on welfare at the time. But we were tired of being always on the back burner. So we moved ourselves to the front burner."[90]

The night of the arrest, Duncan's children waited late into the night for her return. When she finally arrived, the children piled onto the bed around her. David fixed his gaze on his mother. "Mama, I think I'm going to become a lawyer," he said. "This scares me. I don't like the idea that they can just lock you away. Somebody has got to become a lawyer to protect the family." Strange food smells in the house were always a tip-off that their mother had been arrested. "I'd wake up on a Saturday morning," Phillips recalls, "and I'd know when there was somebody different in the house because I'd smell the different breakfast—the thick bacon or ham they'd fry. And I'd know that

Mama was in jail. I'd think: I *knew* she shouldn't have gone to that meeting last night."[91]

George Miller saw no humor in the situation. Citing the violence and the threats, he announced that he was shutting down the Las Vegas Welfare department for a week. "Vince was a little skinny guy and he had courage but he and his family were scared to death," Miller says. Fallon says that he and his staff developed "a kind of combat readiness. The state police were our receptionists for a while." Still, he admits that he was frightened when the women carried him down the stairs. He believed they had a car waiting. "Their idea was to put me in the car and do something." Miller, too, feared the women would target him. He sent his family out of state when he couldn't get twenty-four-hour police protection at his Carson City home. "I'd sit up nights in my house expecting them," he said.[92]

But Miller was unprepared for the greatest blow to his authority, which came not from the protestors but from the federal bench. On March 19, 1971, Judge Roger Foley ruled that Nevada's mass welfare cuts were illegal, and that Miller had "run roughshod over the constitutional rights of eligible and ineligible recipients alike." His ruling was a sweeping victory for the plaintiffs, reinstating everyone who had been cut and ordering retroactive payments to recipients.

George Wiley got word of the decision moments before his plane taxied off the runway at Reno, en route back to Las Vegas with Steinem and Kennedy. The Washoe County sheriff boarded the plane and told Wiley that the flight would be delayed so that he could take an important phone call. Always in a rush, Wiley vaulted over the airport fence and found the nearest bank of phones. The call was from Ralph Lamb, sheriff of Clark County. You can call off any more demonstrations, Lamb told Wiley. Judge Foley had ruled in his favor. Elated, Wiley jumped back over the airport fence and sprinted to the plane.

"We had us a victory in Nevada," George Wiley told the jubilant crowd waiting for him at the Las Vegas airport. "We have shown George Miller and his staff that they can't mess around with poor people. What Miller did was illegal and he should be arrested just like our people for breaking the law." Ruby Duncan turned to the mothers. "Ladies," she said, "We have won because we stood together for the rights and decency that are guaranteed to us." The laughing, crying group then drove to the Moulin Rouge for a victory celebration, with food and drink catered courtesy of Sammy Davis Jr.

Judge Foley's landmark decision had ramifications far beyond welfare, says Mahlon Brown. It established citizens' rights to fair hearings in conflicts with government agencies across the U.S. "Everybody adopted fair hearings as a result of that decision," Brown says. "You got fair hearings in everything from employment security to motor vehicles. And it spread across the country."[93]

To a person, Nevada state officials were unrepentant. George Miller was outraged. "You can get on the rolls with the drop of a hat—it takes an act of Congress to get you off." Miller and O'Callaghan vowed to continue cutting ineligible people from the state's welfare rolls. But from now on, "we will dot our i's and cross our t's," Miller promised. Keith Macdonald, chair of the Nevada Welfare board, told reporters that he didn't plan to schedule many fair hearings, no matter what Judge Foley said. "I've got to earn a living myself," said Macdonald, part owner of a Reno drugstore. "If I spend all my time at hearings for poor people I'm going to end up being one of them."[94]

Conservatives in the Nevada Assembly had their own answer to the court decision: they introduced legislation making welfare fraud punishable by prison terms of up to ten years, with no chance for parole. Father Vitale, a frequent visitor to the statehouse, asked the bill's sponsors if they really wanted to "move Nevada back 500 years to the time poor people were put in prison." "To hell with the poor mother if she's a cheater," one legislator shouted. Staying in session longer than ever before in Nevada history, the legislature passed one angry resolution after another. "They couldn't wait to punish us for the marches," said Harriet Trudell.[95]

A few weeks later, the federal government delivered another blow against the state. The U.S. Department of Health, Education, and Welfare announced that George Miller had grossly overstated the number of Nevada families receiving benefits fraudulently. Federal investigators found only a 7.4 percent error rate in the state's welfare caseload, not 22 percent as Miller had alleged. And one-third of those errors were caused by the state's own sloppy paperwork. Nevada had illegally disqualified thousands of people who were entitled to aid, regulators concluded.[96]

Duncan lost no time in making political hay out of the HEW report, excerpts of which she published in her new weekly column, "Ruby Says," in the *Las Vegas Voice*. If anyone should be charged with defrauding the taxpayers, Duncan wrote, it was the Welfare department. Miller had wasted taxpayers' money on a mean-spirited crusade against the poor. Why was it okay to spend taxpayers' money investigating poor mothers, she asked, instead of feeding, clothing, and sheltering their children?[97]

George Wiley expressed confidence that NWRO's success in Nevada would stop other states from enacting similar welfare cuts, but his declarations of victory were wrong. The backlash came fast and hard in the months after Judge Foley's decision. President Nixon declared himself a born-again antiwelfare hardliner, and state after state cut poverty programs deeply. The National Welfare Rights Organization was unable to marshal much resistance. The Strip marches and legal cases had depleted the organization's resources, and internal tensions between recipient leaders and middle-class organizers threatened to tear the welfare rights coalition apart. Operation Nevada was "the last national demonstration of black people employing mass marches and civil disobedience coupled with supporting litigation in the courts," wrote NWRO cofounders Frances Fox Piven and Richard Cloward. "It was the end of an era that had begun almost two decades earlier in Montgomery, Alabama."[98]

If Operation Nevada was the last great victory for the national welfare rights movement, it was a fertile beginning for the mothers of West Las Vegas. The women's taste for political activism had been whetted. Governor O'Callaghan had challenged them to stop protesting in the streets, and learn how to work for change in a democratic society—and Ruby Duncan was ready to try. She had come to believe that poor mothers could force the state to improve the welfare system. Ahead lay activism in the Democratic party, lobbying, fund-raising, and running for office. In time, they would turn toward community development as well, building clinics, daycare centers, and libraries. No longer clients, this group of poor mothers had come to think of themselves as determined catalysts of change.

CHAPTER 6

DRAGGING NEVADA KICKING AND SCREAMING INTO THE TWENTIETH CENTURY

Ruby dragged Nevada kicking and screaming into the twentieth century.

—Renee Diamond, Democratic party activist and former state assemblywoman

When the cameras, celebrities and poverty lawyers left town after Operation Nevada, Ruby Duncan and the women of Clark County Welfare Rights were euphoric. They'd outmaneuvered Governor O'Callaghan, who they felt was trying to build a national reputation on their backs. And they'd humbled their nemesis, George Miller. "We partied for awhile," recalls Jack Anderson. "There's something so therapeutic about giving someone a swift kick in the ass who deserves it. And we couldn't think of anyone more deserving of that swift kick than George Miller." A few weeks after the Strip marches, the Westside mothers gathered at the Moulin Rouge with Anderson, their friend and advisor, to relive the highlights and to chart their next steps. "The women looked around and said, "Gee, we experienced this tremendous victory,'" Anderson recalls. "But the conditions under which they were living had not changed. You go through all of this and what you have won is the unfettered right to $142 a month. That's not a lottery ticket. It's a loser."

The Las Vegas mothers' movement had plenty of momentum, though— more than Duncan had ever imagined. Five hundred women had joined the Clark County welfare rights group after the door-knocking campaign, fair hearings, rallies, and Strip marches. And Duncan was determined to hold onto the extraordinary coalition she and the women had built. Father Louis Vitale and the Franciscans were in for the long haul. Maya Miller was developing a close friendship with Ruby Duncan, and she made clear that she could be counted on for political and financial support. Democratic party mavericks Harriet Trudell and Renee Diamond—a casino manager's wife from L.A. —vowed to take Duncan to every political meeting they could barge into.

During the summer of 1972, the women of Operation Life renovated and reopened the old Cove hotel as the Westside's first medical clinic. Here Alversa Beals marks the clinic opening. (Courtesy of Ruby Duncan)

Marty Makower secured a meager stipend from VISTA (Volunteers in Service to America)—the domestic Peace Corps—to write grants and do legal research for the women. And the League of Women Voters, while uncomfortable with marches, provided invaluable support on policy issues by publishing in-depth research and analysis. "It seemed strange to me to see these wives of doctors and other professional people with the welfare rights women," says Anderson. "But these women recognized how gifted Ruby was."

With funds pieced together from supporters and the National Welfare Rights Organization, Clark County Welfare Rights rented offices next to Legal Services at the Moulin Rouge hotel. The place exuded a musty activist glamour. Yellowing photos of Dinah Washington, Nat King Cole, and Louis Armstrong hung on the faded lavender walls next to news clippings of 1960s civil rights battles. Supporters like Jane Fonda and Pearl Bailey would stop by when they were in town, often carrying grocery bags full of food and supplies. It was a perfect place to brainstorm the future of their movement, over Versie Beals's pots of chicken and rice, beans, greens, and pans of cornbread. The women pooled their money for the meals. "I was always good at feeding a lot of people on just a little money," Beals says. "Everybody was always eating there," recalls Duncan's son, David. "Or maybe I just remember it that way because I was so hungry then."[1]

Many Nevadans were hungry that summer. Despite Judge Foley's order that the state restore aid to families who had been illegally terminated, and pay $3 million in back benefits, few Westside families saw a penny of retroactive aid. George Miller and O'Callaghan fulfilled their promise to again cut off every recipient whom Judge Foley had reinstated. And those who were thrown off AFDC in 1971 also lost Medicaid coverage for their children. The new cuts, enacted just months after Foley's decision, affected 70 percent of Nevada welfare recipients—and were carefully crafted to avoid legal challenges. "Welfare rights announced their victory and all that," Miller boasted. "But it was a hollow victory because we immediately turned around and took everybody off again. . . . And we took more off the second time because we went thoroughly through it."[2]

The results were not hard to discern. Mahlon Brown took a busload of legislators and two nurses—one from the state Welfare department, one from Clark County—to a Henderson public housing project. They found a group of youngsters with sores on their faces. "These people never wash their children," the Welfare nurse said in disgust. "That's scurvy, not dirt," the Clark County nurse replied. It was a result of diets deficient in vitamin C, fresh vegetables, and fruit. Absence of vitamin C over time slows healing and increases the risk of infection. Governor O'Callaghan told the Los Angeles Times he did not believe that children were going hungry in his state. Clark County Manager David Henry disagreed. "One form of starvation is falling over dead," he snapped. "The other is malnutrition."[3]

Ironically, the Nevada Welfare department had made these drastic cuts in welfare rolls at a time when it had a $408,000 surplus. In fiscal year 1971, Nevada actually returned more than $300,000 to the federal government rather than spend it on AFDC. This was one-third of the entire federal allocation to Nevada for AFDC. But Miller and O'Callaghan were not worried about appearing Scroogelike. They cast themselves as champions of state's rights, fighting an overbearing federal authority. And they acted with confidence, aware that they were riding a cresting wave of nationwide antiwelfare sentiment.[4]

In the aftermath of Operation Nevada, George Wiley had told reporters: "We are turning back the anti-welfare tide." But by late 1971, that tide was higher than ever, threatening to wash away gains made by the welfare rights movement and antipoverty programs. State officials were panicking over the explosion of AFDC rolls, which grew from five million to eleven million between 1967 and 1972. Some of that increase was attributable to recession, which stretched state finances further. In 1971, nineteen states cut welfare benefits, and thirty-one other states debated doing so. Alabama cut thirty-three thousand recipients from the rolls that summer. New York was contemplating cuts that would affect hundreds of thousands. Vietnam War expenditures left little funding for domestic initiatives. But the rejection of federal poverty programs in states across the country was not simply financial. It was ideological as well.

Stung by attacks on his Family Assistance Plan, and feeling the heat from rival Republican stars such as Ronald Reagan, President Richard Nixon recast himself as an antiwelfare warrior. The president now called for "Workfare not Welfare," and his new public assistance program required recipients to work for their benefits at well below the minimum wage. In a shameless reversal, Nixon publicly mocked Democratic presidential candidate George McGovern for proposing a guaranteed income program in 1972. The president even asked country singer Johnny Cash to perform Guy Drake's "Welfare Cadillac" at the White House. "We get peanut butter and cheese," Drake had written in his country ballad, "and man, they give us flour by the sack. 'Course them Welfare Checks they meet the payments on this new Cadillac." Cash refused to sing the song, but the president's much-publicized request helped drive a minor hit to a spot in the top hundred. "Welfare Cadillac" became the anthem of the antiwelfare backlash.[5]

Images of the poor as lazy, immoral, dishonest, and disproportionately black saturated American popular culture in the early 1970s. Media coverage of poverty programs focused on corruption, inefficiency, and bloated bureaucracy. In the early 1960s, Lyndon Johnson had gone out of his way to portray beneficiaries of the War on Poverty as white, working-class men and women who'd fallen on hard times through no fault of their own. After 1969, the percentage of stories about welfare that featured African Americans grew dramatically. Three in four faces shown in television news broadcasts about welfare were those of black women and children.[6]

Testing the effects of such coverage, one researcher divided viewers into two groups: one was shown a story that featured a poor black family, the other, a poor white family. Afterwards, viewers were asked what role they thought government should play in helping the poor. A majority of those shown stories with white protagonists said that government should provide more unskilled jobs and lower interest rates. Most of those shown stories featuring black people said government aid wouldn't help. African Americans, the viewers agreed, had to develop a stronger work ethic. White and black Americans sharply disagreed about dissent, as well. By the early 1970s, two out of three white Americans felt that blacks were asking for too much, and, by a six-to-one margin, they opposed protest demonstrations by blacks or the poor. Two out of three blacks, by contrast, felt efforts to ease poverty and racism were moving too slowly—and only one African American in four thought the government was on his or her side.[7]

Progressive movements were not immune to such divisions. Racial, class, and gender tensions threatened to split the National Welfare Rights Organization. Conflict had long been brewing between female recipients who had volunteered their time for years, and the mostly white male organizers employed in salaried positions. Stereotypes ran rampant on both sides, as the recipients' leaders demanded: "Whose movement is this, anyway?" NWRO president Johnnie Tillmon had lectured male staffers that "you don't just come into somebody's neighborhood and run it." The purpose of paid organizers, she said, was to "support" and "inspire" welfare mothers "in doing our own thing." For Tillmon, the movement had a clear mission: to politicize, train, and empower poor women. Many educated, middle-class NWRO activists had a different goal: to force the federal government to embrace guaranteed minimum income. Empowering poor mothers was, in their view, secondary to systemic reform.[8]

Wiley tried to ease discontent among the recipients' leaders by hiring former recipients for paid positions at NWRO's D.C. headquarters. But an anonymous memo entitled "Power to Recipients" suggests how tense relations had become at the organization by late 1971. The memo accused Wiley of riding "to T.V. fame and glory on the back of recipients." Calling for "total recipient control," the memo writer said that "middle-class professionals should . . . not be involved in policy-making, [should] stop treating recipients like children, [and should] reflect the racial constituency of NWRO members who are predominantly black, Puerto Rican and Mexican-American." Change or dissolve, the memo concluded. "NWRO might as well be dead without a recipient as head."[9]

For their part, Wiley and NWRO staff—many of them white—accused recipient leaders, including Tillmon and Sanders, of becoming autocratic, more invested in protecting their own power than in developing a democratic base. Sanders and Tillmon countered that some men were not comfortable with poor black women exercising power. In 1972, the women on the national board split down the middle over a motion to fire Wiley, who lost his temper. "This board doesn't even have the guts to fire me," he said. One woman grabbed Wiley by the throat, and started to choke him. Others pulled her away —but the organization never recovered. Wiley resigned angrily. A few months later he died in a boating accident.[10]

Ruby Duncan had to face down an insurrection of her own after Operation Nevada. As NWRO organizers prepared to pull out, they decided to wrest the organization from her hands. She had become too powerful and anti-democratic, they felt. "Some of the national organizers just was not satisfied with me," Duncan says, "because I didn't take their orders like they wanted me to take them. I had some respect for my own self. They wanted to pick them a person who they could run from Washington D.C."

During Operation Nevada, Duncan resented the often condescending attitude of some NWRO organizers, who were loath to share decision making with the Westside women they were supposedly championing. Every night, recalled NWRO organizer Andrea Kydd, a black ex–social worker, staffers would hold mass meetings on the Westside. Ruby Duncan presided, and participants were encouraged to feel that their ideas were driving Operation Nevada—but it wasn't true. "Meanwhile, back at the ranch house," said Kydd, she and other out-of-town organizers "already knew what was going to happen." Staffers sensed that this approach angered Duncan, but they felt they had a job to do— one that was more important than spending precious hours listening to the mothers. "There was a struggle going on, and deep and bitter feelings on the part of numbers of people on each side," recalled Ed Sparer. "There were times when it boiled to the surface . . . and had constantly to be patched up again."[11]

What couldn't be patched up was NWRO's determination to dump Duncan and replace her with CCWRO vice president Erma Lee O'Neal. There was no question that O'Neal deserved a leadership position. She had studied federal, state, and local public housing regulations, and had thrown herself into tenants' rights, becoming one of the city's most respected tenant advocates. O'Neal was also a talented organizer with a soft-spoken style, a methodical, clear-thinking woman less likely than Duncan to ruffle the feathers of public officials. But rather than openly promoting O'Neal as leader of a tenants' group, the NWRO staff launched a secret campaign to unseat Duncan.

National organizers had "done a good job of getting new welfare rights memberships," Duncan says. "People were signing up like crazy, and that was wonderful." But as they signed up new members, staffers were urging them to vote Duncan out. "On the day of the election I went over to the building a little early," she recalls. A woman who'd recently joined came up to her and said:

"It's time to get rid of you." Duncan was taken aback. "Why? What have I done?" The woman replied: "You don't listen." In a panic, Duncan called Johnnie Tillmon, who advised her to control the meeting. If you can do that, she said, you can keep your presidency.

Duncan quickly caucused with founding CCWRO members—Versie Beals, Emma Stampley, Essie Henderson, and Eddie Jean Finks. The women laid plans to control the meeting that night. Beals chaired the proceedings, announcing that, according to the bylaws, only full members of CCWRO could vote, and only welfare recipients could be full members. That excluded VISTA volunteers and paid NWRO organizers in attendance. When Duncan was reelected, O'Neal and her supporters walked out, charging angrily that Duncan and her inner circle had hijacked the election. For days and weeks afterwards, whispered accusations nearly destroyed the Westside mothers' movement.[12]

Remarkably, it didn't. O'Neal resigned from the Clark County Welfare Rights Organization to start Poor People Pulling Together, which protested evictions and price-gouging in public housing, and helped families find emergency shelter. Some years later, O'Neal became the first tenant representative on the Las Vegas Housing Authority board, where Duncan later joined her. The two women quickly buried the hatchet. "If they had fights, they kept those private," says Father Vitale. "I respect them for that."[13]

Jack Anderson sees great irony in the attempt to unseat Ruby Duncan. "A few years later, there wasn't a National Welfare Rights Organization," he says, smiling and leaning back in his battered law office chair. "But twenty years later there was a Clark County Welfare Rights Organization. The lesson in it? We don't really know what indigenous leadership is, or what qualities it takes."

> We have these things that we're looking for: a salt-of-the-earth, street-wise person with the education and sophistication of a Barbara Jordan [the Texas Congresswoman who gained a national reputation during the Watergate scandal]. And we fail to see that we have in our midst Ruby Duncans, who are inimitable souls and effective leaders. And we also failed to see what the ladies of the Westside had that made them so strong—a real spirit of sisterhood.[14]

It had taken the women years to feel entitled to a fair shake from the government. Now they were arguing something more daring: that poor mothers deserved a voice in policymaking. They knew more about managing a tight budget than any cost-cutting legislator. They knew firsthand what poor children lacked and what mothers needed to pull their families out of poverty. "At first," says Marty Makower, "the women were saying *you've* got to do this differently. But after a while, they started thinking: *we* can do this better ourselves."[15]

The second round of welfare cuts had forced the women to shift the focus of their movement. "We knew that to be on welfare was a trap," says Henderson. "I didn't want to be trapped by crumbs. I wanted more." The women began thinking about how they could bring new services and programs to their state. Gathering each day at the Moulin Rouge, the women and their attorneys analyzed the regulations of county, state, and federal programs for the poor. "Jack and Mahlon would sit us down and explain everything to us," Essie Henderson recalls. The attorneys were becoming experts in poverty law. The women were seasoned experts on poverty. Together, they translated the arcane language of the law into a language of rights and justice that the women could claim for themselves. The women also learned the nitty-gritty of welfare regulations. Anderson and Brown briefed them so intensively that when the women showed up at hearings they often knew more about the regulations than did the officials.

Allies such as Anderson, Brown, Makower, and Maya Miller offered intellectual, financial, and emotional resources but did not attempt to dictate either the vision or strategy of the mothers. Offended by NWRO organizers whom they saw as condescending toward welfare mothers, middle-class members of the Las Vegas antipoverty coalition were clear that they wanted a different kind of relationship. "The purpose of a good ally," Anderson liked to say, is "to be on tap, not on top." The women deserved a chance to make their own decisions, he said. "And if it's just an opportunity to fail, you have to give that to people because great successes are built on minuscule failures. You're better prepared the next time."[16]

BUILDING A MOVEMENT AROUND HUNGER

In the late 1960s, Americans woke up to the reality that hunger was not restricted to Africa or Asia. Visiting Appalachia, Native American reservations, and the Mississippi Delta, the Harvard-based Physicians' Task Force on Hunger in America reported in 1967 that ten to fifteen million Americans suffered from hunger and malnutrition. Many were children. In 1968, CBS News broadcast *Hunger in America,* a hard-hitting documentary that showed the faces of America's hungry children—and made clear that federal food programs were not reaching the people who needed them most. In the uproar that followed, the Senate pumped $200 million more into food programs and held hearings on their shortcomings.[17]

In 1970, Food for All was created by the American Friends Service Committee, the League of Women Voters, and the National Council of Negro Women to monitor federal food programs. After conducting a two-year survey, Food for All concluded that federal food stamps, commodities, and school lunch programs were being sabotaged by "deliberate under-use of money intended for feeding hungry people. . . . Administrators and legislators simply do not believe that millions of people are hungry." The group estimated that, as a result, twenty-five million Americans were not receiving adequate nutrition. These underfed Americans were probably not wasting away, experts said. But they were likely to be dizzy and fatigued, have difficulty concentrating, and suffer frequent colds and infections.[18]

On the Westside, many mothers were seeing such symptoms in their children. And that seemed just plain wrong. In the city of all-you-can-eat, forty-nine-cent buffets, the Clark County Welfare Rights women were convinced there was enough food to go around. Mary Wesley, who became the group's point person on hunger, talked to church groups and women's organizations to solicit food donations. She and other mothers went door to door to identify families in greatest danger of malnutrition, took down their information, and asked managers of local restaurants and markets to supply them with regular groceries. Wesley asked contributing restaurant and supermarket managers to send a record of their expenses to the County Commission, so politicians would learn what it cost to feed a family in Las Vegas.

When the state Welfare department again cut off thousands of families in the summer of 1971, the poor descended on the county's General Assistance office. But county relief officials could not begin to meet the need; they simply lacked the resources. A budget established for four hundred families could not feed thousands of hungry Clark County residents. While the county investigated whether each family was eligible, Wesley organized a food bank on the Westside. It seemed crazy to her to spend taxpayers' money investigating who was truly hungry. "When you're hungry, you're hungry," she said. Wesley collected canned vegetables and meats, cereals, juices, and milk, and distributed leaflets letting community members know that these supplies, unlike the Clark County commodities storehouse, were available twenty-four hours a day, seven days a week. "You never know when people are going to run out of food," she said. "It could be the weekend when a mother realized she didn't have anything to give her kids." But the women recognized that their small food bank wasn't enough to feed all the needy.[19]

The Clark County school district had been getting federal money to serve hot lunches and breakfasts to poor children, but Westside schools weren't getting them. It had taken almost a year for the women to convince district administrators to serve even cold sandwiches to Westside school children. The mothers felt that wasn't enough. "My children go to school without breakfast," Rosie Seals said at a community hearing in 1971. "They can't concentrate all morning. Then for lunch they give them a sandwich." School administrators insisted that they were not trying to cheat poor children. Westside schools had inadequate kitchen facilities, they said, and the district could not afford to upgrade them.[20]

The mothers were unpersuaded. Most schools in Las Vegas, constructed hastily during the population boom of the 1960s, were built without kitchens—yet white schoolchildren were served hot meals. Duncan and Seals had heard at the 1971 NWRO national convention that school administrators in at least a dozen cities were using federal lunch moneys to provide hot lunches in affluent districts while providing inexpensive cold lunches in poor neighborhoods.

Congress had earmarked funds for hot lunches for schoolchildren, regardless of ability to pay, in 1946. Nearly a quarter-century later, however, few poor children anywhere in the U.S. were getting free or reduced-price school lunches. In 1970, in response to exposés by the National Education Association and protests by welfare mothers in several large cities, Congress amended the National School Lunch Act, requiring that federally subsidized school lunches go first to the neediest. Yet the U.S. Department of Agriculture, which administered the school lunch program, put little pressure on states or school districts to comply. Nevada had one of the poorest records in the country, and Clark County was worst of all, serving fewer than three hundred free hot meals in a district where eight thousand students were on public assistance, and thousands more were eligible for food aid.[21]

In June 1971, Duncan asked Anderson and Brown to file suit against the Clark County school district. The suit was joined by the Las Vegas League of Women Voters, the Clark County Ministerial Alliance, and the Catholic diocese. Within a month, the school district had settled. When school started in September, the district was serving ten thousand free lunches per day. Within a year, sixty-eight of the district's seventy-two schools were serving hot lunches. The women also successfully petitioned the school district to hire welfare mothers as lunchroom aides. These federally subsidized jobs, they argued, while not enough for the women to live on, could supplement their income while educating them about childhood nutrition. "It turned out to be the leading lawsuit in the country," Brown says. CBS *60 Minutes* host Mike Wallace, who had covered the Strip marches, now brought cameras to school cafeterias on the Westside. The publicity triggered similar lawsuits across the country, as poor communities insisted on equitable distribution of federally subsidized meals programs.[22]

Still, school lunches did not reach children under the age of six, pregnant women, or the elderly, all of whom needed better nutrition. With the aid of Marty Makower, the women pored over the small print of county aid regulations. They discovered, to their delight, that the county was required to provide fresh meat and vegetables as well as canned and dried foods. At the next County Commission meeting, the women came prepared to make their case. Children were showing the signs of poor diet, they told commissioners. Commodities did not provide fresh vegetables, and provided only one can of fruit or vegetables per person each month. Beef had not been available for over a year. Unlike more expensive, healthy food, the USDA rations were heavy on starches, corn syrup, and lard. That diet, the women knew, led to rapid weight gain without nourishment—and a higher risk for diabetes and heart disease. Many of the women had watched their own weight balloon on that high-starch intake, and their health was already suffering. Duncan suggested that the county instead give poor families vouchers to purchase fresh and nutritious food in regular supermarkets. She loved the idea of poor mothers "shopping like any other middle-class American."[23]

Duncan, Mary Wesley, and Erma O'Neal met with the County Commission for a series of negotiations about the food crisis. With the memory of the Strip marches fresh in their minds, the commissioners were inclined to listen. "The marches were terribly effective and they continue to be when Ruby negotiates," Mahlon Brown said a few years later. "It's in the back of the minds of the founding fathers. They know that she's capable of mobilization. And that's got to have an effect on the negotiating ability of the lady."[24]

The commissioners voted in July to increase the number of people eligible for assistance, to replace county relief administrator Stella Fleming, and to establish a food voucher program to supplement commodities. The vouchers would be redeemable in local supermarkets. To pay for the services, the county borrowed three hundred thousand dollars from its medical relief program. But commissioners warned the CCWRO women that Clark County could not provide aid on the same scale as the state or federal government. There was a real risk that General Assistance coffers would be empty by fall.

By October 1971, as predicted, Clark County General Assistance was broke. The office had no choice but to close its doors, suspending both the new voucher program and commodities distribution. When county officials asked the state for help, Governor O'Callaghan slammed them for fiscal irresponsibility—the opening shot in an increasingly bitter exchange. George Miller said the County Commission was letting "Welfare Rights run their program for them." He claimed Jack Anderson had convinced them "to spend themselves broke and then the state would have to pick up the tab." County manager David Henry issued an outraged press release, saying that state officials should apologize for their "quickie solutions for a real human problem—welfare. Your solutions not only failed miserably but . . . threaten the financial stability of this county."[25]

When O'Callaghan refused to allocate state funds to reopen the county relief office, CCWRO decided to take action. "Floating around in the halls of the courthouse," recalls Mahlon Brown, "these blue pieces of paper appeared with the outline of the state of Nevada, and the words 'Nevada Starves People.' The women just dropped a few of these around the courthouse. And then they started a rumor that they were going to pass these out at the escalators at the airport." CCWRO members showed the leaflets to hotel managers and city officials, as well. "It's amazing how they found money to open up the county assistance offices," says Brown. "That's political action." Grumbling all the while about having to bail the county out, O'Callaghan convinced the legislature in late November to appropriate one hundred thousand dollars toward the General Assistance program. That was only one-fifth of what the county had asked for. "This doesn't solve the problem," one county commissioner said. The mothers watched the back and forth carefully. The political lesson was clear: poor mothers could call on one branch of government to help them fight their battles with another branch. It was a strategy they would use many times in the years to come.[26]

The women applied for and received a fifteen-thousand-dollar grant from the federal government—through Food for All—to fight hunger on the Westside. In the weeks before Thanksgiving, Mary Wesley and a group of welfare mothers solicited food donations from grocery stores, food wholesalers, and hotels. But that traditional method of aiding the needy at holiday time yielded only 150 Thanksgiving dinners. The women hated having to choose who among their neighbors would get the baskets. The process bred resentment and charges of nepotism. Some women who walked away empty-handed accused their friends in CCWRO of feeding their own children and grandchildren first. Wesley and Duncan began to wonder whether piecemeal charity was worse than no aid at all.

Wesley and Duncan wanted food aid that was more comprehensive and less personal. They were intrigued by the federal food stamp program, which provided government issue coupons that low-income people could redeem in grocery stores for foods of their choice. Nationally the program did not reach a sizable percentage of its target population until the early 1970s. But, as AFDC rolls exploded, and more people learned about food stamps, the number of people receiving them more than doubled, from four million in 1970 to ten million in 1971. Nevada was among the last holdouts. With O'Callaghan embattled and the county commissioners seemingly on her side, Duncan sensed an opportunity.[27]

LEARNING THE POLITICAL PROCESS

Just a few days into the New Year, the county relief agency again ran out of money, and on January 12, 1972, it closed its doors. Only the county's burial fund for indigents was spared. That day, fifty men, women, and children, black and white, marched on the governor's heavily guarded Las Vegas office, carrying signs that said "Feed Us Now, Bury Us Later." Duncan and Wesley passed around petitions to recall Governor O'Callaghan. "We voted for this man," Duncan told the crowd, "not because he would give us cash dollars, but because we thought he would better the lives of poor people." The petition drive, Duncan knew, was a long shot; no recall of a Nevada governor had ever succeeded. So she played diplomat as well, presenting a list of demands to the governor's assistant. "The county says they have no power," Duncan said. "So now we're looking to the governor."[28]

Duncan and the women decided to put pressure on the County Commission, hoping they in turn would use their influence to move the governor. CCWRO women paid a visit to the manager of the Union Plaza hotel, the largest casino in downtown Las Vegas. "We told him we were fairly sure the County Commission that afternoon would vote to cut the vouchers," Duncan recalled. "We felt certain that he would be glad to reserve an area for serving steak dinners to women and children and senior citizens and unemployed and disabled folk who would therefore be hungry, after which we would go to another luxury hotel." The delegation urged the manager to speak to the commissioners about continuing the vouchers. The manager put in some calls to the commission. That night the Clark County Commission, facing a room of angry welfare mothers, declared a "welfare emergency," and called on Nevada to accept food stamps.[29]

Mary Wesley was excited. She was receiving a stipend from the federal government to lobby her county government for expanded food programs, and her efforts seemed to be working. "I thought I'd finally found a profession working on something I really knew about," Wesley says with a shy laugh. "Poor people and kids." Other CCWRO women found their niche as well. Essie Henderson got VISTA funding to work at Clark County Legal Services, where she studied welfare laws and regulations. Henderson found that she loved the law. She was an instinctive researcher and had a knack for remembering and citing relevant welfare regulations. If Henderson could find time and money to finish high school, Legal Services attorney Arlene Joyce told her, she could earn good money as a paralegal.

Henderson was intrigued by the idea. "I handled one case where I got a lady back on Social Security," she recalls. "I put together all the pieces and looked it up in that big book we had with all the codes. I was good in the math part of it." But the prospect of going back to school was daunting. Henderson's four children were still young and needed her full attention. And attending classes would also mean she could no longer work on the Strip or the laundry to supplement her AFDC check.[30]

Instead, Henderson planned to use her new skills to lobby on behalf of welfare rights. Maya Miller, Harriet Trudell, and other allies encouraged the welfare mothers to make their voices heard in Carson City. Johnnie Tillmon, too, thought that welfare mothers could make effective lobbyists. Henderson had attended a NWRO training workshop where Tillmon "showed us how to read a bill, how to find the parts we wanted, and how to use the numbers of different parts of the bill when we testified."[31]

Refashioning welfare mothers as lobbyists, however, was controversial even within the welfare rights movement. Duncan, Wesley, and Henderson had attended the NWRO convention in Providence the previous fall, hoping to sharpen their legislative negotiating skills. To their surprise they found that many organizers "were really troubled by the insistence that the women be lobbying," says Maya Miller. "They felt that white legislative assistants would never be able to understand the women, whereas they could understand the interpreters, the organizers, the scholars. They thought that middle-class people should be the ones who did the lobbying." That attitude upset Duncan and it offended Miller. "If empowerment is what you're after," Miller says, "that is not a useful premise."[32]

Empowerment was what the women of CCWRO were after. And they had come to realize that street protest would get them only a short way down that road. On the advice of Harriet Trudell, Duncan threw herself into Democratic party politics. Trudell was a true believer, raised in Alabama by a devout Roosevelt-loving trade union organizer and a mother who was a political cartoonist. Her father taught her "that nothing was a greater sin than to take a person's human dignity, and that poverty took it in the most violent way of all." Passionate about desegregating the Democratic party, Trudell's father was the only member of the Alabama delegation to the 1948 Democratic convention who did not walk out when Hubert Humphrey pushed through a platform calling for abolition of poll taxes, desegregation of the armed forces, and a federal anti-lynching law. Trudell emulated her father. "I marched with Martin Luther King from Selma to Montgomery," she says. "That's me. Just show me the fight."

In the winter of 1972, Trudell and Ruby Duncan took the Las Vegas Democratic party by storm. "We were like salt and pepper at meetings for a while," Duncan says. "Harriet would come to take me to every meeting. I would say, 'Oh I'm tired.' And she would say, 'Just drink you some water and come on. You gotta go.'" Trudell brought Duncan into the Women's Democratic Club of Las Vegas. "She was extremely controversial at the time," Trudell says. "We just shoved her down people's throats anywhere I had the ability to. And in the end, being the personality she was, Ruby was very successful."[33]

Duncan learned fast. "I began to learn, I began to listen," she recalls.

> So all the meetings in West Las Vegas, I would drag all the ladies. I had an old station wagon and I would fill it up with women and say, 'Let's ride around and just watch and see.' And everywhere we'd see a group of cars, we'd just go in and sit and listen. We wanted to hear what are you doing for us outside of just sitting here talking. And then we started working on the preachers until we made them our friends too.

Trudell explained how political parties hold neighborhood caucuses to elect delegates for party conventions. "You have these meetings right at your house?" Duncan asked. "Yeah, people have them in their houses," Trudell replied. "And you know, in your neighborhood, they haven't had one in years." That was all Duncan needed to hear. Poring over maps of the city's electoral districts, she realized that she, Henderson, and Beals lived in three different zones. "Versa, you're going to have a meeting at your house," she said excitedly. "I'm going to have one at my house, and we're going to have one at Essie's. We've got someone in each of these districts." A few weeks later, Duncan, Beals, and Henderson were elected delegates to the Clark County Democratic convention. "No pun intended," says Jack Anderson, "but they changed the complexion of the Democratic Party in Nevada." Duncan was so effective at mobilizing new troops for the Democratic party that she won a seat on the county Democratic party's central committee. Governor O'Callaghan couldn't help but notice.[34]

By January 1972, Nevada Welfare officials were on the defensive. A county investigator had found a $12 million surplus at the state Welfare department—accumulated by denying aid to eligible children and the medically indigent. "That policy is not only morally wrong but fiscally unsound," Duncan declared in Las Vegas's black weekly, *The Voice*. The state's lawmakers, she wrote, "may benefit from discussions with the consumers of the program." Duncan talked the Hotel and Culinary Workers Union into paying for a bus to take a CCWRO delegation up to Carson City. First stop was a visit to the governor's mansion. Like any polite guest, Duncan had wired O'Callaghan in advance. "Any arrangements you make for feeding our members will be most welcome," she wrote the governor.[35]

SANDALS IN THE SNOW: WELFARE MOTHERS IN CARSON CITY

Essie Henderson, Alversa Beals, Mary Wesley, and thirty other mothers chatted merrily as they boarded a bus for Carson in January 1972. The temperature in Las Vegas was in the sixties, but deep snow awaited them in the mountains of northern Nevada. The women rode all night, eating fried chicken on the bus, and arrived the next morning at the governor's mansion. As they poured off the bus, lugging signs and singing songs, they were met by reporters who asked why they were there rather than at the legislature. Duncan savored the moment. They had repeatedly picketed the governor's office in Las Vegas, to no avail. They had met the governor's plane at McCarran Airport carrying a plump pink pig. It was not easy to ruffle the feathers of this governor. But they were determined to keep on trying.[36]

Twenty-two years later, Mike O'Callaghan still remembered the women's visit. "When I got home there was nobody outside," he says. "But there were all these picket signs on the front porch. So I walked in and Ruby said, 'Hi Governor.' They were all in my dining room having cake and coffee and lunch. My wife Carolyn had brought them in. 'They came all the way from Las Vegas,' she said. 'It's cold weather up here. They're not used to it. They were cold. So I invited them in.' " O'Callaghan strode past the women without a word, grabbed a swimsuit and headed to the nearby hot springs where it was his habit to soak daily. Then he returned to his office without meeting the women. "I had been working since 4 o'clock that morning," he says, "and I had to get back to my office in the capital."[37]

Many of the women felt demoralized by the governor's refusal to speak with them after their long trip up from Las Vegas. Maya Miller, who had invited them to stay at her nearby ranch, noticed how cold and unhappy the women were when they arrived at Washoe Pines that night. "By the time they got to my house there was a big claque that was feeling pretty antsy," she says. Some of the women had not been out of the city for years, and were jumpy about the darkness and the sounds of wild animals. All were chilled to the bone. As they trudged through the snow to the green clapboard cabins nestled against the Sierra foothills, Miller saw that the women were wearing "little Las Vegas sandals" without socks.

That night, Miller served them hot stew she'd been simmering all day, and warm sourdough bread. The food restored some of the women, but others were ready to give up. "I want to go home on the next bus," one woman said. "When does it come by here?" Miller, who lives on a remote, high-desert road, struggled to keep from laughing. "The idea that there was a city bus coming by!" she exclaims. But the women recovered their good humor. "The next morning they put on their best clothes and went down to confront the people in the legislature."[38]

The plan was to lobby legislators to bring in food stamps. "They had told us that food stamps would never get here," says Mary Wesley. "It would be easier to bring in a pink elephant than food stamps." But she never got to make her case. When the women got to the capital, "there was nobody in the offices. They just left the doors open and walked out. I don't know what they thought we were going to do. It was interesting to see just how scared they were of the little peoples."[39]

The Welfare board was in session. And there Duncan cast herself, in classic Western tradition, as the new sheriff in town. "Clark County Welfare Rights Organization hopes to bring law and order back to the Welfare Division," she declared. As Tillmon and Anderson had trained them to do, the women cited sections of the Social Security Act and later amendments that spelled out their rights: to cost-of-living increases, medical care, and continued coverage for children pursuing higher education. The Welfare board was cool to their presentation. But they agreed to open discussions with the U.S. Department of Agriculture about bringing a food stamp program into Nevada.[40]

The women felt that on this point, at least, they'd scored a victory. But two weeks later, the board came out against food stamps, citing a U.S.D.A. study asserting that the commodities program provided enough food, of sufficient quantity, to feed all needy Americans. Clearly, Ruby Duncan commented, the poor were going to have to use "more creative means to bring justice to Nevada." In early February, she unveiled a campaign targeting professional associations planning Las Vegas conventions that winter. "Welcome to Las Vegas where starving people and poor people live," began a series of model letters written by CCWRO. "We are sure that you will be eager to dine with poor people at your expense (those ample expense accounts)." Las Vegas welfare mothers, the letters said, volunteered themselves as convention speakers for anyone interested in learning about the real Las Vegas. The letter-writing and conference-crashing plan was quickly dropped, however, when Mary Wesley came up with a much better idea.[41]

WHY SIT-IN WHEN YOU CAN EAT-IN?

Why *sit-in* again, Mary Wesley asked, when they could *eat-in*? "The eat-ins were based on a simple principle," says Jack Anderson. "The right to eat takes priority over the right to make a profit." That principle had galvanized mothers' protests from eighteenth-century bread riots in Paris to twentieth-century century kosher meat boycotts in New York City. The eat-ins served another purpose, says Emma Stampley. They made hungry children visible. "We decided we were going to go sit down in one of the restaurants after people started saying: 'Ain't nobody hungry on the Westside.' We made up our minds to prove how hungry our kids were."

Duncan and Wesley, who had years of experience in hotel kitchens and restaurants, knew how much food was prepared and thrown out daily in their city. "So we decided to go around to the hotels and ask them if they would feed some of the kids," Wesley says, "show them what real, nutritional food was like." The idea had enormous appeal and humor for the women. "I was so excited at night I couldn't sleep," Wesley says. Instead she imagined how far they might go. "If the eat-in doesn't work we could have a sleep-in next, let the kids sleep in clean new beds," she suggested mischievously. They could also protest at grocery stores.[42]

During the first few days of February 1972, Mary Wesley called the managers of eighteen Strip hotels to ask for free meals for hungry children. Dressed in their Sunday best, Wesley, Duncan, and Henderson then came to call at their offices. The women sat politely before the men and their big desks and explained that Clark County had run out of money for food for the poor. The executives squirmed uncomfortably, insisting that there was nothing they could do about it. "We're in the hotel and casino business, not the welfare business," said a Sahara vice president. There *was* something the hotels could do, Wesley replied. They could feed the children. She pulled out her datebook and asked for a dinner reservation for six hundred. "And every time they said 'No,'" Wesley recalls, "I would write down as if they'd said 'Yes.'" Ruby Duncan says they chose the Stardust for the first eat-in because it had the best food. Wesley says it was because the Stardust manager treated her the most rudely. "No problem if you don't want to make a reservation," she told him. "I guess we'll just come when we're hungry."[43]

The hotel owners met to craft a uniform response to the request that they feed hundreds of children free of charge. "The situation presents a different set of problems to law enforcement and hotels than did the welfare rights march of 1971," wrote *Las Vegas Sun* reporter A. D. Hopkins. The majority of the marchers were adults who did not evoke widespread sympathy. "In this case, many or most of the eat-in participants . . . will be children and the issue will appear to many as one of whether children have a right to be fed."[44]

On February 8, 1972, two hundred and forty Westside mothers and children stepped out of buses and cars and onto the Strip. Tourists and gamblers watched as the children walked in orderly lines into the Palm Room restaurant at the Stardust. "What can I order?" Sondra Phillips, then thirteen, asked her mother. "You can order anything you want," Duncan told her. "You may order the most expensive item on the menu if you wish." The most expensive item on the menu was steak, Phillips recalls. "I had never had steak before, so we all ordered steak and potatoes that night. I could see the manager getting nervous."[45]

Mary Wesley beamed as she watched the youngsters eat. She knew the fresh vegetables would be a shock to children who'd grown up on canned beans. "These children had been eating so poorly that when salads came, some of them started to cry: 'they're giving us raw greens.'" Others were frightened that a rare steak was "bleeding." At that moment, Wesley says, "I knew I was doing the right thing." Allan, Wesley's eleven-year old son, said grace. Two hundred heads bowed, then they dove into the food. "Honey, I ain't never seen kids eat like that," laughs Emma Stampley, who brought four of her children to the Stardust that night. "They cleaned their plates. And we ate good too."[46]

Trying to stay calm, the waitresses asked their supervisors what to do. "Give them bills," came the reply. So the waitresses wrote up 150 separate checks, dutifully delivering them to groups at each table. Wesley and Duncan followed behind, picking up each of the checks. Then, at their signal, the children and parents started to file out. Sondra Phillips watched with both fear and pride as the manager said to her mother: "Miss Duncan, you're going to have to pay this bill." She heard her mother reply: "We want food stamps in Nevada. Our children want fresh food." The manager was firm: "Ma'am if you don't pay I'm going to have to call the police to get you arrested."

Duncan and Wesley offered to pay for the entire group with personal checks but the manager refused; he didn't believe that they had enough money to cover the bill. The two then tried to pay for the meals they and their children had eaten. That offer was also refused. The Las Vegas police arrived, armed and wearing riot gear. Duncan and Wesley did not go peacefully. "Please God don't let anybody beat my mother," Sondra Phillips whispered. "At that time the Vegas police had a very bad image," she recalls. "It took six policemen to handcuff my mother and six to handcuff Mary Wesley."

When hotel security guards refused to let the rest of the women and children leave, the mothers replied: "Our children have to go to the bathroom. They can go here or they can go in the restroom." Managers offered to let the children leave but the mothers would have to stay and wait for the police.

"Be sure not to jump on the crap tables," the women instructed their children. "You be good!" And the manager said, "O.K. maybe you should go with the children." Police escorted the children and mothers through the casino to the restrooms, the procession followed by CBS News cameras.

Pleasantly full after a dinner of crab and salad, a positively mellow Emma Stampley paused to tell reporters how pleased she was that the children of the Westside were "finally getting a decent meal." After months of living on red beans and neck-bone soup, she added, they were more than ready for some good food. Out of the corner of her eye, Stampley saw a man approach the coffee shop manager and try to hand him cash, saying he wanted to cover a hundred dollars of the bill. The manager refused his money, so the man —a local car dealer—instead handed Ruby Duncan a fifty-dollar contribution to CCWRO. "I just don't like to see children going hungry in Las Vegas," he said.[47]

While she and Duncan were waiting to be taken to jail, Wesley chatted with a restaurant employee who had seen her carrying plates to the children. "Where did you train?" he asked Wesley. "I work on the Westside," she said. "Your kids say grace and all that," he said admiringly. "They have good manners." The man seemed surprised, Wesley says with a rueful smile, "as if we were animals or something. The whole time I was talking to him, they were taking our picture. And my baby girl was standing behind my legs, waving a little peace sign for the cameras."

By the time Wesley and Duncan were taken to the city jail and booked, several hundred protesters had gathered outside the jail, singing "We Shall Overcome." After two hours, a woman guard told Duncan and Wesley that they could go. "Why don't you leave us here tonight?" Duncan suggested. She was a bit worried that this newest escapade might have angered the wrong people. "Nobody will hurt us here. We're tired and we just want to rest." The woman insisted that they leave. But Duncan and Wesley were nervous. Before stepping out of the building's elevator, they peeked around the corner to see if anyone was following them. Judge Reid, a black judge who was about to preside over their arraignment, was standing there. "Come off that elevator, you two mischievous devils," he said. The next thing they knew, they were out on the street, weary but ebullient as they greeted the crowd. Hugging their children and friends, the women promised to return to the Stardust "double-strength" and to hold similar eat-ins at Strip hotels until the state and county restored aid to the poor.

One of the first black Las Vegans to win citywide office, Reid was no friend of welfare rights. And the women's vow to continue the protests made him and other civic leaders angry. Even the *Las Vegas Sun*—the more liberal of the city's two dailies—was calling for criminal penalties for the eat-in planners. Judge Reid released Duncan and Wesley that night on their own recognizance. But the next day he announced a "get tough policy" toward protestors: $2,500 bail for first offenders, $5,000 bail for second offenders, and $10,000 for those who persisted.[48]

High bonds did not dissuade the protestors, however. Mary Wesley led a march down the Strip to the Stardust the next night, carrying signs that said "Fire O'Callaghan, Hire Ruby Duncan." The 125 protestors, most of them teenagers and toddlers holding their mothers' hands, found the Stardust doors bolted shut. The Stardust security chief warned them to disperse or be arrested en masse. Wesley led the group back from the hotel entrance to the sidewalk, where they sang civil rights songs and chanted for a while before leaving. Herb Tobman, Stardust manager, told reporters that the demonstration had caused serious and "irreparable" harm to his business, and he promised to prevent a repeat of the eat-in. He said the Stardust would press criminal charges against Duncan and Wesley, and file a civil suit against them, asking for ten thousand dollars in punitive damages.[49]

On February 11, Jay Sarno of Circus Circus—who was the only Strip executive to say yes when called by Mary Wesley—sent two buses to pick up fifty Westside children and ten mothers at the Welfare office and bring them to his hotel. Sarno, a large-living Strip legend who invited all Las Vegans to his hotel's circus shows for free, served the children a meal of fried chicken, french fries, and chocolate-and-vanilla cake. "Mr. Sarno treated us like guests and even helped serve food to the children," Mary Wesley told reporters. With Sarno's blessing, Essie Henderson led a "picket line in reverse" outside the hotel while the children ate. The picketers praised Sarno and condemned the state Welfare board, which that day reiterated its opposition to food stamps. Inside, Circus Circus employees took the children to the amusement section of the casino, where they played arcade games, drove go-carts, and marveled at the pink elephant flying overhead on a monorail.[50]

Sarno, who was raised in modest circumstances, may have felt sympathy for the children. Or perhaps he hoped for some good publicity. Circus Circus had been losing money since it opened. But his action, like the eat-ins themselves, drew mixed responses. "These people on welfare do not want a better way of life or they wouldn't lower themselves by running in packs, demanding something for nothing and deliberately breaking the law," an "Angry Las Vegan" wrote to the editors of the *Sun*. "As long as there are people like you around, Mr. Sarno, we'll be supporting them to infinity." Another letter writer proposed a new civil rights song for taxpayers: "We Are Overcome."

But *Sun* columnist "Vegas Bill" said he doubted the sincerity of the Stardust claims that feeding the children posed an economic hardship. "Ever wonder what the daily hotel tab for complimentary drinks, rooms, dinners and other tokens runs?" he asked readers. Some of the hotels, he noted, "are getting itchy about what all this publicity does to the Las Vegas image, and are fearful of a decline in tourist traffic. This may be a more potent pressure than all the welfare marches put together. Yet if this comes about, you can say that the 'eat-in' conception did it, can't you?"[51]

Stardust officials pressed both felony charges and a civil suit against Duncan and Wesley—but their own economic self-interest soon derailed both cases. Jack Anderson, a former casino pit boss, represented the women in the civil case. He used his inside knowledge of the gaming industry to embarrass Stardust executives and publicize the linkages between gaming interests and the state's power elite. At issue were the "irreparable damages" the hotel claimed it had suffered when the eat-in disrupted gambling. If the Stardust wanted to prove the eat-ins had cost it money, Anderson argued, the hotel would have to reveal how much its casinos took in on an average night, when there were no demonstrations. "The hotels know how much you're going to win or lose," Anderson told the judge. "For them it is not a game of chance.[52]

Anderson knew that Strip hotel owners never revealed how much profit their casinos made on any given night. Such stonewalling had caught the attention of Internal Revenue Service auditors, who suspected the casinos were skimming cash to evade taxes and launder money for "silent investors." But the IRS needed evidence, and hotel owners had no intention of obliging them. Anderson filed a countersuit to compel them to open their ledgers. The case was at an impasse.

Judge William Compton called attorneys for both sides into his chambers, Anderson recalls. "This suit is bad for this city," the judge grumbled. "Can't something be done?" Anderson reminded him that Duncan and Wesley were also facing felony charges that could land them in jail for five years—even though they had offered to pay the eat-in bill. Compton picked up the phone and called Clark County District Attorney Roy Woofter. "Roy, get down here," he said. Compton demanded to know why the prosecutor had indicted the two women. "It was in the grand jury's wisdom to indict," said Woofter. The judge was having none of it. "The grand jury will do whatever you tell them to do," he snapped. "And you'll do whatever *these* guys tell you to do," pointing to the Stardust attorneys. It's a measure of Strip owners' political clout—and their desire to keep their ledger books closed—that the city's criminal charges, as well as the civil suit, were dropped a few days later. The Stardust announced it would pick up costs of the eat-in, and, for good measure, issued a public apology to Duncan and Wesley for besmirching their reputations.[53]

Just one month after the eat-ins, Governor O'Callaghan recommended to the legislature that it give Clark County an emergency appropriation of $160,000 to reopen its relief office. The "lesson in all this," Anderson says, was clear. "They had decided it was better to feed people through General Assistance than through the private sector. This was one of those private-public partnerships, we hear so much about." The eat-ins, and the court proceedings that followed, tore the curtain off the machinery of power in Nevada. The civil suit "vividly portrayed the nexus between the economic might of the state, the gaming-resort hotel industry and the political process," says Anderson. No serious observer of Silver State politics could miss the point: "The decisions in Nevada are made not in the legislature but on the Strip by the Resort Hotel Association."[54]

Ironically, the eat-ins won Duncan and the Westside women some friends among the Strip businessmen they had so recently bedeviled, including Stardust manager Herb Tobman. "From that day on," says Mahlon Brown, "Tobman provided 200 turkey dinners to the poor every Thanksgiving." He became an enthusiastic supporter of the Westside mothers' movement, acting as a liaison between the women and Strip hotel owners. Duncan "socialized" men like Jay Sarno and Herb Tobman, says Brown. "There was an awakening by those guys that there's some really hungry people out there. Tobman has been involved in a lot of social things that he would never have been before. And he can blame Ruby for that. I think she knocked on his door pretty loudly and woke up some of his humanity."

But other power players, says Brown, "just hid a little bit harder and deeper into whatever their darkness was." Many years later, Duncan's son David Phillips—who went on to become a successful attorney—was told by a law client that some rough men in the gaming industry had called a meeting shortly after the Strip marches and eat-ins to decide whether to kill Duncan. Phillips's client, a union leader who claims to have attended the meeting, said that Al Bramlet, the man who had first recruited Duncan into the Hotel and Culinary Workers Union almost twenty years earlier, was among those who met to decide her fate. Many of the largest Strip hotels were built with union pension money, and so the union's financial interest often dovetailed with that of hotel owners. "There was concern that they were losing so much money," the man told Phillips. "So some guys were saying, 'We've got to hit this lady. We've got to take her out.'" But three men ended the discussion. "Nobody touches her," one said as the others nodded. "Hands off on Ruby. All she does is feed kids."[55]

Duncan may well have been changing hearts and minds even in the roughest Vegas back rooms. But in the end, Phillips believes, the decision to spare his mother was made for economic reasons. "Those guys figured: 'We'd just make her a martyr,'" Phillips speculates. "People would say she was killed because she fed poor people. Maybe there'd be riots, with worse disruption and loss of money. Each time they shut down the Strip, it took quite a while to get business back up. Anything that hits the press about violence in Las Vegas, their profits suffer."

Ruby Duncan knew she had angered some dangerous people. Several times in the early 1970s, she says, strangers tried to run her off the road. Her home was not safe, either. Many nights the family returned to find the house ransacked. "Nothing was ever taken," says Phillips. "Someone just wanted to harass her." That harassment took many forms. Without warning, police would sometimes walk in the back door on weekend mornings, saying they wanted to make sure that nothing was wrong. Saturday was cleanup day in the Duncan household. "They'd walk through the house, and then we'd have to clean it all again," Phillips says, laughing. "Because we were afraid maybe they had planted something." That was not just teenage paranoia, he says. People did plant illicit drugs in Duncan's trademark Buick station wagon. "My brother and I had the duty of checking Mama's car. You have to leave the windows cracked here, or they'll break because of the heat. And we'd find marijuana cigarettes on the floor. We would get those out right away, run in the house, and flush it real quick before anybody could catch us."

The scariest incident came late at night, as the family was sleeping. Duncan's son-in-law was coming home from working the night shift, when he spotted an intruder. "We caught this guy coming up to the house with a bottle of gasoline," Phillips recalls. "I look out and there's this tall, thin white guy running with a can of gasoline splashing all over the place." Phillips and his brother-in-law chased the intruder away. Duncan tried to make light of the attempted murder. "It proves that what we're doing is working," she said.[56]

CHANGING THE COMPLEXION OF THE DEMOCRATIC PARTY

For all their media notoriety, the women still hadn't gotten what they wanted: livable welfare benefits, job training, and food stamps. Shortly after the 1971 Strip marches, Governor O'Callaghan had told Harriet Trudell that the women "need to stop marching and learn how to do politics. They need to get into the Democratic Party. They need to learn how to get out the vote." Trudell smiles: "Mike had no idea how far they would go."[57]

Duncan and CCWRO initiated a voter registration drive on the Westside, bringing hundreds of welfare mothers into the Democratic party. "Pretty soon they were a solid voting block, much to the chagrin of the old party hierarchy, whom we absolutely wiped out," says Trudell. "They really didn't know what was coming. They were a sleepy little group." The women also took advantage of the new youth vote. The Twenty-Sixth Amendment had been ratified the previous year, giving eighteen-year-olds the right to vote. At the height of the Vietnam War, voters wanted to recognize the service of young soldiers. "Old enough to fight and die at 18 but not old enough to vote," ran the popular slogan. By 1972, eighteen-year-olds could vote—and CCWRO launched Operation Registration, a countywide campaign to register poor, young, and minority voters for the upcoming presidential election. It was a busy time. On February 8, the day after the Stardust eat-in, young Westside voters helped elect Duncan, Beals, and Henderson as delegates to the Clark County Democratic Convention. It was to be held at the Sahara hotel on February 19, one week after the Circus Circus eat-in.

The mothers lobbied hard behind the scenes before the convention, lining up support from the state's few black elected officials, the Hotel and Culinary Workers Union, and leaders of the youth caucus. The new rank and file were dissatisfied with the governor's handling of the welfare crisis, which they felt had tarnished Nevada's reputation nationally. Nevada "will remain a medieval, almost cannibalistic society unless things change," Father Louis Vitale told the delegates.

Over O'Callaghan's furious objections, the convention passed two resolutions condemning his handling of the welfare crisis, and called for a special session of the legislature—which normally met for only sixty days every two years—to resolve it. In a surprising show of force, the 1,200 delegates voted unanimously to increase the state's welfare grants, accept food stamps, and extend aid to needy families with an unemployed father in the home. "We took over the party," says Trudell. It was a stunning defeat for the state's Democratic leader, who walked out of the convention. "O'Callaghan stormed past me," Trudell recalls. "And when he saw me, he said 'You can *have* your Democratic Party!' " Trudell smiled sweetly. "What are you going to do?" she asked, "change your registration?" O'Callaghan paused. "Of course not!" he muttered, then walked out of the Sahara hotel.[58]

Duncan hailed the convention in the press, calling it "a moral victory for poor people." It was more than that, Essie Henderson recalls. "We made history at the Sahara." The delegation that Clark County sent to the state convention would no longer be all-white and male: it was 15 percent ethnic minority, 20 percent youth, and 50 percent female. Ruby Duncan and Harriet Trudell—"salt and pepper"—were among them. The newly inclusive Clark County Democratic party reflected a national change, as the so-called McGovern rules of 1972 opened up state and national party conventions to grassroots organizations, women, minorities, and youth. No longer could party officials hand-pick convention delegates and tell them whom to vote for, effectively choosing the party nominee.[59]

Overnight, the new rules enabled insurgents such as Duncan and Trudell to challenge traditional power brokers. "Al Bramlet used to come in and vote for the whole damn Culinary Union," says Trudell. "Where are they?" she would demand. "I got their proxies," he'd respond. By February 1972, Bramlet could no longer rely on such gambits, and the platform—usually tightly controlled by party leaders—was up for grabs, as well. At the state convention in

Carson City in March, the insurgents embarrassed O'Callaghan once again, passing a welfare platform that condemned his administration. "Nevada has the fourth-highest per capita income in the nation," Trudell declared from the dais. "We have no morally acceptable reason to deny survival with dignity to all our citizens."[60]

In the months before the 1972 elections, conversations like these were happening in Democratic party caucuses and conventions from New York to Los Angeles. The National Welfare Rights Organization, in its final political offensive, had launched a national campaign to register poor voters and elect sympathetic delegates to the Democratic National Convention in Miami. "There is a very basic reason why our legislators are not reacting to our cries," Beulah Sanders told supporters. "They do not think we represent a powerful voting constituency." NWRO women were elected as delegates from California, New York, Wisconsin, Rhode Island, Massachusetts, and—of all places—Nevada, giving poor women an arguably greater influence on the Miami Democratic convention than at any political convention before or since.[61]

In July 1972, Ruby Duncan, Harriet Trudell, Mary Wesley, Essie Henderson, Rosie Seals, Emma Stampley, and several other Westside mothers flew to Miami Beach, all expenses paid by Maya Miller. Duncan and Trudell were the only official convention delegates. The others joined a large array of protesters who came to Miami to march against the Vietnam War, fight for women's rights, and promote NWRO's "Poor People's Platform" both inside and outside the convention center. With the help of Gloria Steinem and other key allies, NWRO leaders persuaded the Democratic party's Policy Council, led by Hubert Humphrey, to develop a welfare reform platform that was more generous than Richard Nixon's Family Assistance Plan. Emma Stampley was one of those who took to the Miami streets. "People from all over the country marched," she recalls. "There were thousands and thousands of people there." She felt, as never before, that poor women had finally arrived in the Democratic party and that many white activists were embracing them.[62]

Class differences among delegates to the convention were stark, however. The Democratic National Committee and many delegates stayed at Miami's fabled Fontainebleau hotel, with its waterfall-filled swimming pool. The Las Vegas women stayed at a run-down motel with no air conditioning and a pair of marauding owls, who had somehow built nests inside the rafters. But Henderson didn't much mind. Besides the convention action, there was the sweetness of a seaside vacation. "I just loved all of that water," she sighs. And Mary Wesley finally got the rest she'd been craving, but at a cost. Hours after she arrived in Miami, she slipped on the hotel floor and broke her ankle. "I couldn't believe it," she says wistfully. "I got to go to the Democratic convention and I had to spend almost the whole time in my room."[63]

Duncan worked to get the women badges to the convention floor. "All of us would exchange badges. When one was tired, we would go and get someone from the bleachers. We all was stumping for McGovern to become President." It was a chaotic and diverse convention, with advocates for a wide range of causes fighting for airtime: women's rights, gay liberation, peace, civil rights, marijuana legalization, and amnesty for draft evaders, as well as welfare rights. Before it ended, the convention passed a far-reaching welfare resolution that reflected the impact of the welfare rights movement. A thousand delegates voted for NWRO's $6,500 guaranteed income plan; McGovern's counterproposal of four thousand dollars per year was adopted as the Democratic party standard. And NWRO won approval for much of its Poor People's Platform, which called for decent housing for all, enhanced programs for children, and recognition of the welfare movement's role in expanding the party's base. It was the pinnacle of NWRO influence within the party, and an experience that the Westside mothers never forgot.[64]

Ruby Duncan came home from Miami with a bug for partisan politics. Days after stepping off the tarmac, she announced her candidacy for the Nevada Assembly. Duncan vowed to put "People Before Politics." Though she knew she was unlikely to win on her first foray, Duncan used her campaign to reach out beyond the welfare poor. In every speech she made, she linked the concerns of AFDC recipients with those of children, the elderly, and the working poor. She called for a state minimum wage, an investigation into the pro-business policies of the workmen's compensation board, food stamps, and aid to the disabled. These last two programs, she pointed out, were almost completely funded by federal dollars, and yet the state of Nevada still refused to bring them in.[65]

Duncan's campaign, with Henderson and Beals at the helm, ran like a well-oiled machine. The women, now precinct captains in the Democratic party, pasted Duncan's image and slogans on telephone poles and housing project walls. They knocked on doors and urged Westside residents to cast their votes for Duncan. "I'd gotten everyone hyped up and interested in politics," Duncan says. "But I was on them so hard to get every single vote out, they finally said: 'Ruby, they're coming. Relax.'" Duncan lost by a narrow margin in the same election that returned Richard Nixon to the White House.

The loss was disappointing but not enough to slow the women's momentum. After the eat-ins, the victories at the County Commission and the Democratic party conventions, the Westside mothers were flying high. "I began to have a lot of faith," says Duncan, "that practically everything we wanted we could get." They had loved direct action—the excitement, the press coverage, the speeches and rallies. But the adrenaline rush of street protest was wearing thin. After all the sit-ins, eat-ins, marches—and numerous trips to the city jail—they were done with hit-and-run strikes. "We was always walking around in circles singing "We Shall Overcome Someday," Essie Henderson recalls. "You've got Monday, Tuesday, Wednesday, Thursday, Friday, Saturday and Sunday. You ain't never gonna see Someday." By the spring of 1972, the women wanted to build something lasting. "I got to dreaming," says Duncan. "We all did. We began to think it might be time for us to start running some programs. We thought: if George Miller could run the Welfare department the way he had been doing it, surely we could do a better job."[66]

If poor mothers ran their own community-based welfare programs, they could educate and empower the poor while providing quality social services. They could treat the poor with dignity rather than scorn, and design programs that promoted self-sufficiency. In Las Vegas, where jobs had always been plentiful, perhaps they could even create a successful job placement program. The women believed that they could do all of that—*and* create jobs for themselves. "We can do it," they said, "and do it better." They had the dream and the will. But they needed a plan—and a lot of money.

I GOT TO DREAMIN': CREATING OPERATION LIFE

A group of friends met at Ruby Duncan's house to chew over ideas for their newest and most ambitious project yet: a community social service agency run by and for the poor. Everyone was throwing out names, recalls Essie Henderson, until Mahlon Brown suggested one that stuck. Since the purpose of their new program was to raise the standard of living on the Westside, "why not call it Operation Life?" he asked. The women liked the sound of it. "That was before 'life' got a bad name," Duncan says with a wry grin. Operation was a military metaphor used by many antipoverty groups in the 1960s and 1970s, most notably Operation Breadbasket, created by Martin Luther King Jr. in 1962 to distribute food and promote job opportunities in Chicago and eleven other cities. As the women envisioned it, Operation Life would do that and more: it would bring their neighborhood back from the dead after years of neglect, by planting the roots of a healthy new community in the barren soil of the Westside.

Operation Life, the women told community leaders and prospective funders, would offer an array of services for the poor: job training and placement, a daycare center, free hot breakfasts for children, doctors' offices, consumer counseling, home-owner counseling, and drug rehabilitation. Small business development and support would also be available. And the women-run agency promised to centralize social services for poor families in the heart of the Westside. The women knew how exhausting it was dragging children on and off buses, climbing stairs at one agency after another, in their spread-out city.[67]

They had no intention of dissolving the Clark County Welfare Rights Organization. Poor women still needed a political organization. Besides, Duncan thrived on campaigning, speechmaking, back-room negotiations. She wasn't about to give it up. And the other CCWRO leaders—Henderson, Wesley, and Beals—enjoyed advocating for poor mothers at state and federal offices, helping them apply for food aid, Medicaid, housing, and clothing allotments, and making sure that caseworkers treated them respectfully. Operation Life would not replace welfare rights. It would add to and transform them.[68]

But first, Operation Life needed a headquarters. And there were few buildings, even on the Westside, that the women could afford to rent. Mahlon Brown suggested that they approach retired Air Force general R. G. "Zach" Taylor, the former commander of Nellis Air Force Base, who had just been appointed chairman of First Western Savings and Loan. The bank owned many abandoned buildings on the Westside with few development prospects. Taylor, who was new to the business world, was willing to give unorthodox ideas a chance. And he had a white elephant on his hands: the five-story Cove hotel.

Like so many Westside businesses, the Cove hotel had been a casualty of integration. In the 1950s, it had been a flourishing nightspot where Sammy Davis Jr., Nat King Cole, Pearl Bailey, and other big-name black performers would stay while playing at Strip hotels. But by the late 1960s, the Cove was frequented mostly by petty criminals, drug dealers, and the police who came in regularly to arrest them. Now the Cove stood closed and empty, a hulking building with a swimming pool full of trash and five stories of cracking windows. Spiderwebbed glass tinkled eerily when the wind blew. Homeless people camped on the upper floors; junkies used the darkened banquet rooms to mainline drugs. Locals avoided the corner where the hotel stood. Once the commercial heart of the Westside, Jackson and D Street had by 1972 become known as Nevada's most dangerous corner.

The women liked the symbolism of opening Operation Life in a building whose history so closely paralleled the history of the Westside. "This is a neighborhood that many people are afraid to walk through," Duncan wrote in her proposal to First Western. "We believe that our project will change this situation. The Cove hotel will become a center of community action." Several government agencies agreed to lease space or provide financial support for the project. Clark County promised funds for a twenty-four-hour childcare center to serve mothers who worked nights. Juvenile Services would fund a temporary haven for neglected minority children awaiting foster care. Clark County Juvenile Court said it would fund Youth with a Purpose, Operation Life's proposed program to combat juvenile delinquency. Legal Services promised to rent an office in the building. And the federal Office of Economic Opportunity would subsidize a daily hot breakfast program for two hundred to five hundred Westside children.[69]

Several nonprofit community development and advocacy groups, tapped by Jack Anderson, Maya Miller, and Father Vitale, also offered support. Food Advocates, a California think tank, promised to send experts to help Operation Life develop a food bank and a Food Stamp distribution center (should Nevada ever adopt food stamps.) The National Employment Law Project in New York offered to help develop an employment referral service. The Nevada Consumer's League and Food for All said they'd rent offices in the building. And salaries for some of the Operation Life staff would be paid by the Campaign for Human Development, created by the Catholic Church in 1970 to help community groups develop jobs, improve schools, and "foster self-sufficiency." (Vitale was on the group's national board.)[70]

At the heart of the women's vision for the Cove was a complex of small businesses run by poor mothers. Mary Wesley wanted to open a dress shop featuring African fabrics. Essie Henderson and her sister planned a beauty shop. Versie Beals, chef and baker for every welfare rights gathering, was thinking of opening a bakery or a restaurant. To help promote economic development projects large and small, the National Housing Law and Economic Development Center in Berkeley committed two of its attorneys for sixty days each to train community residents at the Cove.[71]

With all these building blocks in place, the women delivered their proposal to General Taylor and other First Western board members. "We found out where they lived and put it in their milk boxes with the morning milk," Duncan recalls. The board was impressed both by the women's plans, their endorsers, and the vital services they promised to provide. "We already had received half a dozen proposals," recalled Taylor. "All of them included a gambling set up. More slot machines didn't seem to be what the Westside needed." Taylor hoped that the project could enhance the value of other First Western properties on the Westside. He agreed to lease the Cove and a building across the street to Operation Life rent-free for a year. If he deemed the new program a success, Taylor would give the women the option to buy both properties.[72]

All summer and fall of 1972, the women worked feverishly to reclaim the Cove. Commandeering the labor of friends, husbands, boyfriends, and children, along with enthused white supporters, the women painted, plastered, rewired, and hauled truckloads of trash out of the hotel swimming pool. It was an overwhelming task, Mary Wesley recalls. "The more we cleaned, the more dust there was. It was nerve-racking to work so hard and never think you'd get a better building." Still, the women were excited. "Paid or not, hot or cold," says Alversa Beals, "we stuck together to make it work." Teenage children grumbled at first but soon got into the spirit. "We all got close. We got to be like one big family," says Beals's daughter Glendora. "Us and Ruby's kids and Miss Mary's children too."[73]

Most of the doors in the Cove and all of the windows on the first three floors had been shattered. Neighborhood boys from the summer Youth Corps, supervised by local tradesmen, hung doors, installed windows, laid pipe, and painted walls, using sixty gallons of donated paint. A local drug rehabilitation program helped tar the leaking roof. The firm that monitored underground detonations at the Mercury nuclear test site gave the women office equipment, furniture, and a small offset press to turn out announcements. By the end of the summer, the Operation Life women even received grudging greetings each morning from the dopers and drug dealers who hung out on Jackson and D. "These moms were old hands at confrontation," wrote *Review-Journal* reporter Bill Vincent. "The rough character of the corner didn't bother them. The hoodlums got the message and disappeared."[74]

In August 1972, the women published a birth announcement for Operation Life in the city's black newspaper, pledging "a new approach to the problems of the walled city of West Las Vegas." Shedding their old skins as welfare clients, the women pronounced themselves "well springs of creativity in the black community" and vowed to succeed where other poverty programs had failed. "This is a self-help project," Duncan wrote. "Though we have supporters traveling all over the nation to seek out help from foundations, the decisions will be made here and will be made by poor people."

Operation Life opened for business in September 1972, even though most of the hotel was not yet renovated. The women had reclaimed just enough space to give Operation Life a storefront office, a meeting room, and a daycare center. The old casino would house the daycare center. The employment center, drug counseling program, and Legal Services Office were housed in hotel rooms. Hot breakfasts would be prepared in the hotel kitchen and served to children and the elderly in the dining room.[75]

Robert Egans, a Grambling College football star, was hired to be an assistant director for Youth with a Purpose, an Operation Life program for local teenagers who'd been in trouble or might soon be. The program, funded with a sixty-thousand-dollar grant from Clark County Juvenile Services, paid for neighborhood boys to make over Jackson Street, cleaning and painting storefronts. Youth with a Purpose also provided tutoring and dropout prevention counseling for high-school students, and opened a restaurant called the *Muigwithwania* ("we're together" in Swahili). First using the old Cove hotel kitchen, and later renovating the building across from the Cove, Westside adults with cooking and food-service experience ran a restaurant-school to train local youth for jobs in hotels and restaurants.[76]

In November, days before the hot breakfast program was scheduled to begin—with local women hired to cook and serve food to children and the elderly—the federal government rescinded its grant. Duncan called George Wiley in Washington to see if he could find out what had happened. Wiley quickly accused Governor O'Callaghan of sabotage, saying he'd personally intervened to block the Office of Economic Opportunity money. Federal officials in Washington told the *Las Vegas Voice* that the governor had not intervened, but that Nevada OEO director Frank Matthews had. Matthews denied the charges, saying Duncan had bungled the grant by failing to work through proper channels. Red tape frustrates everyone, he said, but "grandstanding" and "ill-advised bullheadedness" don't serve the needs of the poor. "Laying the blame on state officials is an old and cynical attempt for power grabs at the expense of needy people."[77]

Angry allies called for another Strip march, but Duncan was no longer interested in playing that game. She was playing a winning hand in Las Vegas. This wasn't the time to burn bridges. She resubmitted the hot breakfast grant —and set her sights on winning support in Carson City. With the new legislative session about to begin in Carson City, she thought she could accomplish more for Operation Life and Nevada's poor by working inside the system. Food stamps would feed far more people than even the most ambitious breakfast program. Maya Miller offered to provide her with meals, a house, and a car for the duration of the session. The other women could hold down the fort at Operation Life for a couple of months, while Duncan and Miller tried to persuade legislators at long last to modernize the state's welfare system. Their main goal for the session was to bring food stamps to Nevada, the last holdout in the nation.

Before Duncan left for Carson City, the CCWRO women worked to build support for food stamps in the Nevada business community. Using Food for All information brochures, Mary Wesley and Essie Henderson met with supermarket managers and grocery store owners to explain that food stamps could substantially increase their sales volume and profits. The women knew that getting Albertson's and Safeway on their side would matter far more than any argument that Duncan could make to legislators. In January 1973, Duncan left for Carson City, vowing not to return empty-handed.[78]

THE LAST STATE IN THE UNION TO ACCEPT FOOD STAMPS

Stares and laughter greeted Duncan when she boarded a plane full of politicians bound for Carson City at the opening of the 1973 legislative session. "Ruby where you going?" one of the men asked. "I'm going up with y'all," she answered. "I'm going to lobby y'all for some food stamps." The men started laughing. "Oh come on now," they said, guffawing and rolling their eyes. The reception was not much better when she walked into the statehouse. "I was the only big, black something walking around those halls," Duncan says. "And a female at that, and a welfare mama."

Duncan joined a team of seasoned activists. Sister Carole Hurray of the Las Vegas Franciscan Center was at the statehouse, along with Maya Miller and Nancy Gomes, the welfare expert who had written the bombshell report revealing the Welfare department's $12 million surplus. The four women were determined to bring in food stamps and boost monthly AFDC benefits from twenty-five dollars to sixty-seven dollars per child. They also argued for extending aid to the disabled and to unemployed fathers. The federal government had authorized both years before, but Nevada refused to adopt them.

Rising early each day at Maya Miller's ranch, Duncan would "trudge through the snow to go down for the early morning finance committee hearings," Miller recalls, returning late at night. Then she would stay up into the wee hours studying pending bills. Miller's fourteen-year-old son, Eric, would wake to the sound of Duncan pacing in the kitchen. She read long passages to herself, stumbling over the awkward legal language but refusing to give up until a bill made sense to her. "Eric was my company-keeper at night," Duncan says. "He kept the fire going and he had the TV on low. I said to myself, 'this child is sitting here with me to make sure that I'm staying warm, and to keep me from feeling lonely.' He would sit there with me and I would be reading bill after bill, making sure that nothing got past me."

Duncan's ninth-grade education was hardly sufficient to enable her to make sense of the impossibly complex language that regulated the lives of the poor. Jack Anderson and Mahlon Brown were more than willing to help with such technical matters. But Duncan hated to be told that she couldn't do something, Maya Miller recalls. She'd been tagged as a rabble-rouser, a street protester, a loudmouth. No one really believed that she could master the intricacies of legislative politics. So she took up that challenge with a passion. "It was interesting to me that Ruby was willing to play this game," Miller says. "But she had an inquiring mind, and she wanted to know whether you could make change that way."

Duncan says her first experience as a lobbyist was an eye-opener. "I'd go at 6 o'clock in the morning, and I would stay with those legislators till 12:30 at night. And I learned to do what they did." Policy decisions, she quickly realized, were often made after hours, not in offices but in restaurants and bars. A large, chocolate-skinned woman with a taste for pink and turquoise dresses, Duncan spent her evenings during that session trying to blend in at lily-white Carson City watering holes. "If there was a whole crew of them sitting together I would go over. And I'd say, 'Oh, excuse me Gentlemen, maybe I could come and sit with you?' So I would sit with them and hear different kinds of language on welfare, on business. It was quite interesting to learn how to read between the lines of bills."

Duncan also had to learn to read the culture of white male politicians. "I watched them. I would go to the parties where they were just gulping down, gulping down. I wasn't drinking, just studying their heads." Cornering legislators on the mornings after, Duncan reminded them of conversations they might have forgotten. "Last night you were drinking very heavy so I don't know if you remember, but you told me you was gonna help us.' And they'd say, 'Did I say that?' And I'd say, 'Yes you did. You told me. I wasn't drinking so I remember.' And they'd say, 'Okay. Well I guess I have to do what I said.' "[79]

"Commodities luncheons" were another tactic Duncan used that year to cajole Nevada legislators into voting for food stamps. Riffing on Upton Sinclair—author of *The Jungle,* the novelistic exposé of the meat-packing industry—she and the CCWRO women hoped to change lawmakers' hearts by turning their stomachs. "The mothers brought their commodities and prepared a lunch," Jack Anderson recalls. "They waited until the key legislators were present to open these funky cans of meat, real foul-smelling stuff." Most of the lawmakers avoided it, opting for peanut butter instead. "The Spam pretty much went untouched"—except by two assemblymen, who ate it and promptly got sick, says Anderson. But lawmakers weren't yet ready to say that commodities weren't fit for consumption by the poor.[80]

The contempt that many Carson City lawmakers felt for welfare mothers was profound. Maya Miller was speaking with Duncan in the anteroom of the state senate "when a good-old-boy senator" stopped to gaze at Duncan in mock amazement. He took out an imaginary tape measure and pretended to measure her breasts. "I think I'm going to enter you in a contest," he said leeringly, then walked out of the room. His colleagues were scarcely more respectful. Archie Pozzi, a Carson City Republican, got irritated when Duncan told the Senate Finance Committee that living costs in Las Vegas were more than twice the welfare grant. "Don't you people look for jobs, or do you just hang around the house?" he said. "We'd like to work," Duncan responded. "But there are no jobs available."

In 1973, the nation was mired in a recession, and southern Nevada was hit particularly hard. Even George Miller acknowledged the problem. "The jobs are not there," he told reporters, justifying why he opposed providing daycare to job-seeking welfare mothers. "We can't find jobs for women who want to work now. Daycare centers so these women can do what? Pull slot machine handles?" Lawmakers were, if anything, more hard-nosed than Miller. When Washoe County—facing bankruptcy—asked for state relief, legislators instead suggested that commissioners cut "frills": mental health care, contraceptive clinics, and programs to combat alcoholism.[81]

The session wore on into late March, long past the usual sixty-day limit. Duncan and Miller had been lobbying hard for three months with nothing to show for it. The legislature refused to discuss food stamps or to raise AFDC benefits by even five dollars per child. But slowly, some of the arguments put forward by the women and their allies started to sink in. Jack Anderson told the Senate Finance Committee that the Welfare department's failure to spend its allotted budget the previous year had cost Nevada $8.5 million in federal matching funds. If the state simply took what the federal government was offering for public assistance programs, Nevada could increase monthly AFDC grants by $25 per child, expand programs for the medically indigent, the elderly, and the blind, and pay for both a commodities and food stamp program—all for $5 million less than the Welfare department was budgeting. After Anderson's testimony, Senate and Assembly finance committees voted to fund a food stamp program for Clark and Washoe counties. But their colleagues continued to drag their feet.[82]

Maya Miller paid for Mary Wesley, Erma O'Neal, Rosie Seals, Eddie Jean Finks, and several other Westside welfare mothers to bus up from Las Vegas to press the case for food stamps. The women testified about the effect of food shortages on children, while legislators fiddled with papers and watched the clock. At noon, the lawmakers sent out for hamburgers, french fries, and root beer from an A&W across the street—on the County Commission's tab, because the session had gone on so long that the legislators were no longer drawing a salary. But no one thought to offer food to the welfare mothers. While the politicians and reporters ate, Miller, Duncan, and the welfare mothers stood watching.

A reporter asked Miller for a comment. "I can't believe that you let those welfare women sit there while you all fed your fat faces," she said. Startled, he handed Miller his partially eaten burger. "You can have this, Maya," he said. "I don't need your leftovers," she snapped. "I have the money to eat in a restaurant. But that you were willing to feed yourselves and let these welfare mothers go hungry is incredible. There's not one of you who would come to my house and not expect to be given a cup of coffee." The legislators filed out. The press followed. Miller sat there stewing.[83]

The men had left their hamburger wrappers and soda cans behind in the Assembly lounge. Reflexively, Miller started picking up the refuse, "because that's what women do, even when they're really irritated," she recalls. "Then I checked myself. I sat down. And I threw the carton of hamburgers and sodas I'd picked up on the floor." She saw a guard watching her. "Notice that I'm the one who did that," she told him. "The welfare mothers did not do that." Miller stalked out of the room. A state policeman hurried after her and ordered her to clean up the mess. She refused. When he took her arm, Duncan and the other women "gathered round me so protectively that he backed off," Miller recalls. She told reporters she would come back to clean up the mess when the distinguished legislators came back to help. Then she drove home.

That evening, Miller looked out her window to see a sheriff's car with red lights flashing drive up to her house. Two uniformed officers came to her door and handed her a letter. By unanimous vote, the Nevada State Legislature had resolved that Miller must issue a public apology or be banned from the statehouse. As Miller brooded over how to respond, national newspaper editors—who two years before couldn't find Carson City on the map—pounced on the story. In the wake of Operation Nevada and the eat-ins, which had generated national press, the Hamburger Incident made great copy. "Environmentalist Litters Legislature," wrote the *New York Times*. "Irate Welfare Activist Irks Legislators," noted the *Los Angeles Times*. The *Boston Herald* made Miller one of its "People in the News." The local papers were all over the story as well. "Legislative Session Dishing up Hash," wrote the *Las Vegas Review-Journal*.[84]

Miller used the opportunity to air her views on the Nevada welfare crisis. She wrote a letter to legislators, which she sent to local papers as well. "I am sorry for the litter, but I cannot tell you I am sorry for my impatience or my sense of outrage at the violence Nevada does daily to its poor children," she wrote. "I am concerned about your spending your honorable body's time and attention on me and my frustrated small act, instead of on the real issue involved: how to cure the disgrace of poverty that persists in Nevada in the midst of our affluence." Duncan followed Miller's letter with her own, describing her own "taste of rage that none of us can swallow any longer." Legislators offered welfare mothers "luncheon leftovers just as you offer meager grants on which our children must grow," she wrote.[85]

Wire services and syndicated radio networks from Los Angeles to New York carried the story of the hamburger battle, and Maya Miller happily agreed to be interviewed. On the air, she compared the Nevada welfare system to plantation agriculture. The state had crafted its welfare system to subsidize casino hotels that paid "$1.38 an hour for scrubbing walls and making beds and cleaning toilets all day," Miller said. An L.A. radio host asked her if she was charging collusion between the governor, the legislature, and the gambling industry. "It does make you wonder why the governor of the state and the legislature would work together to keep the grant so low for women and their children," Miller said. "Maybe it is to keep a cheap pool of women laborers—maidservants in the hotels—and in our legalized prostitution industry?" That comment struck a nerve, a senior state senator told Miller privately, but it didn't incline the legislature to increase funding for welfare.[86]

Maya Miller and Ruby Duncan decided to change course, and pour all their resources into the food stamp battle, which they felt might be winnable that session. Food for All, which was funding the Clark County Welfare Rights Organization's emergency food programs, suggested that the women get the grocery store lobbyists on their side. "The food stamp program is a financial boon to grocery stores," Food for All noted in a 1972 report. "It is not uncommon for the food stamp program to mean an increase of $1 million in food sales per month in many areas."[87]

The women quickly realized that poverty programs benefited others besides the poor. Supermarket chains stood to profit handsomely from food stamps. "The women saw that hundreds of millions of dollars in food stamps would be spent in this state," says Anderson. "Store owners would be the beneficiaries. Farmers would be beneficiaries. The developers who build the stores would benefit. And where would Safeway take their money? Safeway will take their money to the bank. And so the banks would be beneficiaries."

With a new sense of confidence, the CCWRO women called the National Association of Grocers in Washington, D.C., in the spring of 1973. "Look what the food stamp program would bring you," they told the association's director. "You must come up or write a letter to the Ways and Means Committee." He was only too happy to oblige. "The food stamp program is the greatest program in the world," the director said. "It's a shame that you don't have it in Nevada." The grocers' lobby contacted its Nevada members—including the largest supermarket chains in the West—and provided CCWRO with the names of store managers throughout Nevada. The women contacted them, asking them to write letters to legislators advocating food stamps.

The Nevada senate was deluged with letters from supermarket executives. "They were ten times more forceful than the models we had prepared," Anderson says with a twinkle. "They spoke about the tremendous wealth that we had, and the benefits of this program. It would bring tears to your eyes how concerned these men were for the plight of poor women and children." They also noted that the state would profit from sales taxes on every food stamp purchase.[88]

In April 1973, the Nevada legislature passed a bill bringing the federal food stamp program into Nevada, the very last state in the union to do so. Senator Floyd Lamb walked out of the chamber to offer Duncan his congratulations. "You won," he told her. "I was so happy I literally cried right there," Duncan recalls. But when the silver-haired senator told Duncan she could now return home, she shook her head. "Y'all could change your mind any time," she said, laughing. "I'm not going home until *you* go home." Besides, she noted, George Miller had the final say about food stamps—who got them, and when.

Lamb, a gruff ex-cowboy, coolly sized up the woman who'd been his adversary for so long. Then he offered her his arm. "OK," he told Duncan, escorting her up to his office. "Let's go up and call him." Lamb had a reputation for being a ladies' man, Duncan says, so she made sure to keep his door open. But the powerful Finance Committee chair was true to his word. "George Miller," he roared into the phone, enjoying the moment. "What about the food stamp program? Ruby's sitting here and she wants to know when you're going to start working on it." Lamb told Duncan to stick around for a meeting on food stamps the next morning. She stayed for weeks. "I would sit in the back of the room while George and all them was down at the front," she says. "And if I shook my head no, they would say, 'George, go back over that again. I don't think you got it quite right.' I really enjoyed lobbying then."

"I love being aggressive," Duncan says. "Aggressive is my middle name. But I can be as sweet as anybody let me be. I can be as good as anybody let me be. Or I can be very, very ugly. And so therefore I choose in between. A little sweetness, and a little ugliness. And somehow I wiggle through."

She corrects herself. "*We* wiggle through."[89]

Ruby Duncan returned to Las Vegas with the trophy she'd promised her community—federal food stamps—and a reputation as a player in Nevada politics. Previously seen as little more than a street agitator, Duncan had come to be recognized by some county, state, and federal officials as an authority on poverty issues and as a savvy, influential lobbyist.[90]

Duncan's months in Carson City had changed her. The battle for food stamps had taught her how to marshal business executives, Legal Services attorneys, grass-roots organizers, federal funders, and in-your-face lobbying to bring essential services to poor Nevadans. Operation Life had made a good beginning. But the Westside had so many more needs, and the federal government—despite deep cutbacks by the Nixon Administration—still offered a glittering array of programs to meet them. Newly confident in her ability to bring federal antipoverty programs to Nevada, Duncan was determined to turn the federal tap fully on. Twenty years after she and thousands of others had made that hopeful journey from the Delta, Ruby Duncan had finally figured out how to make the desert bloom.

CHAPTER 7

"WE CAN DO IT AND DO IT BETTER":
REVITALIZING A COMMUNITY FROM THE BOTTOM UP

*Operation Life, the new baby of the welfare struggle, was put
together for survival.... What had been mothers' dreams came true.*

—Ruby Duncan, "Welfare Mothers Push for Justice,"
Operation Life Community Press, January 29, 1974

The Cove hotel quickly became a legend in its own time. There had never been
a building hotter, colder, damper, or darker. "It never rained in Las Vegas—
except when we were in the Cove Hotel," recalls David Phillips. "It rained constantly. And the building leaked like a sieve." The first winter in the Cove was
one of the coldest in the city's history. Snow fell on the Las Vegas Strip, while
inside the hotel, women bundled on sweaters and blankets. To make matters
worse, pipes inside the old hotel burst regularly, flooding the office. "People
would arrive at the Cove to do their morning's work and suddenly you would
hear a torrent of water rushing," recalls Marty Makower. "It was always a little
spooky going back through the hotel to try to find the leak, because it was big
and vacant." You never knew who you might run into. Homeless people had
been sleeping there for years. Some remained even after Operation Life took
over the building. The smell of their cooking fires would hang in the hallways.[1]
    When it wasn't bone-chillingly damp, the Cove was suffocatingly hot.
During the summer of 1973, temperatures in Las Vegas reached 115 degrees.
Clients hoping for help with their welfare or Medicaid benefits dripped with
sweat as they crowded onto two threadbare sofas in the Operation Life waiting area. The organization had no money for air conditioning, says Makower,
so, "when it was hotter than blazes, electric cords ran crisscrossed everywhere
from little fans set up to keep people breathing." The heat was so intense that
even the Cove soda machine stopped working. "Now if the pop machine had
sense enough to stop working, we shouldn't have been working either," says

Operation Life veteran Leola Harris. "But we came in every day because we loved it. We loved that we could help kids."[2]

The Operation Life office was "surreal," recalls Diane Guinn, who came to work as a grant writer in 1973. A life-sized, cardboard cutout of Sammy Davis Jr. dominated the front. People patted his head as they walked by. Keno boards still hung on the walls. "In a five-story hotel with all those rooms, we were all crunched in one teeny, eight-by-ten office with all the file cabinets," Guinn recalls. "We were crawling over people. It was very dark, and very dingy." Rising up from the chaos was a gleaming, new photocopy machine. "State of the art," says Guinn. "The women loved that machine. It was a beauty. It was the heart of the operation." Behind the office was a cavernous, empty casino and bar. Sometimes the Operation Life staff would retreat from the heat to the little Naugahyde booths. Chatting and laughing, they could almost hear the faint chimes of long-gone slot machines, the tinkle of ice in glasses, the horns of late-sixties disco.[3]

The daughter of a Las Vegas bartender and a coffee-shop owner, Guinn knew first-hand about racial tensions in Las Vegas. Her school was segregated, and so were the clubs where she and her friends danced during the late 1960s. One black friend who worked at a club she liked wouldn't dance with her there because he was afraid he'd get fired. "It just wasn't done," she says. Guinn, then twenty-two, had just graduated from the University of Nevada when she wandered into the Clark County Legal Services offices looking for an interesting job. Duncan was there, working with Anderson. "What are you doing?" Duncan asked her. "I'm job hunting," Guinn said. "No you're not. You're starting for me Monday." Guinn stayed at Operation Life for the next fifteen years. "It was exciting because you felt like you were part of the *zeitgeist* of the time," says Guinn. "That's a great feeling for anyone to have. You're a part of what's in."

Versie Beals, Operation Life's secretary, was the first face one saw at the Cove. She sat at the front desk and answered the phones. Smiling that slow, infectious smile, Beals set people at their ease—and held the office together. She ordered and kept track of office supplies, opened the mail, and wrote the checks. She also defused heated situations, talking an agitated young mother down from her panic or soothing a tough street kid who seemed ready to explode. Beals was the first one to arrive in the morning and the last one to leave at night. Sometimes she trembled as she turned her key in the lock. Jackson and D was still a rough place. "Kids would break in all the time, climb over the fence, break the window, go through our pop machine," she says.[4]

By the summer of 1973, Operation Life was abuzz with activity. Essie Henderson, treasurer, huddled with young mothers who were having trouble with welfare caseworkers. She and the other self-described "ladies" of Operation Life also ran food stamp workshops, explaining eligibility rules to AFDC recipients, the elderly, the unemployed, and the working poor. (Nationally, only 23 percent of those entitled to food stamps applied for them.) Down the hall, three dozen children played in the Operation Life childcare center, carved out of the old bar and casino. Nearby, teacher-trainees from the University of Nevada tutored middle- and high-school children.

At the old registration desk in the Cove lobby, teenagers with Youth with A Purpose checked their clipboards before setting out to survey Westside residents about crime and how to prevent it. The group, composed of at-risk youths, was directed by the Reverend Albert Dunn, an on-again, off-again Duncan ally. The reverend also organized a series of public discussions with judges, lawyers, and ex-convicts about the criminal justice system and how it affected the poor. These talks were held in the old Cove showroom, newly renamed the PanAfro auditorium. Icons of black pride were everywhere, from portraits of Martin Luther King Jr. and Coretta Scott King to idealized depictions of African goddesses and posters lauding "black excellence" in the schools.[5]

In an adjoining Cove room, volunteer John Dombrink worked with students to write and publish the *Operation Life Community Press,* a lively, monthly gazette of news, interviews, consumer and legal tips, and political analysis. Billing itself both as voice and resource "for the poverty community," the *Community Press* devoted each issue to a special concern of the poor. One enumerated the rights of poor defendants in the county, state, and federal court systems, printed addresses and telephone numbers of Clark County Legal Services attorneys, and detailed the services that those lawyers performed. Another issue traced the checkered history of public housing in Las Vegas. A third examined redlining, the refusal of banks to lend money in poor, minority neighborhoods. The *Community Press* printed forms for small claims court filings, housing grievances, and consumer complaints, explaining how to fill out the forms and file claims. It printed eviction notices, and explained to tenants what to do if they received one.

In an innovative departure from traditional letters to the editor, the newspaper launched the "Operation Life Line" which took telephone messages twenty-four hours a day, enabling Westsiders to discuss their "reactions to laws, law enforcement, courts, government agencies or anything that gripes you." The lifeline, the editor noted, was for people who "don't have the time to write a letter to the newspaper."[6]

BRINGING FEDERAL DOLLARS AND SERVICES TO THE WESTSIDE

Support for Operation Life poured in from near and far. Georgia civil rights activist Julian Bond, an admirer of Duncan since the Strip marches, flew to Las Vegas to host a fundraiser for Youth with a Purpose. Nevada's Catholic bishop, Joseph Green, lauded the group. And newspaper writers waxed effusive: "Jackson and D was the rotten heart of the Black Ghetto," wrote the *Las Vegas Review-Journal* in 1973, "a textbook example of the civic cancer eating the vital center of so many of America's cities.... Last summer it was saved, or at least brought back from the dead. New shops have been opened, buildings have been painted, women and children are busy on a dozen different projects.... No longer is it a sex, drug and crime scene. This surprising turnabout was accomplished not by the Federal Government, the state or the city but by a most unlikely partnership between mothers on welfare and a financial institution."[7]

But with all this, the Westside still did not have a single medical facility where poor children could get treatment. Even as they worked on the Cove, the women dreamed of opening their own clinic. Seeds for that idea were first planted at the 1972 National Welfare Rights Organization convention in Miami, when Essie Henderson, Alversa Beals, and Ruby Duncan heard Beulah Sanders talk about a new federal program called Early Periodic Screening and Diagnostic Testing (EPSDT). The program provided funds for physicians to perform free medical screenings of poor children. The women listened carefully. Medical care for poor children on the Westside was practically nonexistent. Many of the Operation Life founders had children with medical problems that had gone untreated. Thousands of other poor families in Las Vegas, and throughout Nevada, were in similar straits.

Five years earlier, a national study by the U.S. Department of Health, Education, and Welfare had found that between 10 and 25 percent of American children from low-income families suffered from untreated orthopedic, neurological, vision, hearing, mental, and emotional conditions. President Lyndon Johnson cited that report in a speech to Congress in 1967 asking for a new medical program to detect, prevent, and treat major illnesses in poor children. "We must provide help to strengthen a poor youngster's limb before he becomes permanently disabled," Johnson said. Popular support for the War on Poverty had ebbed. Congress was not in a mood to authorize expensive new poverty programs. Still, few elected officials wanted to go on record as voting against care for sick children. Johnson's Early Screening program passed easily in 1967, becoming one of the last legislative victories in his War on Poverty. Getting the program up and running was another matter. As with so many other federal poverty programs, the states dragged their feet, and federal

Operation Life earned accolades from civil rights leaders near and far. Here Georgia activist (now NAACP chief) Julian Bond, arriving in Las Vegas in 1973 to raise funds for the group's Youth with a Purpose program. (Courtesy of Ruby Duncan)

officials were reluctant to pressure them. The deadline for states to begin screenings was July 1969. Few met that goal.[8]

Early medical screening for poor children in most states did not become a reality until welfare rights activists sued in federal court. In 1972, federal judges ordered the states to begin screening poor children by the end of the year, for the first time opening up the possibility of regular medical care for millions who had never had it. Congress appropriated money for each state to hire outreach workers to publicize the program and encourage poor mothers to bring their children to the new government-funded clinics. At the 1972 National Welfare Rights Organization convention in Miami, Beulah Sanders described the Early Screening program and encouraged welfare mothers to apply for the outreach jobs.[9]

Excitedly, Henderson, Beals, and Duncan returned to Las Vegas and told Jack Anderson about what they'd learned. EPSDT had been so poorly publicized that Anderson, a poverty lawyer with expertise in federal programs, had never heard of it. The women were particularly pleased with its focus on prevention. Beals's daughter had suffered from an untreated eye disorder that left her nearly blind. Many Westside women had similar stories to tell. The 1966 HEW report, which Sanders described at the convention, confirmed what they had long suspected: poor children were far more likely to become seriously ill than children who visited doctors regularly.

The women had wanted better medical care for their children since leaving cotton country. Now, after two decades in Las Vegas, they finally saw their chance. They had learned in the food stamp battle that they needed powerful allies. During the winter and spring of 1973, the women called on medical professionals and politicians to bring Early Screening to Nevada. The Clark County Medical Association came on board, welcoming a chance to expand the number of patients it could reach in Las Vegas. With the help of Clark County doctors, Operation Life was able to convince physicians' groups across the state to support the program. George Miller opposed Early Screening, claiming that "Nevada already provides the highest quality of medical treatment for the kids and for the mothers on welfare." When his Medicaid director decided to support the program, however, Miller withdrew his formal opposition. After all, the EPSDT program was 100 percent federally funded.[10]

But Miller made no secret of his dislike for the program. Poor mothers "overdoctored" their children, he said.

> If a welfare mother had a kid with sniffles, she'd take him out to the doctor. If I had a kid with sniffles, I'd give him a cold tablet.

Operation Life provided medical care to a higher percentage of eligible children than any federally funded Early Screening clinic in the nation. Here is the clinic's outreach team: Essie Henderson, Alversa Beals, an unidentified woman, Mary Wesley, an unidentified woman, Joann Byron, and Dorothy Jean Poole, in the late 1970s. (Courtesy of the Las Vegas Sun*)*

> You *don't take your kid to the doctor because you know it's a cold and they're going to get over it, so why give up the money. There was no point in them* not taking the kid in because it was available to them for free.

Miller made plans to bring the program to Nevada but, privately, he vowed to monitor the clinics closely.[11]

The women of Operation Life immediately asked for the contract to conduct outreach for the Las Vegas clinic, which was to open in the spring of 1973, staffed by physicians from the Clark County Medical Association. The doctors said they'd consider hiring Operation Life, and invited the women to present their outreach plans. In the weeks leading up to the meeting, Anderson and Sister Carole Hurray of the Franciscan Center conducted role-playing exercises in which they pretended to be the doctors, while the Westside mothers explained why they should get the outreach contract. The Operation Life women were already known and trusted on the Westside, they argued. And they were willing to ferret out any child who needed medical care. As the day of their meeting approached, however, the mothers grew increasingly nervous. They were going toe-to-toe with rich, white doctors; their own pitifully lacking educations never seemed more glaring. "*We can do it and we can do it better*. We would say it but we didn't always believe it," Anderson recalls. "Fortunately we never admitted this to one another.[11]

The Medical Association doctors opened the April 1973 meeting by talking about money. They had a contract from the state Welfare department to open a clinic and would be paid $32 for every child they screened. The physicians were open to the idea of hiring Operation Life to do outreach, but they wanted the women to sell themselves. Why should the clinic hire them? What did they have to offer? Although the women had expected those questions and had carefully prepared answers, something about the way the doctors had begun the session irritated Essie Henderson. The doctors hadn't described the services they would provide. They had simply stated how much they would be paid. "What kind of examinations are you planning to do for the children?" Henderson asked, her voice disarmingly sweet. "Health exams," one doctor snapped, barely disguising his disdain. Anderson looked over, saw Henderson's eyebrows arch, and took a deep breath.

From that moment on, he says, Essie Henderson ran the meeting. "Will you measure each child?" she asked. "Yes," one of the doctors replied. She put on her glasses and recorded the men's answers on a clipboard. "Will you weigh the child?" Yes. "Are you going to measure their heads?" Yes. "Will you do vision screening?" This time the doctors hesitated. Henderson asked again: "Will you do vision screening?" "Well, we haven't thought about it," one of the doctors said haltingly, "but yes, I think we would." Without missing a beat, Henderson asked, "Will you use a Snellen eye chart?" The doctors just looked at each other. Consulting her notes, Henderson asked if they planned instead to use some other new eye-testing equipment she'd read about. She showed one doctor the article she'd been reading. Clearing his throat, he replied, "Well, I don't know. We'd have to think about that."

Anderson studied the faces of the women. Henderson was all business.

Duncan was sizing up the room. Versie Beals stifled a smile. Henderson looked down at her notes, then raised her head and continued. "Will you develop a hematocrit?" she asked. There was a long pause. "Yes," one doctor finally replied. "Will you be testing for sickle cell?" she asked. The doctor nodded. "Yes, we'll use the hematocrit for that," he replied. "What's the threshold you'll use?" Henderson asked. "Did you read Dr. Paul's article that they're getting a lot of false negatives and false positives on that test? That they're suggesting that electrophoresis really is better?" The doctors fell silent. Anderson says that he could see them sweat.[13]

The ranking physician stood up, signaling that the meeting was over. The Clark County Medical Association, he said, would like Operation Life to submit an official proposal describing its outreach strategy and what it expected to be paid. The doctors ushered the women out the door. "We'll get back to you in a few days with a decision," they said, closing the door behind them. The women were excited, although a bit worried that they had alienated their prospective employers. "But after about five minutes," says Anderson, "the women understood that the docs knew nothing about this program except that they were paid $32 per child. The women realized that they knew more about this program than the docs did." Henderson just wanted to see how much these doctors cared about the children they were proposing to serve. "And that," says Anderson, "was a test the doctors failed."

Anderson and the Operation Life women developed a plan, and submitted it as promised, two days after the meeting. When weeks passed with no word from the Clark County Medical Association, the women asked Anderson to call. It was an awkward conversation. The physician made pleasantries for a while. Then he delivered the bad news. A screening clinic had already been opened across town at Sunrise Hospital, he told Anderson, and Operation Life would not be needed to do outreach. Anderson watched the women deflate as he told them the news. Then Henderson piped up: "Why don't we visit the clinic and see what they're doing over there?" The women already knew one essential fact about the Sunrise clinic: it was nearly impossible to get to from the Westside. It would take three transfers to reach the clinic by bus. Given the city's substandard bus service, that could take three hours. Whomever else this clinic was supposed to serve, it was clearly not intended for the children of the Westside.

The women piled into Jack Anderson's car, drove from the Westside to the white side of town, and strode into their city's only EPSDT clinic. Henderson asked if she could speak to the medical director. "He's not in," the receptionist said. Henderson asked by name for each of the six doctors listed as clinic staff. Not one of them was there that day. "We're being considered as outreach workers," Henderson said. "Would it be all right if we watched a screening?" The receptionist made a phone call, and a clinic aide came out to take the women to an examination room where a white child was being screened. Henderson began taking notes. The child was asked whether he could hear a tuning fork ring. When he nodded, his ears were pronounced sound. The screener then applied a tongue depressor, looked briefly at the child's teeth and declared them fine. After they had watched several examinations, the women began questioning screeners about their credentials. "And, what's your title?" the women asked. "I am an audiologist," one screener replied. "What training do you have for that?" "Oh, they just hired me a few days ago. I'm a housewife and they showed me how to do this." The women thanked their hosts, filed out of the hospital and drove back to the Westside.

None of them had seen a physician anywhere in the clinic. They hadn't met many nurses working there, either. And the clinic workers they'd spoken with told the women that they had been certified by the state to conduct EPSDT screenings after minimal training. Most had been stay-at-home mothers before taking these jobs. "You know," Henderson said, looking around at her friends with a twinkle in her eye, "we could do that." The women thought about that for a second, says Anderson, and then they began to talk all at once. Maybe they could open a clinic on the Westside. Maybe they could hire welfare mothers to conduct outreach *and* screenings. "We're going to do it," Henderson said firmly. "We're going to run a clinic."

The women got back to the Cove and set to work. They pored over EPSDT regulations and literature to see what illnesses they should screen for and what lab tests they would have to conduct. Renee Diamond and Pat Van Betten, a local nurse and Operation Life supporter, helped them find names of labs and physicians to consult. Cost was a key question. Although federal researchers had estimated that EPSDT screenings could cost as much as ninety-seven dollars, the Nevada legislature had allocated just thirty-five dollars per screening. And George Miller had decided that the state would pay no more than thirty-two dollars per child. The women called hospitals, commercial laboratories, physicians, nurses, optometrists, and dentists.

In just a few weeks, the women learned volumes about the economics of for-profit health care. When one Las Vegas hospital laboratory quoted them a fee for a single lab test that was more than the entire thirty-two dollars per child allotment, the women grew discouraged. Perhaps this wasn't going to work after all. Wait a minute, one of the women said. Why not send the blood and urine samples to out-of-town labs? Furiously, the women began calling labs throughout the Southwest, until they found one in Los Angeles that agreed to run a whole battery of tests for less than the first lab wanted to charge for a single test. That was the emotional turning point, Anderson recalls. Once the women knew they could afford the lab tests, they began to hatch detailed plans for the clinic they did not yet have. They created a price chart for services, called physicians to solicit donations of used medical equipment, and located African American doctors and dentists who agreed to work for a minimal fee.

Few observers thought the women could pull it off. "People laughed when we said that we were going to do an EPSDT program," Jack Anderson recalls. Even his colleagues in poverty law were incredulous. "Jack, you've been smoking some bad dope," they told him. "How in the world are these women going to operate a health screening center? They've got sixth-grade educations and you're going to turn them loose on Las Vegas?" At the very least, critics said, a failure by Operation Life would make it harder for other grass-roots organizations to run their own clinics. Anderson was unperturbed. Children on the Westside presently had no medical facility at all, he replied. It seemed worth a try for that reason alone. "These women deserve an opportunity. And they can't fail, because they're going to learn something."

Besides, Anderson told skeptics, it was not his place to tell clients what they could and could not do. "When Ruby and the women come in here and want to do something, I just pretend that they have laid a $10,000 retainer on the table. When they ask 'Can you help us?' I respond as any red-blooded American attorney would. I say 'Certainly.' What they want from Legal Services is our best advice. They don't come here for me to tell them they don't have the capacity to do something. They can make their own assessment as to whether they can do it."[14]

Two months after the Clark County Medical Association turned them down for an outreach contract, the women of Operation Life had everything they needed to open their own clinic in the Cove. On August 27, 1973, the Operation Life Community Health Center opened its doors—the only EPSDT screening center in the United States run by as well as for poor families, and the first medical facility to open on the Westside, more than thirty years after large-scale black settlement began there during World War II.[15]

The Operation Life clinic was funky. But it was theirs. The women rehabilitated a suite of rooms on the ground floor of the Cove for a storefront

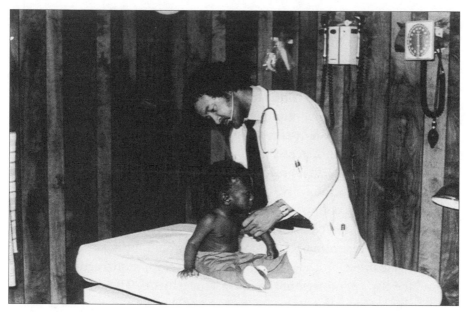

Doctor Garnet Ice, chief medical officer for the Operation Life clinic, examines a baby at one of the newly renovated Cove hotel rooms, 1974. (Courtesy of Glendora Washington)

clinic. Over the entrance was emblazoned Operation Life's motto: "For the Poverty Community, in the Poverty Community." The medical director was a black physician named Garnet Ice. The chief dentist was James McMillan, a founding member of the Las Vegas NAACP, and someone who had long been skeptical about Ruby Duncan and her militant tactics. As word of the clinic got out, a growing number of medical professionals volunteered their time. By year's end, a team of physicians, nurses, dentists, and optometrists was treating neighborhood children in the same spot where, two years earlier, drug dealers had hired children to make deliveries.[16]

Operation Life's Jackson Street clinic offered screening, diagnosis, and treatment for ADC children, blind children, foster children, and mothers under the age of twenty-one. The clinic offered patients every service that federal regulations would allow: heart scans, tuberculosis tests, screening for sickle cell anemia (a disease prevalent among African Americans), eye and ear tests, and dental care. Henderson had gone over the regulations with a fine-tooth comb, and realized that EPSDT offered treatment for physical problems that were not covered under Medicaid. Many children on the Westside could get dental and eye care for the first time. Over the next few years, the Operation Life clinic screened more than ten thousand children. Eighty percent of them needed dental work. Half had never seen a dentist in their lives. Four out of every ten children who came to the clinic needed eye care. One in three had a physical ailment serious enough to require a physician's treatment.[17]

The Operation Life clinic soon screened 80 percent of all eligible children in Clark County, the highest outreach rate of any EPSDT clinic in the U.S. And it served an unprecedented number of needy children at a time when many EPSDT clinics were underused. A remarkable achievement, said other clinic administrators. Common sense, the Operation Life women replied. In a community that had long had no medical care, it stood to reason that every child needed to see a physician.

Nowhere in the country were federal EPSDT outreach funds used more effectively than on the Westside. Essie Henderson, Versie Beals, Mary Wesley, and a changing cast of neighborhood women would meet each morning at the Cove, pile into Dorothy Jean Poole's beat-up old station wagon, and drive around the city's poor neighborhoods seeking patients. They knocked on every door and refused to take no for an answer. They roused depressed mothers and sleepy children and drove them to the clinic for checkups. When a woman would say "I've got too many children. I can't do this," Versie Beals would reply, "If I can get my eleven kids out the door, you can get yours down to the clinic." Sometimes, says Beals, "we would have to dress the children ourselves and drag them out the door."

No other EPSDT clinic in Nevada came even close to Operation Life's rate of disease detection, a statistic dourly noted by doctors at the rival Sunrise Hospital Clinic, run by the Clark County Medical Association. Less than two years after it opened, the Operation Life Community Health Center was screening 250 more children per month than all other EPSDT clinics in Nevada combined, treating fully 60 percent of the state's eligible children. Its success catapulted Nevada, long near the bottom of the list for its medical care for children, to the very top, with treatment rates ten to twenty times higher than those of New York and California. Congress twice lauded Operation Life for running one of the most effective EPSDT clinics in the nation. Even hawkish Casper Weinberger, then Secretary of Health, Education, and Welfare under President Gerald Ford, held up Nevada's EPSDT program as exemplary.[18]

With new credibility among city and county officials, the women of Operation Life set to work on another long-held priority—to open a public library on the Westside. At first glance, the women conceded, a library might not seem as important to the community as food, shelter, or medical care. But, growing up in cotton country, many Westside adults had been unable to complete school. "I only learned to read and write a little bit," Versie Beals says with a hint of shame. Ruby Duncan, too, felt keenly how a lack of education limited her. "If I could write," she liked to say, "I'd be really dangerous." The women of Operation Life wanted to ensure that their children would not be held back in the same way. Westside residents had been asking county library officials for years to open a branch in the black community. A mobile library van visited the neighborhood twice a month. Clark County Library officials thought that was sufficient—people on the Westside, they contended, just didn't read that much.

Ruby Duncan felt that such policies were rooted as much in racism as in contempt for the poor. Black children in Las Vegas schools were treated disrespectfully by teachers and administrators alike, Duncan's children say, and physically disciplined for minor infractions. Duncan's older daughter, Georgia Phillips, was repeatedly dragged down the hall on her knees to detention because her skirt—which she shared with her younger, shorter sister—was too short for the school dress code. She still has scars on her knees from the experience.

"We never saw white children mistreated, just us," Phillips says. Both of her older brothers were similarly mistreated at their high school and organized sit-ins by black students in protest. Not to be outdone, Georgia Phillips led a sit-in at her junior high school. "We got tired of being treated like nothing," she says. "So we demanded respect. They closed down the school one of those days. They sent all the white children home and kept us on the lawn. There were police with guns." She shakes her head, still amazed. "We were just young kids. They brought police for a bunch of 13-year-olds."[19]

By 1973, Westside children and teens were helping to set the agenda for their mothers' activism. With nearly everyone jammed into tiny, overcrowded homes, study space was a key issue for the children. Everyone but the Clark County library district seemed to agree that the Westside needed a community library. The women's first response had been direct action. Westside mothers and children held a series of "read-ins" at city libraries in white neighborhoods. They got uncomfortable stares, but no move was made to open a branch on the Westside. The women filed a lawsuit against the Clark County library district, but it went nowhere. By mid-1973, the women of Operation Life decided on a different tack. They decided to open a library of their own.

Women who had, for too long, heard themselves described as without intellect or culture now created an intellectual and cultural center for their community. "We didn't have time to argue with the other side of the community that called us dumb and stupid," says Duncan. "The only thing we were after was to . . . make sure the children were able to have this service in their community." Their children needed more than a safe, quiet place to read and study. They also needed to read books, hear music, and see films and plays that gave them a sense of belonging and pride. Well before the University of Nevada began to offer courses in African American studies, the Operation Life women raised enough money to amass the largest collection of African and African American studies books in the state, covering black history, culture, and politics. "It was just like giving food to our children," says Duncan. "They were hungry and we wanted to feed them."[20]

The women had the books. Now they needed a physical space for their library. Once again, they approached General Taylor with a proposal. Would he give them another abandoned Westside building, this time for a library? The general was intrigued. If Operation Life got the go-ahead from the Clark County library district, he said, First Western would provide the building. Library officials told Duncan that the new library would have to meet certain standards if it was to become part of the county library system. If the building was brought up to code, the library district would rent it from Operation Life for $1,200 monthly. The women were elated. If this worked, they would not only have a community library, they would also be earning the first return on their labors—rent for a building they owned: not government program dollars or private foundation grant moneys, but legitimate business income.

First they would have to reclaim another derelict building from the wrecker's ball. And this building, across the street from the Cove, was in terrible shape. The wallboard was full of holes. The building lacked a full cement foundation. The women contributed sweat equity, but they needed funding to hire earthmovers, masons, and electricians. Nervously, they went back to General Taylor. To their delight, he agreed to underwrite foundation and electrical work, and he convinced three other local banks to pitch in money for building renovations. At a time when banks were under attack for their unwillingness to invest in poor communities, turning an abandoned building into a library could only bring good publicity. Taylor came to the Westside—with a police escort—to visit the Cove and inspect renovations at the proposed library site.

The opening of the Westside's first library, in December 1973, was a grand affair. Versie Beals and Mary Wesley cooked chicken, collard greens, rice, pinto beans, and tea cakes for a crowd of hundreds. The women of Operation Life celebrated both a victory for the children and what they hoped was the organization's first step toward economic self-sufficiency. The rent they received from the library district would first have to go toward repairing and maintaining the building. But, eventually, the women hoped it would help support other Operation Life programs. After years of bleak Christmases, these Westside mothers had finally given their children a present that mattered. Westside youngsters now had a place to study, among ten thousand books selected to celebrate black history and culture. The community had a gathering place full of comfortable seating nooks and fresh new meeting rooms. And a group of welfare mothers were the owners of the building. Sometimes Duncan had to pinch herself.[21]

The new West Las Vegas library was filled with people day and night. The county supplied four librarians, including Nevada's only black male children's librarian. Operation Life ran tutorial programs for school-age children, and a daily story hour for younger children. The building was open until eight each evening, so that middle- and high-school students could have a place to study after school hours. The building, which had meeting rooms and an auditorium as well as stacks, soon hosted community meetings, family reunions, African festival days, and Thanksgiving dinners for five hundred. Heavyweight boxing champion and conscientious objector Muhammad Ali came to visit. He talked to a crowd of children and adults, signed autographs, and praised the community's determination in creating the library.[22]

As Operation Life grew larger and more complex, the organization needed a skilled office manager. Duncan found one in her cousin Aldine Weems, a woman of many talents. Weems had migrated from Tallulah to Las Vegas as a girl and had completed high school in Las Vegas. As a result, she had better literacy and math skills than did Operation Life's founding mothers. A single mother of three, Weems was on welfare between 1966 and 1968. She asked caseworkers to enroll her in a state-sponsored training program for welfare recipients that would allow her to attend college, but was repeatedly told that she was not qualified. Weems asked Duncan for help. Duncan made phone calls and asked questions, and eventually Weems was admitted to the program. In a city where African Americans made up 10 percent of the population and 40 percent of the poor, fewer than 4 percent of those in the program were nonwhite. Weems made the most of the opportunity. Graduating with a two-year college degree, she was hired as a secretary in a federal agency in Las Vegas.

In 1973, when Weems lost her job as a result of federal budget cuts, Duncan pulled her into Operation Life. "You've got some skills that I know we don't have," Duncan told her, "office skills." Weems agreed to work part time.

"Within a few weeks I was working eight-hour days and some nights," she later recalled. Weems's position at the Cove meant more to her than an ordinary job. When she was offered her government job back, she turned it down. "I just couldn't leave. When you get into this and good things are happening and you're a part of it and you're helping people . . . you just don't walk out on it." Weems's ability to research, write, and manage people soon made her invaluable to Duncan.[23]

While Weems streamlined and professionalized operations at the clinic, the youth programs, and the daycare and feeding programs, Duncan, Anderson, and the women discovered a panoply of new federal programs they wanted to apply for. "There was a world of possibilities out there from the federal government," Diane Guinn recalls. Duncan and the other women would leave notes full of suggestions on the desks of grant writers Guinn and Makower. "A one-page memo became a three-week nightmare for us," Guinn laughs.

Duncan wanted to forge a direct relationship between the federal government and Operation Life, sidestepping the state wherever possible. The Comprehensive Employment and Training Act (CETA), passed by Congress in 1973, enabled Operation Life to hire poor Westsiders for a previously unthinkable number of jobs. A few years later, more than one hundred women and men worked as Operation Life CETA workers, visiting homebound elderly, tutoring schoolchildren, providing job counseling, and working on the community press, among other tasks.[24]

Guinn's first dramatic success came in January 1974, when the U.S. Department of Agriculture gave Operation Life more than two hundred thousand dollars to run the first Women and Infant Children (WIC) nutrition and medical program in Nevada. In the early 1970s, a series of studies was published showing that pregnant and breast-feeding women and infants were among the highest-risk groups in the country for malnutrition, and that existing federal food programs were not meeting their needs. In September 1972, Congress voted funds to create WIC, providing protein-rich food, nutrition education, and medical screening to low-income pregnant women, lactating mothers, and children under the age of five. But President Nixon signed the bill grudgingly, and well into 1973, no funds were released. "Nixon was trying to stop WIC from coming into being," says Guinn. "So they were making impossible regulations for state officials."[25]

While USDA officials dragged their feet, the Food Research and Action Center (FRAC) in Washington, D.C., filed a class-action lawsuit on behalf of a small group of poor mothers. Duncan got a call from Ronnie Pollack, the lead attorney for Operation Nevada, who was now working for FRAC. He asked her to join the suit, and she, as well as one of Versie Beals's daughters, agreed. On August 3, 1973, the court ruled in favor of the plaintiffs, ordering the federal government to release WIC funding to states across the country. "We weren't the only ones fighting for this, but we were in the first group that made the WIC program happen, anywhere in the country," Duncan says proudly. Winning the WIC suit thrilled Duncan because she believed her actions would improve the health of poor mothers across the United States.[26]

But, once again, Duncan had to wrestle with state officials to bring a federal poverty program to Nevada. To receive WIC funds, states had to submit an administration plan to the U.S. Department of Agriculture. "Nevada had no intention of applying," says Guinn. It was the only state in the U.S. that did not. "So we not only had to do our part, we had to write the state part too." Operation Life wrote a WIC plan for Nevada, lobbied the legislature to accept it, then applied to the federal government to run its own WIC clinic. In January 1974, Operation Life received word from Washington that it had won a federal grant to open a Women and Infant Children nutrition program on the Westside—one of the first WIC clinics in the U.S., and the first in the country run by poor mothers themselves.[27]

"It was a great feeling to know that these women and children were getting milk, cheese, peanut butter," Duncan recalled. "All this high-protein food is very important for the body of a pregnant woman, or for a child, or for an infant." With WIC funding, the Operation Life clinic could now hire obstetricians and gynecologists, offering care to pregnant women and lactating mothers. During the first month, the WIC clinic treated 1,400 families; within a few years, it was providing food to 5,000 families.[28]

The Operation Life WIC program provided jobs as well as food and nutritional advice for poor women. Federal regulations required WIC eligibility screeners and nutrition educators to have a high-school degree, which excluded most of the founding mothers of Operation Life. But WIC opened up opportunities for young women in the community who could read charts, perform eligibility calculations, and write reports. The program ushered a new generation of Westside women into Operation Life, both as workers and as clients. "The mothers who came in there were treated with respect," says Beals's daughter, Glendora Washington, for many years a WIC worker at the Cove. "They liked that. It wasn't just the food. Going into Operation Life felt different than other social service offices."[29]

Duncan invited reporters to tour the new Operation Life WIC clinic. "West Las Vegas has a high rate of anemia, low-birth weights and infant mortality, and good food will correct this," Duncan told them. Adding that protein is vital to brain development, Duncan predicted that WIC would also improve Westside children's school performance. And a full schedule of pre- and postnatal exams would enhance mothers' health as well. Before the WIC clinic opened, she said, too many pregnant women in West Las Vegas got no prenatal care at all. Now that would change. Both on the Westside and nationally, Duncan's optimistic predictions were borne out as incidences of low birthweight and infant mortality dropped among participants in the program.[30]

Mary Wesley's daughter might have died without the Operation Life WIC clinic. She was seven months pregnant when the clinic opened and had yet to see a doctor. At her first exam, she was found to be severely anemic and a carrier of sickle cell anemia, a life-threatening disease. Clinic physicians launched an intensive treatment program to strengthen her before she gave birth. She received six shots a week, Wesley recalled, all free of cost, and mother and baby emerged healthy. Wesley, who had previously shown little interest in the clinic, was enormously relieved—and electrified. She jumped into clinic work with the zeal of a convert, knocking on doors and urging mothers to bring themselves and their daughters in for exams. Eventually, Wesley became Operation Life's health access coordinator, informing poor women about their rights to healthcare and where to get it.[31]

The WIC clinic brought enormous satisfaction to the Operation Life women. Duncan could almost see the children in her community grow stronger, healthier, and brighter-eyed. But the sickly mothers and children who came into the clinic every day made clear that hunger was still widespread on the Westside. Federal school lunch and breakfast programs fed adolescents and teenagers during the school year, but during summer months, the women knew, many children did not get enough to eat. In 1974, Operation Life applied for USDA funding to feed poor schoolchildren during summer break. With federal backing, the women provided fifteen thousand lunches that year. Impressed by the success of the Westside program, the USDA continued funding Operation Life's summer lunch program for a decade, providing upwards of two hundred thousand meals in total.[32]

As the mercury climbed that summer, the women sat in the Cove and tallied their achievements. They had given their community essential food, medical care, a library, and a community center. But what about a little fun and relief from the heat? There were no public pools on the Westside, although summer temperatures routinely exceeded one hundred degrees. The only city-funded pools were in white neighborhoods. Operation Life women approached the Southern Nevada pool builders' association, which agreed to donate labor and materials to refurbish the Cove hotel pool—a donation that amounted to over ten thousand dollars. Operation Life reopened the pool to great fanfare, as neighborhood youths flocked to it in droves.

"The Cove Hotel had been written off by many as an abandoned ghetto structure," the *Las Vegas Review Journal* enthused in June 1974. "Now it has been revitalized and is a popular spot for children to swim and to receive the nutritional hot lunches they may not be able to get at home." Versie Beals was hired to cook hot meals for 250 children a day. "My grandkids was in the bunch," she says happily. "And my sister's kids. Everybody that you knew, all the kids was there. And they could walk there. The kids would just stay there all day and we would watch them swim. Night times we would have to close the pool. But the kids stayed to the last minute. They never did want to leave."[33]

STILL STRUGGLING TO SURVIVE

For every victory, though, there were always more battles. Ruby Duncan and allies had to fend off George Miller's constant attempts to scuttle the food stamp program. Applicants "were flooding in like vultures to the kill," Miller claimed. People were trading in the stamps for cash, he said, using the money to buy liquor and illegal drugs. It was time to launch another statewide investigation, this time to root out food stamp fraud.

Welfare administrators in many states were behaving in much the same way. In the fall of 1974, Operation Life joined a lawsuit by poor mothers from seventeen states who alleged that state Welfare departments were illegally denying food stamps to millions of eligible citizens. The suit charged that state Welfare departments had so completely failed to publicize the program that a majority of those eligible did not even know it, and caseworkers were harassing applicants so severely that many ultimately gave up. In 1973, seventy percent of Americans eligible for food stamps were not receiving them, and $280 million appropriated for the program went unspent. The mothers won the lawsuit, forcing Nevada and other states to begin publicizing the food stamp program a decade after it was passed by Congress.[34]

That same year, Duncan took her battle to bring federal programs to Nevada onto the campaign trail, running again for Nevada Assembly. The odds were long because redistricting forced her to run in a predominantly white, conservative district. She ran on the Bread and Justice ticket along with Maya Miller, who ran for U.S. Senate, and Mahlon Brown, who ran for Justice of the Peace. Politically, Operation Life could not affiliate with the campaign, but the mothers of Clark County Welfare Rights worked hard for the candidates, as did their children. "It was so exciting for us," recalls Beals's daughter, Renia Glasper. "It was the first time we thought we could have a say in who got elected." But only Mahlon Brown emerged victorious.[35]

Ultimately, Duncan lost by three votes, and she would never again run for public office. But the campaign marked a turning point on her road from rabble-rouser to legitimate political actor. She broadened her base of political allies in the state, making common cause with Democrats who agreed that the state had needlessly soured its relationship with the federal government. The race also helped establish Duncan as a liaison between federal agencies and Nevada communities, a role that she cultivated as she worked to bring a raft of federal programs into her state and city.

Duncan's New Year's message for 1975 was triumphant, reflecting her sense of how far she and her band of Westside mothers had come in just a few years. "The accomplishments of the women who make up the Clark County Welfare Rights Organization have been startling," Duncan wrote in her "Ruby Says" column. "Four years ago they were welfare recipients struggling just to survive. Today they operate their own welfare programs, own an $80,000 building, and are attempting to purchase a five-story hotel worth several hundred thousand dollars." In many ways, she wrote, the poor mothers of the Westside owe their success to George Miller's "excesses." Before 1971, most welfare recipients were afraid to fight. "The mass termination ended their fears. They had nothing to lose and everything to gain by organizing and demonstrating against the bureaucrats who abused them."[36]

The community came to see the women-run Cove as just that: shelter from the storm. In a state where hysterectomies were performed on poor women at eight times the national average, poor women in Las Vegas knew they would receive quality medical attention at the Cove, with a wide array of birth-control options and no coercion. In a state where caseworkers were trained to deny people assistance, Operation Life founders expertly navigated families through the social services labyrinth. But welfare advocacy was volunteer work. No public agency or private foundation was willing to fund social workers without high-school degrees.

Duncan's reputation, however, was growing with each Operation Life success, and that would soon translate into grant dollars. She was flying around the world, climbing the ladder professionally and politically—with no more education than the other women, and that created some tensions and jealousies. She was flown to Moscow for an international women's peace conference, and asked to speak to community healthcare providers across the U.S. about the success of the clinic. In 1975 Duncan was a delegate to the International Women's Conference in Mexico City, where she talked with women from Africa and Latin America about healthcare for poor mothers, job training, and food programs. She returned from her travels to write about what she had learned: that despite a world of differences, many of the issues faced by poor mothers transcended national boundaries.[37]

"She came back from Moscow a wiser person," recalls David Phillips, who was then in college.

> We sat for hours talking about what she saw. She'd seen the so-called Red Terror, and she realized something she called the politics of poverty, which is international. Because here we were saying: If we don't cut down on welfare and increase military spending, the Soviets will be in our backyard. After a few nights of not having eaten, we'd think: Let the Soviets come. Maybe they'll bring some bread.

David asked his mother: Is there really something to be afraid of? "It's just the fear of the unknown," she told him. "We don't have anything to fear. There are poor people there as well as here."[38]

Duncan herself survived on a modest income. Despite her acclaim, she lived on dribs and drabs of money from speaker's fees and temporary grants. She got a small stipend from NWRO until the group folded in 1975. But for all intents and purposes, she and the other Operation Life women were dedicated volunteers. It bothered Duncan immensely that the women who had worked with her from the early days of Clark County Welfare Rights Organization still were not earning enough to enable them to break free of public assistance.

"*Soon we're going to be off of welfare. When the money comes in.* That's what we would always tell ourselves," Mary Wesley says. "That's why we worked so hard, worked our heads off and our hearts off because we wanted to get off welfare. But when money did come in, my check was so low I still qualified for welfare." Duncan wrote scores of letters to churches and philanthropies, trying to raise money to give the women salaries. But the grants were always temporary and never enough to live on.[39]

Without decently paying jobs, the women of Operation Life, like millions of other poor mothers, would never be able to move off public assistance. By 1975, Duncan was ready to move into high gear on the issue of jobs. Now vice-chair of the Clark County Democratic Party, Duncan went to Carson City for the 1975 legislative session with greater clout than she'd had two years earlier. As before, she pushed for an expansion of welfare benefits, but now she had an even more ambitious agenda—she wanted the state to develop job training and placement programs for poor mothers and to provide subsidies for quality daycare centers. And her eye was on Washington as well. As the country prepared for the first presidential election since Watergate, Duncan hoped that her new position in Nevada Democratic politics might enable her to project her voice beyond Carson City to the national stage.

"DON'T CREATE JOBS THAT I DON'T QUALIFY FOR"

Political winds were shifting, Duncan realized, and in ways she had not expected. By the mid-1970s, Washington had become a less friendly place for antipoverty activists than it had been a few years earlier. But years of political work in Nevada seemed finally to be yielding fruit in Carson City. When Duncan, Beals, Henderson, and Maya Miller testified before the Nevada senate in 1975, asking for increases in monthly AFDC grants, the response was dramatically different than it had been two years earlier. Finance Committee Chair Floyd Lamb made an eloquent speech in support of a welfare increase, telling astonished colleagues that he didn't see how families could possibly live on Nevada's meager AFDC grants. While a satisfied Ruby Duncan watched, nodding her head at every positive vote, the Nevada legislature authorized a 20 percent increase in monthly welfare grants. It wasn't as much as Duncan had asked for, but it was the first time since the state initiated its ADC program in 1955 that legislators had voluntarily increased allotments.

"It was so beautiful to see legislators listening to poor people and expressing honest concern," Ruby Duncan wrote in her column afterwards, "no confrontations, no arguments, and no distorted facts. Just a group of poor people, welfare administrators, and some honestly concerned legislators who were all talking about making life better for Nevada's needy families." The change in attitude, Maya Miller told reporters, was a direct result of years of lobbying by Ruby Duncan and other Nevada welfare mothers who had finally shaken loose some of the stereotypes held by men like Lamb and also by many middle-class women. "Welfare is a women's issue," Miller said, echoing Johnnie Tillmon. Poor mothers are "the very baseline of the movement for equality and elimination of discrimination toward women."[40]

Energized by their victory in Carson City, Miller and Duncan turned their attentions to national politics. Amidst a national recession, as the economy contracted after a two-decade war, President Gerald Ford had slashed the AFDC budget and tightened eligibility requirements, ordering states to collect child support from absent fathers or lose federal aid dollars. He asked Congress to raise the price of food stamps, from one-fifth of a family's monthly income to one-third. Finally the president asked Congress to eliminate the WIC supplemental nutrition program.

Operation Life stood to lose everything its founding mothers had fought so hard for: the Women and Infant Children nutrition program, food stamps, job training, public service employment, even poor women's right to retain Medicaid on jobs that did not give them medical coverage. Duncan urged Nevadans to call their representatives and condemn the cuts. "No fancy economic theories will convince hungry families that less food is really helping them," she wrote in her column. The president was trying to save federal dollars "at the expense of feeding hungry people."[41]

Frustrated at being so far from the center of political power, and hoping to influence welfare policy and legislation, Maya Miller moved to Washington, D.C., in the spring of 1976. There she helped to create Women's Lobby, the first organization in the nation's capital devoted full-time to lobbying on women's issues. Miller invited Duncan to join her in trying to secure adequate welfare benefits, job training, and employment rights for women; reproductive rights; and greater support for victims of violence. Duncan jumped at the chance and flew to Washington to join her friend and mentor. The two made quite a sight in the Capitol. Duncan, always flamboyant, sported a large Afro and brightly colored African dresses. The diminutive, silver-haired Miller wore woven Guatemalan skirts and Birkenstocks. Together, the unusual pair of lobbyists tried to convince a mostly white and nearly all-male Congress to provide incentives for employers to hire poor women in well-paid, traditionally male fields such as construction, industry, and tourism. They knew they were waging an uphill battle, but Duncan thoroughly enjoyed the journey.[42]

In the spring of 1976, the two women got a chance to address the Democratic National Platform Committee. The party was gearing up for the presidential election, and the likely candidate, Georgia governor Jimmy Carter, was interested in fresh ideas about welfare and employment. A self-proclaimed New Democrat, he was eager to court the votes of women and blacks. Maya Miller spoke first, explaining what was then a new concept: "the feminization of poverty." Of the nation's 24.3 million poor, she told them, 19.6 million— over 80 percent—were mothers and their children. Poverty programs of the past had failed, she said, because they had focused only on male breadwinners. A successful poverty program would have to include flexible hours, benefits for part-time workers, and federally subsidized childcare.

"Welfare can be viewed as a great way to live," Duncan told delegates, "if you died yesterday. However if you are alive, it is the most humiliating experience you will ever suffer." The Democratic Party had participated in stereotyping welfare mothers, she said. Now that welfare mothers were active in the party, perhaps they could see that such a strategy was self-defeating.[43]

Welfare mothers wanted to work, Duncan said. It was policymakers, employers, and trade unions who had labeled them unemployable. Nixon's Work Incentive (WIN) Program had turned millions of poor mothers away, refusing to train them because they had too many children. Union hiring halls in Las Vegas refused to hire poor mothers, even when there were openings, because most union jobs not requiring a high-school degree were considered "men's work." The jobs that are earmarked for poor women across the U.S.— maid work, clerical work, kitchen work—will not pull a family out of poverty, Duncan told the DNC. "The Democratic Party must develop a national policy for full employment that includes us."[44]

One month later, Duncan testified before the Senate Finance Committee, which was considering full employment legislation for the first time since World War II. The Humphrey-Hawkins Full Employment bill had strong support from the AFL-CIO and civil rights groups. Coretta Scott King and NAACP chief Benjamin Hooks testified shortly before Duncan. Duncan found a more respectful audience than she had expected, perhaps because the senators were surprised that a welfare rights advocate was asking for jobs.[45]

"We want to work," Duncan said. She scanned the faces of committee members, looking especially for the chairman, Louisiana senator Russell Long, who had been so dismissive of Johnnie Tillmon, and who had called welfare mothers brood mares. "Count us in when developing a policy for full employment," Duncan said forcefully. She paused to make eye contact with Long, who seemed to be listening. "Don't create jobs that I don't qualify for. Remember that traditional qualifications of white and male exclude me. A job that forces me to abandon my children to the streets is not acceptable. A job must provide a decent wage so that health care and child care are possible."[46]

Congress should finally recognize the economic value of women's labor in the home, Duncan said, and factor it into full employment policy. Government grants to women who stay home to raise children should be seen as fair compensation for performing one of society's most important jobs: raising the next generation. "Employment for all will not occur overnight," Duncan concluded. Mothers' stipends would provide an economic buffer for women who cannot work because they have young children or who cannot find work in hard times.

"We like to believe in the bootstrap theory," Duncan said, looking straight at Senator Long. "But remember, it is a cruel jest to tell a bootless person to pick herself up by her own bootstraps." Welfare mothers are not born, Duncan said. "Most welfare mothers have been discriminated into welfare and then discriminated against for being there. We have always been ready to move out, but the barriers have to be replaced with bridges. Let us today start the building."[47]

Perhaps emboldened by her newly amicable working relationship with Nevada's Senate Finance Committee chairman, Floyd Lamb, Duncan decided to buttonhole Senator Long the next day. She stationed herself between his office and the Senate chamber. "I paced the hallway until he came out his office," she recalls. "He was on his way to go vote down on the floor." Duncan took a deep breath and said quickly, "Senator Long, how are you? We are both from the same home state and I'd like to talk to you about the issue of poor women in America." Duncan had expected him to push right past her, so she was caught off-guard when he said: "Yes. That's a good idea." Duncan offered him a business card and asked him to call on her to speak when his committee was considering welfare or jobs legislation for poor women. To Duncan's surprise, he did.[48]

Over the next year, Duncan testified before the Senate Health and Labor Committee, the Budget Committee, and the Economic Opportunity Committee, as well as Long's Finance Committee. Duncan's message was consistent: "It's time people in Washington realize that if you can get good jobs with good pay, we'd be happy to get off welfare. . . . People are tired of having welfare officials tell them how to run their lives, when they can get sick, how much food they can eat. We want to rule our own lives. We want a piece of the American pie. We want jobs that will provide our families with a decent life."

Duncan soaked up the atmosphere and language of Capitol Hill. "When I was done talking," she says, "I would stay in those hearings, and I would sit where I could get the attention of the people on the committees. And I'd shake [nod] my head if I liked what they said, so they'd know it was right." Maya Miller recalls one welfare reform hearing in 1976 where Duncan got the attention of the two deans of Senate welfare politics, Russell Long and Daniel Patrick Moynihan. They both had fairly retrograde ideas about women and work. Moynihan was deeply ambivalent about the idea of mothers working outside the home at all. Long worried that welfare enabled poor women to avoid taking low-wage jobs. Even so, says Miller, "both senators understood that the population for whom welfare is the basis was women with their children." And by the mid-1970s both men were talking about how poor women needed jobs. Each time one of them called for putting welfare mothers to work, Duncan would try to catch their attention and nod vigorously. After a while, she says, "they would look at me to see if I was nodding."

After one hearing at which Long had taken positions that Miller and Duncan saw as starting points for negotiation, Miller said to Duncan, "Let's go out and talk to him." Long was pleased when he spotted Duncan. "I thought I must be saying something right," he said wryly, "because I saw you nodding away." Then he shook his finger in mock reproach and said: "I remember years ago when we had hearings on welfare, you were one of those women who shook their fists and me and said 'We're not going to iron your shirts, Senator Long.' So I thought, well there's somebody now who's agreeing with me."[49]

Duncan knew that Long was not really an advocate for poor women. He worried about Southern labor shortages and tried to block jobs programs that might limit the supply of low-wage labor, while Duncan fretted about poor women being stuck in low-wage jobs, without healthcare coverage for their children. He fought federal work programs that paid more than the prevailing Southern wage for menial work, while she resisted workfare or training programs that forced poor mothers into dead-end jobs. And yet, Duncan sensed that Long could be an ally on jobs for welfare mothers. And she understood the symbolic importance of forging even a temporary alliance with such a well-known foe of welfare rights.

It was a smart call. Described by President Ronald Reagan as "one of the most skillful legislators, compromisers, and legislative strategists in history," Long was one of the most powerful senators of the twentieth century. A Southern Democrat first elected in 1948, the year of the Dixiecrat rebellion led by Strom Thurmond, Long shared many of the class and race prejudices of his fellow white Southern elites. Still, his father—the legendary Louisiana governor, senator, and maverick presidential candidate Huey Long—was no ordinary Southern patriarch. Russell Long echoed his father's calls for greater income equality in the U.S. During fifteen years as chair of the Senate Finance Committee, he worked on tax reform to benefit working families, most notably the earned income tax credit. Was Long genuinely drawn to Duncan's calls for a piece of the pie for welfare mothers? Perhaps. Or maybe he was enough his father's son to recognize the political possibilities of making common cause with a black, feminist welfare mother from his home state. Long and Duncan shared little ideologically, but both were masters of political theater, and both enjoyed upsetting the status quo in the halls of power. In the late 1970s, the two crafty Louisianans developed an oddly convivial working relationship. Winning Long's ear was one of Duncan's most interesting and politically unlikely achievements.[50]

"I GOT TO SIT IN THE PRESIDENT'S CHAIR": A WELFARE MOTHER IN THE CARTER WHITE HOUSE

Duncan's influence in national Democratic Party politics reached its peak when she attracted the attention of the party's rising star—former Georgia governor Jimmy Carter. By the spring of 1976, Carter was on a fast track to the party's nomination for president, and he wanted to put Nevada in his column. To win Nevada, the black vote would be crucial. Carter had just gotten himself into hot water with black voters in April 1976 by saying, in answer to a reporter's question about public housing, that people should be allowed to maintain the "ethnic purity" of their neighborhoods. It took him several days to apologize for the remark, and in its wake, he redoubled his efforts to win black voters' support.[51]

So when his advisors suggested that he meet Ruby Duncan, the black vice-chair of the Clark County Democratic Party, Carter ran with the idea. The candidate and the activist both turned on the Southern charm for the occasion. But it quickly became clear that there was genuine rapport between the former peanut farmer and the former cotton picker. Duncan told Carter and his wife Rosalynn about Operation Life and the programs it had brought to the Westside. She got the impression that they were really listening. "Jimmy Carter is a straight down home person that cares about other people," she wrote in her column. "He wants to provide jobs for those who want to work and uniform benefits for those who cannot work." Though she had previously been supporting the presidential candidacy of Idaho senator Frank Church, Duncan switched her allegiance. "Speaking of candidates of your choice," she wrote, "Jimmy Carter is mine."[52]

That summer, Duncan, Essie Henderson, Versie Beals, and several other welfare mothers were elected delegates to the Clark County Democratic Convention, where they helped to pick the Nevada delegation to the Democratic National Convention in New York City. Duncan was voted chair of the Nevada delegation. She declined in favor of former governor Grant Sawyer but held onto her seat on the floor of Madison Square Garden. She wanted to be there to cast a vote for Jimmy Carter for president.[53]

As they had in 1972, the women of Operation Life decided to attend the convention as a group. To raise money for the trip, they baked and sold tamales, tea cakes, and sweet potato pies. In July 1976, several Operation Life women and their children took a Greyhound bus to New York City. They shared rooms in a midtown hotel and took in the sights, both on the convention floor and around the island of Manhattan. Duncan took the opportunity to reacquaint herself with the candidate and his family. She was impressed when they addressed her by name and asked specific questions about Operation Life.

The next day she became an exuberant, if unexpected, poster woman for the Carter campaign. "They were coming around to get our votes on one of Carter's resolutions," she recalls. "And the music was so beautiful that I got up and I was standing there waving my arms. I said, 'Come on. Everybody get up.' People on the other side of the aisle got up. After a while I heard zing, click click. It was the press. They said, 'Don't stop. Keep doing it.' I said, 'Everybody get up. I don't want to be up there dancing by myself.'" The next morning a closeup of Duncan's face, dancing with her Carter placard, smiled from newsstands across the city.[54]

After the convention, Duncan returned home full of the fervor of the party faithful. She launched a fierce and furious voter registration drive in the city's poor neighborhoods, assuring black and Latino voters that Carter was a candidate who cared about poor people. The candidate's daughter-in-law, Judy Carter, came to visit the Operation Life offices at the Cove. Versie Beals was asked to show her around. She tried to get out of it. "Oh No. I can't talk. I'm almost tie-tongued," she said. Beals stumbled over her words at first, telling Carter: "I can't talk. I hope you understand." But Carter seemed impressed, even excited by what she was seeing. "She told us how Jimmy set up a whole system of mobile health care units that would travel through Georgia to take care of people," Duncan recalled. Then Beals herself got excited and poured out the story of how she and the other women had created the clinic. Talking about what poor women could do if they put their minds to it, Beals says, "I wasn't ashamed any more. I was proud."[55]

The upcoming election, Duncan told Westside voters, represented an unprecedented chance for poor people to have their concerns heard at the highest levels of American politics. But it would not happen, she warned them, unless they turned out at the polls. "Politicians listen to labor members because they're registered and they vote," she said. "Politicians listen to men with big pocket books and not to people like us, because they are registered and they vote. . . . To help our community become as it should be, a dream I've held for many years, your help is needed."[56]

Duncan got out the vote for Democratic candidates that fall like an old-fashioned urban boss. The women of the Westside were her machine. They provided rides to campaign meetings for elderly people, cooked food for prospective voters, and printed up educational literature. "Politicians say poor people don't vote so why should they listen to their cries for justice?" Duncan wrote. "It is time that we unite, stand up and show them we are here." It is vital for "every living, breathing, warm-blooded human being between the ages of 18 and 118 years to register to vote." Leaving nothing to chance, Duncan and the Operation Life women drove people to city offices to register and took them to the polls on election day.

When Jimmy Carter returned to Las Vegas toward the end of the campaign, Duncan was invited to speak with him. "I was late," she says. "His staff was getting kind of nervous. When I walked in, they said, 'Oh good, there's Ruby.' And the first thing he did—I will never forget this—he broke from everybody and he ran over and put his arms around me. He hugged me." Photographers took a picture that Duncan displays to this day, of a smiling Jimmy Carter with his arm around Ruby, their faces close and beaming. Her story—up from the cotton fields to become a dynamic provider for the poor—fit well with Carter's New Democratic politics of personal renewal.[57]

As a candidate, Jimmy Carter had promised to enact sweeping welfare reform. He liked Duncan's focus on giving welfare mothers jobs, a message that pleased conservatives as well as liberals. Her alliance with Senator Long burnished her image as a maverick among black activists. And Carter seemed to like her personally. In November 1976, shortly after his election, Carter invited Duncan to Washington to a brainstorming session he was hosting for community development groups. "The first thing Carter did when he got elected was have meetings with low-income people from throughout the United States," recalls Duncan. Participants felt that Carter was genuinely interested in what they had to say. "There were all kinds of community development people there and we were all excited thinking about what we wanted to do," Duncan says.

That January, she was one of a handful of Nevadans invited to attend Carter's inauguration. "I still can't believe it," an incredulous Duncan told reporters that winter. "If people had told me a few years ago that I could be at-

By 1976 Ruby Duncan was vice chair of the Clark County Democratic Party. During the 1976 presidential campaign she was visited in Las Vegas by candidate Jimmy Carter, who hoped that the black vote might prove crucial in swinging Nevada into his column. (Courtesy of Ruby Duncan)

tending a Presidential inauguration, I would have thought they were crazy.... We now have a President who is willing to work with all types of people while in office. He is a man of the people, genuinely concerned with their needs." Simply by treating her with respect and warmth, Carter convinced Duncan that he was different from his predecessors. "Low and middle income people, women, minorities—all the cast-asides of our populace, have never been able to have a rapport with a president prior to Carter." His election, she told allies in Nevada, would yield important breakthroughs in poverty policy.[58]

She was both right and wrong. Duncan's belief that she had a personal connection with the new president, her hope that his serious-minded wife would open up new opportunities for women, and her euphoria that the poor were finally being listened to, were strikingly reminiscent of the feelings that many working-class women activists expressed at the election of Franklin Roosevelt, forty-four years earlier. Like those earlier activists, many community leaders who flocked to Jimmy Carter's side in 1976 would end up disappointed by the limited gains they were able to achieve during his presidency. And yet there *were* real gains and—for a few short years—Ruby Duncan, a poor black single mother, had access and influence at the White House. That, in itself, was extraordinary.

The new president cared about poverty and sought counsel from a wider range of Americans than most previous presidents. Like Roosevelt, Jimmy Carter synthesized the ideas of varied activists into creative fiscal and employment policies. Carter would also try to jump-start a sluggish economy through large-scale investment in public service jobs. He more than doubled spending for jobs and training programs, and shifted their focus increasingly toward what the Department of Labor described as "the most disadvantaged groups in our society." And Carter did seem genuinely interested in finding ways to open up job opportunities for women.[59]

Jimmy Carter's personal gestures to Duncan and other community activists in those early days of his presidency may have been more symbolic than politically substantive. But the First Family's public performance of listening to the poor mattered; it marked a significant departure from the Nixon-Ford years. "I thought he was a very warm man and understanding," Duncan recalls. Six years earlier, Richard Nixon had invited Johnny Cash to sing "Welfare Cadillac" in the White House. In 1977, Jimmy Carter invited Ruby Duncan to the Oval Office.

"It was the first time I had ever been in the White House, in the Oval room," she says. "The president was having a meeting with his Cabinet members. There he was, sitting in this big chair." Duncan, never shy, asked Carter if she could sit in his chair. The most powerful man on earth stood up and beckoned her to do so. "So I sat in the President's chair," Duncan says, still marveling. It was as close to real power as she had ever come. She chatted briefly with Carter and his advisors about her ideas. For that brief moment, Duncan felt, real change for poor women seemed possible.[60]

Duncan knew her way around Washington by the time she had her moment in the president's chair, and she knew how difficult it was to bring about substantive change. On the other hand, her own trajectory inclined her to believe that anything could happen. Even before Carter's election, she had been asked by the director of the Work Incentive Program (WIN) to consult with the U.S. Women's Bureau to share her knowledge of the obstacles facing minority women in low-wage jobs. After Carter's election Duncan would work even more closely with Alexis Herman, the young black labor activist appointed by Carter to run the bureau.[61]

By the time Duncan began working with the Women's Bureau she had come to believe that women's poverty was rooted in the gender segregation of the labor force. Breaking down those walls was key to improving the condition of poor mothers. A woman could work her whole life as a maid or in a laundry and never lift her family out of poverty. Strong unions, such as the

Hotel and Culinary Workers Union in Las Vegas, certainly improved wages and benefits for hotel maids. But Duncan wanted to see "nontraditional" work opened up to poor mothers: union jobs in heavy manufacturing, in construction, on highway crews, in prisons, as custodians in hospitals, prisons, and schools. The best union jobs in the tourist and entertainment industries, she pointed out, had historically been reserved for men—as parking valets, lighting techs, and stage crew workers. "We are not asking to be hired as college professors," Duncan told Department of Labor officials and members of Congress. But there was an array of private and public sector jobs that did not require a college education and that were unfairly closed to women. Duncan urged the federal government to create incentives and imperatives for employers to hire poor mothers.

She also pushed Congress, the Small Business Administration, and other federal agencies to support poor women seeking to open small businesses. "Within the next six months," she wrote on the eve of the 1976 election, "poor women and black women are going to be heading strongly in the area of economic development. It is important that we don't get left out when government and men are talking about jobs, business, development and the like."[62]

In the first years of the Carter presidency, Duncan saw progress on those goals. In a series of landmark employment bills passed in 1977 and 1978, Carter and Congress doubled the number of public service jobs available under CETA; reached out to private employers, establishing Private Industry Councils to promote training and placement for the chronically unemployed; and expanded youth training programs, opening training slots for hundreds of thousands of young people in their own communities.[63]

Duncan haunted the halls of the Department of Labor, urging officials to prioritize poor women. She made sure that she was at the table when federal officials developed goals and timetables for female and minority participation in the construction industry. She pushed for equal employment opportunity for poor mothers in apprenticeship and training. And she consulted with Women's Bureau chief Alexis Herman in identifying the barriers that kept poor mothers from earning enough to support their families. Using data from the Las Vegas hotel, restaurant, construction, sanitation, highway maintenance, plumbing, and defense industries, Duncan argued that race and sex discrimination, and lack of childcare, were the key factors keeping poor mothers out of jobs that could pull their families out of poverty.[64]

Duncan hoped that the Humphrey-Hawkins Full Employment and Balanced Growth Act, finally passed by Congress in 1978, would open up abundant new resources for job training and placement for poor women. By the time it passed, however, the bill had been so watered down that it bore little resemblance to the original legislation introduced by Senator Hubert Humphrey (D-Minn) several years earlier. The act recognized the right of all Americans to decently paid work, but it was missing the piece most desired by its advocates: concrete government action to achieve full employment. The final bill simply called for "the right to full opportunities" for all Americans who wanted to work. It was a nice sentiment.

Still, Carter's jobs policies were not as empty as critics charged. Between 1976 and 1980, Congress approved a vast expansion of public service employment, job training, and placement programs. These programs not only created jobs but brought a wide range of services to poor communities—translators for immigrants, repairs on dilapidated housing, home aides for the elderly. Carter officials and Congressional supporters attempted to address major shortcomings of earlier poverty policy: insufficient job creation and investment in impoverished communities, and no expansion of job opportunities for women. These were the final salvos in the War on Poverty. These programs were in place just a short time before the retrenchment of the Reagan years. Humphrey-Hawkins became a favorite whipping boy of those who saw big government as, in Reagan's words, "the problem, not the solution." Horrified by the growth of government jobs programs under Carter, candidate Ronald Reagan attacked the Humphrey-Hawkins Act as a "blueprint for fascism" and called for its repeal. Public service jobs dried up quickly after Reagan's election in 1980, and the Reagan revolution shifted American politics so decisively that these significant experiments in job creation were quickly swept from the public memory. But on the Westside, and in hundreds of other poor communities, federal job creation dollars made a difference for a while. And on those still poor streets, memories of groups like Operation Life linger.[65]

During 1976 and 1977, Duncan also worked with Carter's chief welfare advisor, Franklin Delano Raines, to come up with a proposal for a guaranteed minimum income for all Americans. A twenty-eight-year-old African American wunderkind from a poor Seattle family, Raines was brought to Washington by Daniel Patrick Moynihan, who was his professor at Harvard. He did his first presidential briefing, for Richard Nixon, when he was just twenty. When Carter asked Raines to serve as his Special Assistant on Welfare, the policymaker was just seven months out of law school. Duncan was not comfortable with high-powered African American professionals, as a rule, and few people with Raines's résumé paid much attention to welfare mothers. But Raines had grown up in poverty, and Duncan felt he understood her concerns. She spoke candidly with Raines about her ideas for welfare reform, and they continued to confer up to the day before he presented his final proposal to the president.[66]

As introduced to Congress, Carter's Better Jobs and Income Program was not what Duncan had hoped for. It had elements she believed in, most importantly a federally subsidized minimum income grant for the poorest Americans. But the plan contained punitive work requirements for mothers of older children and paid less to single-mother-headed families, no matter what their size, than to two-parent households. There was no significant allocation for federally subsidized childcare. And the proposed maximum benefit of $4,200 per year was not enough to raise anyone out of poverty, Duncan told Congress. Still, she came out in support of the plan, with deep reservations.[67]

Duncan's former allies in the welfare struggle were not so willing to negotiate. Carter's plan drove a wedge between old allies. Poverty activists condemned the proposal for forcing mothers to take dead-end jobs at below-minimum wage. Feminists criticized the plan for paying women a pittance to stay at home rather than providing real work opportunities outside it. League of Women Voters president Ruth Clusen said the proposal reflected an "outmoded conception of who the family breadwinner should be." Ruby Duncan and Maya Miller, who found the plan workable, wanted more generous mother stipends *and* expanded work opportunities. Any support for the bill, critics said, amounted to condoning workfare, anathema in the antipoverty movement. Instead of condemning the plan, Duncan and Miller urged, try to improve it. "Women are the poorest of the poor," Miller wrote. "That is a fact of life stemming directly from the unpaid work of women in the home *and* the low and discriminatory wages of women in the labor force."[68]

Carter's final proposal never even made it to a vote. Like Nixon's first Family Assistance Plan, it was killed by fierce opposition from the left and the right. The time for a guaranteed minimum income proposal, if there ever was one, had come and gone. No president from that time on would even take the idea seriously. Some veterans of the welfare struggle, including NWRO's Johnnie Tillmon, would later wonder whether poverty activists made a mistake by working so hard against the Nixon and Carter plans. Perhaps, Tillmon said, it would have been wiser to rally behind them, even if the proposed monthly grants were insufficient. Activists could have pushed for increases over time. Instead, they lost what may have been their last chance to enshrine in federal law the principle of a guaranteed minimum income for all Americans.[69]

Duncan agreed with Tillmon, ruing yet another lost chance at strengthening economic democracy. By the late 1970s, she was also seeing the truth of another of Tillmon's insights: "Welfare is a women's issue," Tillmon had written in *Ms.* magazine in 1972. "For a lot of middle-class women in this country, Women's Liberation is a matter of concern. For women on welfare, it's a matter of survival."[70]

Duncan had come to feel that "sex means more than race when it comes to income." Poor women, in her experience, stayed poor because they lived in a culture that discounted their value. And her dealings with many black male leaders on the Westside did little to convince her that they had poor black women's interests at heart. As Tillmon had tried to steer NWRO into alliances with the larger women's movement, now Duncan brought poor mothers into the Nevada chapter of the National Organization for Women (NOW). Her ideas for creating new coalitions between poor and middle-class women got her elected to the national executive board of NOW. Duncan championed an Equal Rights Amendment to the U.S. Constitution, and a state amendment in Nevada. Increasingly, her arguments for Operation Life's funding took on a feminist hue. "Ruby never played the race card," says Mahlon Brown. "She played the sex card again and again."[71]

Highlighting gender as a factor in fighting poverty alienated Duncan from just about everyone in Washington, Maya Miller noted:

> . . .the unions and the Department of Labor, who wanted to pretend that poverty was primarily a problem of no jobs for men; the Office of Management and Budget and the Congressional Committees, who saw the price tag for finding jobs for women as mind-boggling; representatives of the racist and sexist southern and wild western states, who fear the consequences of letting black and hispanic women share in their states' affluence; even the coalition of advocates for the poor who worry that welfare reform will never come about if Congress understands how poverty. . . is tied to women and their children.[72]

Still, Miller observed, Duncan wielded remarkable influence in Washington during the Carter years. Few poor black women, at any time, participated in federal policymaking to the extent that she did. It was an uphill battle always, and a lonely one. "The Welfare Reform hearings of 1977 and 78 were rife with white men and women technicians," Miller wrote, "but notably lacking [were] the black women who had been the backbone of the welfare movement of the 60s. . . . It is not easy to keep a presence in Washington for poor black women." Ruby Duncan persevered through sheer determination, but also because she had a keen sense of when to change tacks.[73]

"Welfare doesn't provide the solution, food stamps don't provide the solution," Duncan began to argue in 1977. "They only keep the problem going. We need economic independence." Welfare reform was dead and Duncan was not looking back. She was ready to practice what she called "down-home capitalism" to bring self-sufficiency to Operation Life and the women of the Westside.[74]

CHAPTER 8

CAN WELFARE MOTHERS DO COMMUNITY ECONOMIC DEVELOPMENT?: THE TRIUMPHS AND TRIALS OF OPERATION LIFE

It has come time that women get on with the business of doing business.

—Maya Miller

In the spring of 1976, Las Vegas was rocked by the largest strike in its history, as twenty-two thousand members of the Hotel and Culinary Workers' Union walked off the job. The strike was sparked by decades of frustration over hotel owners' refusal to hire or promote black workers into any but the most menial jobs. Seeking a $1.35 per hour raise for the lowest paid among them, thousands of black maids, porters, and kitchen workers slipped out of their uniforms and walked out the front doors of a dozen Strip hotels. White stagehands, bartenders, and waitresses joined the strike, shutting down the Strip. As tens of thousands of tourists left town, the *Los Angeles Times* compared the scene on the Las Vegas Strip to the emergency evacuation of three hundred thousand Allied troops when the Nazis invaded France in 1940.[1]

Hoping to break the strike, Caesars Palace sent managers into the Westside to hire nonunion labor. They found some willing recruits, but to no avail. Five years after Ruby Duncan and the mothers of the Westside marched through the casino at Caesars Palace, hundreds of striking workers—many of them African American—blocked entrances to the hotel to keep out strikebreakers. Caesars lost millions before the strike was settled, half a million dollars from one canceled convention alone. By the end of the two-week walkout, Caesars, like every other major hotel in Las Vegas, granted raises to their lowest paid workers.[2]

It took considerable courage to strike in Las Vegas. The 1976 strike was not only the largest but the first major strike in the history of the Strip. Powerful labor unions had been as integral to the growth of Las Vegas as gambling, drinking, and desert sunshine, but the tacit agreement between labor and management was that there would be no strikes. There were many reasons why local union president Al Bramlet ended up dead in the desert less than a year later, but the 1976 strike did not endear him to less savory figures in management. "People had a way of ending up face down in the desert," Duncan says. "That was the mob's idea of problem solving."[3]

Many Operation Life women were among the strikers, and the Westside rocked with celebrations when the union won its demands. But, even as they cheered the strikers' victory, Duncan, Essie Henderson, Mary Wesley, and Versie Beals laid plans to pressure the hotels for a wider range of jobs for black women. A quarter-century after most of the Operation Life women came to Las Vegas, the vast majority of black women in Las Vegas were still working as maids, laundry workers, and kitchen help. Poor women wouldn't need federal jobs programs if unions and management made room for them in mid-level positions, Duncan declared. "We don't mind hard work and we wouldn't mind climbing the ladder," she wrote, "if it would get us somewhere."[4]

A 1971 federal court decision by Judge Roger Foley had ordered the city's largest hotels to open upper- and middle-level jobs to women and minorities. Eighteen hotels agreed to comply, and to publish quarterly reports indicating the race and sex of every employee they hired. Five years later, 80 percent of minority women and 89 percent of black women working on the Strip were still employed in low-paid service positions. "Look at our town," Duncan wrote. "We have hundreds of good paying jobs such as bartender, bell 'boy,' door 'man,' stagehands, security guards, etc.—and no women have any of these jobs." As soon as the 1976 strike was over, Operation Life set out to place poor women in some of those jobs.[5]

In the fall of 1976, Duncan and Reverend Al Dunn mounted a publicity campaign to draw attention to hiring practices on the Strip. Each week they published damning statistics from the Strip hotels' quarterly reports in the *Las Vegas Voice*. They invited Governor O'Callaghan, Judge Foley, Nevada legislators, and state officials to the Westside to explain to black voters why they were not withdrawing the gambling and liquor licenses of hotels that were flagrantly violating the 1964 Civil Rights Act and Judge Foley's orders. Turning up the pressure, Duncan and Dunn issued press releases calling on tourists to boycott Strip hotels, whose policies they compared to those of the Jim Crow South.

"Las Vegas Hilton Making Progress—Toward White Supremacy," Dunn and Duncan charged in their first press release, which the *Las Vegas Voice* ran in its entirety. At the time of the 1971 consent decree, all Las Vegas Hilton managers were male and all but nine were white. Five years later, the Las Vegas Hilton management was still all-male and, though the hotel had hired fifty-five new managers, all were white. The Las Vegas Hilton, by far the most profitable hotel in the Hilton chain, had promised in 1971 to "take aggressive action" to move blacks into managerial positions. Yet the results, Duncan and Dunn charged, "could not be worse if they were Bull Connor." Hilton executives were not pleased at the comparison with the Birmingham, Alabama, public security chief who had used police dogs and fire hoses to disperse protestors in the 1963 children's civil rights march.[6]

The most scathing and colorful criticism was reserved for Caesars Palace. The women who cleaned the faux Roman statues, scrubbed mold from the fountains, and vacuumed dust from the red velvet drapes were working in "neo-slavery," according to Duncan and Dunn. "The Roman Empire enslaved women, Africans from across the Mediterranean and neighboring Spaniards," they wrote. "Today there is a new Caesars World. . . . Mops and brooms have replaced chains and leg irons. . . . The new victims, as the old, are women and persons of African and Spanish ancestry."[7]

Strip hotel owners had long insisted that the only reason they did not hire women or people of color in better-paid positions was that there were no qualified applicants. Prejudice, they said, had nothing to do with it. In the fall of 1976, Duncan got her hands on a leaked document that proved otherwise: a secret memo from billionaire recluse Howard Hughes to the chief of staff of his Summa Corporation. Hughes was, at the time, the Strip's largest employer. He owned the Desert Inn, the Sands, the Castaways, the Landmark, and the Frontier hotels. "I know there is tremendous pressure upon the Strip owners to adopt a more liberal attitude toward integration, open housing and employment of more negroes," Hughes wrote. "I can summarize my attitude about employing more negroes very simply—I think it is a wonderful idea for somebody else, somewhere else. . . . The negro has already made enough progress to last 100 years."[8]

Duncan published the memo in the *Voice* in September 1976, when other newspapers refused. The pressure campaign yielded phenomenal results. Less than two months later, Caesars promoted twenty women and men of color to management positions, and launched a management training program for low-level employees. The Las Vegas Hilton and MGM Grand hotels quickly followed suit, as did several other large hotels.

Forming a new group, the Coalition of Low Income Women (CLIW), the women of Operation Life received funding from the Catholic Church to hire poor women as inspectors to monitor these new programs. The CLIW inspectors also conducted a survey among black and Latina mothers in Clark County to determine which hotel jobs they most desired. The women's list of desired jobs included bartender, showroom captain, stagehand, spotlight operator, gardener, truck driver, projectionist, and parking lot valet. In 1977, these jobs, which paid significantly better than maid work, were filled entirely by men—95 percent of them white.[9]

But hotel management was only part of the problem. Duncan and the leaders of CLIW—Essie Henderson and Mary Wesley—knew that they would have to pressure the hotel workers' union to end decades of tacit and active cooperation with the hotels' racist and sexist hiring practices. "Women can drive cars as well as men," contended Joyce Broussard, a young CLIW activist. "A woman can seat people as well as any man. This is clearly discrimination and it has to change."[10]

Change was not easily won. When women went into the union hall to apply for traditionally male jobs, those with union cards were offered housekeeping or kitchen work instead. Women who did not belong to the union were told they could not be considered for jobs until they joined. But they could not get a union card until they were offered a job. Occasionally, one of the Westside women was able to convince a supervisor to hire her as a lighting technician, a stagehand, or a valet. When she returned to the union hall to report her luck, she was told that there were more senior union members who had priority.[11]

The Coalition of Low Income Women announced a new form of protest: a series of "join-ins," during which poor women descended on union hiring halls to try to sign up as members. If the unions did not let the women join, the Coalition warned that it would file complaints with the state Equal Rights Opportunity Commission. Duncan, Beals, Wesley, Henderson, and other Operation Life leaders divided Clark County welfare mothers into twenty occupational groups based on their stated job preferences. Several hundred women signed up. Leaders of each group spoke with union hiring hall dispatchers to find out the qualifications for each job, and the race and sex of everyone they had sent out in the past year for jobs. The women then called job dispatchers several times daily to see if they had any openings. They continued this practice on and off for years.[12]

The women did not limit their attention to the hotels. In 1977 Mary Wesley became the second woman in the city of Las Vegas to be hired as a union sanitation worker. Wesley had dogged the union dispatcher until he could ignore her no longer. "I went out every day for six months before they sent me out," she laughs. Some of her black male coworkers felt that Wesley should not be encroaching on their territory. But the hostility did not last. "The guys wanted to help me do my work," she recalls. She told them she didn't need help. "At home, if I have to move a refrigerator, I do it. Why do I need a man to help me lift a little garbage can?" Everyone asked her how she could handle working on a garbage truck. She smiles. "When I came home at the end of a day on the garbage truck, I was so relaxed, I took a shower and painted the house. When I came home at the end of a day of being a maid, I was so tired I just fell across the bed. I couldn't move. That's when I thought, the mens have so much easier jobs and they get paid so much more."[13]

Mary Wesley's success at infiltrating an all-male trade inspired hundreds of other poor women to do the same. By 1979, the Coalition of Low Income Women had placed more than five hundred women in union jobs. The organization would continue its efforts for the next decade. Over the years, Duncan says, she lost track of how many women they were able to move off welfare and into good jobs around the city. "I still run into them all over the place," Duncan muses. "We proved we could do what the feds kept saying they wanted to do: get welfare mothers back to work."[14]

NOT ENOUGH ACCOUNTABILITY OR TOO MUCH SUCCESS?
WHAT REALLY HAPPENED TO THE WAR ON POVERTY?

While the women of Operation Life were investigating hotel and union officials, George Miller was once again investigating them. He disliked the idea that a group of uneducated welfare mothers was managing large sums of public money. Miller wanted greater accountability, especially at the Operation Life clinic, which received funds directly from the state Welfare department. By 1976, Miller had become convinced that the women were abusing the public trust, and he began taking action to shut down the clinic. The ensuing battle was played out in ways that were quite similar to struggles between community groups and government officials in cities across the country.

Miller was blunter than the social service officials in other states, and more obsessive about rooting out fraud, but his concern about misuse of public moneys was widely shared. From the moment War on Poverty dollars began flowing into poor neighborhoods, state and local officials charged that "poverty pimps" masquerading as community leaders were diverting funds for their own enrichment. Fraud charges, court battles, rescinded grants, and financial audits became weapons of choice for government administrators who opposed channeling public money directly to community organizations. In some cases they found evidence of fraud. In others they did not, but the charges stuck anyway—draining local antipoverty coalitions of energy and political support.[15]

In fall 1976, Miller announced that he was revoking Operation Life's contract to run the crown jewel of their program—the Early Screening clinic. Miller argued that welfare mothers were overusing the Operation Life clinic, taking their children in to see doctors when they were not seriously ill. "There'd be three on welfare that would see a doctor to every one time that a regular family would," he said. In February 1976, Miller informed federal officials that Nevada was pulling out of EPSDT entirely, saying that administering the program had become too expensive. The governor and the legislature supported the decision and were willing to accept the expected penalty: a 1 percent reduction in federal health care funds. HEW officials quickly replied that Nevada would lose far more if it shut down the program. It would lose its entire Medicaid budget, tens of millions in federal dollars.[16]

Miller backed off but announced other drastic cuts in state medical aid to the poor. Nevada Medicaid would no longer cover dental care, mental health, physical therapy, or prescription drugs. "I guess they think poor people don't really feel pain," Duncan shot back. The state had to draw a line somewhere to prevent frivolous use of state Medicaid funds, replied Welfare department counsel Marilyn Romanelli. Welfare mothers were taking children to the doctor to get their toenails clipped, she said. From now on, AFDC recipients who wanted to have their children screened at EPSDT clinics would have to get advance approval from a caseworker.[17]

Testifying before the state Welfare board, Maya Miller and Jack Anderson challenged Miller's claims that EPSDT costs were out of control. Nevada had a $40 million surplus, they said, in part because the state had refused to spend federal dollars allocated for the Early Screening clinics. Unfazed, the Welfare department reported to Operation Life that it was trimming state payments for medical screenings. If the women wanted to keep the clinic open, they would have to agree to the cuts. Duncan and clinic medical director Dr. Garnet Ice stalled for time while they consulted with attorneys and federal officials about their options. Meanwhile, Operation Life's contract with the state Early Screening program expired. Miller announced that the clinic, now without a contract, would have to close.[18]

Duncan turned again, as she had so many times, to the federal government, asking the U.S. Public Health Service to investigate Miller for attempting to sabotage Nevada's EPSDT program. The welfare chief counterattacked, asking the state attorney general to file fraud charges against Duncan and Ice for billing the state as if all children who came to the clinic were screened by physicians, when many were being seen by nurses or lay staff. Duncan and Ice denied the charges, to no avail.[19]

On Thanksgiving day, 1976, Miller padlocked the Operation Life clinic. Duncan decried the act as a "death knell to the black children of this community." She demanded that Miller present hard evidence of fraudulent billing or reopen the clinic. Welfare department counsel Romanelli told reporters that Operation Life was also under investigation by the federal government. Duncan called federal EPSDT officials, who refuted Romanelli's statement, but the clinic doors remained bolted. Once again the Westside was without a medical facility. "We always hear about poor people pulling themselves up by their bootstraps and Operation Life was doing just that," Duncan wrote. "But no, the state won't have it. So they take your only boots."[20]

The courts had, in the past, proven strong allies against the state Welfare department, so Duncan decided to sue Romanelli and Miller for libel. It was a mistake. Her case was assigned to Howard Babcock, a judge who strongly opposed federal intervention in state affairs and who had ruled against black plaintiffs in earlier school desegregation suits. Babcock unceremoniously threw out Duncan's libel charge, warning her not to bring it again. "Do you remember the days when we were in the streets, screaming, marching and yelling to get real programs for poor people?" a dispirited Duncan asked supporters waiting outside the courthouse. "I was told, 'Now wait a minute Ruby, all this is not necessary. Why don't you stop all this and work within the system instead of always fighting it?' So I did. We negotiated, we compromised, I smiled and entered into agreements with the powers that be in good faith. I have been continuously harassed every step of the way."[21]

In the last weeks of 1976, Duncan and Ice were indicted for conspiring to defraud the state. Renee Diamond, Operation Life's treasurer, who was white and married to a well-known casino manager, accompanied Duncan to court. Diamond wanted to provide support, and she wagered that her presence might help ease the court's hostility toward a black welfare mother who had challenged the state at every turn. "They were brutal to Ruby," Diamond says.

Marilyn Romanelli was so vituperative in her accusations against Duncan that, according to Diamond, the judge told her to present the evidence and "stop performing for your boss in Carson City." That didn't stop Romanelli from making unsubstantiated charges out of court. Maya Miller remembers the Welfare department counsel ridiculing Duncan on the TV news, "saying that she drove a Cadillac at taxpayer's expense." (Duncan drove a Buick, and it was not paid for by Operation Life.) Diamond wondered why the state would invest so much energy trying to close a clinic that treated poor children. Maya Miller thought she knew: "Ruby had become a real symbol of challenge to George Miller's way of running the state's welfare programs." (Romanelli now says she cannot remember the case.[22])

The personal attacks in court and on the news, and Duncan's fear that the clinic might never reopen, wore her down. The poverty activist was only forty-three years old, but a lifetime of poor nutrition and a decade of political struggle had taken their toll on her health. One day, after being grilled on the stand for hours, "Ruby collapsed and had to be carried out of the courthouse," Diamond says. "She took it all physically. It almost destroyed her. I never thought she'd come back from that." But Duncan quickly rallied. George Miller was willing to "destroy good things in an attempt to destroy me," she told reporters. "I won't die, George. I learned to survive a long time ago."[23]

Duncan pulled every political string she had, from the Clark County Commission to Capitol Hill, to reopen the Operation Life clinic. "Taxpayers are always screaming for welfare mothers to get up and do something productive," she wrote. "We have done that here without any help from the State. I won't stand by and watch the efforts of so many hard-working poor women go down the drain because of a few men who believe in only political muscle and not in the needs of people."[24]

Duncan's years of cultivating friends in high places paid off. Many community groups in other parts of the country withered under similar attacks, but Duncan was able to rally her allies. The Clark County Health Department stepped in—allowing the Operation Life clinic to reopen less than six weeks after Miller padlocked the doors, offering more medical services than ever before. With staff and funding from the county and the federal government, the Operation Life clinic could now care for poor women of all ages, providing gynecological and obstetric care, prenatal checkups, and pediatric screening. Finally the clinic could serve the women who had created it.[25]

Though the clinic survived, and even thrived, the Nevada Attorney General's office pursued the fraud case against Duncan for five more years, until a federal appeals court judge finally threw out the charges. Duncan was completely exonerated. But, for five years—from 1976 to 1981—Operation Life was ineligible to apply for funds from a wide array of federal poverty programs.

The group did not become eligible for these funds again, Maya Miller says, "until we went to the attorney general and rallied a lot of political support.... It just shows what mean-spirited, vengeful people can do to try and stop a simple positive effort for women and children." George Miller insisted that vengeance had nothing to do with it. It was his job to be prudent about how the state spent taxpayer dollars. It was a line that Ruby Duncan and other community activists would hear many times in the years to come.[26]

THE ROCKY ROAD TO ECONOMIC SELF-SUFFICIENCY

In the six years since the Strip marches, Duncan and the women of Operation Life made only limited progress toward economic self-sufficiency. VISTA provided small stipends; the Catholic Church, federal programs, and private foundations provided short-term grants. But mostly the women who had founded Operation Life volunteered, relying on hotel work, welfare, or men for support.[27]

By 1977, Alversa Beals had not been paid in so long that she had to fall back on skills honed during her Delta childhood to feed her eleven children. Every Friday night, Beals and her boyfriend Robert would go fishing at Lake Mead. "They would stay out there the whole night," her daughter Glendora recalls, "eating bologna sandwiches and reeling in fish. Mama was good. She caught a lot of fish. The rule when she brought them home was, if you didn't help clean them, you didn't eat." Beals also trapped turtles in nearby lakes and ponds that she turned into a hearty soup. And she grew collard greens in strips of earth near her little house in the Westside projects.

Those nights by the lake were Beals's escape from the pressures of her life. "It was how she kept her sanity," says her daughter Renia. "She needed that time. Imagine raising eleven children on your own." Beals had finally found a man she was happy with. But those late-night fishing trips also enabled her to fulfill a vow she had made to her children. "I used to tell 'em, you won't have new shoes or new clothes. I can't buy you those. But I can promise you'll never go hungry."[28]

Some Operation Life women resorted to other time-honored means of supporting themselves. One Monday morning, Beals was setting up the Cove office when one of the volunteers smiled and confided, "I made $600 on the Strip this weekend." She'd been turning tricks. Beals let her emotions show on her face. "I do what I have to," her friend retorted, "to get money for my children." And nothing, she said, felt as bad as dealing with caseworkers at the Welfare office. She would not go back to that, no matter what.[29]

Still, too many years of living on the edge wore the women out. One night in 1977, Jack Anderson came into the Cove and found the women talking about giving up. There had been too many years of wondering how they'd feed their children, and too many fights just to keep their programs going. It was winter and the office was freezing. Beals, Henderson, and a few others were huddled together for warmth. "Damn, we got to get rid of this building," one said. "This is the last day I'm coming here," said another. The litany went on for so long that Anderson thought: "The Cove is history. This is down the tubes." He told them he understood how they felt. "So, do you want to give it back?" he asked quietly.

For a few minutes, there was silence in the room. Everyone just sat, weighed down by the cold and the dampness and the dinginess of the Cove. Then Essie Henderson, who had been complaining as loudly as the rest, changed her tune. "We've got the CLIW and we've got the clinic," she said. "We've got the library and we have this hotel. And when I drive by here, the kids point to it and say, 'You know that's ours.'" Henderson paused. "This is *ours*," she said. "Think about it. Let's pretend we've given it up. Where are you going to go tomorrow morning? I'm coming back here." The next morning everyone was back on the job.[30]

The women were particularly proud of Operation Life's early childhood centers, which they had opened in 1975 in a low-income housing project built and abandoned in the 1960s by the U.S. Department of Housing and Urban Development (HUD). The agency was only too happy to hand two empty houses over to Operation Life because the shuttered project had become an eyesore and a menace. With HUD funding, the women hired local contractors to fix up the decrepit buildings—and give area teens on-the-job training in carpentry, sheetrock installation, and electrical work. The Operation Life day-care program had one center on the Westside, another in North Las Vegas. Again and again, the women felt, they had found ways to breathe new life into dead and dying corners of their community.

The U.S. Department of Agriculture paid for local mothers to cook and serve breakfast and lunch to the children daily. An early childhood education program trained local women to become daycare teachers. Professors from Clark County Community College taught the classes, and women could earn their GEDs (high-school equivalency diplomas) as part of their coursework. Some of Operation Life's founders and many of their sons and daughters benefited from the program, which helped graduates find work in existing childcare centers or get state licenses to open their own. Duncan's daughter Georgia Phillips and her friend Ruby Pryce had dropped out of high school

THESE HOUSES ARE BEING BUILT BY
OPERATION LIFE
ELOPMENT CORP. Mrs. Ruby Duncan PRES.
ADA STATE BANK: INTERIM FINANCING
RITY PACIFIC MORTGAGE CORP: PERMANENT FINANCING
SSISTANCE FROM NEV. STATE HOUSING DIVISION DEPT.
MERCE & FEDERAL HOUSING ADMINISTRATION
CONTRACTOR Mr. Robert Fortson
NICAL ASSISTANCE BY Mr. H.P. Fitzgerald
RECTOR CITY OF LAS VEGAS WESTSIDE COMMUNITY DEVELOPMENT

In the 1980s, Operation Life received a series of grants from the U.S. Department of Housing and Urban Development and the city of Las Vegas to construct new housing for low-income families. Here Ruby Duncan greets Rosie Seals and Mother Ethel Pearson as she opens the first houses built by Operation Life. (Courtesy of the Las Vegas Sun*)*

when they became pregnant. Through the program, the two nineteen-year-olds completed their high-school degrees and found paying jobs caring for children.[31]

Like the Johnnie Tillmon Child Development Center in Los Angeles, the Operation Life daycare program reflected poor mothers' desire to gain economic self-sufficiency and instill pride in their children. The program taught black history, music, and culture, and provided meaningful work for local mothers. But daycare teachers often earned less than unionized hotel maids. And few daycare centers provided medical coverage. In those ways childcare was like other fields in which poor women were concentrated. Satisfying as it was, it would not lift poor mothers out of poverty.[32]

Nor would the daycare program move Operation Life toward economic self-sufficiency. The program was always overenrolled because there was a great need for quality childcare on the Westside. But tuition was minimal because no one could afford to pay much. And the buildings were incredibly costly to maintain. Many Westside HUD houses had been "so poorly put up that nobody could live in them," says Renee Diamond, now Commissioner of Modular Housing for Nevada. "The heating bills would eat you up in the winter and the cooling bills in the summer were like some third world country's national debt."[33]

Struggling toward what seemed like a certain financial collapse, Operation Life was rescued by a sudden infusion of federal funds at the end of 1977. Benefiting from the vast expansion of jobs programs under President Carter, the organization mushroomed virtually overnight. By 1978, Operation Life had become one of the largest employers on the Westside. The federal government was spending eight billion dollars annually for public service employment during the late 1970s. And Department of Labor officials, lobbied hard by Ruby Duncan, were willing to channel significant funding to neighborhoods like the Westside, with large populations of the chronically unemployed.

In December 1979, Operation Life received a bonanza in CETA funds, enabling Duncan to hire a hundred people, many of them former welfare mothers. Diane Guinn had been writing CETA grants for years but had never received anything this large. "Ruby would keep telling me to ask for more people," says Guinn. "Then they all got approved at once." Each of the positions paid about eight thousand dollars a year—hardly a princely sum, but, by the standards of the Westside, a very desirable salary.

Duncan used CETA money to hire poor Westside mothers as early childhood educators, healthcare aides, voting educators, job counselors, and social service advocates. "The Operation Life women used a lot of ingenuity to find work not only for themselves but also to create work opportunities for other women in the community," says Marty Makower. And money attracted more money. Las Vegas and Clark County officials, who credited Duncan with bringing in millions of dollars in federal aid, steered more money in her direction. The fortunes of the organization improved dramatically as grants started coming in both from government agencies and private philanthropies. Soon, Operation Life was the largest employer on the Westside.[34]

Versie Beals received a salary for three years running. Essie Henderson and Mary Wesley worked first as job placement counselors, then as clinic managers. Henderson supervised the nonprofessional clinic staff; Wesley coordinated healthcare outreach. "I could have made more money on the garbage truck," Wesley says, "but I got so involved, I couldn't leave. I loved helping the kids get doctors' care."[35]

CETA moneys also enabled Duncan to hire a cadre of energetic younger women who brought fresh energy and ideas to Operation Life. Joyce Broussard, a young Westside activist, took over the Coalition of Low Income Women and expanded the group's activities. She helped poor mothers find jobs as flag-women on highway construction crews, as road pavers, and as entry-level construction workers. Broussard also challenged public employers to eliminate what she saw as unnecessary hiring credentials. One of her successes was opening up jobs as prison guards to former welfare mothers. Previously, applicants had to have high-school degrees. Broussard convinced state prison officials that women could do the job just as well without a degree. And in prison positions where they needed more education, the women promised to attend school at night.

Operation Life was now a full-scale social service agency with a large and diverse staff: black and white, old and young, women and men. Duncan's skill at attracting federal funding greatly enhanced her status as a political player in Las Vegas, and won her appointments to the local CETA granting council, the Housing Authority, and other quasi-governmental city posts. "Ruby had an incredible capacity to hustle money and she really liked doing it," recalls Maya Miller, then chair of the Operation Life board.[36]

Duncan would pore over the latest federal program announcements to educate herself about the ever-changing array of funding opportunities. She would figure out what grants Operation Life was eligible for, then fly to Washington and walk the halls of HEW, the Department of Labor, the Department of Education, and the Department of Agriculture. "Ruby would poke her head into one office after another, finding little pots of money everywhere," Miller recalls. "She had a nose for it. She went right in and would ask the questions that needed to be asked.... And she was willing to move from one funding program to another just as the whims of the federal government were moving from one to another."

Following the trail of federal money, Duncan took Operation Life in new and unexpected directions. The organization became a HUD-certified mortgage counseling service, helping poor homeowners avoid default. With Department of Energy money, the group hired contractors to install solar energy collectors on Westside roofs, reducing residents' utility costs. And Operation Life–funded carpenters built ramps on poor people's homes to make them wheelchair accessible.[37]

Duncan says she adopted a talk-till-she-dropped style to exhaust officials into giving her money. "Sometimes I think they just gave me money to get me out of their office," she says with a grin. But her fund-raising skills grew more sophisticated over time, says Diane Guinn. "It took Ruby a while to tame down. When she first started speaking in public she had a shrill sound. But as time passed, she got very good. Ruby charmed and charismaed grant monies into being." And she knew how to generate excitement about her ideas. "She was like a hurricane right next to you," says Guinn. "It was exciting to be near her and to work for her." Marty Makower felt the excitement too. Inspired by Duncan to attend law school, Makower replaced Jack Anderson in the late 1970s as Operation Life's chief attorney.[38]

Duncan's warmth and magnetism, Makower says, forged unlikely and enduring political alliances that enabled Operation Life to last far longer than most 1960s-era community organizations. "Political allies had to be found. Relationships had to be built. Ruby was a genius at doing that, Makower says. "She just ran right past the racism that was always in her face. And because of the terrific human being she was, the people who at first seemed least likely to take her seriously often turned around in extraordinary ways."[39]

The Operation Life board, chaired by Maya Miller, reflected some of the odd but powerful alliances Duncan built. Few people could have drawn together such influential mainstream leaders as then–gaming commissioner (later U.S. Senate minority leader) Harry Reid, Stardust manager Herbert Tobman, NAACP head James McMillan, and state senator Joe Neal with representatives of the Association of Black Social Workers, the Black Panther Party, the Nation of Islam, and the Clark County Welfare Rights Organization.

Board meetings were chaotic, fertile, interesting—and notoriously long, former members recall. But it was here that an endless array of new ideas was introduced, fleshed out, and either dropped or pursued. In the late 1970s, Duncan and the board became intrigued by the idea of making Operation Life an incubator for business development. The founders of Operation Life had long been interested in opening small businesses, but now President Carter was willing to invest in innovative strategies for redeveloping poor communities. For a brief moment, there was federal money for community groups with an interest in capitalism. Duncan was anxious to tap that well.

OPERATION LIFE AND THE CDC MOVEMENT

The buzz in Washington during Duncan's frequent visits in the late 1970s was about community development corporations, a strategy for urban renewal that was suddenly attracting lots of government support. Run by neighborhood residents, CDCs were receiving seed money from federal agencies and private philanthropies, and encouraged to collaborate with local banks to build affordable housing, start businesses, generate jobs, and enhance the quality of life in poor neighborhoods. CDCs differed from their predecessors, Community Action Programs, because they could profit from the houses they built and the businesses they created, potentially becoming self-supporting. The federal government funded hundreds of community development projects in the Carter years.

The goal of CDCs was community revitalization, and the federal government's Title VII program was the gold standard: it selectively funded model CDCs that officials felt had the potential to regenerate entire communities. Only forty-seven community projects were designated Title VII CDCs in 1977, and federal officials were known to favor minority-run agencies. Duncan wanted Operation Life to be one of them.

Ruby Duncan was first drawn to the idea of community-based economic development, because it was born in the streets, not in government agencies or academic think tanks. Most government poverty programs focused on providing aid and training to individuals so they could leave poverty-stricken areas. Advocates of community development wanted to make those neighborhoods livable again by planting the seeds for self-sustaining economic growth. Initially funded by the Ford Foundation, the idea was then championed by New York senator Robert Kennedy, who sponsored the first federal legislation funding community development corporations in 1966. Community development corporations found an unlikely backer in President Richard Nixon. Bedeviled by civil unrest in his first term, Nixon was intrigued by the possibility of transforming black urban radicals into true-believing capitalists. In 1969, Nixon created the Office of Minority Business Enterprises; two years later, Congress passed Title VII, guaranteeing substantial ongoing federal support.[40]

Community development corporations quickly sprang up in rural and urban areas, and federal funding expanded dramatically after Jimmy Carter's 1976 election. The U.S. Departments of Labor, Housing and Urban Development, Health and Human Services, and the Small Business Administration all got into the act. During Carter's presidency, the federal government pumped as much as $2.6 billion annually into community development, and Congress reformed banking laws to stimulate construction and business loans in poor and minority neighborhoods.[41]

Ruby Duncan was ready to jump into the world of CDCs, but she needed to learn more before applying. In 1976, she and Maya Miller attended a meeting in Washington, D.C., of community development leaders from across the country. They were the only women in the room. "I can remember all these well-dressed men," says Miller. "Eskimo men, Latino men, Asian men. All these people came out of poverty communities. But there wasn't one woman head of a CDC."[42]

That was no accident. The shift of federal government resources from Community Action Programs to community development corporations had been, in part, a response to the criticism that local boards of earlier poverty programs were "dominated by women and preachers." As one veteran of the Office of Economic Opportunity put it: "The failure to involve men, the working or unemployed fathers has been the single most important failure of the Poverty Program. But economic development is different. Business is man's work. It promises power and status. They come out for that." With the goal of promoting men's participation in the program, federal community development funds flowed almost exclusively to male community leaders into the late 1970s.[43]

Duncan was impressed by the scale of the community organizations represented at the 1976 meeting and listened open-mouthed as male CDC heads described the money pouring into their organizations: "I got $500,000 from HEW." "I got $250,000 from the Labor Department." Duncan laughs: "Here was all of these men, some of them from the welfare rights movement but all of them men. And I thought, if they can do it, so can I. I'm not going to sit back and let all those men get all that money and we don't get anything."[44]

For a year Ruby Duncan waited anxiously for word on Operation Life's application. She took it as a good sign when she was invited to the Carter White House in the fall of 1977 to join a working group of urban renewal leaders. It was. She came home from Washington to find that Operation Life had been selected as a Title VII CDC.[45]

It was a tremendous coup. Only a handful of groups were funded through Title VII. Operation Life was the only one run by poor women, and the only one attempting to get women off welfare by hiring them to deliver social services. The Westside mothers' group had suddenly jumped into a different class. Federal officials gave Operation Life $180,000 to draw up plans for the economic revitalization of the Westside, and promised millions more to create new housing, businesses, and jobs. "We plan to help the nitty-gritty people, particularly welfare mothers, to develop businesses and get off welfare," Duncan gleefully announced.[46]

What had begun as a grass-roots movement was becoming an established institution. But the transition was not painless. Federal money came with strings attached. Operation Life needed to hire a panoply of experts: developers, business consultants, economists, health management professionals. Every job description for a position funded with federal dollars came with a strict list of qualifications, and uneducated welfare mothers could not hope to compete for the new positions. This influx of professional managers came at the same time that Operation Life got the go-ahead to hire one hundred new CETA workers. Suddenly, the offices were full of faces that the founders did not recognize, many of them white and from outside the community.

Some Westsiders began to complain that Operation Life was slipping away from the control of the poor mothers who'd founded it. "Before, it was like a big family," said Mary Wesley. "Everybody knew everybody, and everybody knew what was going on. Now it's more businesslike.... Sometimes I don't even know who is working here." To some extent, the founding mothers agreed, the professionalization of Operation Life was good. It enabled the organization to deliver an expanding array of high-quality services to a growing number of the city's poor families. "But it still needs an atmosphere where people care," said Wesley. "Poor people, when they go to places that are businesslike, get turned off. They are afraid they won't get helped there, figure somebody will look down on them."

Rosie Seals wondered if the organization was diluting its founding principles by chasing federal money down too many different paths. She had always felt uneasy with that strategy. "People would say there's money for this program and money for that," Seals recalls. "But I'm not interested in every little program. I just want to help the welfare mothers."[47]

Seals's question would not go away. Could Operation Life really get its core constituency off welfare by chasing every new federal program that came down the pike? Duncan maintained that jobs for welfare mothers were still her priority, and insisted that CDC business development money provided the best opportunity yet to create job opportunities for Westsiders. The money was already flowing: The city of Las Vegas awarded Operation Life more than a quarter of a million dollars to develop new businesses in the black community. CETA funded a Minority Youth Enterprise Project to encourage and train young black entrepreneurs. Operation Life launched Project Assets, which urged Westsiders to open accounts at the Westside Credit Union, with the option of investing in Operation Life businesses.

Duncan and the Operation Life women were ready to try their hand at small-scale capitalism. Essie Henderson and her sister Earlene wanted to run a beauty shop. Versie Beals wanted a bakery. Mary Wesley wanted to design and sew clothes. Like millions of other American women who started their own businesses in the 1970s and 1980s, these former welfare mothers believed that entrepreneurship might be the best way to elude sexism and race-discrimination in the job market. Besides, the Westside needed shops that local residents could walk to. Board chair Maya Miller endorsed this new direction. "It has come time," she said, "that women get on with the business of doing business."[48]

GENDER POLITICS AND DOWN-HOME CAPITALISM

Essie Henderson and her sister Earlene Weatherall became the first Operation Life women to open a small business. Their beauty shop and beauty supply distributorship was financed by Operation Life CDC and by a local Nation of Islam mosque, where Henderson had become an active member. Operation Life's goal of building economic self-sufficiency among poor women dovetailed with the Nation of Islam belief that black consumers should buy from black businesses. The sisters' beauty shop became a gathering place for neighborhood women. The beauty supply business, featuring African American hair- and skin-care products, flourished as well. Henderson and Weatherall were able to support their families and hire a small staff. Duncan pointed to the sisters with pride, arguing that women-run businesses were a viable route out of poverty for former welfare mothers.

Many of the Operation Life women wanted to open small businesses— bakeries, dress shops, restaurants. They had been hatching plans for years. But Washington pushed them to think bigger: Why not open factories? Better yet, why not an entire industrial park, taking advantage of the Westside's proximity to the railroad tracks? Federal officials wanted Operation Life to develop an enterprise that could employ hundreds. "There didn't seem to be any room in the overall economic development planning to talk about the kind of small entrepreneurial activity that people could understand and that tapped the strengths that the women had," says Marty Makower. "The federal expectation was that we think big."[49]

And so the women set aside their hopes for their own small shops. Operation Life's new federally funded consultants helped them draft more ambitious business proposals, instead. One idea was to open a small factory to manufacture home security devices. Burglary was a constant problem on the Westside; why not stop crime and make money at the same time? With a grant from the Law Enforcement Assistance Administration, the women researched which devices were most effective, testing alarms already in use on the Westside. But no banks wanted to invest in their factory.

Another idea was to take advantage of the region's most reliable asset—the sun. The women wanted to manufacture and sell low-cost solar panels to reduce utility costs in poorly insulated Las Vegas homes. Federal grant money enabled them to hire a solar panel designer and train local residents to install the prototypes in Westside homes. But the women hit a wall when it came to manufacturing. Local banks weren't interested in bankrolling the venture. The federal government's desire for Operation Life to "think big" unfortunately meshed poorly with what Nevada investors considered feasible.[50]

Ratcheting down their plans—and thinking of local needs—the women turned to food issues. Food prices on the Westside, as in poor urban neighborhoods across the country, were high. Duncan believed that the growth of massive supermarket chains made the problem worse. "Let's open and support local food businesses," Duncan wrote, "instead of giving all our money to fast food chains whose central offices are located out of state." In 1979, Operation Life started a food-buying cooperative, where members purchased food at just 10 percent over wholesale prices. The staff also coordinated a community gardening project that provided fresh vegetables to local families at minimal cost.[51]

Operation Life had the most success generating jobs by providing essential social services. That was the women's original idea, and it worked. By 1980, the organization employed over one hundred people, the vast majority of whom were current or former welfare recipients. Operation Life's cash flow approached $3 million annually. And each dollar was earmarked for the needs of women and children.[52]

Operation Life's clinic remained the group's most prized program and its best job generator, providing scores of positions for professionals and community residents. Duncan was always scouting out ways to expand the clinic further. As a member of Senator Edward Kennedy's health advisory panel, and a board member of the National Council of Free Clinics, Duncan learned about a program that would enable the clinic to become the Westside's only full-scale medical facility. If the clinic won recognition as a federal Community Health Center, it could receive funding and medical staff from the U.S. Public Health Service—and become the only clinic in Las Vegas that took patients regardless of ability to pay.

The idea for community health centers had been around for fifteen years. HEW officials under Lyndon Johnson had drawn up plans for one thousand centers to serve 25 million poor people. By 1977, however, only 125 community clinics had opened, serving just 1.5 million people. Senator Edward Kennedy pushed through funding to open eight hundred more centers. Soon, community health centers were treating more than 4 million poor Americans. Many were staffed by the National Health Service Corps, which allowed recently graduated physicians and nurses to pay off loans by working for several years in poor communities.[53]

Operation Life's 1979 application to open a Community Health Center on the Westside was initially greeted with skepticism by federal officials. "By all traditional standards, they did not have the capacity to deliver health services," says Jack Anderson. But when officials reviewed Operation Life's record of healthcare delivery, they decided to take a chance. In 1979, HEW awarded the group more than two hundred thousand dollars to upgrade and expand the clinic. The U.S. Public Health Service provided additional nurses and physicians, enabling the clinic to provide geriatric, internal medicine, and psychiatric care. By 1980, the Operation Life Community Health Center provided forty regular jobs for local women.[54]

While Duncan spun out development plans and hunted down grants, her old welfare rights comrades kept Operation Life's volunteer programs thriving. With donations from major bakeries, the women distributed between three hundred and five hundred pounds of free bread and rolls daily to needy families, singles, and seniors. Always conscious of nutrition, the Operation Life bread program provided rye, whole wheat, black, and raisin bread. This program ran five days a week for more than fifteen years. Poor black, white, Mexican American, Native American, and Asian families flocked to Jackson Street from as far as thirty miles away. Families could take as much as they needed. But "we'd like for everyone to be aware that some women have 7 or 8 children," Leola Harris, bread program director, announced in the *Community Press.*[55]

Every two years, in the months leading up to elections, Leola Harris geared up another initiative: Operation Life's Voter Education and Registration Project. Harris, with an edgy mix of pragmatism, humor, and fiery conviction, trained a team of senior citizens, teenagers, and welfare mothers to canvass the city's poor neighborhoods, making sure that everyone eligible to vote was registered. She also informed voters about positions taken by politicians on issues of importance to the Westside. "The time is gone when we sit passively and let politicians play with our lives," Harris wrote in the *Community Press.* "Voter education, political awareness and participation in the electoral process are part of our struggle."[56]

In Washington, D.C., where President Carter had appointed veteran activists to head poverty agencies, Ruby Duncan was anything but passive. Instead of wandering the hallways, she was now invited to the head offices. Graciela Oliveras, the founder of Food for All, now directed the Community Services Administration (CSA), the umbrella agency for most social service and economic development programs. Oliveras considered Operation Life a model for community development, and in 1978 she asked Duncan to help set guidelines for CSA-funded projects. Rosalynn Carter appointed Duncan to the First Lady's Communities Symposium, where Duncan advocated hiring the unemployed to rebuild poor neighborhoods. In 1979 President Carter appointed Duncan to his National Advisory Council on Economic Opportunity, to be a voice for the poor.

Significantly for Duncan, who was keenly aware of being a black single mother, Carter also asked her to join the steering committee for the White House Conference on Families, which sought to strengthen American families at a time when the public perceived them to be under unprecedented stress. Planning for the conference quickly erupted in controversy when Carter appointed a divorced black Catholic mother as chairwoman. She was forced to step down. Duncan, however, remained on the committee, and the new chairman wrote her a personal note, saying how much he appreciated her ideas and her calming influence in a stormy political moment.[57]

Not everyone was so fond of Duncan, particularly people who thought that welfare mothers with limited educations should not be running social and health programs, influencing national policy, or handling millions of -taxpayer dollars. From Westside business leaders to federal agency directors, many were offended by Duncan's ambition, aggressive style, and success. "Ruby was attacked savagely," recalls Father Vitale. "Almost anyone who had some kind of position took a shot at Ruby." Vitale says state officials launched a disinformation campaign to discredit Duncan. Rumors spread that she took bribes to deliver votes on the Westside. "There was griping about how often she flew around the country and to Washington, and nasty cracks about her friendship with affluent white women like Maya Miller," Vitale says. Some of the complaints came from other poor mothers, who suspected that Duncan had enriched herself at their expense. "When you're leading a movement of people who have nothing," says Marty Makower, "it doesn't take much to provoke resentment."

But most of the criticism came from people who couldn't stand the idea of a black welfare mother achieving renown and a measure of power. On the Westside, some local leaders accused Duncan of selling her soul to white politicians. In 1978, she was the target of blistering criticism from a group of black politicians and businessmen who had recently purchased the *Las Vegas Voice*. They scrapped her long-running "Ruby Says" column, and ran a series of editorials charging Duncan with financial corruption and voter manipulation. "It is apparent that the Mayor and Commissioners along with the City Manager owe Ruby Duncan a debt," the *Voice* editorialized. "What special favor did she do for these men?"

The editors charged that Duncan was illegally using CETA funds to pay welfare mothers to work on the campaigns of her white cronies. "I thought we were out of slavery and being forced to do things against our will," the *Voice* opined. "But when you are associated with Operation Life and Ruby Duncan, slavery just begins."[58]

Other editorials revealed the sexism behind *Voice* editors' resentment of Duncan. "Everything that has to be done in the community, we have to go through women," the editors complained. "They are heading all of our programs, all organizations and now are in charge of all the big money coming into Las Vegas. As bad as I would hate to do business with women it seems as though that is who I will have to go to. We should now get them elected to offices and we stay home and watch soap operas and fix dinner for the head of the household." Some might call this "women's liberation," the editors said, but it was really "slave and welfare mentality" promoted by the white man. "He makes sure that the welfare mother controls while shoving the Black man aside, as always. . . . What do these welfare mothers know about pulling a business together for you and me? Remember that Black women have always been less threatening to the white man."[59]

The venomous fury of the attack on Duncan was shocking, says Louis Vitale, but the backlash was not unexpected:

> *When somebody comes in and—through the very force of their personality, the political moment and the social mood—starts cutting across lines that usually keep people down, they're going to get hit from all over. People are going to have their foot out to trip them and that's exactly what I saw with Ruby. Some of it came from people on high, because she was speaking for and with people who had nothing besides the power of their presence, of their cause, and of their courage. And some of it came from the community.*[60]

Duncan's family was outraged, and they smelled both envy and male chauvinism. "When you have a single mom standing up and moving more than they can ever consider moving, that's where the jealousy comes in," says Duncan's son Kenneth Phillips. "That's where the backstabbing comes in. *I'll undercut you here. I'll shortcut you there.* Some so-called black leaders, they had a problem with her. It was a power struggle. She didn't have all the education. They felt that she really should have stayed in her place. They would undercut her by whispering, by their attitude."[61]

By 1980, Duncan was beginning to have problems in Washington as well. Some Carter administration officials were uncomfortable with Operation Life's overt feminism and with its attempt to turn social service delivery into a form of economic development. In August 1980, Duncan and Maya Miller were summoned to Washington by Gerald Mukai, associate director of the Office of Economic Development. Mukai wanted Operation Life to take on a project that would move it away from social services into the realm of pure capitalism. Maya Miller says the idea made her skin crawl: the federal government wanted Operation Life to buy and run the troubled Aladdin casino hotel on the Las Vegas Strip.[62]

Miller was deeply opposed to the idea of Operation Life running a casino. Gaming hotels took the money of people who could ill afford it, which ran counter to everything Miller felt their movement had been about. She also suspected a setup. "It was built on a smoke-and-mirrors economic notion," she said. "It was fraudulent." Even the mob had failed at making the Aladdin profitable. Harry Reid, then gaming commissioner, had told Miller that the debt-saddled property was available for as little as $250,000.

Duncan was torn. On the one hand, she was up for any challenge—particularly one that so many others had already failed at. Besides, the irony was delicious: a welfare mother running one of the green-felt palaces! But the real draw was survival; she worried that Mukai would pull Operation Life's funding if she refused. She'd heard that two other CDCs had lost funding when Mukai judged them unprofessional, and she feared that Operation Life—the only woman-run CDC funded by Mukai's office—might be particularly vulnerable. "I need to keep the program going," she told Miller that night as they pondered the proposal. "I've got to go with him."[63]

Mukai turned up the pressure the next day. "It will do no good to pretend that your production is stellar," he told Duncan and Miller. "It is not. If you want to do it your way, then you'll have a problem a year from now." Operation Life, he said, had to shed its "welfare rights mentality" and stop talking about racism and sexism. "The real color of prejudice is green. The name of the game is money. You've got political power," Mukai said, looking hard at Duncan. "Now do you want economic power?" If so, he was prepared to offer

Operation Life four hundred thousand dollars to buy and renovate the Aladdin. He urged Duncan to hire a Las Vegas consultant he knew who could broker the deal. Operation Life's "strong thrust on giving people back their dignity" had been successful, he said. "Now you need to show green."

Mukai was blunt: Many people in Washington thought Operation Life couldn't turn a profit. And Duncan was partly to blame for spending almost every penny she received to hire local people. Stop investing everything in "people capital," he told Duncan. "You'll end up with nothing." Mukai wanted Operation Life to involve more "real business people." Hire a real estate developer, invest in property and business assets. And don't be dissuaded by Maya Miller's reluctance, said Mukai. Feminism and economic development don't mix. As the women stood up to leave, Miller asked Mukai: "What is the urgency about doing all this now?" He replied: "The urgency is this administration's time." But Duncan never got to make the decision. By August 1980, Jimmy Carter's time was running out.[64]

OPERATION LIFE IN THE REAGAN YEARS

"Government is not the solution," President Ronald Reagan said during his inauguration in January 1981. "Government is the problem." From his first days in office, Reagan set out to dismantle what was left of federal poverty programs. He proposed deep cuts in housing subsidies, child nutrition programs, food stamps, public assistance, student loans, low-income energy assistance, and Medicaid payments to the states. He asked Congress to dismantle the Community Services Administration, Legal Services, and VISTA. He called for an end to Basic Educational Opportunity Grants for college students, which had enabled an entire generation of middle-class young people to attend college, and minimum Social Security payments, which guaranteed a decent standard of living in old age to people who had not been able to accrue adequate Social Security benefits. This included most domestic and agricultural workers.[65]

Liberal Democrats in Congress saved some small-budget programs, including VISTA and Legal Services. But Congress passed Reagan's Omnibus Budget Reconciliation Act, which House Budget Committee chairman James Jones (D-Oklahoma) called "the most monumental and historic turnaround in fiscal policy that has ever occurred." It banned public assistance payments to strikers and reduced the income that recipients of public assistance could earn from jobs before benefits were cut. It limited the assets a family could hold while receiving public assistance, and gave states flexibility to impose strict work requirements. It cut three million children from the school lunch program, one million from food stamps, half a million from the breakfast program, and half a million women and children from AFDC. More than seven hundred thousand children lost Medicaid benefits. Rents in public housing increased, pushing three hundred thousand American families into substandard private housing, and an unknown number into the streets.[66]

Congress dissolved the Community Services Administration and repealed Title VII. Block grants to the states replaced the direct grants that federal agencies had previously made to local antipoverty organizations. Community groups could no longer appeal directly to the federal government for funds. And the Basic Educational Opportunity Grants program was ended, sparking a sharp decline in the percentage of high-school graduates attending college. In just two years, black college enrollment dropped 7 percent.[67]

The poorest Americans were hit hardest by these cuts. Although programs serving low- and moderate-income Americans constituted less than 10 percent of the total federal budget when Reagan was elected, they absorbed one-third of his budget cuts. As a percentage of income, the bottom 20 percent of income earners lost income at seventy-five times the rate of families in the top 2 percent. The average black family lost three times as much in cash and non-cash benefits as did the average white family.

Black Americans fell below the poverty line at twice the rate of whites. Gains made as a result of federal poverty programs evaporated quickly. Reagan's first term saw a 72 percent increase in the number of African Americans among the "long-term unemployed"—those who had been out of work for six months while actively looking for a job. By 1985, 36 percent of all black Americans were living in poverty, more than at any time since the Census Bureau began collecting that data in the 1960s.[68]

Programs that were not eliminated were dramatically restructured. The women of Operation Life would no longer be able to go over the heads of hostile state administrators to plead their case before friendlier officials in Washington, D.C. After a brief transition period, all social services and community development grants would now be administered by the states. Reagan claimed that state control over social services would cut down on waste. But his consolidation of seventy-seven federal programs into nine new block grants had more to do with ideology than efficiency. He was following through on his promise to dismantle the New Deal state and weaken the grip of "special interest groups." He wasn't referring to the Western defense contractors or energy companies that had bankrolled his candidacy. What alarmed the new president and his conservative constituency was the influence of civil rights and feminist groups in the nation's capital, and of urban leaders such as Ruby Duncan.[69]

The Reagan administration did not immediately defund community development corporations. Liberals in Congress managed to protect moneys already allocated to community groups. But organizations such as Operation Life would now have to navigate an alphabet soup of new agencies, none of which was friendly. Community workers were forced to spend much of their time submitting grant applications to, or filling out paperwork for, myriad public and private agencies, each with its own rules. The cumbersome process drained vitality from all but the largest CDCs.[70]

The toughest problem, however, wasn't strictly financial. Every precious federal dollar now came with a visit from zealous new Reagan appointees who insisted that Operation Life adhere to every change in grant regulations. Answering to federal officials consumed an ever-growing share of staff attention and energy. Most of the Operation Life founders were still poor in 1980, but at least they had earned respect as poverty program administrators. Now Duncan began to receive terse letters from Washington accusing her of hiring unqualified staff. She was ordered to provide Washington with the résumés of everyone on staff whose salary was paid, in part or in full, by federal funds.[71]

The implications for many of Operation Life's founders were clear. One of the first targets of government officials' ire was Aldine Weems. In 1981, she was supervising the medical program, the WIC nutrition program, the daycare centers, and all CETA workers. To the founding mothers of Operation Life and to longtime allies Harriet Trudell and Renee Diamond, it seemed that Weems performed miracles. She had kept Operation Life's array of programs running, day in and day out, for nearly a decade. To a new crop of federal appointees, Weems was out of her depth, an uncredentialed beneficiary of Democratic boss Ruby Duncan's patronage, running programs she was not qualified to manage. Weems was to them a glaring illustration of how Operation Life was abusing the public trust.

Federal officials also raised questions about Operation Life's office manager, Alversa Beals, who received a small stipend from CETA. They did not see a woman who had, for a decade, been the heart of the organization. Reagan health and social services officials saw a woman with almost no formal education, who was managing an office that channeled millions of dollars in public funds. Pressure came down on Duncan from all sides to stop using federal moneys to pay the women who had built Operation Life. "We were smart enough to bring the programs in," says Mary Wesley bitterly, "but when the money came in we were too dumb to run them." And when she tried to defend the women who had worked with her at Operation Life for a decade, Duncan was asked about her own qualifications. Many of those questions came from the regional offices of U.S. Health and Human Services in San Francisco, where Ronald Reagan had appointed Duncan's old nemesis, George Miller, as director.[72]

The Community Services Administration was asked to justify investing millions in a group of uneducated welfare mothers. The agency hired an independent research firm to assess Operation Life. Duncan and the women answered the investigators' questions, opened up their ledgers, and waited in trepidation to find out if Operation Life would survive.

The report's findings surprised them—and many in Washington. It described Operation Life as one of the great success stories of the CDC program. The numbers alone told the story, the author wrote. Operation Life had brought $7.5 million into an impoverished community and held physical assets worth more than $1 million. It provided healthcare to an area that previously had none, launched rehabilitation, weatherization, and solar energy projects, and was creating a public-private partnership to construct housing for low-income buyers.

The report also lauded Operation Life's collaboration with business groups and noted that, far from being reliant on the federal dollar, the group had won 100 percent bank financing on several projects. Herb Tobman, formerly General Manager of the Stardust, was now working as Operation Life's business developer. And Duncan's campaign to bring women into male-dominated trades had changed the views of many Las Vegas union officials and business owners about what kinds of work poor mothers could do.[73]

"In a critically underserved area," the report concluded, "Operation Life stands as a very real presence . . . and [has] perhaps [come] closer to the model of community controlled and supported economic development than any other CDC." The report recommended that those deciding the future of federal poverty policy study Operation Life closely. Since the majority of the poor were women and children, Operation Life's strategy—an agency run by poor women, generating jobs by delivering services—could be an important model for other CDCs. That example could and should be replicated, the report urged, and recommended increased federal funding.[74]

Officials in the Reagan administration seem to have been at least partly convinced. Against all odds, appointees of the president who had coined the term "welfare queen" gave millions of dollars to Operation Life in the early 1980s for housing and medical programs, when other community groups were being slashed to the bone. The glowing 1981 evaluation unquestionably improved the group's image in Washington. Duncan's rhetoric about the women having pulled themselves up by their bootstraps fit conservative self-help notions. Reagan's defense secretary, Casper Weinberger, had himself lauded the group a few years earlier. And in Nevada, the group's decade of success—and Ruby Duncan's expertise at winning federal funds—had won the organization powerful friends. She had brought in tens of millions of federal dollars that benefited the entire state, through food stamps, WIC, EPSDT, and various economic development grants. Grateful allies in city and state government urged federal officials to preserve the program, at least for a while.[75]

Funding for community health centers was cut by 25 percent during Reagan's first term, but the Operation Life clinic continued to thrive. The clinic actually grew larger in 1983, when it received a grant from the U.S. Public Health Service to treat any patient who walked through its doors, including unemployed and elderly men and women. Operation Life also received funds to hire local women to work as home health aides for the homebound elderly. A large number of senior citizens now used the Operation Life clinic as their primary healthcare facility. The clinic was flooded with patients dealing with life-threatening diseases, including diabetes, emphysema, high blood pressure, and heart disease. Many were so ill that they had to be hospitalized immediately. With no money to pay for medical care, poor Las Vegans had been staying home and growing sicker. A decade after it first opened, the Operation Life clinic continued to serve new communities of the needy.[76]

Former test-site and defense plant workers were among the most seriously ill. Their high rates of cancer led Operation Life clinic doctors to suspect a radiation link. In the *Community Press* and public forums, Operation Life reached out in the mid-1980s to "atomic veterans" organizations to learn more about the symptoms affecting people exposed to high doses of radiation. Clinic doctors saw the symptoms firsthand. Years of work at Henderson weapons plants and at the nuclear test site had left now-aging Westside men with an array of maladies, from leukemia to thyroid cancer.[77]

Seeing radiation-related cancers up close at the clinic changed Ruby Duncan's view of the Nevada antinuclear movement. She had chastised Father Louis Vitale when he first started demonstrating at the Nevada test site. "Why are you protesting *there*, Father?" she asked. "That's the only place where black people can get decent work and get training and benefits." So when Vitale decided to commit civil disobedience at the test site in 1982–1983, he didn't ask

Duncan or anyone from the black community to come along. Vitale and the Franciscans jumped the fence and erected five hundred cardboard bombs to symbolize the nuclear tests performed there. "I didn't know if we'd get five years in prison," says Vitale, "because this was the first time anyone had ever entered the Nevada Test Site for a protest." The Franciscans were hauled off to jail. Supporters flocked to the federal building in downtown Las Vegas for a vigil, lining up along a rope studded with cardboard bombs.

All of a sudden, a friend told Vitale, a large black woman walked up, ducked under the rope, grabbed a sign and joined the protest. "I was driving in my car and I heard that Father Vitale got arrested at the Test Site," she explained to the baffled protesters. "He was always there for us, so I want to be here for him." Vitale gets emotional telling the story. "It was Ruby. I was so touched by that. I didn't ask her to go to the Test Site but I really appreciated that kind of testimony."[78]

Ruby Duncan's political vision was maturing and growing more expansive, but the building that housed her dream wasn't aging nearly as gracefully. The increased volume of patients and services had outstripped the Cove's capacity, and the building was becoming a costly burden. It was still a magnet for the homeless, and the city was demanding that Operation Life cement up several unused floors. HUD and the city of Las Vegas had provided large sums to renovate the old hotel, but never quite enough. Duncan and Trudell, Operation Life's physical developer, submitted ever-changing proposals to transform the Cove into senior citizen housing, a nursing home, or transitional housing for the homeless. But none of these projects won funding. The truth became inescapable: Operation Life had to move out of the Cove.[79]

The organization purchased a double-wide trailer to house the clinic while Duncan worked feverishly to raise money for a new building. On the strength of Operation Life's ten-year record, Duncan was able to raise seven hundred thousand dollars to construct a handsome, glass-and-brick building. The new headquarters would house the Operation Life clinic, the WIC program, and the community development corporation. Duncan ran into a bit of luck in her fund-raising. The Fleischmann Foundation, which had long admired Duncan, was dissolving, and grant officers were looking for a few farewell projects. They provided nearly three hundred thousand dollars; city commissioners and the federal government provided the rest. Donning hard-hats and wielding shovels, the Operation Life women posed for photographers at the ground-breaking ceremony.

Four hundred dignitaries joined a sea of Westside mothers in the fall of 1982 to celebrate the opening of the Operation Life building. After years in the decaying Cove, the mothers could not quite believe the sight of the brand-new tan-and-cream-colored building with the Operation Life logo on the front. Duncan described it as "a need indeed and a dream come true." All in the midst of the Reagan revolution.[80]

This sweetest of victories was accompanied by troubling winds blowing from Washington. At the request of the president, Congress repealed CETA in 1982, ending the public service employment program that had offered training and job placement to more than one million people annually. CETA had been one of the most successful initiatives of the War on Poverty, reducing welfare dependency and increasing income, particularly among women participants. But CETA had been easy to kill, because the public associated it with welfare recipients. At the time of its repeal, it was the second most unpopular social program in the nation, ridiculed by conservative politicians as a patronage mill and a multibillion-dollar swindle of taxpayers. Only AFDC was more hated. The end of CETA was a crippling blow for community groups. It would now be much more difficult for Operation Life to employ poor mothers.[81]

The Reagan administration also waged a relentless war on the Legal Services program. Jack Anderson, Marty Makower, and Mahlon Brown continued to advise the Operation Life women well into the Reagan-Bush years, but other community groups struggled as funding for Legal Services was cut again and again. In 1983, a *New York Times* editorial lauded the success of Operation Life and used it as an argument for continued federal funding of Legal Services. "This ambitious organization has turned its very poverty into venture capital," the *Times* wrote. And "lawyers provided the know-how." The *Times* cited the Westside mothers' group as a model for community development. "If the Reagan administration won't actively help such enterprises," editors asked, "can't it at least stop making it harder?"[82]

But the writing was on the wall. Operation Life could no longer rely on federal funding. Money for staff salaries and economic development was about to dry up. Ruby Duncan sent a series of increasingly anxious letters and phone calls to New York's Ford Foundation, which had contributed over $110 million to community development corporations since 1969. Duncan asked Ford to sponsor three Operation Life initiatives: a job training and self-esteem-building program for AFDC mothers, a construction campaign to build homes and promote ownership among low-income families, and an industrial park on the Westside that the group hoped would generate many new jobs.[83]

Ford was impressed. Operation Life had continued to attract $2 million in county, city, state, and federal dollars, even in a time of severe budget cuts. A relatively modest investment from the foundation would keep the organization afloat. In December 1982, Ford program officers flew to Las Vegas for a meeting at the Desert Inn with key Operation Life staffers, General Taylor of First Western Savings and Loan, and representatives from HUD, the city, and the County Commission. Ford officers came out of the meeting ready to fund Operation Life—and convinced that the group's greatest asset was Ruby Duncan.

"Since the mid-seventies," a Ford analyst wrote, "she has been the force which transformed the group of welfare mothers who gathered to protest welfare cutbacks into an important and creative community development corporation." Ford not only funded Operation Life but insisted on paying Duncan a fifty-thousand-dollar annual salary. After decades of scraping by, Ruby Duncan was finally being paid for her work as a spokeswoman and advocate for the poor.

The salary, which seemed astronomical to the other women, was hardly enough to make Duncan affluent, but it made a profound difference in her life. Her decades-old back injury caused chronic pain, and her doctors and medications were expensive. Duncan was able to buy a one-bedroom house. Ford also provided funds to cover Duncan's work trips so that she did not have to go hat-in-hand to donors for every flight and car rental.

Ford officers were pleased with Operation Life's productivity between 1982 and 1984. In addition to its new, ten-thousand-square-foot headquarters, the organization built ten homes for low-income families and drew up plans for twelve more. Duncan and Marty Makower met with executives from Howard Hughes's Summa Corporation to discuss a proposed seventy-acre industrial park on a lot donated by North Las Vegas. In 1984, Ford renewed its support of Operation Life to help develop revenue-producing businesses. Duncan was investigating three possibilities: a medical laboratory, a landscaping company to service the big Las Vegas hotels, and a drapery business that would take advantage of the women's sewing skills.[84]

Ford also provided money for the Coalition of Low Income Women (CLIW), which now engaged in welfare and tenant advocacy as well as job placement. Henderson, Wesley, Beals, Seals, and Emma Stampley kept CLIW alive throughout the 1980s, and Ford's support gave them small stipends.[85]

Throughout the Reagan and Bush presidencies, the women of CLIW continued to move poor mothers off the welfare rolls and into good jobs. "We are a group of welfare mothers and we'd like to come in and talk to you about a job," CLIW women said to Las Vegas personnel directors. "Because we definitely want to work." Duncan says the women's perseverance and boldness worked. "Many people said 'O.K.' Once we came in they hired practically everybody we wanted them to hire."

The Coalition of Low Income Women met with the managers of the city's major hotels to secure waitress jobs for poor women. They placed women who had been trained in Operation Life secretarial and computer programs as clerk typists and computer programmers. They met with construction company heads to persuade them to open up entry-level positions for women. And, with an eye toward both fashion and self-esteem, they solicited donations of classy outfits so that applicants would have something respectable to wear on job interviews.[86]

Duncan believed that rebuilding the self-esteem of poor mothers was central to moving them back into the workforce. In 1979, Duncan hired Sharon Glover Wilson to be Operation Life's assertiveness trainer. Wilson grew up on the Westside admiring the mothers' movement and became friendly with Duncan's son David at the University of Nevada. Duncan noticed Wilson's impeccable clothing and polished way of speaking, and asked the younger woman: "Could you teach women how to dress up and feel good about themselves?" Wilson agreed. For the next several years, she taught courses at Operation Life, advising Westside welfare mothers "how to dress, depending on the job they were seeking, and how to conduct themselves in interviewing for jobs." Wilson said she stressed the importance of being punctual, and gave "tips on how to be most productive at whatever job they were doing."[87]

One of CLIW's most creative fund-raisers was its June 1982 "Big Girls Bundle of Joy Fashion Show," held at the Fremont Hotel in downtown Las Vegas. The "Big Girls" show was more than a benefit. It raised consciousness about problems of body image among poor women of color. Years of inadequate nutrition, starchy commodities diets, and fried Southern cooking had left many of the women overweight and out of shape. Operation Life nutritionists taught healthy ways to lose weight. But it often seemed impossible for large women to find plus-sized clothing that was suitable for going to work.

Duncan had talked for years about opening up a clothing store for large women that would offer an array of stylish fashions. "Lack of 'becoming' clothing reinforces negative self-images that many large women hold," Duncan wrote the Ford Foundation. "Large women do want to look good. They hold professional positions, have careers, date, dance, make love and can be sensuous and attractive and wear good looking clothes. They have the same feelings, engage in the same activities and do the same work as smaller women." At the Big Girls Show, Operation Life women modeled fashions designed to make large women look and feel good. A Westside beauty shop did the women's hair and offered advice to audience members on the best hairstyles for different skin tones and body types. Many of the "big girl" fashions were designed and sewn by Mary Wesley and other Operation Life women. Essie Henderson and her sister offered neighborhood women a chance to sell cosmetics created by and for black women.[88]

Through the WIC program, Operation Life sought to promote a healthier diet among the Las Vegas poor. Nutritionist Ana Luna, a recent émigré from the Philippines, taught young mothers and grandmothers the gospel of fresh vegetables, offering six-week courses on diet and cooking, as well as parenting classes. Many of the mothers who came into the clinic were so young that they didn't know how to feed or take care of their children, Luna recalls.

WIC staffers believe that they improved eating habits among a large percentage of Westside residents. "We saw thousands of mothers every month," says Luna. They were a very diverse group. In 1973, when the clinic opened, it served an almost exclusively black clientele. By the 1980s, Hispanics, Asians, and poor whites were sitting side-by-side in the waiting room. "Along with hard times in this country, you saw the clinic changing dramatically," recalls Renee Diamond, Operation Life's treasurer. "We served all colors." The WIC program was, in many ways, the most vibrant part of the agency by the late 1980s. Operation Life WIC served nearly seventy thousand clients during that decade.[89]

The clinic also responded to pressing new community problems. In the mid-1980s, crack cocaine flooded the neighborhood, leaving devastation in its wake. Operation Life created a pioneering, state-funded drug and alcohol education program for young people. Peer counselors ran seminars, Alcoholics Anonymous–type meetings, and rap groups, while clinic staff worked to get clients into drug treatment. A twenty-four-hour drug crisis hotline offered information and referrals for people with substance abuse problems. In tandem with the drug program, Operation Life ran stress-reduction classes for low-income parents, to reduce drug and child abuse.[90]

Despite Operation Life's efforts to stem the tide of drug abuse, some of its own employees fell prey to crack. Twice, Duncan had to fire young women she found dealing drugs out of the Operation Life WIC office. Retribution came swiftly. One young junkie sought to avenge his girlfriend's firing by spraying the back door of the clinic with bullets. Fortunately, no one was hurt. But addicts hit Operation Life in other ways as well, stealing equipment, office supplies, and money. The theft problem got so bad, says Georgia Phillips, that "if it wasn't nailed down it wasn't going to stay—chairs, tables, pictures, it went. The same thing with the day care center. Even toys." And there was no money to replace them.[91]

By the middle of Reagan's second term, federal funding was drying up faster than pools of water in the desert. But in 1987, HUD provided $1.5 million to fund one last major Operation Life initiative: the Westside's first senior citizen housing project. In recognition of Duncan's longstanding advocacy for the elderly poor, the new thirty-apartment complex was named Ruby Duncan Manor. Harriet Trudell told reporters she hoped this would be just the beginning of Operation Life's work in senior housing. In a city where affordable housing was becoming ever more scarce, said Trudell, "we need 300 units, not just the 30 we got, but you have to make the best of what you have. If we can get more federal money, which has been tight, we would consider building more housing."

Trudell knew that was unlikely to happen. She, Aldine Weems, Renee Diamond, and Duncan had traveled to San Francisco a year earlier to sign the papers making Operation Life eligible for the HUD money. They were joined at the HUD offices by Marty Makower and Jack Anderson, both of whom now practiced economic development law in Oakland. The reunion was sweet. They all felt lucky to have something to celebrate at a time when funding for the poor was disappearing. The celebrations continued in Las Vegas at the grand opening of the project early in 1988. The whole coalition was present for that occasion: Maya Miller, the board, the Franciscans, the League of Women Voters, city and state political allies, and all of Operation Life's founders— now old enough, and still poor enough, that they all qualified for housing in Ruby Duncan Manor.[92]

It was a bittersweet time, says Harriet Trudell. Even as the women celebrated the launch of Ruby Duncan Manor, Health and Human Services officials told her that federal support for community health clinics across the country was on the chopping block. Funding for Operation Life's clinic was about to be cut. "It's over," they told Trudell grimly. She thought she saw tears in one official's eyes. "We hung on way longer than most of the CDCs," Trudell asserts with gruff pride. "We produced again and again. We had such a good reputation and track record that it took them a long, long time to destroy us." But that didn't make it any easier when the ax fell.[93]

CHAPTER 9

MAYBE WE WERE FIGHTING HISTORY: THE LEGACY OF OPERATION LIFE

We were fighting the community, the courts, the welfare department and the government. And maybe we were fighting history.

—Renee Diamond, on the end of Operation Life

HOW A DREAM DIES

One by one, the programs the Operation Life women had worked so hard to build were taken away. The first to go was the library. In the summer of 1986, Clark County announced plans to construct a new library on the Westside. The women weren't sure how to feel about the news. For the first time, their neighborhood would have a state-of-the-art library facility, with computer terminals, film-screening rooms, and a performance space. Thirteen years earlier, the women had rescued a derelict building from the wrecker's ball to create the Westside's first library. And they had done it, Ruby Duncan pointed out, "without a dime of public money." Without Operation Life, it is likely that the Westside would have gone on as it had for years, with no library at all. So the announcement was a victory, of sorts.

Once the new library was completed, however, Operation Life would lose one of its primary sources of monthly income—the rent from the library district. And one of its prime properties would again stand empty. Duncan couldn't shake the feeling that the organization had begun to slide downhill. Renee Diamond helped the women look for another tenant, but nothing came of their negotiations.[1]

Duncan changed tactics. Why spend millions on a new library, she asked county officials, when the Westside already had a good one? She tried to convince officials to spend the money instead on something Clark County desperately needed: a homeless shelter. Las Vegas had one of the highest rates of homelessness of any U.S. city its size, and the numbers of homeless in the city continued to grow exponentially with each year. After the 1987 stock market crash derailed the full-speed-ahead economy, many poor families who came to Las Vegas seeking work found themselves stranded. Unable to afford even the least-expensive housing in this high-rent city, they lived in cars, parks, and parking lots, or camped out in empty buildings. After Operation Life's move to the new building, the Cove was once again vacant. With five floors of bedrooms, and downstairs offices set up for social service programs, the hotel would be a perfect site for transitional housing, Duncan argued. Here was a chance both to tackle a pressing problem and to make good use of the white elephant. But city and federal officials repeatedly rejected her applications.[2]

The library district, too, rebuffed Duncan. The neighborhood needed a larger library with modern amenities, officials said. No amount of plaster and paint could hide the fact that the Operation Life facility was inadequate. Duncan's protests, they said, were not in the interest of the community. Unspoken, says Mahlon Brown, was the city's discomfort with the Nation of Islam, which was using the library building for its youth group. Officials felt that libraries should not be sites for political or religious proselytizing. They worried that the Black Muslims were indoctrinating Westside youth to hate whites. Operation Life women thought the Nation of Islam was doing some good, preaching self-respect and urging young people to avoid drugs and alcohol. Essie Henderson was a liaison with the local mosque, where she was a member. Henderson, who became a strict vegetarian and took to wearing a white turban, sometimes called white allies "blue-eyed devils." She says she was teasing, but it made good friends of Operation Life uncomfortable and it made less sympathetic observers livid.

For Henderson and the other women who had worked so hard to make the library a vital community center, the sight of the Operation Life building standing empty again was heartbreaking. Its flaking walls held thirteen years of memories. Children with no quiet space in their homes had come there to study. Old people had nestled into the library's comfortable chairs for warmth in the winter, or simply to break out of their isolation. Welfare mothers had taken classes there in math, literacy, and computers. Drug addicts seeking to quit had found support in Operation Life rap groups. Teenage mothers had learned the basics of diapering, feeding, and comforting their children in parenting classes. On weekends, the library had hosted community dinners, African culture festivals, and films.

"I first saw Paul Robeson as *The Emperor Jones* in that library," Renee Diamond reminisces. A group of Operation Life women had watched the film together, huddled close in the dark, whispering their appreciation of the great black actor and singer. Eugene O'Neill's play about the contradictions of black power-seeking hit the women hard, perhaps because it echoed so many of their own experiences over the past two decades.[3]

Ruby Duncan thought of the film's antihero when her long-time ally and friend, the Reverend Al Dunn, was convicted of running a counterfeit operation that had printed $2 million in phony U.S. currency. Mahlon Brown, by then the U.S. attorney for Southern Nevada, had investigated Dunn. The episode was extremely painful for Duncan, whom Dunn accused of betrayal. "She's a bought—lock, stock and barrel—black woman," he told reporters. "She must be quarantined politically." Duncan professed nothing but compassion for her old friend. "What has the poor man got, but frustration like all black folk?" she asked. Too many years of rejection and racism can push a black person over the edge, she said. Some of Duncan's friends wondered if she was not describing her own descent into despair. As Operation Life's programs fell under the ax, Duncan lashed out with a fury that stripped away her reputation as a seasoned political strategist and administrator. She started to sound again like the fire-breathing militant who burst onto the Las Vegas scene in 1969. In her own mind as well, Duncan was once again the righteous poor mother locked in battle with cruel and capricious officials.[4]

The blows fell quickly on Operation Life in 1986. After the library closed, the next program to go was the organization's foray into affordable housing. Thirty years after the women first arrived in Las Vegas, housing on the West-side was still overcrowded and substandard. Using federal funds, Operation Life had begun building houses for poor and moderate-income residents in 1980. The women had researched the best low-cost construction methods and materials. Duncan had convinced the city of Las Vegas to donate land, and the Ford Foundation helped underwrite the construction. The first round of building had been an unqualified success: the organization had constructed and sold ten homes, and planned to build at least ten more. Profits from the homes were to be placed in a revolving loan fund to pay for future construction projects. Duncan was confident that Operation Life had finally launched a business that would lead to economic self-sufficiency.

But, at the same time that the county announced it was opening a new Westside library, city officials reclaimed funds they had awarded Operation Life to build another ten low-cost homes on the Westside. City planners cited a HUD memo that criticized the Operation Life building campaign for being too sluggish—although Ford had commended its speed. The city also claimed

The Operation Life Day Care Centers offered prekindergarten education, warm meals, and an introduction to African American history, culture, and music to Westside children. Here is a group at the center in the 1980s. (Courtesy of Ruby Duncan)

that some of the new homeowners earned too much money to qualify for the houses, endangering federal support. But the real reason for the city pullout was economic. Private developers were now building houses for low-income families. Las Vegas no longer needed to subsidize such efforts. Mayor Ron Lurie ordered Duncan to return more than $132,000. The demand hit Duncan like a body blow.[5]

City and county officials had been allies of Operation Life for years. They had sided with the women in battles with state officials in the 1970s. After 1980, they had spoken up on behalf of Operation Life when federal officials threatened to defund the group. Now, Duncan began to feel that there was no place to turn. "The federal government gave cities the authority to do as they wish," she complained to reporters. "Poor communities have no power or jurisdiction to hang onto anything." In a stinging press release, Duncan and Trudell charged city officials with punishing Operation Life for its successes. The women of Operation Life had expected the city "to laud our achievement and hasten to support our next redevelopment venture," they wrote. The city's "changed priorities are a bitter pill to swallow." In an intemperate outburst that she would later regret, Duncan branded city officials racists and refused to return the money. "We are stung, disappointed, and angered by this turn-about," she raged. But she knew her fury was impotent.[6]

In July 1986, Duncan went to City Hall to return the money. When told that the mayor was not there to accept the check personally, she turned around and walked out of the building. As she had so many times, she paused to speak with reporters. Operation Life had brought millions of dollars in federal aid to Las Vegas, and hundreds of millions in buying power generated by the programs they had brought into the state. Years of work by Operation Life women had brought tax revenues to the city and benefited business as well as the poor, she said. "Hereafter you may not exploit our labor and skill, and then take away from us and our community the benefits for which we strive."[7]

Duncan's attempt to claim the moral high ground did not intimidate the mayor. Like many others in city government, he had watched her career for a long time. Lurie dismissed her outrage as little more than political theater. "If I had known she was going to put on a complete show," the mayor said, "I would've cancelled my other appointments to be here." He warned Duncan that grandstanding would not pay off. "She's playing games with us," he told reporters. "If that's the way she wants to play, we'll play the same way. She's not running city government. We are." Duncan's tactics would endanger Operation Life funding in other areas, he said. "We may have to have a full-blown investigation of all of the programs." Federal housing officials sided with the mayor, ruling that Operation Life violated HUD regulations by selling two houses to families whose incomes slightly exceeded allowable levels for families participating in its program. A dispirited Duncan quietly returned the money.[8]

Duncan wrote a friend from her Washington days, Massachusetts Congressman Joe Kennedy, to ask for help and advice. The letter suggests just how desperate Duncan was feeling as she watched Operation Life's fortunes ebb. "I am frustrated," she wrote. "If they want to go to war, I sure do know how to fight and I'm ready for 'em. I'm mad as hell and half crazy, but I do know what I am capable of doing.... I respect and listen to your advice. Please, please tell me what would you do if you were in Operation Life's shoes?"[9]

Duncan did still have some friends in Washington, and amidst the blows came surprising victories. Just two months after the city terminated the housing program, Operation Life received large federal grants to add a dental clinic and new administrative offices to the health center. HUD gave Operation Life money to hire more staff for its mortgage counseling program, still the only federally funded service in Nevada helping homeowners avoid foreclosures. Publicly, Duncan pronounced herself "thrilled to death." But, behind closed doors, confusion reigned.[10]

Operation Life was receiving such mixed signals from funders that no one knew for sure whether the organization was on its way up or down. The uncertainty took its toll. People who worked at Operation Life in the late 1980s say that Duncan became increasingly anxious and short-tempered. The feel of the office changed. Recriminations and finger-pointing became common, heightened by tensions over race and gender. The coalition that had for so long sustained Operation Life began to fray, as did Ruby Duncan's nerves. Intense stress aggravated the old back injury that had first landed Duncan on welfare so many years before. Her spinal disks began to dissolve. There were mornings when she could not move her feet from the bed to the floor without sending knife-sharp pain coursing through her legs, back, and neck. Duncan's own body was turning against her.[11]

So, too, were federal health officials, although Operation Life was not singled out. Community health centers came under attack across the country. Health and Human Services (HHS) officials in San Francisco had warned Harriet Trudell in 1987 that clinic funding was coming to an end. Nevada Health Division chief Larry Matheis told Nevada legislators in spring 1987 that federal officials had "made it extremely clear that it's not their intention to fully fund any community health centers in the future." Matheis said it would be a mistake for the state to allow clinics like Operation Life's to close, because they filled "cracks in our primary health care system." Nevada and other states did increase funding for community health centers, but they could not compensate for the federal cuts.[12]

No one disputed the quality of such clinics, which provided "better health care at lower cost" than private clinics, said Princeton University health policy analyst Paul Starr in 1986. So why was HHS withdrawing support for the program? "The answer," Starr wrote, "was clearly ideological," a single-minded "repudiation of the War on Poverty."[13]

Withdrawing federal funding from community health centers, Renee Diamond says, allowed Reagan administration officials to redress what they saw as one of the worst mistakes of the nation's antipoverty crusade: using federal funds to underwrite militant community groups. Without that money, organizations such as Operation Life would die quickly and quietly. Diamond, who was elected to the Nevada Assembly in the late 1980s, watched closely as federal health officials systematically transferred funding from community groups to professional health maintenance organizations.[14]

Across the country, community health centers were told to lower their costs, raise their income, hire staff with better credentials, and increase the numbers of people they served, if they wanted to keep federal funding. George Miller's office issued "minimum qualifications and experience" standards for community health center personnel in Nevada and California, forcing Duncan and the clinic board to fire several Operation Life stalwarts who were now deemed unqualified. One was longtime clinic director Diane Guinn, who had been working for Operation Life since 1972.[15]

Rosie Seals was there the day that clinic board members voted to ask Diane Guinn for her resignation. Everyone felt sick about it. Guinn had dedicated thirteen years of her life to Operation Life, but board members felt that they had to safeguard the clinic's future. Guinn felt betrayed, as they knew she would. To this day, Guinn thinks Duncan could have fought harder to protect her. And she was not the only longtime staffer forced out in the mid-1980s. Duncan says she argued passionately to try to save her staff, especially Guinn, expending dwindling political capital in the process. But in the end, Duncan and the board did what was asked of them, hoping to save the clinic.[16]

The firings enabled Operation Life to preserve federal funding in the short run, but the organization paid a high price. Suspicions ran rampant as staff and supporters waited anxiously to see who would be fired next. Some of the Westside women voiced doubts about the commitment of white allies, believing that politically connected women such as Harriet Trudell and Maya Miller could somehow save the group if they really wanted to. Some white supporters began to pull away, hurt and incredulous that anyone could question their loyalty after so many years of service. And as jobs became more scarce, jealousies festered among the Westside mothers. Why had some of the founding mothers drawn salaries when others hadn't? Whose children had benefited most from Operation Life? There had always been pressure from Washington, and George Miller's political vendettas were drearily familiar—but the women could no longer hang tight against them. The trust and intimacy that had for so long held the Operation Life coalition together began to unravel.

Determined to hold everything together, the endlessly competent Aldine Weems became acting clinic director while Duncan and the board searched for a credentialed director to replace Guinn. But Miller's office rejected their choices, and laid down an ultimatum. If Aldine Weems was still acting director in four months, HHS would withdraw funding for the clinic. The search process shifted into high gear. "The searches were long, painful, exhausting and expensive," says Makower. They drained Operation Life of energy and resources. "I think we did the best that we could to hire good people," she says. "But they didn't fit the organization. The relationships didn't gel. The work that we could have done didn't happen because we had to deal with personalities and ideas that were just not appropriate for our organization."[17]

The final straw was Miller's insistence that Operation Life hire, as clinic director, a white academic with no connection to the community. Tensions flared quickly between Duncan and the woman, who had a strong managerial style and was closely allied with George Miller. The clinic was slipping out of Ruby Duncan's control—and out of Operation Life's grip, as well. A few years earlier, George Miller's HHS office had forced Operation Life to enter into a financial partnership with Vegas Verdes, a North Las Vegas clinic that served the city's growing population of Mexican and Central American immigrants. Operation Life was wary of being held responsible for a clinic whose board they did not know and whose billing and hiring practices they did not control, but it complied. By 1986, regional HHS officials told Operation Life that the clinic was not growing fast enough. Shortly after the new director was hired, Miller's office gave Operation Life six months to increase its monthly patient visits or face closure.

Duncan says Operation Life was seeing plenty of new patients. "They gave us a hoop to jump and we jumped through it. So they raise it and we jumped through that. Then they raised it again. We jumped over it." The combined clinics were logging between thirty-six thousand and fifty-thousand patient visits a year, Duncan says, serving sixteen thousand patients too poor to pay for private medical care. Where, she asked federal officials, would those families go if the Operation Life clinic shut down?[18]

Duncan's protests fell on deaf ears. In December 1986, Miller's regional HHS office announced that it would no longer fund the clinic. Operation Life was ordered to transfer patient records to other health centers. No other clinics could absorb so many patients, Duncan replied. A University Medical Center clinic had opened near the Westside, but its managers warned federal officials that it would not be able to handle all of Operation Life's patients. Duncan desperately asked political allies for help. "We see this action," she wrote Nevada Democrats, "as part of the administration's larger effort to deprive poor people of their rights as citizens."[19]

In a letter to Maya Miller, Duncan called the decision to defund the clinic "a deliberate and diabolical attack" by George Miller "to avenge old Nevada political wars." Contacts in Washington confirmed Duncan's suspicion that Miller had played a direct role in defunding the clinic, although he denied the charge. HHS regional directors, he said, had no say in federal health policy. In fact, Miller claimed, he had tried to save Operation Life. "Ruby had her heart in the right place," he said toward the end of his life. "I tried to explain her to the Public Health Service boys. She wasn't always so good on the paperwork, though. And when you're spending taxpayers' money, you've got to have accountability."[20]

As she had so many times before, Duncan pulled every string she could. She wrote to every official in city, county, and state government who had expressed support for the clinic over the years. U.S. senators Harry Reid and Richard Bryan, together with congressman Jim Bilbray, met with the federal chief of the Community Health Center program. They convinced him to continue funding Operation Life and to provide the clinic three additional National Health Service Corps physicians. But he insisted that the current clinic board resign. The new board would be composed of elected officials and health professionals. Rosie Seals and other veterans who'd been on the board for years were forced off. Of clinic founders, only board member Essie Henderson was allowed to remain.[21]

The new board came together very quickly. There were many in Las Vegas who wanted to see the Westside clinic survive. But few on the new board believed that poor people should run their own clinics. The new Operation Life clinic board was prestigious: it included a congresswoman, a county commissioner, and a healthcare administrator from the University Medical Center.[22] But it was out of touch with the population it was supposed to serve, perhaps intentionally so. Board members imposed new layers of bureaucracy at the clinic and introduced a strict new set of patient fees. Essie Henderson complained that new clinic rules required her to pay eighty dollars for copies of her grandchildren's health records. That was a hardship for any poor family, she said.[23]

The clinic was mostly out of their hands by now, but Operation Life's founding mothers had the satisfaction of knowing that its funding was secure—for at least the near future. Operation Life still had WIC and the homeowners' counseling program, and the Ford Foundation continued to sponsor the group's job placement program for poor women. Harriet Trudell worked with a committee of casino and hotel owners, bankers, airport commissioners, and state economic development officers through 1989 to develop new business opportunities. And there were a few bright spots for the founding mothers: with Operation Life CDC backing, Mary Wesley opened a small restaurant.[24]

A 1987 Ford Foundation report singled Duncan out for praise, calling her and other CDC leaders "architects of a new society" and practitioners of "corrective capitalism," who were bringing investment dollars to communities that private sector capital had long since abandoned. But, in truth, by that time Operation Life's fires were burning lower. And so were Ruby Duncan's. In 1988, when a Nevada newspaper described Duncan as the embodiment of Martin Luther King Jr.'s legacy and asked her to reflect on her two decades of organizing, she sounded dispirited. "There are too many people who are unemployed," she said, "too many people not getting a good education, too many who are homeless, unhealthy and sick." Duncan wondered if it might not be time to return to direct action protest. "Nothing ever works unless you make a lot of noise and move real heavy," she said, sounding more like the rabble-rouser of the late 1960s than the seasoned lobbyist and political negotiator she had been for the last decade.[25]

That summer, Duncan flew to Atlanta to attend the Democratic National Convention with her son David, who was a delegate for the Reverend Jesse Jackson. Duncan wept as she listened to Jackson, who had run a historic campaign for the presidency, describe the highs and lows of the civil rights movement. Thirty years of black activism, and her own hard work, had indeed carried her far from the cotton fields of the Ivory Plantation. But it was a constant struggle to keep from sliding backwards. Unbeknownst to her, one final battle was taking form at that very moment.[26]

While Duncan was in Atlanta, George Miller ordered Vegas Verdes to merge completely with the Operation Life clinic and move into the Operation Life building. To make room, he told the Operation Life CDC to move out. Miller claimed the Vegas Verdes clinic needed the office space and that Operation Life had ample office space in its other properties. Duncan protested. She had just secured a federal grant to expand the Operation Life headquarters building. If the move could just wait a few months, she pleaded, there would be room enough for the CDC and the expanded clinic. The answer came quickly: Miller's office wanted the new merged clinic operational in weeks. If Operation Life CDC did not move out, there would be no clinic at all in the building.[27]

Rosie Seals felt as if the floor had been pulled from under her feet. "How can they come in and demand this?" she asked, perplexed. "There must be a screw loose somewhere. We are going to fight like hell before they move us from this building." The women contemplated moving the CDC to the vacant library building. Maybe there was a silver lining in this. Perhaps, by charging the new combined clinics a higher rent, the Operation Life CDC could fund new ventures in the community. But then the women got the chilling news that the new clinic board—on which Henderson was completely isolated —planned to change the name of the clinic and then remove the Operation Life logo from the facade of the building they had worked so hard to erect. It seemed to the women as though their enemies were determined to erase all traces of their twenty-year movement.[28]

At Duncan's request, Senators Reid and Bryan and Congressman Bilbray visited George Miller and the regional director of the Public Health Service in San Francisco and tried in vain to negotiate a compromise. Reid called Duncan and told her the director would not budge. Operation Life would have to move. Maya Miller didn't buy it. Something was fishy, she told Duncan. "It isn't every day that two Senators and a Congressman get faced down by a regional agency rep." It would make it easy for the politicians, Maya Miller wrote, "for us at OL to say, 'we'll do it gracefully for the community.' But then I think of the dreaming and scheming, the writing and re-writing of grant proposals, the respect you earned at the legislature, the time and foot leather spent in Washington . . . all the pains and strains . . . all these efforts to bring health care to the community." Thinking back on all of that, Miller concluded, "I can only dig my heels in deeper with the rest of you and say with Rosie: 'There must be a screw loose somewhere.' "[29]

The women opted to stay in the Operation Life building, which they still owned, but they were left with an empty shell. Rather than wait six months for the Operation Life addition, George Miller stripped the Operation Life clinic of its federal funding and ordered the board members of the new combined health clinic to move. Federal moneys that had already been allocated for the Operation Life addition were transferred to the new health management group, which renamed the clinic the Community Health Center of Southern Nevada. "They literally moved a block away," Renee Diamond says, still exasperated. "They spent a half million dollars in public funds rehabbing a shopping center to get their community health center, leaving this building, that had been built specifically for health care, empty."[30]

Pillaged is perhaps a closer description. Duncan, Beals, Seals, and Mary Southern walked through their clinic after the move to see what repairs needed to be done. They were stunned at what they found. "They had torn the place up," Mary Southern said bitterly, tears in her eyes. "Ripped the faucets out of the wall. Tore down the seats, the cabinets. And they left us empty champagne bottles in the trash to let us know they enjoyed doing it. One minute you got everybody on your side, all the officials, all the politicians. And then, like that, it's 'damn you.' "[31]

Ruby Duncan says the strength ebbed from her legs as she walked through the wreckage. But she refused to let city officials or Westside leaders see how the loss affected her. "Never let the man find out what your weak spot is," she often told her daughter Sondra. "Once they find your weak spot, they'll destroy you." Instead, as she had so many times before, Duncan picked up the pieces and kept on. Operation Life still had the WIC program, and federal administrators wanted WIC centers connected to a health clinic. So Duncan negotiated with the University Medical Center to bring a small satellite team of nurses to the building, and the clinic reopened. It was smaller, and the women no longer ran it. But there was once again a clinic for women and children in the Operation Life building.

The Cove, even shuttered and cemented, was still worth $250,000. The women tried to parlay it into something of use, applying yet again for federal funds to turn the Cove into either a homeless shelter, senior citizen housing, or a nursing home. "It could be a dynamic project," Duncan enthused. "We have loads of low-income seniors and handicapped people who have no place to stay." But the federal government turned her down. Meanwhile, the building was costing Operation Life more than $10,000 a year to seal off, so that no transient could set a fire there that might spread through the neighborhood.[32]

Early in 1989 city commissioners issued a warning to Operation Life. Unless the group found money to rehabilitate the Cove, the city would have to knock it down. The hulking edifice had become a haven for gangs and drugs, authorities said. Operation Life paid to have the building bricked up, but transients and homeless families still found ways to get back in. The Cove, with its eighty-eight bedrooms, was irresistible to people with no place to sleep—of whom there were more in Las Vegas with each passing month. The Clark County Commission allocated a small amount of money to begin repairs on the Cove, but on July 26, 1989, the historic old hotel caught fire.

Duncan was awakened by a phone call late that night. "Do you know the Cove is burning?" a male voice asked. The caller would not give his name but told her that friends of Duncan's were sitting on the corner that evening and saw two official-looking trucks drive into the parking lot. The trucks stayed for a half hour. Minutes after they left, the hotel burst into flames. No one was ever charged with arson, but fire officials told reporters that the fire had spread too quickly and too fiercely to be anything but intentional. "Fire Bug Torches the Cove," headlines blazed the next morning.[33]

The city demolished the building so fast it was eerie, Father Vitale recalls. "They knocked it down overnight. Even that late on, they were anxious to get rid of anything associated with Operation Life. They had the wreckers in there the day after the fire. A lot of people felt that wasn't necessary. But they really wanted to get rid of that building." Looking back, Vitale says, "I don't know if it was a great boon or a total disaster getting the Cove Hotel. It was the greatest ego booster in the entire world when they took over that hotel. But, God, it took an enormous amount of energy out of the organization over the years to keep that building going."[34]

The Cove's significance may have been mostly symbolic. When first refurbished, the hotel-turned-clinic had been a visible sign that the women were bringing new life to a devastated neighborhood. When the building was reduced to ashes, many who had worked in the crowded, damp, unbearably hot or cold—yet somehow utopian—Cove office came back to the corner of Jackson and D streets. They hugged. They rubbed their eyes, closed them, opened them. It was really gone. It felt as though they were the only ones left who could still see it. Much of Operation Life's history had been locked in the old Cove office. Now, many of those records, photographs, and letters were lost. The women wondered if anyone would remember what they had built there.

Operation Life did not fold with the loss of the clinic, or even the burning of the Cove. The organization still had large grants for WIC, drug and violence prevention programs, mortgage counseling, and job development. But the loss of the clinic, the torching of the Cove, and twenty-five years of stress and struggle finished the work that federal budget cutters had begun. Aldine Weems died early in 1990, just fifty years old. She had been sick for years from kidney disease and smoking-related emphysema. Duncan was grief-stricken and scared. Everything—and everyone—seemed to be slipping away too fast. Renee Diamond was elected to the state legislature and had to curtail her involvement with Operation Life. Maya Miller resigned as chair in 1990; at seventy-five she could no longer make the regular trips south. Duncan's nerves and her spinal disks grew more inflamed every day, until she walked out of her office in the middle of 1990 and was ordered by her physician not to return.[35]

The younger generation rushed into the breach. Duncan's oldest daughter, Georgia Phillips, returned to Operation Life after an eight-year absence to run the homeowners' counseling program and to manage Ruby Duncan

Manor. Ana Luna taught nutrition classes, counseled pregnant women and lactating mothers, and screened WIC patients. There were too few people to run the WIC program by then, she says, so everyone had to pitch in wherever they were needed. Women in their thirties, who had marched on the Strip and come of age in the Cove, poured into the Operation Life building to keep the programs afloat.

Duncan couldn't get out of her bed, but "she called in the old fighting troops at the end," says Marty Makower. And they came. Essie Henderson, Rosie Seals, Versie Beals, Mary Southern, Emma Stampley, and other neighborhood women who had been involved from the beginning created a new board. Duncan convinced the Ford Foundation to provide one last $150,000 grant. The board called in Jack Anderson to help them reassess where to go from there. They asked two black professors from the University of Nevada— an Upward Bound director and an education professor—to lend their expertise as well.[36]

But with Duncan and Weems gone, the organization became unmoored. The state Economic Opportunity Board, charged with dispensing state poverty program moneys on the Westside, worried that there was no one at the helm. While Duncan lay in bed, in her words, "half crazy with pain and drifting from all the painkillers and other drugs," the state announced that Operation Life would no longer be eligible for funding. Mid-paycheck, Harriet Trudell's salary was suspended. She walked away from the Operation Life building with tears in her eyes. She still can't figure out how or why everything came to such a crashing end. "I guess in the end it was just Reaganism that did us in," she says.[37]

The Ford Foundation decided to cut ties. Operation Life seemed to have little vision or energy left. Foundation head Robert Curvin asked Duncan what she might like to do after Operation Life. She still fantasized about opening a dress shop for large women, Duncan replied. But, for now, she could have only one goal: to regain her health sufficiently that she didn't have to take painkillers so strong that it took her half of every morning to clear her head.[38]

In that fog, Duncan wasn't even fully aware that the last of Operation Life was passing. The homeowners' counseling program ended in 1991 when a HUD official visited the Westside unannounced and found no one at the Operation Life offices, and no sign telling clients where else to go for help. The WIC program was the last to go, shutting its doors on September 30, 1992. Some of the staff had been working without paychecks for months. "The very last day was so depressing," says Ana Luna, "not just because we were losing our jobs but because we enjoyed working together. Everybody was quiet on the last day. We ate together. We didn't go out for lunch. We had a few patients. I remember closing the door. Everyone was crying."[39]

Ruby Duncan was in so much back pain that she slept through that last day. A few days later, she and Georgia, who was now managing Ruby Duncan Manor, the sole surviving piece of Operation Life, headed to the office, as if they expected it to be open, with mothers and their babies lining up. When they crossed Owens street, the reality hit them. They stood in silence for a long time, just taking it in. The building was dark. In offices that had been crowded since the building opened, there was not a soul to be seen. For a long time afterward, Renee Diamond says, she would go out of her way to avoid the street where the Operation Life building stood. "It was just too sad to see the building empty. I couldn't stand to see it that way." It was better to remember it full of people, shouts of laughter, crying babies, wisecracking teenagers, and the irresistible smell of Versie Beals's sweet potato pies.

Operation Life had survived, even thrived, during the Nixon, Ford, and Carter administrations, eight years of Ronald Reagan, and almost the entire presidency of George H. W. Bush. For twenty years, often without salaries, the women kept the office going, wrote grant proposals, met with politicians, and countered the charges of fraud and nepotism that came as regularly as summer storms. They fed the hungry, provided medical care to the poor and elderly, nourished infants and pregnant women, built homes and senior citizen housing, ran job placement and daycare programs, created a library and pool, taught nutrition, built self-esteem, and mounted innovative efforts to combat drug abuse, domestic violence, and sexual assault. Operation Life truly was the social and economic anchor of the Westside, exactly what the architects of community development had envisioned.

Ruby Duncan and the women of Operation Life were unusual in many ways, says Louis Vitale, who is a scholar of grass-roots social justice movements. First and most remarkable, theirs was truly a poor mothers' movement. The women conceived it, drove it, and sustained it. And they attracted a talented and dedicated pool of allies who worked alongside them for twenty years. "To make a movement work," says Vitale, "you have to have a really broad base." Duncan and the mothers of the Westside drew together an amazingly broad coalition—of women and men, young and old, black and white. The Westside mothers and their children, Vitale and the Franciscans, Jack Anderson, Mahlon Brown, Marty Makower, Harriet Trudell, Renee Diamond, and Maya Miller devoted two decades of their lives to their shared dreams: empowerment for poor women and a minimum quality of life for all. To a person, their hearts are still in it.

Vitale, who is still ministering to the urban poor, marching with migrant farmworkers, and getting arrested at U.S. military installations, believes that Operation Life—and the coalition that created and sustained it—are models for bottom-up social change. "That movement probably came as close as anybody ever has to the goal of community-based groups developing their own destiny. The women went into the arena of running an organization and yet they still maintained their grassroots identity." In the process, the women of Operation Life not only strengthened their city and neighborhood, they created a new community—what civil rights workers called a "beloved community," nurturing bonds of love, friendship, and political commitment across lines of racial, religious, and economic difference.[40]

The women's continued enthusiasm and refusal to accept defeat kept the movement going long after most community organizations dependent on federal poverty program dollars had folded and been forgotten. But eventually even the staunchest Operation Life veterans were forced to reckon with a political climate that was growing ever more hostile to community-based organizations, not only in Washington, but also in the nation's cities. The nation's commitment to fighting poverty had evolved and transformed itself many times since 1964, from the War on Poverty to a war between poverty programs, and from there to a war on the poor. By 1992, few remnants of the early idealism remained. To many Americans, the very idea of a presidential war on poverty seemed naive. It was at that moment, with Bill Clinton promising to end welfare as we know it, that I first met Ruby Duncan and the women of Operation Life.

THE YEARS AFTER OPERATION LIFE

I was first introduced to Ruby Duncan, Alversa Beals, Rosie Seals, Essie Henderson, Emma Stampley, Mary Wesley, Leola Harris, and Mary Southern on Labor Day 1992, three weeks before the Operation Life WIC clinic closed its doors for the last time. Ruby suggested the Union Plaza Hotel for our meeting because it was just across the tracks from the Westside. Long ago it had been a railroad station. Now, it was a run-down but still busy hotel—its casino thronged with gamblers of every conceivable racial and ethnic variety, its showroom headlining a drag performer named Jimmy James, who was that night impersonating Marilyn Monroe.

The restaurant was empty when I arrived. A few minutes later, I saw a line

Fifty years after moving to Las Vegas, Alversa Beals still fishes, traps turtles, and grows fresh greens in a backyard garden to feed her family. (Annelise Orleck)

of suspicious-eyed, elderly black women heading toward me, led by a large, chocolate-colored woman coiffed in cascading curls. "Ladies," Ruby Duncan announced in the ringing soprano voice that her children and friends love to imitate, "this is the history professor who wants to write our story." She paused theatrically, then swept her arm out in a gesture that embraced them all and finally came to rest on her own chest. "Ladies," she declared, "We are History!"

As soon as we sat down, the women grew animated. They seemed happy to be together again. The sudden end of Operation Life had scattered them with a force that left them feeling bruised. They ate heartily, joked with each other, touched each other's arms, caught up on gossip.

They told the funny stories at first. There was the time Duncan burned the cornbread at Jack Anderson's birthday party, but the white folks ate it anyway and said how good it was. "Yeah," Rosie Seals laughed, "till I asked them, 'What you doing eating that black bread?'" "Isn't it supposed to be this way?" Anderson asked. Then there was the time they served sausage to children from a Nation of Islam mosque whose leader had specifically asked them not to feed the children any pork. Mary Southern warned Duncan: "Those kids are gonna tell." Duncan was unrepentant. "Hungry as they are," she laughed, "they are not gonna say a thing." The women still remembered cooking red beans over sterno in their rooms at an exclusive Aspen retreat, where they'd been invited to attend a Ford Foundation board of directors training session. "We couldn't even afford breakfast there," one of the women shouted. "The cheapest thing on the menu was seventeen dollars." Tears of laughter rolled down their cheeks.

The green satin wallpaper around us had lost its sheen, but these old ladies still burned with passion. Raw with anger at how the clinic had been taken from them, they shifted with breathtaking speed between fury, tears, and raucous humor. They told stories of when they first arrived in Las Vegas, recounted their moments of political triumph, prodded each other's memories, argued with each other's interpretations, told embarrassing anecdotes at each other's expense. And every once in a while, they admitted how confused they were by the ugliness of the way it ended. As I sat there, the women began to puzzle through what had happened and just what their legacy might be.

People did seem to remember them, Duncan said, with more fondness than she expected. When the Westside exploded after the Los Angeles police officers who beat Rodney King were acquitted, there were only two buildings on the Westside that were completely untouched: the Operation Life building and Ruby Duncan Manor. "There's not even graffiti on those buildings," Duncan said proudly. Seals nodded, banged the floor with her cane, and shifted a wad of chewing tobacco in her cheek. "They respect us," she said. "That's why they leave those buildings alone."

Duncan says her phone started ringing as soon as news of the verdict came down, and the streets of the Westside flared into violence. A city official she had worked with for years asked her to help restore peace to the Westside streets. "They knew I wasn't afraid of those gang kids," she said softly. "I knew them when they were babies. Their mothers used to come to the clinic. They got to grow healthy and strong on all that WIC milk and eggs." She gave a full and throaty laugh, satisfied at what she and the other mothers had done for their community. "All that good food we gave them."

Those Westside girls and boys, now adults, still recognized the women. They would stop Duncan, Beals, Seals, or Henderson on the street and ask them when they were going to bring the community back together again. For a while, they thought they might revive Operation Life. But now, Henderson tells young people: "We're old. We did our share. If anything's going to happen, it will have to be you young people who make your own."

Emma Stampley says she wouldn't feel safe now going door to door, the way they did twenty years earlier. "I'd be afraid I might get shot." Crack cocaine swept the neighborhood like a hurricane in the late 1980s, savaging families and spreading gang violence. Cheap, powerfully addictive, and notorious for its links to crime, crack changed the once close-knit Westside. Some of the Operation Life women have lost children to drug overdoses. All have been touched by gunshots. As Los Angeles gangs exported members to run the Las Vegas drug trade, drive-by shootings and executions became all too common.

In the years since Operation Life closed its doors, three of Stampley's children have died. Her youngest was shot by gangsters as he left a dance club. Stampley's house was guarded by police for several weeks afterward, fearful that an assailant might target the rest of the family. Versie Beals says that many of Stampley's friends were afraid to attend the funeral for fear that shooting would break out. Eddie Jean Finks has lost three children as well: two daughters to depression and drugs, her son to a hail of gangsters' bullets. Another Operation Life activist, Roma Jean Hunt, lost her daughter to a drive-by shooting. The young woman was sitting on the living room couch feeding her newborn infant when bullets tore through the front window and into her chest. She had just enough time to lay her baby safely on the floor before she died. With each tragedy, old friends and comrades from Operation Life rally around, bringing food and words of solace. Marshaling strength, finding energy they didn't know they still had, weary grandmothers take in their children's children and try to set them on a steady path.[41]

Emma Stampley lives far from the Westside now, in a house full of children, grandchildren, and great-grandchildren who look to her for solidity and warmth. For many years after Operation Life folded, Stampley was a tenants' rights organizer, fighting to improve housing opportunities for poor families in a city where construction of high-priced gated communities has far outpaced affordable housing. Middle-class black Las Vegans have been able to rent or buy homes across the city for two decades, but poor black Las Vegans are still largely isolated on the Westside. To the extent that this has changed at all, it is through the efforts of activists like herself.

Mary Wesley was still hoping to graduate from high school and attend college with one of her grandsons when I met her in 1992. With seven grandchildren, she was packing up and heading out to Rialto, California, to live near her son. He was doing well financially, and she wanted her grandsons to grow up with a positive male role model. By the end of the 1990s, Wesley was raising nineteen grandchildren and was riding herd to make sure that none got involved in drugs or gangs. She made strict rules for that household, and held regular family meetings. Everyone had to tell her where they were going, and when they were returning. Grandma Mary slept upright in a living room recliner, partly to ease her high blood pressure, and partly to make sure she knew what time the children came home. "No one moves out of my house unless they are going into college or the military," she says in her hoarse, melodic voice, then flashes a dazzling grin. So far, she's batting a thousand.

In the mid-1990s, Wesley's health declined rapidly. She fought daily headaches from pounding high blood pressure. Doctors warned her that she risked a stroke unless she took off weight and carefully regulated her diet. With the help of her grandchildren, she lost almost one hundred pounds. These days her health is better than it has been for years. The trademark high cheekbones that she says are legacies of Native American heritage look more carved and imposing than ever. Her large, dark eyes are luminous, somehow peaceful, even after everything she's been through. She says she's reached a plateau. Some time back, she returned to Mississippi for a large family reunion, where she was honored for her tireless efforts to keep her family whole and healthy. A grandson in military dress uniform took her arm, escorting her as she walked to the front of the room, basking in the applause of her relatives. It felt good, she mused later, to allow herself the pride and happiness of that moment. Good things can happen as long as you're still alive. In 2003, Wesley returned to Las Vegas, her youngest grandchildren still with her. She hasn't ruled out going back to school.[42]

Versie Beals has taken in some grandchildren too. At various points she's had two, three, or six living with her. The violence of the Westside has not spared her, or them. One of Beals's granddaughters was murdered by an ex-boyfriend while she was sleeping. She left behind eight children. Beals's daughter Ida is now raising them as her own. While I was visiting Las Vegas in 2003, Beals's nephew was shot point-blank by unknown assailants and died before he could identify them. He was just walking down the street with two friends, Beals says. After twenty years in the military, he had come home to begin the next phase of his life. "Sorrow," she told me, "is a steady train running through our lives."

Still, Versie Beals derives a lot of joy from children and grandchildren, most of whom are solid as the hills. Her children attribute their success as a family and as individuals to the strict but loving care of their mother. As they raise their own children, they marvel at how well she raised eleven on her own. All of them, nine daughters and two sons, live near their mother. They visit regularly, their doors always open to each other, their homes always busy with children and dogs, and sisters catching up, cooking, gossiping. It was near Mother's Day when I saw them last. Glendora was collecting funds from her siblings for a gold necklace "for Mama" that would dangle medallions with everyone's names inscribed.

Beals is now taking care of her frail elder brother. When he took ill, she moved into his small cottage on the Westside, passing up a chance at a shiny, new two-bedroom senior citizen apartment. "I would not ever put him or any of them in a home," she says in that sweet, low voice. "I just wouldn't. I couldn't." She doesn't mind, she says. She's got some land around her. Beals makes the hardpan Nevada desert earth bloom with collard greens, mustard greens, and flowers. She bends over them solicitously, tenderly—still a Louisiana country girl after fifty years in Las Vegas. Beals catches fish and turtles at nearby Lorenzi Park, and cooks feasts for family gatherings, even though a family dinner for Versie Beals can be enormous. With eleven children, forty-seven grandchildren, forty-four great-grandchildren, ten siblings, and scores of nieces and nephews, Beals doesn't blink at cooking for hundreds. She is happy that her family stays close. That's what gets Beals through. That's her life, she says quietly.

It took years, Beals says, but she has finally gotten over her sadness at the way Operation Life ended. She won't deny there were years when the women were almost consumed by bitterness over what they had lost. But these days, Beals says, the women seem to have found peace. "We did an awful lot those twenty years," she says shyly, happily. "Most important thing was that we loved each other. When Ruby called us, and said 'Let's go do something,' we all went. And if she called me right now, and said 'Come on, let's go out,' I would go. Right now."

Essie Henderson also comes when Ruby calls. The two are tighter now than they've ever been. Henderson says she counts on Ruby to drive her places. At a recent Operation Life reunion, she and Harriet Trudell roared with laughter recalling road trips the two had taken, and the trouble they'd stirred up in their halcyon days. Still drawn to finely tailored clothing and soft, shimmery fabrics, Henderson looks the part of the longtime beauty salon owner. She was near seventy before she retired. The beauty shop, a Westside institution, is still providing income and still doing hair.

One of Henderson's sons is a nurse; another works as a bartender at the Tropicana hotel. Her daughter is raising six children, all doing well. The only little one Essie has to care for is a great-grandson who lives with her and his other great-grandmother while his parents are serving time for drug offenses.

In 1997, five years after the Operation Life WIC clinic closed its doors for the last time, Ruby Duncan returned to the scene of her first political success twenty-six years earlier—Caesars Palace. (Courtesy of Kit Miller)

They'll be out soon, Henderson says. And she is ready to help her grandson find work, and stay clean.

Much of her good humor and faith, says Henderson, arises from the happy relationship she had for more than thirty years with a "sweetheart of a man" named Curtis Norris. Although she met Norris not long after arriving in Las Vegas, she didn't marry him until her "baby" was out of high school, because, she says, her children did not want a stepfather. A Tallulah-born man who could "do anything at all," Norris contributed to Henderson and her children from his paycheck as a porter, and then as a bartender at the Sahara hotel. He was "jolly, jolly, jolly," she says happily. She still reels from losing him to lung cancer, but he was the love of her life and she savors even the mention of his name.[43]

Henderson has tried to keep the name Operation Life alive, together with Eddie Jean Finks, Georgia Phillips, Sharon Glover Wilson, Ana Luna, and Ruby Pryce. They run a small counseling program for poor mothers and their children, using rental income from the Operation Life building, now occupied by the Elks club. Phillips, Luna, and Wilson work with women approaching the five-year lifetime limit on receiving federal aid, imposed by the 1996 welfare reform bill. They train the women for job interviews, help them to dress properly to look for work, and, when necessary, provide emergency assistance to make sure their families have housing and food. The Operation Life offices are located in the garage next to the law office of Duncan's son David. The small counseling service, with its three-thousand-dollar monthly budget, is a mere shadow of what Operation Life once was. Still, the women say, it's heartening to carry Operation Life into the twenty-first century.[44]

At eighty, Rosie Seals is still a regular at the church that she and Duncan have attended for years. Religion has been central to her life, and she's passed that on to her children. Of Seals's surviving seven children, three are ministers. Her twins, Charles and Timmy, are Pentecostal preachers. Her son Tyrone, who lives in Dallas, heads a Baptist congregation. Seals's daughters Cynthia and Clementine live in Las Vegas. Family keeps Seals going, but so does community. Lunching at a Westside fried fish and chicken restaurant, "Mother" Seals is greeted with love and respect by everyone who sees her shuffle in on her walker, from the cooks behind the counter to a homeless man who comes by to bless her for all her help. Seals squeezes his hand and gives him her lunch.

To me, Seals is as gruff as ever, although I think I've detected some softening after more than ten years of acquaintance. "Since the last time I saw you

I've had three back surgeries and I'm still black," she begins one visit. Though she has been doubtful from the start that this book would ever see the light of day, she wants to make sure I get it right, and to let me know that she was there from the beginning to the end, twenty-five years of working for the poor. Like many in this migrant generation, Seals still daydreams about "getting away from here, going back to Louisiana or maybe Mississippi. I'd like to plant me a little garden." Will she really do it? "Probably not," she huffs. "It takes money and that's one thing I don't have." Seals takes satisfaction in the simplest thing Operation Life did. "We fed a lot of hungry children," she says. "They can't take that away from us. And when you put food in the bellies of little children, you can feel you did something with your life."[45]

Ruby Duncan, now seventy-two, is also surrounded by family. Five of her seven children live in Las Vegas. So do most of her fourteen grandchildren and great-grandchildren. Her son David runs a successful law practice on the Westside and has served as a regent of the University of Nevada. Georgia is the longtime manager of Ruby Duncan Manor. Kenneth is a limousine driver. After years in the gaming business, Duncan's youngest son, Roy, is now a food services manger for the city's court system. And her eldest, Ivory, after working for years in Atlantic City casinos, is now a floor manager at a Las Vegas casino. Sondra lives in Washington, D.C., where she has been a union organizer, a social worker, and an artist. Of Duncan's sons, only Ronnie lives outside of Las Vegas.

It was not always easy being the child of such a powerful matriarch, Duncan's children admit. Their mother ruled them fiercely, determined that they make successes of themselves. Duncan makes no bones about it. She did what she thought she had to, and firm directives to her children were often stand-ins for her actual presence. She was away an awful lot during her children's early years—going to meetings and marches, traveling to Carson City, New York, and Washington, D.C., to lobby, testify, and raise money for Operation Life. Her ex-husband, Roy Duncan, frequently stayed with the children when she was gone—a role that endeared him to them, and earned Ruby's gratitude. But her feelings are clear. Mention his name and her eyes flare. The anger and pain still fester.

She raised her sons to be strong but gentle, as comfortable in the kitchen as they are under the hood of a car. "Our mother taught us to be men," says Roy, as Kenneth nods his agreement. "She taught us to be independent. She taught us to cook, and clean and sew." A real man doesn't depend on anyone to keep him clean, dressed, and fed, Ruby taught them.

In 2003 some of the Operation Life women came together at a Las Vegas restaurant to share a meal and reminisce: clinic nurse Pat Van Betten, Essie Henderson, Harriet Trudell, Alversa Beals, Renee Diamond, Ruby Duncan, Emma Stampley, and, seated, Rosie Seals. (Annelise Orleck)

She'd hoped all her children would wait to have children until they were educated and settled in careers. Despite their mother's firm warnings, Georgia and David had children young. Duncan insisted that they find jobs to support their babies. But she also made sure that Georgia and David stayed in school. If that was difficult, it was all right with Duncan. Says Georgia: "I heard a lot of people complain they didn't get enough from Operation Life. People had too many kids. They dropped out. It was hard. But Mama taught us to take advantage of every opportunity."[46]

Since Duncan ended her career with Operation Life, the accolades have flowed in—often from unlikely quarters. Former Governor Mike O'Callaghan escorted her in 1998 to a dinner where she was named a Distinguished Nevadan. "We're good friends these days," Duncan said cheerfully, shortly before O'Callaghan's death in 2004. Even George Miller, toward the end of his life, had nothing but good to say about Ruby Duncan's accomplishments. "Ruby did a lot of good," he told me. "I really mean it from my heart. If you happen to run into Ruby, tell her George Miller still loves her and says God bless her." The University of Nevada has compiled Duncan's papers in its women's history archive, and she still sits on the board of the National Economic Development Law Center, assisting community groups that are trying to enhance the political and economic clout of poor mothers and children.

Duncan sees Jack Anderson when she travels to Oakland for board meetings. Every once in a while, she talks to Mahlon Brown. She checks in regularly with Maya Miller, who is nearing ninety. Miller has remained active in the peace movement, traveling to Iraq to deliver food and medicine to Iraqi women, assisting Native American rights groups, and fighting the Yucca Mountain radiation dump in Nevada. As soon as her back improves, Duncan says hopefully, she'll travel up to Carson to see her old friend and mentor. She talks on the phone with Marty Makower, who has worked for years to improve housing and schools in Oakland, California. And Duncan has promised both Harriet Trudell and Renee Diamond that she'll jump back into Democratic politics (Trudell is now political director of the Nevada Democratic Party; Diamond is a state housing commissioner).

Ruby Duncan has stopped asking herself what went wrong. She chooses to focus on all that she and Operation Life accomplished. "We brought millions and millions in direct aid and program money into this state, this city and this community," she says. "We fed people. We gave women prenatal care to make healthy babies. We got women jobs. We helped a lot of people feel better about themselves. There's a lot we didn't get to do that I wish we did." She pauses. The anger trembles just beneath the surface of her skin. But then she calms. "But we did a lot. We really did." She laughs that throaty, high laugh, then looks away.

WHAT DOES IT MEAN TODAY?

When President Bill Clinton signed the Personal Responsibility and Work Opportunity Act in 1996, he ended sixty years of guaranteed federal aid to this country's poorest citizens. Gone was the much-maligned Aid to Families with Dependent Children. Federal aid to poor families was frozen at 1996 levels, and in 2003, the House voted to continue the freeze through 2008. America's poor families can now receive aid for only two consecutive years—and five years total. States receive bonuses for sharply cutting their public assistance rolls, and for reducing rates of out-of-wedlock births. Conversely, states can be penalized if they do not force mothers to work a minimum of twenty hours and terminate aid to families who fail to meet that requirement.[47]

In 2003, President George W. Bush proposed a still tougher public assistance program: PRIDE, Personal Responsibility and Individual Development for Everyone. The proposal, which the House approved, would double the number of hours recipients are required to work, from twenty to forty. It would also reduce states' flexibility to create innovative job training programs, and deny recipients the chance to count education, drug treatment, or job counseling toward their work requirements. The House also voted to approve the president's request for "superwaivers" that would enable federal agency heads to override rules for virtually every federal poverty program. In passing that bill, the House relinquished its right to set eligibility criteria for food stamps, public housing, childcare, job training, adult education programs, and aid to poor families.[48]

Elected officials have glibly stated that PRIDE's harsh new rules will be good for poor women. "Making people struggle a little bit," Pennsylvania Senator Rick Santorum opined while arguing against federal funds for childcare, "is not necessarily the worst thing."[49]

Today's lawmakers place little stock in Franklin Roosevelt's belief that a civilized society provides a safety net for its poorest and most vulnerable. Lyndon Johnson's vision of ending poverty in our time seems almost laughable in our cynical age. The income gap between the richest and poorest Americans is greater than at any time in our history, and the number of Americans living in poverty continues to rise. Today nearly thirty-five million people— 12.4 percent of the U.S. population—are poor. One in five American children grows up in poverty. Tens of millions more adults work full-time and still worry that they will run out of food before their next paycheck. Their ranks, too, are growing.[50]

Can't we do better? What if we tried another approach toward poverty policy and asked poor parents what they need to revitalize their communities and lift their families out of poverty? The history of Operation Life has much to tell us about the rich potential of a poor women's movement for economic justice—if only we can remove the ideological, cultural, and racial blinders that keep such histories hidden from view. A thick haze of race and gender stereotyping hangs heavily over every discussion of welfare reform in this country. It is my hope that seeing and hearing from welfare mothers in all their complex, contradictory humanity can cut the distance between *them* and *us*—a necessary first step toward envisioning a more humane way of providing aid to poor families.

Still, it is difficult for people to relinquish deeply ingrained prejudices. It's hard to trust those who have fallen by the wayside on the road to prosperity, because it raises the possibility that we too might fall. Ironically, as the women of Operation Life found, when poor women take action on their own behalf, they become even more unsettling. When those who have been reviled, marginalized, and reduced to little more than projections of our deepest cultural anxieties begin to stare back, talk back, and fight back, it makes nearly everyone uncomfortable.

Maybe that's a good thing. It forces us to reevaluate our most cherished assumptions about poverty—what causes it and how to ameliorate it. After a cacophonous, half-century debate about America's so-called underclass, few creative or genuinely new ideas have surfaced. Perhaps that's because we have been largely unwilling to listen to the poor and support the bottom-up community revitalization programs they have created. The successes of Operation Life should make scholars and policymakers rethink the conventional wisdom that the War on Poverty was a failure, and that its call for "maximum feasible participation" by the poor was at best naive and at worst a slush fund for corrupt community leaders. The history of Operation Life invites a very different conclusion. When the lived experience of poverty is seen as a valid credential, entitling poor mothers and fathers to build their own antipoverty programs, the results can be astounding, both materially and psychologically.

"Go back and look at the hundreds of millions of dollars that have been pumped into the Nevada economy through Food Stamps, the WIC program and the community development money that Operation Life brought in," says Jack Anderson. "When you look at all that, there is no organization in the history of Nevada that has brought more money into the Nevada economy than a group of women that a few years earlier had twelve members and not enough money in their treasury to do a mailing to them."[51]

Hundreds of thousands of poor Nevadans continue to benefit from the federal health and nutrition programs that state officials had refused until Duncan and other poor mothers forced them to reconsider. Millions of women and children continue to enjoy improved health as a result of the Women and Infant Children nutrition program. Ruby Duncan and other Operation Life women were among the lead plaintiffs for the lawsuit that forced the U.S. Department of Agriculture to release money for that program after years of officials dragging their feet. An equally large number of poor Americans benefited from Duncan's fierce lobbying of the Carter administration to channel job training and workforce investment dollars toward poor and minority women. And the Westside has a library, medical care, and quality senior citizen housing, where before there was none. What is remarkable is not that the women of Operation Life failed to achieve their vision, but that they went as far as they did. Their successes are astonishing not only because they started with so little, but because those who opposed them were so fierce and so relentless.

Can we blame the women of Operation Life for not ending poverty in their community? Can we blame federal War on Poverty programs, or the CDC movement, for failing to end poverty in our time? Critics of federal poverty programs argue that billions of taxpayers' dollars were poured down the drain in poor urban communities that remain mired in poverty, violence, and drug addiction. The Westside of Las Vegas is still a troubling, even a frightening, place. But that doesn't mean that Operation Life—or the thousands of local groups funded through Great Society poverty programs—should be seen as failures.

If we view these programs in the way that Ruby Duncan does, we can celebrate every hungry child who was fed, every house that was built, every illness that would not otherwise have been treated. If we think in larger terms, we see millions employed, fed, educated, and given medical treatment, neighborhoods at least partially rebuilt, and the political enfranchisement of poor people who became active in political parties and demanded a voice on welfare hearing boards, school boards, city councils, and county commissions. Federal poverty programs were not simply top-down manipulations but also invitations for the poor to become engaged at all levels of American politics. Their involvement generated turbulence and conflict in many cities, but it was a healthy, vigorously democratic process.

Economic development of neglected neighborhoods takes patience, money, and political commitment—qualities usually in short supply where the poor live. "CDCs operate in neighborhoods where the free market failed in the first instance," a Ford Foundation report reminded readers in 1987. A little "down-home capitalism" is not enough to bring prosperity to communities where schools, medical facilities, and the political system have failed as well. "We can't pretend market forces are going to revive these communities," cautions Paul Brogan, a leading funder of community development groups. Federal support is indispensable, and no amount of aid will eliminate poverty overnight. It will take time, training, and partnership with the poor.[52]

In the last twenty years, dozens of new welfare rights groups have jumped into the void left by the decline of groups such as Operation Life. Perhaps the best known is the Kensington Welfare Rights Union (KWRU) in Philadelphia, run by firebrand Cheri Honkala, who pries open abandoned HUD buildings to provide housing for homeless families. When she and five other mothers found there was no safe place for their children to play, they took over a closed welfare office and turned it into a community center. After being held in jail for six days, Honkala and the others were found not guilty by a jury that was so impressed by the defendants that jury members asked if they could join the welfare rights group.[53]

Defining poverty as an international human rights issue, members of Honkala's group and other economic human rights organizations have traveled to the Mexico border to meet poor women who live and work in polluted and dangerous American-owned factory towns. KWRU has also forged links with the labor movement, particularly the Hospital and Health Care Workers Union. Hospital workers in New York City realized the need for such alliances when Mayor Rudolph Giuliani replaced nine hundred union workers in public hospitals with unpaid women forced to work off their public assistance benefits. When welfare recipients join labor unions, it is more difficult for cities and state governments to use workfare programs to undermine union wage standards.

In Oakland, California, the Women's Economic Agenda Project (WEAP), a group much like Operation Life, has been running job training and computer literacy programs since 1982. Through its Family Resource Center, the organization offers parenting workshops, a food pantry, tenants' rights advocacy, and social service referrals. "While we help to feed the stomach, we know that we have an obligation to feed the mind," the group says.[54]

Developing human potential, Jack Anderson believes, is just as important as developing economies. Political organizing has helped poor women transcend the humiliations of poverty, heal battered egos, and discover untapped talents and strengths. When we assess the success and significance of a group such as Operation Life, says Anderson, we should measure not only in dollars, buildings, and programs, but in the people it sparked. "Different people blossomed in each campaign we did. The light bulb went on. And each time, it was a ray of hope."

Operation Life and the newer organizations that have followed in its path remind us that the light of social change burns brightest and longest where people build real coalitions—between affluent and poor, black and white, men and women. The "beloved community" built by Operation Life activists enhanced the lives of all who participated. Renee Diamond calls her Operation Life years "the most meaningful of my life." Maya Miller recalls her part in the struggle as "one of the treasures of my life." Jack Anderson says bluntly: "I think the greatest beneficiary of the Operation Life years was me, because I was able to see that light bulb go on so many times in so many people. You're working with an impoverished woman of color who's a single mom with an eighth-grade education. What potential does that person have? The traditional scale says their potential is zip. You know that a thousand employers would have passed that woman over. And then you see that person become an administrator of a massive program that is successful not just for Las Vegas but nationwide. I feel fortunate to have been part of it."

Mary Wesley is still proud not only that Operation Life "brought programs in but that we made them start to treat poor people more fairly." Just as importantly, she feels that the women of Operation Life modeled effective social justice organizing for the generations that followed. "The kids really learned that they could do these things too. They could speak out. If you just sit there one person, and be silent, you'll never get anywhere. But if you come in masses, in droves, it'll work."

The example of Wesley's generation made a big difference for the younger generation, says David Phillips. "I think at that time we had the highest rate of college students from an impoverished area. Out of one project, we had like fifteen kids who went to college. A lot of school teachers. Three of us are lawyers. We've got two doctors. We had an engineer. And a few made careers in the military." Lee Gates, the young man who was handcuffed to Ruby Duncan when they were arrested at the second 1971 Strip march, went on to become a judge. Another graduate of Operation Life's youth programs became one of the highest-ranking officers in the Las Vegas Fire Department. "That would never have happened without Operation Life," Phillips insists.

If there is one major lesson in the success of Operation Life, says Anderson, it is this: we will never eradicate poverty until we stop dehumanizing the poor. "As a society, we have designed welfare systems that have attempted to kill the spirit." Nothing better illustrates that contention than the 2003 PRIDE bill, which proposes marriage as the solution to poverty, when an estimated two-thirds of women seeking aid have left physically abusive spouses. The perversely named PRIDE proposal also denies welfare mothers the opportunity to receive drug treatment, education, or career training instead of working a dead-end job. If we could instead "tap the tremendous potential and energy that poor women have and design programs to build on their spirit and hope," Anderson says, "then, in a relatively short period of time, we would no longer need a welfare system."

Ruby Duncan felt that she was on her way to eradicating poverty in her community. Now she's well past the age when she can think of going back to organizing. But the key to her approach is as relevant today as it ever was. You have to feed the children. But you also have to build self-esteem among their mothers, women who have been despised for so long that they've begun to despise themselves. Duncan's great hope is that today's young women will carry on her challenge: to break down the barriers against decent jobs, healthcare, daycare, housing, and education for poor women and their children, and to establish those goals as a birthright for all Americans.

On a hot day on the Westside of Las Vegas, Duncan sits in her car near a bakery where she's picking up sweet potato pies for an Operation Life reunion. The bakery, a concrete block with a hand-painted sign, stands in an unpaved lot like many on the Westside. Duncan is watching four skinny, teenaged black girls on the corner talk excitedly. Long-limbed and gawky, like still-wobbly colts, the girls whisper among themselves, head-down serious, then burst into loud peals of laughter. Duncan grins at them, and sighs. "I wish we still had the programs, so that we could get these girls involved," she says. "We've got to go back to education and reach out to the younger women. There's so much potential there." She worries about the future of these girls, who seem fragile and vulnerable.

But Ruby Duncan is irrepressibly hopeful. She turns on the ignition, guns the accelerator, and cruises smoothly out of the lot. "I just get to dreamin' sometimes, all over again," she says. "Poor women must dream their highest dreams and never stop."

ACKNOWLEDGMENTS

No author writes a book alone, least of all a book like this, which is—after all—about community. For twelve years I have been privileged to spend time with the remarkable group of people who made Operation Life an anchor on the troubled Westside of Las Vegas and a beacon to community-based movements for economic justice across this country. Getting to know them has been, without question, the very best part of working on this book.

My first thanks are due to Maya Miller—activist extraordinaire, inspiration, and dear friend—first for introducing me to the story of Operation Life, then for revealing that she had a basement full of papers documenting its history that no one else had yet seen. She opened up her home to me more times than I can count, fed me warm sourdough bread before an open wood stove, and most importantly shared her vast knowledge of Operation Life, the national welfare rights movement, and the politics of the gaming industry in Nevada. Maya Miller's career as a pacifist, environmentalist, feminist, and fighter for economic justice is far more complex and expansive than I had space to convey in this book. She deserves—and will undoubtedly soon get—a history of her own. I am also most grateful to Kit Miller for sharing her memories and for taking some of the beautiful portraits of the women of Operation Life that appear in this book.

This book, like the movement it chronicles, could not have happened without Ruby Duncan. Her generosity has been unstinting. From our very first phone conversation through the final revisions of this book, Ruby Duncan has cheerfully and thoughtfully answered endless questions, searched for documents, phone numbers, and names, and made contacts for me with scores of people who were active in Operation Life and in the Clark County Welfare Rights Organization. Her memory for details, dates, and numbers was astonishing, giving me insight into the amazing mind and spirit that drove the Las Vegas poor women's movement for more than twenty years. Ruby was anxious to ensure that everyone involved received due credit . "You should talk to so and so," she'd say, writing down the number. "Be sure and talk to her and to him. I'll call if you want me to." And she did not give names of only her closest friends but also of people she knew would criticize her. Ruby wanted this book to be fair and nuanced, and she did everything she could to make it so.

I owe more than I can repay to the women of Operation Life and the Clark County Welfare Rights Organization: Rosie Seals, Essie Henderson, Alversa

Beals, Mary Wesley, Emma Stampley, Eddie Jean Finks, Betty Jean Clary, Leola Harris, and Mary Southern. They put up with twelve years of phone calls, visits to their homes, questions, requests for photographs, requests to interview their children and their friends. For their good humor, their patience, the delicious cooking they shared, child-rearing tips, and their faith that one day I would really finish and publish this book—I am very grateful.

Heartfelt thanks as well to Renee Diamond for opening her home to me and sharing her expertise in state politics, the gaming industry, and the history of Operation Life; to Harriet Trudell for her pithy stories and insights into how all of this tied in to Democratic Party politics; to Marty Makower for carefully explaining to me the ins and outs of Operation Life's community economic development activities and for her keen insights into the interpersonal dynamics of the movement; to Diane Guinn for conveying the intensity and fun of the Operation Life office; to Jack Anderson and Mahlon Brown for so vividly detailing the vital role played by Legal Services in the history of this movement. Father Louis Vitale, a lifelong activist and scholar of social justice movements, helped me to see Operation Life in larger contexts as both a political and a spiritual phenomenon. l am grateful to all of them, too, for making clear how important friendship, love, and loyalty were to this movement.

I also want to thank the children of Operation Life, now mature and successful adults: David, Georgia, Kenneth, Ivory, and Sondra Phillips, Roy Duncan Jr., Renia Glasper, Glendora Washington, Dorothy Love, and Grace Beals. It is not always easy to be a child of activists. Their loving, candid, and sometimes painful descriptions of growing up "in the movement" added greatly to my understanding of the meaning and the legacy of Operation Life.

I want to also acknowledge those who devoted years of their lives to Operation Life but whose contributions are not recounted in this book: Stella Nelson, Dorothy King, Lena Tatum, Ruby Pryce, Roma Jean Hunt, Donald Clark, John Dombrinck, and so many others. This group of women and men sparked and sustained a truly community-wide movement. I was simply not able to relate the stories and accomplishments of everyone who participated. But this book, and the movement, owe them a great deal.

Last but not least, in Las Vegas, I'd like to thank Joanne Goodwin, a fine historian and friend, for years of conversations about Operation Life, the national welfare rights movement, and the significance of the movement. She was also instrumental in helping Ruby Duncan to donate her papers to the women's archive at the University of Nevada, Las Vegas. I am also grateful to Su Kim Chung, UNLV's highly skilled archivist, for her flexibility, good cheer, and invaluable assistance with archival research. Thanks, as well, to the fine archivists at the University of Nevada at Reno for their help with the Maya Miller collection.

Friends on the faculty and staff at Dartmouth have supported this project for more than a decade now, listening to ideas and talks, reading and commenting on drafts of chapters and conference papers. Thanks to my colleagues in the history department for their interest, camaraderie, and day-to-day support. Special thanks to my dear friends Leo Spitzer and Marianne Hirsch for close and careful readings of several chapter drafts, for sharing with me their own superb work on migration, trauma, and nostalgia, and for challenging me to be honest about how I—a white, middle-class academic—fit into and shaped this story of a movement of poor, black women. My love and thanks, also, to Susan Brison, Melissa Zeiger, Mary Kelley, and Ivy Schweitzer who read this book, believed in it, and understood what I was trying to do, at times when a lot of other people didn't. My thanks to Diana Taylor for helping me bring Ruby Duncan to Dartmouth as part of the unforgettable "Redefining Motherhood" conference in 1993.

Thanks to Laura Lovett, Irene Kacandes, Judy Byfield, Angelia Means, and Christina Gomez for reading and commenting on pieces of this book as part of Dartmouth College's Gender and Migration faculty seminar, and to Linda Fowler, Fayan Nelson, and Roxanne Waldner at the Rockefeller Center for Public Policy at Dartmouth, who supported this project in big and little ways. Francis Oscadal at Dartmouth's Baker Library was a great help with research more times than I can count.

This book would never have been completed without grants from the National Endowment for the Humanities, the American Council of Learned Societies, and Dartmouth's Rockefeller Center. I am grateful to these foundations for enabling me to take time off from teaching to write and revise this book.

The Dartmouth College Presidential Scholars' program has brought me the most talented, dedicated group of research assistants any author could desire. This book has been much enriched by the work of Mattie Richardson, Julie Morganstern, Karen Tani, Diana Vernazza, Kyle Gilbride, Sean Levy, Catherine McCormick, and Lydia Gensenheimer. Julie Morganstern, Karen Tani, and Diana Vernazza went on to do their own research and writing on poverty activism and policy, and I have learned a great deal from these fine young scholars.

Thanks to Nell Painter, Charles Payne, and Linda Gordon for insightful comments on this work at various conferences. I am grateful to Linda Gordon, Alice Kessler-Harris, and Jacqueline Jones for the inspiration of their work and for helping me get the grants that made it possible for me to write this book.

My agent, Lisa Adams, has been a marvelous shepherd for this book. She read drafts and spent many hours talking with me about my vision and hopes for this book. I am most grateful for her enthusiasm and her belief in this project.

Thanks are due as well to Joanne Wyckoff and Brian Halley at Beacon Press for their editorial suggestions, hard work on the manuscript, and faith in this book.

If it takes a village to raise a child, it also takes a village to produce a book. I feel fortunate to be part of the community of friends and neighbors in Thetford, Vermont. Thanks for the emotional support, dinners, childcare, and drinks during the intense last few months it took to finish this book. Thanks, too, to the marvelous young women of Dartmouth and Thetford who took care of my children while this book was being completed.

To my daughter, Evi, and my son, Raphael, who have been forced to coexist with this book for their entire lives, my apologies—and my eternal gratitude for their love, warm hugs, and patience, even when they were rightfully jealous of all the time and attention it took away from them. Evi learned to crawl at the Luxor Hotel in Las Vegas. As a newborn, Raphael liked to fall asleep to the soft chiming of slot machines. I hope they'll look back with some fondness on our research trips, or at least that they'll forgive me.

To my mother, Thelma Orleck, my brother, Jerry, and my nephews, Lawrence and Jonathan Orleck, all my love and gratitude for a lifetime of warmth and support.

To my life partner, Alexis Jetter, I owe more than I can convey here. We have shared twenty years of love, support, adventures, co-parenting, and the pleasures and labors of family life. But our relationship is also an intellectual collaboration. That has never been more true than on this book. At one time, we thought of writing it together. Ultimately we didn't, but Alexis has been intensely involved in every phase of the research and writing, generously sharing her years of experience as a journalist, her meticulous attention to detail, and her scrupulousness about telling all sides of a story. She participated in every interview, asking questions that I would never have thought of and pushing me to interview government officials whom I might have been content to let speak through newspaper accounts and public records. As for the writing, it would be a pale shadow of the truth to say that Alexis edited me. She held up every idea to the light to see if it could bear the scrutiny. She wrestled every transition to the ground to make sure that it behaved. She went back through the evidence, not only to check my facts, but to see if there were any gems that had to be added to the story. And she reflected on her own memories of our interviews to add important insights to the characters developed in this story. Her passion, intellect, and wit are reflected on every page of this book. It is a more vibrant, readable, balanced, and lucid narrative than I could ever have created without her help.

NOTES

ABBREVIATIONS

BESN   The Black Experience in Southern Nevada collection,
        James R. Dickinson Library, University of Nevada, Las Vegas
CCWRO   Clark County Welfare Rights Organization
LVV   *Las Vegas Voice*
MMP   Maya Miller Papers, University of Nevada, Reno, Nevada
NWRO   National Welfare Rights Organization
NYT   *New York Times*
RDP   Ruby Duncan Papers, Nevada Women's Archive, Lied Library,
        University of Nevada, Las Vegas, Nevada

INTRODUCTION

1. See Rhonda Williams, *The Politics of Public Housing: Black Women's Struggle Against Urban Inequality* (New York: Oxford University Press, 2004); Christina Greene, *Our Separate Ways: Women and the Black Freedom Movement in Durham, North Carolina* (Chapel Hill: University of North Carolina Press, 2005); Marc Rodriguez, *Migrants and Citizens: Labor and the American Struggle for Civil Rights in Texas and the Midwest, 1930–1980* (book in progress); Thomas Kiffmeyer, "From Self-Help to Sedition: The Appalachian Volunteers in Eastern Kentucky, 1964–1970," *Journal of Southern History* 64:65–94; Lisa Hazirjian, *Negotiating Poverty: Economic Insecurity and the Politics of Working-Class Life in Rocky Mount, North Carolina, 1929–1969*, Ph.D. dissertation, Duke University (2003); Karen Tani, *Asian Americans for Equality and the Community Based Development Movement*, undergraduate honors thesis, Dartmouth College (2002); and Diana Vernazza, *Who Killed the Child Development Group of Mississippi?: The Local Politics of the War on Poverty*, undergraduate honors thesis, Dartmouth College (2001).

   I am grateful to all of these fine historians and to Robert Bauman, William Clayson, and Felicia Kornbluh for helping me to see the national context of grass-roots organizing in the era of the War on Poverty.

2. My understanding of the double-edged nature of the U.S. welfare state has been greatly influenced by the work of Alice Kessler-Harris, Linda Gordon, Michael Katz, Mimi Abramovitz, Frances Fox Piven, and Richard Cloward. Their important works are too numerous to name here, but books that have been particularly influential on my thinking in this study are: Alice Kessler-Harris, *In Pursuit of Equity: Women, Men, and the Quest for Economic Citizenship in 20th Century America* (New York: Oxford University Press, 2001); Linda Gordon, *Pitied But Not Entitled: Single Mothers and the History of Welfare* (New York: Free Press, 1994) and *Women, the State, and Welfare*, edited by Gordon (Madison: University of Wisconsin Press, 1990); Michael Katz, *The Undeserving Poor: From the War on Poverty to the War on Welfare* (New York: Pantheon, 1989) and *The Underclass Debate: Views from History*, edited by Katz (Princeton, 1993); Mimi Abramovitz, *Regulating the Lives of Women: Social Welfare Policy from Colonial Times to the Present* (Boston: South End Press, 1988); Frances

Fox Piven and Richard Cloward, *Regulating the Poor: The Functions of Social Welfare* (New York: Pantheon, 1971).

3. This approach grows out of my first book, *Common Sense and a Little Fire: Women and Working-Class Politics in the United States, 1900–1965* (Chapel Hill: University of North Carolina Press, 1995). My understanding of the links between larger structural forces and personal poverty, and of the particular place of poor black women in the history of American poverty, was very much shaped by the work of Jacqueline Jones, particularly in *Labor of Love, Labor of Sorrow: Black Women, Work and the Family from Slavery to the Present* (New York: Basic Books, 1985) and *The Dispossessed: America's Underclasses from the Civil War to the Present* (New York: Basic Books, 1992).

CHAPTER 1: FROM THE COTTON FIELDS TO THE DESERT SANDS: LIVING AND LEAVING THE DELTA LIFE

1. Unless otherwise noted, all comments by Joanna Klein in this chapter are taken from the author's interview with Joanna Klein, November 26, 1995, Tallulah, Louisiana. For a discussion both of the African roots of the shotgun house and its history in Louisiana, see John Michael Vlach, *By the Work of Their Hands: Studies in Afro-American Folklife* (Charlottesville: University Press of Virginia, 1991), pp. 185–213.

2. John Dollard, *Caste and Class in a Southern Town* (New York: Doubleday, 1957). Originally published by Yale University Press in 1937, the book reached a wide enough audience that it was picked up and reissued by two trade publishers, first at the end of the 1940s and then again on the twentieth anniversary of its publication when the civil rights movement focused national attention on the politics and culture of the segregated American South. For statistics on emigration from the South from 1940 to 1970, see page 46 of Jacqueline Jones's "Southern Diaspora: Origins of the Northern 'Underclass'" in Michael Katz, ed., *The Underclass Debate: Views from History* (Princeton, NJ: Princeton University Press, 1993), pp. 27–54.

3. Unless otherwise noted, all quotes from Alversa Beals are taken from the author's interview with Alversa Beals, March 19, 1997, Las Vegas, Nevada.

4. Information about Ruby Duncan taken from the author's interviews with Ruby Duncan, September 2, 1992; September 5, 1992; December 7, 1994, Las Vegas, Nevada; telephone interview, May 13, 1998.

5. Author's interview with Joanna Klein; author's interview with Ruby Duncan, September 5, 1992; and Earnest N. Bracey, "A Shock to the System: Vegas changed for good after Ruby Duncan gave silent minorities a voice," *Las Vegas Life*, April 1999.

6. Unless otherwise noted, all quotes from Angie Coleman in this chapter are from the author's interview with Angie Coleman, November 26, 1995, Tallulah, Louisiana.

7. Neil Foley, *The White Scourge: Mexicans, Blacks, and Poor Whites in Texas Cotton Culture* (Berkeley: University of California Press, 1997), pp. 118–140. Foley offers a compelling account of the "growth of corporate cotton culture." As the family farm became increasingly less viable in competition with mechanized "business plantations," what little chance there had been for sharecroppers to rise to land ownership evaporated, even as a myth. Tenant farmers became farm workers.

8. Author's interview with Ruby Duncan, by telephone, June 26, 2004.

"Free black labor," Jacqueline Jones has argued, was considered by Southern planters to be a contradiction in terms. They believed it was necessary to enforce their labor "standards." Since the withdrawal of married black women from the labor force dramatically affected the plantation economy as well as the management of housework in white households, a nearly hysterical rhetoric about lazy black women emerged after the Civil War. This discourse racialized notions of women's work: white women's work took place within the home, but for black women, only work outside of their homes counted as work. Work for their own families left them open to charges of laziness or idleness or "playing the lady." Jones notes that even some Northern officials of the Freedman's Bureau accepted the argument that a certain amount of compulsion was required to force black women to work. These are the roots of twentieth-century welfare policy and administration. Jacqueline Jones, *Labor of Love, Labor of Sorrow: Black Women, Work and the Family, from Slavery to the Present* (New York: Basic Books, 1985), pp. 48–60.

Jones offers illustrations of brutal chastisement of black women in the post–Civil War rural South for all sorts of work-related "offenses" and for having the tenacity to engage in wage disputes (pp. 71–72). Elizabeth Clark-Lewis cites a 1908 comment from one planter: "When there's trouble I just go down with that [a hickory wagon spoke] and lay one or two of them out." Elizabeth Clark-Lewis, *Living In, Living Out: African-American Domestics and the Great Migration* (New York: Kodansha, 1996), p. 23. See too Clark-Lewis, Chapter 2, fn. 21.

9. Jones, *Labor of Love, Labor of Sorrow,* p. 59.
10. Jones, pp. 218–219. For a crystal-clear description of the racial politics of New Deal relief, see Jill Quadagno, *The Color of Welfare* (New York: Oxford University Press, 1994), pp. 17–25.
11. Jacqueline Jones describes the daunting housework facing sharecroppers' wives in the late nineteenth and early twentieth centuries. See *Labor of Love,* pp. 86–87.
12. Author's interview with Alversa Beals, March 19, 1997, Las Vegas, Nevada.
    The fortunes of tenant farmers working cotton in the Mississippi, Arkansas, and Louisiana Delta counties, and throughout the South, declined steadily after World War I. See James Cobb, *The Most Southern Place on Earth: The Mississippi Delta and the Roots of Regional Identity* (New York: Oxford University Press, 1992) and Donald Holley, "The Plantation Heritage: Agriculture in the Arkansas Delta," in Jeannie Whayne and Willard B. Gatewood, eds., *The Arkansas Delta: Land of Paradox* (Fayetteville, AR: University of Arkansas Press, 1993), pp. 238–271.
13. For information on living conditions in the nearby Arkansas Delta, see Elizabeth Anne Payne, "'What Ain't I Been Doing?': Historical Reflections on Women and the Arkansas Delta," in Whayne and Gatewood, eds., *The Arkansas Delta,* pp. 128–149.
14. Ibid. See too Kenneth R. Hubbell, "Always a Simple Feast: Social Life in the Delta," in Whayne and Gatewood, *The Arkansas Delta,* pp. 184–203, for a description of common Delta diets and the important role of gardens, hunting, and fishing. In the first chapter of her dissertation, entitled *Heaven Bound: Black Migration, Community and Activism in Cleveland, 1915–1945* (Yale University, 1992), Kimberly Phillips describes the importance of women's household gardens in feeding sharecropper families. But as she notes on page 21, "Gardens only supplemented diets for part of the year . . . most rural workers faced frequent bouts of inadequate housing and malnutrition."
15. For a beautiful discussion of dress styles as statements of resistance to the dehumanizing of

black workers, see Robin Kelley, *Race Rebels: Culture, Politics, and the Black Working Class* (New York: The Free Press, 1996), Ch. 2: "We Are Not What We Seem: The Politics of Pleasure and Community." On page 50, Kelley cites Asa Gordon, *The Georgia Negro: A History* (Ann Arbor, MI: Edwards Brothers, 1937), p. 91.

16. In Arkansas, black students made up 27 percent of the state's total enrollment, but were allotted merely 2 percent of transportation moneys. See Charles S. Johnson, *Backgrounds to Patterns of Negro Segregation* (New York: Thomas Y. Crowell, 1943), as cited in Gretchen Lemke-Santangelo, *Abiding Courage: African American Migrant Women and the East Bay Community* (Chapel Hill: University of North Carolina Press, 1997), pp. 14–15.

17. Author's interview with Ruby Duncan, December 7, 1994, Las Vegas, Nevada. See also Theresa Traber, *The Impact of Operation Nevada: An Organizational Campaign of the National Welfare Rights Organization,* unpublished senior honors thesis, Department of History, University of Michigan, Ann Arbor (1980), p. 49.

18. Cobb, *The Most Southern Place on Earth,* p. 194.

19. Ibid., pp. 190–194; Foley, *The White Scourge,* p. 179; Jones, *The Dispossessed,* p. 222.

20. Jack Temple Kirby, *Rural Worlds Lost: The American South, 1920–1960* (Baton Rouge, LA: Louisiana State University Press, 1987), pp. 51, 152; "Cotton," in *Louisiana 1941* (Baton Rouge: Louisiana Department of Agriculture and Immigration, 1941), pp. 21–23.

21. For accounts of officially recorded lynchings in Mississippi between 1930 and 1950, see Charles M. Payne, *I've Got the Light of Freedom: The Organizing Tradition and the Mississippi Freedom Struggle* (Berkeley: University of California Press, 1995), pp. 7–28. Cobb, pp. 212–213, documents the rise in racial violence in the Mississippi Delta in the months and years following World War II. Payne challenges Moore's statistic; Cobb accepts it.

22. Jones, *The Dispossessed,* pp. 107, 114. Unless otherwise noted, all quotes from Rosie Seals in this chapter are taken from the author's interviews with Rosie Seals, March 20, 1997, and April 19, 2004, Las Vegas, Nevada.

23. Telephone interview with Ruby Duncan, May 13, 1998.

24. I am grateful to Nell Irvin Painter for showing me her paper "The Shoah and Southern History," presented at a Center for Arts and Cultural Policy conference at Princeton University, October 11, 2002. In the paper, Painter argues that "after much excellent scholarship on the sequelae of Post-Traumatic Stress Disorder, child abuse, sexual abuse, and personal violence, historians are in a stronger position than a generation or two ago to make sense of both the psychological and physical injuries of slavery." That same work, I would argue, needs to be done in examining the resettlement and adaptation of black migrants from the Jim Crow South, as it has begun to be done in examining Jewish World War II refugees and Soviet, Haitian, and South Asian refugees of the 1970s and 1980s.

25. Nancy Naples has interviewed African American women activists in New York and Philadelphia and found that many attributed their sense of obligation to community and an expansive notion of activist mothering to the Southern models set by their elders. See Nancy Naples, "Activist Mothering: Cross-Generational Continuity in the Community Work of Women from Low Income Neighborhoods," *Gender and Society* 6, no. 3 (September 1992): 441–463.

26. Duncan interview, telephone, May 13, 1998; Klein interview; Arthur Raper, *Sharecroppers All* (Chapel Hill: University of North Carolina Press, 1941), pp. 262–263; Cobb, *The Most Southern Place on Earth,* p. 191.

27. Unless otherwise noted, all comments by Mary Wesley in this chapter are taken from the author's interview with Mary Wesley, March 22, 1997, Las Vegas, Nevada.

28. Lillian Smith, *Killers of the Dream* (New York: Norton, 1949), pp. 141–145.

29. Charles Payne, *I've Got the Light of Freedom*, pp. 13–14.

30. Unless otherwise noted, all comments by Essie Henderson in this chapter come from the author's interview with Essie Henderson, December 11, 1994, Las Vegas, Nevada.

31. Author's interview with Rosie Seals, March 20, 1997, Las Vegas, Nevada.

32. Postwar blues songs, memoirs, and letters reinforce the reminiscences of women refugees from cotton country interviewed for this book. See Angela Davis, *Blues Legacies and Black Feminism* (New York: Random House, 1998), pp. 25–33. In two important articles, historian Darlene Clark Hine draws from wide-ranging qualitative data on women migrants to the urban Midwest to argue the need to examine more closely a "rarely explored 'push' factor, that is, the desire for freedom from sexual exploitation, –especially rape by white men, and to escape from domestic abuse within their own families." See Darlene Clark Hine, "Black Migration to the Urban Midwest: The Gender Dimension, 1915–1945," in Joe Trotter, ed., *The Great Migration in Historical Perspective: New Dimensions of Race, Class, and Gender* (Bloomington, IN: Indiana University Press, 1991), pp. 126–146 and "Rape and the Inner Lives of Black Women in the Middle West: Preliminary Thoughts on the Culture of Dissemblance," *Signs: Journal of Women and Culture in Society* 14 (Summer 1989): 912–920. Phillips, "Heaven Bound," p. 42, also notes the appearance of domestic abuse stories in oral histories of Southern black women migrants.

33. Author's interview with Ruby Duncan, September 7, 1992, Las Vegas, Nevada; Duncan phone interview, May 13, 1998.

34. Unless otherwise noted, all quotes from Emma Stampley in this chapter are taken from the author's interview with Emma Stampley, March 21, 1997, Las Vegas, Nevada.

35. Subcommittee on Employment, Manpower and Poverty, *Examination of the War on Poverty: First Session on Hunger and Malnutrition in America*, 90th Congress, 1st Session (July 11–12, 1967), p. 264, cited in Cobb, *The Most Southern Place on Earth*, p. 263.

36. Bessie Smith, "Lonesome Desert Blues," cited in Davis, *Blues Legacies and Black Feminism*, p. 307.

37. James McMillan, *Fighting Back: A Life in the Struggle for Civil Rights* (Reno, NV: University of Nevada Press, 1997), p. 65; Jacqueline Jones, *The Dispossessed*, p. 208; author's interview with Mary Southern, March 20, 1997, Las Vegas, Nevada.

38. Eugene Moehring, *Resort City in the Sunbelt: Las Vegas, 1930–1970* (Reno, NV: University of Nevada Press, 1989), pp. 14–15, 174–177.

39. "Las Vegas, Nevada," AOL Hometown, http://members.aol.com/Gibson0817/lasvegas.htm.

40. Moehring, *Resort City in the Sunbelt*, pp. 34–37; "Resort Rising: 'Magnesium Maggie,'" *Las Vegas Review-Journal* (Stephens Media Group, 1999). See also the transcript of "Oral Interview of Woodrow Wilson," collected by Gwendolyn Goodloe, February 28, 1975, ed. Elizabeth Nelson Patrick, in the Black Experience in Southern Nevada collection (hereafter referred to as BESN), James R. Dickinson Library, University of Nevada, Las Vegas.

41. Interview with Lucille Bryant (December 1, 1995) in Claytee D. White, *The Roles of African American Women in the Las Vegas Gaming Industry, 1940–1980*, unpublished master's thesis, Department of History, University of Nevada, Las Vegas (August 1997), p. 1.

42. Ibid., pp. 21–22; author's interview with Dolores and Sam Rainey, Fordyce, Arkansas, November 27, 1995.

43. "Oral Interview of Lubertha Johnson," collected by Larry Buckner, February 10, 1978, Las Vegas, Nevada and "Oral Interview of Cora Williams," collected by Kathleen E. Wilson, March 11, 1975, Elizabeth Patrick, ed., BESN. See also White, *The Roles of African American Women in the Las Vegas Gaming Industry, 1940–1980*, p. 21.

44. Jones, *The Dispossessed*, pp. 211–212; author's interview with Mary Wesley, March 22, 1997; author's interview with Emma Stampley, March 19–20, 1997, Las Vegas, Nevada.

45. Author's interview with Ruby Duncan, September 6, 1992, Las Vegas, Nevada.

46. *Jackson Daily News*, Jackson, MS, January 20, 1956. See also Deke Castleman, *Las Vegas* (Oakland, CA: Compass American Guides, 1991), p. 16.

CHAPTER 2: "THE MISSISSIPPI OF THE WEST": JIM CROW IN SIN CITY

1. See Joanne Goodwin, "She Works Hard for Her Money: A Reassessment of Las Vegas Women Workers, 1945–1985," in *The Grit Beneath the Glitter: Tales from The New Las Vegas*, Hal Rothman and Mike Davis, eds. (Berkeley: University of California Press, 2002), p. 247. For descriptions of the migrants camping out downtown, near the old Union Plaza station in the 1940s and 1950s, see comments by Sarah Ann Knight in *West Las Vegas at the Crossroads: A Forum*, Nevada Humanities Council (July 19, 1977), p. 5. Transcript in the Black Experience in Southern Nevada collection (hereafter, BESN), James R. Dickinson Library, University of Nevada, Las Vegas.

2. See Eugene Moehring, *Resort City in the Sunbelt: Las Vegas, 1930–1970* (Reno, NV: University of Nevada Press, 1989), p. 22.

3. Author's interview with Ruby Duncan, Las Vegas, Nevada. September 6, 1992.

4. Unless otherwise noted, all comments in this chapter by Mary Southern, Rosie Seals, and Mary Wesley are taken from the author's interviews with: Mary Southern, March 20, 1997, Las Vegas, Nevada; Rosie Seals, March 20, 1997, Las Vegas, Nevada; and Mary Wesley, March 22, 1997, Las Vegas, Nevada.

5. In *City of Quartz*, his wide-ranging history of L.A., Mike Davis discusses the role of restrictive housing covenants and Klan activity in shaping both black and white communities in L.A. through the 1950s (New York: Vintage, 1992), pp. 160–164. See also Michael Konig, *Phoenix, Arizona, 1920–1940*, unpublished Ph.D. dissertation, Arizona State University (1983), pp. 187–188, and Robert T. Wood, *The Transformation of Albuquerque, 1945–1972*, unpublished Ph.D. dissertation, University of New Mexico (1980), pp. 335–336.

6. Arna Bontemps, *They Seek a City* (New York: Doubleday, 1945), p. xv.

7. Ibid.

8. Moehring, *Resort City in the Sunbelt*, pp. 173–176.

9. Ibid., pp. 18, 174–175.

10. Author's interview with Joanna Klein, Tallulah, Louisiana, November 25, 1995.

11. Moehring, *Resort City in the Sunbelt*, pp. 36, 177. See also Emily N. Bristol's "Henderson History: 'City of Destiny,' " in *View Neighborhood Newspapers*, April 2, 2003, online at http://viewnews.com/2003/VIEW-Apr-02-Wed-2003/anthem/20977049.html.

12. Bontemps, *God Sends Sunday* (New York: Harcourt and Brace, 1931), pp. 118–119, cited in

Gerald Horne, *The Fire This Time: The Watts Uprising and the 1960s* (Charlottesville: University Press of Virginia, 1995), p. 27; Moehring, *Resort City in the Sunbelt*, p. 176; author's interviews with Alversa Beals and Mary Southern, March 19, 20, 1997.

13. Moehring, *Resort City in the Sunbelt*, p. 37.

14. Moehring, *Resort City in the Sunbelt*, p. 178; Kathryn Joseph's reminiscences in *West Las Vegas at the Crossroads: A Forum*, Nevada Humanities Council (July 19, 1977), BESN.

15. "Oral Interview of Ruth Sweet," conducted by Bonnie Baucham, February 7, 1977, BESN.

16. A. Costandina Titus, *Bombs in the Backyard: Atomic Testing and American Politics* (Reno, NV: University of Nevada Press, 1986), p. 14.

17. "Oral Interview of Cora Williams," conducted by Kathlyn E. Wilson, March 11, 1975, BESN.

18. Author's interview with Ruby Duncan, December 7, 1994, Las Vegas, Nevada.

19. "Oral Interview of Lubertha Johnson," collected by Larry Buckner, February 10, 1978, Las Vegas, Nevada, BESN; author's interview with Sarah Ann Knight-Preddy, December 7, 1994, Las Vegas, Nevada.

20. "Oral Interview of Cora Williams," BESN.

21. "Oral Interview of Lubertha Johnson," BESN.

22. Moehring, *Resort City in the Sunbelt*, pp. 178–179.

23. "Oral Interview of Cora Williams," BESN; "Oral Interview of Lubertha Johnson," BESN; Moehring, *Resort City in the Sunbelt*, p. 180.

24. Moehring, *Resort City in the Sunbelt*, p. 180. The Ivins quote is from Larry Hott and Tom Lewis's PBS-TV documentary, *Divided Highways: The Interstates and the Transformation of American Life* (Florentine Films, 2003). See too the encyclopedia article "Urban Renewal," at WorldHistory.com, http://www.worldhistory.com/wiki/u/urban-renewal.htm.

25. Author's interviews with Mary Wesley, Mary Southern, and Rosie Seals; author's interview with Ruby Duncan, March 24, 1997, Las Vegas, Nevada; author's interview with Emma Stampley, March 22, 1997, Las Vegas, Nevada; Moehring, *Resort City in the Sunbelt*, pp. 178–182.

26. Author's interview with Alversa Beals, March 19, 1997, Las Vegas, Nevada.

27. Eric N. Moody, *The Early Years of Casino Gambling in Nevada, 1931–1945*, unpublished dissertation, University of Nevada, Reno (1997), pp. 330–331.

28. For a sensationalist account of the rise of Las Vegas, see Ed Reid and Ovid Demaris, *The Green Felt Jungle* (New York: Trident Press, 1963). On diverted Teamsters Union pension funds, see "Hoffa's Fountain of Pension Juice," in Reid and Demaris, pp. 98–109.

29. Author's interview with Sarah Ann Knight-Preddy, December 7, 1994, Las Vegas, Nevada; "Oral Interview of William H. (Bob) Bailey," conducted by Betty Rosenthal, March 16, 1978, BESN.

30. Demaris and Reid, *The Green Felt Jungle*, pp. 11–12.

31. See Sergio Lalli, "Cliff Jones: 'The Big Juice'" in Jack Sheehan, ed., *The Players: The Men Who Made Las Vegas* (Reno, NV: University of Nevada Press, 1997), pp. 23–34. See also Jones's obituary, *Las Vegas Review-Journal*, November 18, 2001.

32. Lalli, "Cliff Jones," pp. 23–25; Moody, *The Early Years of Casino Gambling in Nevada, 1931–1945*, pp. 132–133.

33. Lalli, "Cliff Jones," pp. 23–25. See also John L. Smith, "The Ghost of Ben Siegel," in Sheehan, ed., *The Players: The Men Who Made Las Vegas*, pp. 81–91; Reid and Demaris, *The Green Felt*

Jungle, pp. 18–34; Claytee White, *The Roles of African American Women in the Las Vegas Gaming Industry, 1940–1980*, unpublished master's thesis, Department of History, University of Nevada, Las Vegas (August 1997).

34. All comments by Rachel Coleman in this chapter are taken from author's telephone interview with Rachel Coleman, January 5, 1999; author's interview with Ruby Duncan, December 11, 1994, Las Vegas.

35. Author's telephone interview with Rachel Coleman; author's interview with Mary Wesley, March 22, 1997, Las Vegas, Nevada.

Historian Dorothy Sue Cobble describes the emergence of what she calls "the new service ideal: personality and pulchritude" in the post–World War I era. "The sexual tease aspects of the service encounter peaked in the 1960s," she writes, in *Dishing It Out: Waitresses and Their Unions in the Twentieth Century* (Champagne-Urbana: University of Illinois Press, 1991), pp. 46–48. She also documents the decline of real numbers of black women waitresses, beginning in the Depression, and charts the continued difficulties that black women had breaking into the waitressing profession into the 1970s. See particularly pp. 25–26, 123–125.

36. Demaris and Reid, *The Green Felt Jungle*; John L. Smith, "Moe Dalitz and the Desert," in Sheehan, ed. *The Players*, pp. 35–47.

37. Information on Al Bramlet's recruiting trips is included on the Culinary Workers Union, Local 226, Web site, http://www.culinaryunion226.org/english/pages/history.html.

38. White, *The Roles of African American Women in the Las Vegas Gaming Industry, 1940–1980*, p. 40; author's telephone interview with R. Coleman.

39. For a discussion of black Southerners' exposure to unionism prior to migration, see Kimberley L. Phillips, *AlabamaNorth: African-American Migrants, Community, and Working-Class Activism in Cleveland, 1915–45* (Urbana: University of Illinois Press, 1999), pp. 30–44.

40. Author's interview with Ruby Duncan and Essie Henderson, December 5, 1994, Las Vegas, Nevada; author's interview with Rachel Coleman.

41. Author's interview with Alversa Beals, March 22, 1997, Las Vegas, Nevada. For an analysis of black domestic workers' working-class consciousness, see Bonnie Thornton Dill, " 'Making Your Job Good Yourself': Domestic Service and the Construction of Personal Dignity," in Ann Bookman and Sandra Morgen, eds., *Women and the Politics of Empowerment* (Philadelphia: Temple University Press, 1988), pp. 33–52 and Sharon Harley, "When Your Work Is Not Who You Are: The Development of Working-Class Consciousness Among Afro-American Women," in Darlene Clark Hine, Wilma King, and Linda Reed, eds., *"We Specialize in the Wholly Impossible": A Reader in Black Women's History* (New York: Carlson Publishing, 1995), pp. 25–37.

42. Author's interview with Mary Wesley, September 7, 1992, Las Vegas, Nevada.

43. Moehring, *Resort City in the Sunbelt*, pp. 49–50; Reid and Demaris, *The Green Felt Jungle*, pp. 153–155.

44. Author's interview with Leola Harris, March 19, 1997, Las Vegas, Nevada.

45. Author's interview with Ruby Duncan, September 5, 1992.

46. Ibid; Theresa Traber, *The Impact of Operation Nevada: An Organizational Campaign of the National Welfare Rights Organization*, unpublished senior honors thesis, Department of History, University of Michigan (1980), p. 50.

47. See A. D. Hopkins, "The First 100 Persons Who Shaped Nevada—Al Bramlet: The Organizer," *Las Vegas Review-Journal,* available online at http:www.1st100.com/part3/bramlet .html.

48. Author's interview with Essie Henderson, December 5, 1994, Las Vegas, Nevada.

49. Author's interview with Frank Wright (Curator of the Nevada State Historical Museum), December 11, 1994, Las Vegas, Nevada; James B. McMillan, *Fighting Back: A Life in the Struggle for Civil Rights* (Reno, NV: University of Nevada Press, 1997), pp. 79–89.

50. McMillan, *Fighting Back,* pp. 79–89.

51. Author's interview with Mary Wesley, March 19, 1997. Las Vegas Nevada. For a brilliant analysis of the fluidities and complexities of black working-class resistance in contexts where black workers had little or no power, see Robin D. G. Kelley's "Shiftless of the World Unite," in *Race Rebels: Culture, Politics and the Black Working Class* (New York: Free Press, 1994).

52. Nevada State Museum Exhibition, "Life on the Westside During Segregation," December 1994; author's interview with Frank Wright, December 11, 1994.

53. Author's interview with Ruby Duncan, September 5, 1992, Las Vegas, Nevada; author's interview with Mary Wesley, September 7, 1992; author's interview with Sarah Ann Knight-Preddy, December 9, 1994, Las Vegas, Nevada.

54. Author's interview with Ruby Duncan, September 5, 1992, Las Vegas, Nevada.

55. Ibid.; author's interview with Frank Wright.

56. Author's interview with Frank Wright.

57. "Oral Interview of William H. (Bob) Bailey," conducted by Betty Rosenthal, March 16, 1978, BESN, pp. 14–15.

58. "Oral Interview of William H. (Bob) Bailey," p. 25; "A Vision of Glory," *Las Vegas Review-Journal,* September 27, 1992.

59. "Oral Interview of William H. (Bob) Bailey," pp. 5–13; "Las Vegas: Is the Boom Overextended?" *Life* magazine, July 20, 1955.

60. "Oral Interview of William H. (Bob) Bailey"; author's interview with Sarah Ann Knight-Preddy.

61. Hampton quote from the *Valley View Visitor,* Las Vegas, Nevada, September 1955.

62. Author's interview with Frank Wright.

63. "Oral Interview of William H. (Bob) Bailey," pp. 3–4; see also the interview with Hazel Gay in Claytee White, *The Roles of African American Women in the Las Vegas Gaming Industry, 1940–1980,* p. 51.

64. Moehring, *Resort City in the Sunbelt,* pp. 184–185; McMillan, *Fighting Back,* pp. 93–94.

65. McMillan, *Fighting Back,* pp. 95–97.

66. Moehring, *Resort City in the Sunbelt; Las Vegas Sun,* March 26, 1960; McMillan, pp. 94–95; *Las Vegas Review-Journal,* March 21, 1994.

67. McMillan, p. 98.

68. Author's interview with Mary Wesley, March 22, 1997.

69. McMillan, *Fighting Back,* p. 101; author's interview with Mary Wesley, March 22, 1997.

70. "Oral Interview of William H. (Bob) Bailey," p. 33; Moehring, *Resort City in the Sunbelt,* pp. 186–189.

71. The Hughes quote is cited in Sergio Lalli, "Howard Hughes in Las Vegas," in Sheehan, *The Players,* p. 141. Moehring also discusses Hughes's "high-pressured lobbying" against open

housing in Las Vegas, as does Michael Drosnin in *Citizen Hughes* (New York: Holt, Rinehart, Winston, 1985), pp. 188–189.

72. "Oral Interview of William H. (Bob) Bailey," p. 33.

CHAPTER 3: "BAD LUCK AND LOUSY PEOPLE": BLACK SINGLE MOTHERS AND THE WAR ON POVERTY

1. Author's interview with Ruby Duncan, by telephone, June 26, 2004; author's interviews with Ruby Duncan, September 2, 5, and 6, 1992, and December 11, 1994, Las Vegas, Nevada.

2. See Rickie Solinger, *Wake Up Little Susie: Single Pregnancy and Race Before Roe v. Wade* (New York: Routledge, 1992), pp. 79–82. Solinger cites, among other studies, Mignon Sauber and Janice Paneth, "Unwed Mothers Who Keep Their Children: Research and Implications," in the *Proceedings of the National Conference on Social Welfare* (New York: Family Services Association of America, 1965); Deborah Shapiro, "Attitudes, Values and Unmarried Motherhood," in *Unmarried Parenthood: Clues to Agency and Community Action* (New York: National Council on Illegitimacy, 1967); and Patricia Knapp and Sophie T. Cambria, "The Attitudes of Negro Unmarried Mothers Toward Illegitimacy," in *Smith College Studies in Social Work* 17 (September 1946–June 1947). For the national survey of attitudes about marriage, see Stephanie Coontz, *The Way We Never Were: American Families and the Nostalgia Trap* (New York: Basic Books, 1992), p. 25.

3. For statistics on poor families in the U.S. in the 1950s, see Coontz, *The Way We Never Were*, pp. 29–30.

4. Author's interview with Roy Duncan Jr., September 12, 1999, Las Vegas, Nevada.

5. Author's interview with David Phillips, September 7, 1992, Las Vegas, Nevada.

6. Duncan and Manning quotes are from *Ruby Duncan: A Moving Spirit*, a short film made by the Franciscan Communications Center, Los Angeles, CA, in the mid-1970s.

7. Susan James and Beth Harris, "Gimme Shelter: Battering and Poverty," in Diane Dujon and Ann Withorn, eds., *For Crying Out Loud: Women's Poverty in the United States* (Boston: South End Press, 1996), pp. 56–65.

8. Author's interviews with Alversa Beals, March 19, 1997, and April 19, 2004, Las Vegas, Nevada.

9. Ibid.

10. Subcommittee on Employment, Manpower and Poverty, *Examination of the War on Poverty: First Session on Hunger and Malnutrition in America*, 90th Congress, 1st Session, (July 11–12, 1967), p. 264; Solinger, *Wake Up Little Susie*, p. 54.

11. See Solinger, *Wake Up Little Susie*, pp. 46–48.

12. Author's interview with Leola Harris, March 22, 1997, Las Vegas, Nevada.

13. Author's interviews with Mary Wesley, September 5, 1992, and March 22, 1997, Las Vegas, Nevada; Theresa Traber, *The Impact of Operation Nevada: An Organizational Campaign of the National Welfare Rights Organization*, unpublished senior honors thesis, Department of History, University of Michigan, Ann Arbor (1980), p. 46.

14. Traber, p. 46. See also Mimi Abramovitz, *Regulating the Lives of Women: Social Welfare Policy from Colonial Times to the Present* (Boston: South End Press, 1988), p. 338.

15. Alice Kessler-Harris, *In Pursuit of Equity: Women, Men, and the Quest for Economic Citizenship in 20th Century America* (New York: Oxford University Press, 2001), p. 96.

For information on black workers and the Social Security Act, see page 131 of Kessler-

Harris. For a lucid description of the race-based division of social insurance and public assistance benefits in the Social Security Act, see Joanne Goodwin, "Employable Mothers and Suitable Work: A Re-Evaluation of Welfare and Wage-Earning Women in the Twentieth Century United States," in *Journal of Social History* 29, no. 2 (Winter 1995): 253–274.

16. Author's interview with Rosie Seals, March 20, 1997, Las Vegas, Nevada; for women labor reformers' warning, see Kessler-Harris, *In Pursuit of Equity*, p. 152.

17. Regina Kunzel elegantly sums up these competing racialized narratives of single motherhood in "White Neurosis, Black Pathology: Constructing Out-Of-Wedlock Pregnancy in the Wartime and Postwar United States," in Joanne Meyerowitz, ed., *Not June Cleaver: Women and Gender in Postwar America, 1945–1960* (Philadelphia: Temple University Press, 1994), pp. 304–331.

18. For a nuanced analysis of how larger cultural views of mothers in this era dovetailed with a new postwar discourse on prejudice and the emasculation of black men, see Ruth Feldstein, *Motherhood in Black and White: Race and Sex in American Liberalism, 1930–1965* (Ithaca: Cornell University Press, 2000), pp. 40–61.

19. Solinger, *Wake Up Little Susie*, p. 7. Osofsky, notes Solinger, was sympathetic to unmarried mothers, "devoting his career during this period to improving services for poor single mothers." Ruth Feldstein, in *Motherhood in Black and White: Race and Sex in American Liberalism, 1930–1965*, page 15, offers a persuasive argument that liberals and conservatives both, from the Depression through the mid-1960s, "located sources of political problems, including economic stress and racial inferiority, not in a socioeconomic political system but in families."

20. Solinger, *Wake Up Little Susie*, p. 193; Abramovitz, *Regulating the Lives of Women*, p. 321.

21. In *Wake Up Little Susie* (page 3), Solinger argues that white and black single mothers were assigned "political value by race. In this way, the reproductive capacity and activity of single girls and women in this period were used to explain and present solutions for a number of social problems." For Solinger on the construction of black mothers, see page 43. For the Russell Long quote, see Kessler-Harris, *In Pursuit of Equity*, pp. 272–273. See also *Illegitimacy and Its Impact on the ADC Program*, Bureau of Public Assistance, Social Security Administration (Washington, DC: Government Printing Office, 1960), p. 36.

22. Helen Perlman, "Unmarried Mothers," in Nathan E. Cohen, ed., *Social Work and Social Problems* (New York: National Association of Social Work, 1964), cited in Solinger, *Wake Up Little Susie*, p. 83.

23. See Kunzel, "White Neurosis, Black Pathology" and Solinger, *Wake Up Little Susie*, pp. 31–32.

24. Author's interview with Mary Wesley, September 7, 1992, Las Vegas, Nevada; Florida Department of Public Welfare, "Suitable Home Law" (Jacksonville, FL, 1962), pp. 25–26, quoted in Winifred Bell, *Aid to Dependent Children* (New York: Columbia University Press, 1965), p. 132.

25. See E. Franklin Frazier, *The Negro Family in the United States* (Chicago: University of Chicago Press, 1939), Chapter 16, and John Dollard, *Caste and Class in a Southern Town* (New York: Doubleday, 1957). See also Ruth Feldstein's sensitive readings of Dollard and Frazier in *Motherhood in Black and White*, pp. 28–33.

26. Maurice R. Davie, *Negroes in American Society* (New York: McGraw Hill, 1949), as cited in

Patricia Morton, *Disfigured Images: The Historical Assault on Afro-American Women* (Westport, CT: Praeger, 1991), pp. 88–89; Thomas Pettigrew, *A Profile of the Negro American* (Princeton, NJ: D. Van Nostrand Co., 1964), pp. 16–19, 22–26, cited in Morton, p. 89.

27. Daryl Michael Scott, *Contempt and Pity: Social Policy and the Image of the Damaged Black Psyche* (Chapel Hill, NC: University of North Carolina Press, 1997), pp. 148–150.

28. Hubert Humphrey, *War on Poverty* (New York: McGraw Hill, 1964), p. 13.

29. Doris Kearns Goodwin, *Lyndon Johnson and the American Dream* (New York: St. Martin's Press, 1976), p. 305; Elinor Graham, "The Politics of Poverty," in Marvin Gettleman and David Mermelstein, eds., *The Great Society Reader* (New York: Vintage, 1967), p. 227.

30. Lyndon Johnson, "Total Victory Over Poverty," excerpted from his January 8, 1964, State of the Union address, in Gettleman and Mermelstein, eds., *The Great Society Reader*, pp. 181–185.

31. See Bruce Schulman, *Lyndon B. Johnson and American Liberalism* (New York: Bedford, 1995) p. 82 and 92–93.

32. Doris Kearns Goodwin, *Lyndon Johnson and the American Dream*, p. 216.

33. Author's interview with Duncan, December 11, 1994, Las Vegas, Nevada. Theresa Traber's interview with Jerry Furr on October 27, 1978, cited in Traber, *The Impact of Operation Nevada*, page 60, describes the rite of handing out food from the courthouse steps.

34. For a discussion of the delay in enforcing the Food Stamp Act of 1954, see Martha Davis, *Brutal Need: Lawyers and the Welfare Rights Movement, 1960–1973* (New Haven: Yale University Press, 1993), pp. 75–76.

35. Author's interview with Maya Miller, September 14, 1999, Carson City, Nevada.

36. See Joanne Goodwin, "Employable Mothers," pp. 254–261, and Abramovitz, *Regulating the Lives of Women*, pp. 252–254, 313–319.

37. Author's interview with Michael O'Callaghan, March 18, 1997, Las Vegas, Nevada. See also Diane Nassir, "Nevada's Welfare Assistance Caseload and Gaming," in *Nevada Historical Society Quarterly* (Summer 1994), p. 116.

38. Author's interview with Michael O'Callaghan. See also Nassir, "Nevada's Welfare Assistance Caseload and Gaming," p. 118.

39. Bureau of Governmental Research, *Welfare in Nevada: Report of the Nevada Assembly on Public Assistance* (Reno, NV: University of Nevada Press, 1974).

40. Traber, *The Impact of Operation Nevada*, p. 41; author's interview with Jack Anderson, September 9, 1992, Oakland, California; author's interview with Maya Miller, September 14, 1999.

41. Traber, *The Impact of Operation Nevada*, pp. 37–40; *Welfare in Nevada: Report of the Nevada Assembly*, pp. 10–15.

   Although I have not found evidence of this for the 1950s, in his November 30, 2003, column in the *Daily Sparks (Nevada) Tribune*, Andrew Barbano refers to a story he reported in 1995: "Hilton has a track record of providing those laid off in the winter with information on how to apply for public assistance." He also asserts that managers were trained to do this. See *Barbwire*: "500 Reno Hilton employees fear pink slips Monday," available online at http://www.nevadalabor.com/barbwire/barbo3/barb11-30-03.html.

   Author's interview with Essie Henderson, December 8, 1994, Las Vegas, Nevada.

42. Traber, *The Impact of Operation Nevada*, pp. 40–42; author's interview with Maya Miller

and Marty Makower, September 2–3, 1992, Carson City, Nevada. Ralph J. Roske, "Nevada Welfare Services: From E Clampus Vitus to Umbrella Agency," an official Nevada history of its Welfare programs (Reno, NV: Nevada State Historical Society, 1975), p. 21.

43. Traber, *The Impact of Operation Nevada*, pp. 60–61; author's interview with George Miller, December 4, 1994, Carson City, Nevada.

44. United Press International, "Nevada Food Stamp Permissiveness 'Ripoff,' " October 10, 1974.

45. Author's interview with George Miller, December 4, 1994.

46. Bruce Schulman, *Lyndon B. Johnson and American Liberalism* (New York: Bedford Books of St. Martin's Press, 1995), pp. 96–97; U.S. House, *Examination of the War on Poverty Program*, Hearings Before the Subcommittee on the War on Poverty Program, Committee on Education and Labor, 89th Congress, 1st Session (April 12–30, 1965). See, too, Nancy Rose, *Workfare or Fair Work: Women, Welfare, and Government Work Programs* (New Brunswick, NJ: Rutgers University Press, 1995), p. 85; Scott Stossel, *Sarge: The Life and Times of Sargent Shriver* (Washington, DC: Smithsonian Books, 2004), p. 398; "Four Decades of Success Training Youth," available on the National Job Corps Association, Inc. Web site, www.njcaweb.org/njcapublic/fastfacts/history.htm; "What is Job Corps?" available on the Earle C. Clements Job Corps Academy Web site, www.clementsjobcorps.org/WhatisJobCorps.htm.

47. Carlucci memo to Elliot Richardson, cited in Jill Quadagno, *The Color of Welfare* (New York: Oxford University Press, 1994), p. 125.

48. Author's interview with Maya Miller; author's interview with Jack Anderson.

49. *Las Vegas Review-Journal*, April 23, 1968.

50. Author's interview with Maya Miller; author's interview with George Miller, December 4, 1994, Carson City, Nevada.

51. George Miller interview; Traber, *The Impact of Operation Nevada*, pp. 42–43; author's interview with Ruby Duncan, March 25, 1997, Las Vegas, Nevada; Joe R. Feagin, *Subordinating the Poor: Welfare and American Beliefs* (Englewood Cliffs, NJ: Prentice Hall, 1975), p. 64.

52. Author's interview with Emma Stampley, September 5, 1992, Las Vegas, Nevada; Teresa Traber's interview with Alversa Beals, May 24, 1977, cited in Traber, *The Impact of Operation Nevada*, pp. 51–52.

53. Author's interview with Rosie Seals.

54. Author's interview with Eddie Jean Finks and Betty Jean Clary, September 14, 1999, Las Vegas, Nevada.

55. Martha Davis's interview with Tanya Sparer, February 29, 1989, cited in Davis, *Brutal Need*, p.36.

56. Author's interview with Alversa Beals.

57. Solinger, *Wake Up Little Susie*, pp. 193–194; Abramovitz, *Regulating the Lives of Women*, p. 338.

CHAPTER 4: "IF IT WASN'T FOR YOU, I'D HAVE SHOES FOR MY CHILDREN": WELFARE RIGHTS COME TO LAS VEGAS

1. All quotes in this chapter by Alversa Beals are from the author's interviews with Alversa Beals on March 19, 1997, and September 5, 1992, in Las Vegas, Nevada.

2. Author's interview with Alversa Beals, March 19, 1997; Guida West, *The National Welfare Rights Movement: The Social Protest of Poor Women* (New York: Praeger, 1981).

3. All quotes in this chapter by Rosie Seals are from author's interviews with Rosie Seals on March 20, 1997, and September 5, 1992, in Las Vegas, Nevada.

4. Unless otherwise noted, all quotes in this chapter by Emma Stampley are from the author's interviews with Emma Stampley on March 21, 1997, and September 5–6, 1992, in Las Vegas, Nevada.

5. All quotes in this chapter by Essie Henderson are from the author's interviews with Essie Henderson on December 9, 1994, December 11, 1994, and September 14, 1999, in Las Vegas, Nevada.

6. Unless otherwise noted, all quotes in this chapter by Eddie Jean Finks are from the author's interview with Eddie Jean Finks, September 14, 1999, Las Vegas, Nevada.

7. Author's interview with Rosie Seals, March 20, 1997.

8. Author's interview with Father Louis Vitale, December 9, 1994, Las Vegas, Nevada; "Priest is Single Minded in Quest for World Peace," *Contra Costa Times,* March 31, 2003.

9. Unless otherwise noted, all quotes in this chapter from Father Louis Vitale are from the author's interview with Vitale, December 9, 1994. For a description of the role of Catholic clergy in establishing the nation's largest welfare rights group, in Brooklyn, New York, see Jacqueline Pope, *Biting the Hand That Feeds Them: Organizing Women on Welfare at the Grass Roots Level* (New York: Praeger, 1989), pp. 40–54.

10. There has been little scholarly attention paid to Johnnie Tillmon's life and career. What there is can be found in Guida West, *The National Welfare Rights Movement*; Deborah Grey White, *Too Heavy a Load: Black Women in Defense of Themselves, 1894–1994* (New York: Norton, 1999), Chapter 7; and Nick Kotz and Mary Lynn Kotz, *A Passion For Equality: George A. Wiley and the Movement* (New York: Norton, 1977). Tillmon's comments on ANC Mothers' choice of the name "Anonymous" come from Kotz and Kotz, p. 220. For an NWRO organizer's recollections of the early years of ANC Mothers, see George Martin, *The Emergence and Development of a Social Movement Organization Among the Underclass: A Case Study of the National Welfare Rights Organization,* unpublished Ph.D. dissertation, University of Chicago (1972), p. 73.

11. White, *Too Heavy a Load,* p. 225.

12. West, *The National Welfare Rights Movement,* p. 92.

13. Marvin Gettleman and David Mermelstein, eds., *The Great Society Reader* (New York: Vintage, 1967); Scott Stossel, *Sarge: The Life and Times of Sargent Shriver* (Washington: Smithsonian Books, 2004), p.360; Robert Wood, "The Great Society in 1984: Relic or Reality," in Marshall Kaplan and Peggy L. Cuciti, eds., *The Great Society and Its Legacy: Twenty Years of U.S. Social Policy* (Durham, NC: Duke University Press, 1986), pp. 21–22.

14. Kotz and Kotz, *A Passion For Equality,* p. 185.

15. Ibid.

16. For quote, see pages 14–15 of Hobart Burch, "A Conversation with George Wiley," *Journal of Current Social Issues* 9, no. 3 (1970): 10–20.

17. Kotz and Kotz, *A Passion For Equality,* p. 182.

18. Ibid.

19. For information on Sanders, see Julie Morganstern, *Raising Hell: Tracing the Lives of Welfare Rights Activists Johnnie Tillmon and Beulah Sanders,* unpublished honors thesis, History Department, Dartmouth College (2004). See also Burch, "A Conversation with George Wiley" and Kotz and Kotz, *A Passion For Equality,* p. 80.

20. Kotz and Kotz, *A Passion For Equality*, pp. 182–183, 213. See also "Low Income People and the Political Process," by Richard Cloward and Frances Fox Piven (originally written as training materials for staff at Mobilization for Youth) in *The Politics of Turmoil: Essays on Poverty, Race, and the Urban Crisis* (New York: Pantheon, 1974) and Martha Davis, *Brutal Need: Lawyers and the Welfare Rights Movement, 1960–1973* (New Haven: Yale University Press, 1993), p. 72.

21. *NYT*, July 1, 1966; *New York Daily News*, June 29, 1966; *National Guardian*, July 9, 1966; *Christian Science Monitor*, June 29, 1966. See also Kotz and Kotz, *A Passion For Equality*. For information on poor mothers' activism during the 1930s, see Annelise Orleck, "We Are That Mythical Thing Called the Public: Militant Housewives in the Great Depression," in Vicki Ruiz and Ellen Dubois, eds., *Unequal Sisters*, 3rd ed. (New York: Routledge, 2000).

22. Kotz and Kotz, *A Passion For Equality*, p. 199.

23. *NYT*, July 1, 1967.

24. Burch, "A Conversation with George Wiley," p. 15. There is a small body of social science literature on the origins of the National Welfare Rights Organization that places it in the complex context of 1960s politics. Most of these analyses were written in the 1960s and 1970s by scholars who were still, or had formerly been, active allies of the movement. The most complete account of NWRO's rise and fall is West's *The National Welfare Rights Movement*. See pages 15–75 for her analysis of the formation and political forces fueling NWRO. Organization cofounders Frances Fox Piven and Richard Cloward offer their own version of NWRO's early history on pages 264–359 of *Poor People's Movements: Why They Succeed, How They Fail* (New York: Vintage, 1979). See also: Helene Levens, *Bread and Justice: A Participant Observer Study of a Welfare Rights Organization*, unpublished Ph.D. dissertation, Madison: University of Wisconsin (1971), pp. 57–110; George Martin, *The Emergence and Development of a Social Movement Organization Among the Underclass;* and William Whitaker, *The Determinants of Social Movement Success: A Study of the National Welfare Rights Organization*, unpublished Ph.D. dissertation, Waltham: Brandeis University (1970).

25. Richard A. Cloward and Frances Fox Piven, "We've Got Rights! The No Longer Silent Welfare Poor," *The New Republic*, August 5, 1967, pp. 23–27; *NYT*, August 29, 1967.

26. *NYT*, September 20, 1967; author's interview with Ruby Duncan, September 5, 1992, Las Vegas; author's interview with Maya Miller, September 2, 1992, Carson City, Nevada. See, too, Kotz and Kotz, *A Passion For Equality*, p. 251.

27. White, *Too Heavy a Load*, pp. 214–215; Kotz and Kotz, *A Passion For Equality*, pp. 248–249.

28. Minutes of meeting between Citywide and labor groups, Moorland-Springarn Archives, Howard University, NWRO Papers, Box 2093, Morganstern, "Raising Hell."

29. For an insightful description of Sparer's role in shaping welfare rights legal strategy, see Chapter 3, "The Welfare Law Guru," in Martha Davis, *Brutal Need*.

30. Sparer described the history of the 1960s litigation strategy in Edward Sparer, "The Right to Welfare" in Norman Dorsen, ed., *The Rights of Americans: What They Are, What They Should Be* (New York: Pantheon, 1970), pp. 65–93. Just before his death in 1984, Sparer looked back on the successes and failures of strategy and elaborated on its links to the social protest of welfare mothers, in "Fundamental Human Rights, Legal Entitlements and the Social Struggle: A Friendly Critique of the Critical Legal Studies Movement," *Stanford Law Review* (January 1984): 1–49.

31. Author's interview with Eddie Jean Finks, September 14, 1999.

32. "Mothers Complain on ADC," *Las Vegas Sun,* May 16, 1968; "Welfare Rules Disputed," *Las Vegas Sun,* June 15, 1968; "Welfare Moms Grilled on Sex Life," *Las Vegas Review-Journal,* June 19, 1968; *Reno Evening Gazette,* June 21, 1968; *Nevada State Journal,* June 24, 1968.

33. *Las Vegas Sun,* November 16, 1968; author's interview with George Miller, December 4, 1994, Carson City, Nevada.

34. Edward Sparer, "The Right to Welfare," p. 69, citing 392 U.S. 309, 334 (1968).

35. Cited in Sparer, "The Right to Welfare," p. 75. From 394 U.S. at 631–632. See too Elizabeth Bussiere, *(Dis)Entitling the Poor: The Warren Court, Welfare Rights, and the American Political Tradition* (University Park, PA.: Penn State University Press, 1997), pp. 104–108.

36. Author's interview with Ruby Duncan, September 5, 1992; *Nevada State Journal,* June 23, 1969; *Reno Evening Gazette,* July 11, 1969.

37. Author's interview with Ruby Duncan, September 5, 1992.

38. Sondra Phillips, interviewed by Alexis Jetter, September 14, 1992, Washington, D.C., in possession of author.

39. Unless otherwise noted, all quotes by Ruby Duncan in this chapter are from the author's interviews with Ruby Duncan on September 2, 1992, September 6, 1992, December 12, 1994, March 23, 1997, and September 16, 1999, in Las Vegas, Nevada. See also "Welfare Militant on the Way Up," *NYT,* May 27, 1969.

40. Author's interview with Vincent Fallon, December 11, 1994, Las Vegas, Nevada.

41. *LVV,* July 3, 1969; *Reno Evening Gazette,* July 11, 1969; Theresa Traber, *The Impact of Operation Nevada: An Organizational Campaign of the National Welfare Rights Organization,* unpublished senior honors thesis, Department of History, University of Michigan, Ann Arbor (1980), pp. 57–58.

42. *NYT,* July 2, 1969; *Reno Evening Gazette,* July 11, 1969.

43. Traber, *The Impact of Operation Nevada,* pp. 58–59.

44. Ruby Duncan to Honorable Governor Paul M. Laxalt, August 8, 1969; "We the Undersigned" August 1969, in the papers of the Clark County Welfare Rights Organization, personal collection of Ruby Duncan.

45. *NYT,* March 9, 1969.

46. *Amsterdam News,* April 19, 1969, cited in Morganstern, *Raising Hell,* pp. 90–91.

47. *NYT,* May 26, 27, 1969.

48. For an insightful analysis of the NWRO credit card campaign and activist welfare mothers' claims to rights as U.S. citizens, see Felicia Kornbluh, "To Fulfill Their 'Rightly Needs': Consumerism and the National Welfare Rights Movement," *Radical History Review* 69 (Fall 1997): 76–113. See, too, Kotz and Kotz, Nick Kotz and Mary Lynn Kotz, *A Passion For Equality,* pp. 235–236.

49. *NYT,* May 28, 1969. *NYT,* July 4, 1969. See also Kotz and Kotz, *A Passion For Equality,* p. 236.

50. "Statement by Beulah Sanders before the Presidential Commission on Income Maintenance," June 5, 1969, George Wiley Papers, Wisconsin Historical Society, Box 17, Folder 3, cited in Morganstern, *Raising Hell,* p. 105.

51. "Nixon Asks Overhaul of Welfare," *NYT,* August 6, 1969. For a fascinating political analysis of the controversial proposal and the fate of Richard Nixon's FAP, see Jill Quadagno, *The Color of Welfare* (New York: Oxford University Press, 1994), Chapter 4.

52. *NYT,* August 6, 1969; Quadagno, *The Color of Welfare,* p. 130.

53. *NYT,* August 22, 1969.

54. *NYT,* August 23, 24, 26, 1969.

55. *NYT,* August 23, 24, 26, 1969; author's interview with Ruby Duncan, September 5, 1992.

56. Author's interviews with Emma Stampley, Ruby Duncan, and Rosie Seals, September 5, 1992, Las Vegas, Nevada.

57. *Las Vegas Sun,* January 20, 1970.

58. *Reno Evening Gazette,* October 8, 1969; *Nevada State Journal,* October 12, 1969.

59. *Nevada State Journal,* November 16, 1969.

60. *NYT,* October 28, 1969; Beulah Sanders, "Testimony Before the U.S. House of Representatives Ways and Means Committee," *Congressional Reporter,* October 1969, pp. 1013, 1036.

61. Ruby Duncan to President Richard M. Nixon, December 12, 1969; HEW Commissioner Stephen Simonds to Ruby Duncan, February 20, 1970, in the papers of Clark County Welfare Rights Organization, personal collection of Ruby Duncan; *Reno Evening Gazette,* November 20, 25, 1969.

62. *Reno Evening Gazette,* December 15, 24, 1969.

63. Ronald Reagan's speech and the quote are from Robert Coles's *The Middle Americans: Proud and Uncertain* (Boston: Little Brown, 1971), both cited in Joe R. Feagin, *Subordinating the Poor: Welfare and American Beliefs* (New York: Prentice Hall, 1975), pp. 5, 9.

64. *Reno Evening Gazette,* December 15, 24, 1969.

65. Sondra Phillips, interviewed by Alexis Jetter, September 14, 1992.

66. Author's interviews with Mary Wesley on September 7, 1992 and March 23, 1997, Las Vegas, Nevada; telephone interview, September 14, 1999.

67. Quadagno, *The Color of Welfare,* pp. 140–146; Feagin, *Subordinating the Poor,* p. 64. For a clear discussion of the relationship between ideas about race, mothers' employability, and public assistance policy, see Joanne Goodwin, "Employable Mothers and Suitable Work: A Re-Evaluation of Welfare and Wage-Earning for Women in the Twentieth Century United States," *Journal of Social History* 29, no. 2 (Winter 1995): 253–274. See also Mimi Abramovitz, *Regulating the Lives of Women: Social Welfare Policy from Colonial Times to the Present* (Boston: South End Press, 1988), p. 31.

68. "She Criticized Now Her Job Is Threatened," *Las Vegas Review-Journal,* October 28, 1970.

69. *Reno Evening Gazette,* February 20, 1970.

70. *Reno Evening Gazette,* January 22, March 23, April 21, May 21, 1970; *Nevada State Journal,* February 22, 1970; *Las Vegas Sun,* May 23, 1970.

71. Author's interview with George Miller, December 4, 1994, Carson City, Nevada; author's interview with Rosie Seals, March 20, 1997.

CHAPTER 5: STORMING CAESARS PALACE:
POVERTY AND POWER IN LAS VEGAS

1. Author's interview with Mahlon Brown III, April 22, 2003, Las Vegas, Nevada.

2. See Frances Fox Piven and Richard A. Cloward, *Regulating the Poor: The Functions of Social Welfare* (New York: Pantheon, 1971), p. 306. See, too, Scott Stossel, *Sarge: The Life and Times of Sargent Shriver* (Washington: Smithsonian Books, 2004), p. 441.

3. Stossel, *Sarge,* p. 443.

4. Author's interview with Mahlon Brown III, April 22, 2003, Las Vegas, Nevada.

5. Author's interview with Mahlon Brown III, December 8, 1994, Las Vegas, Nevada.

6. For a detailed analysis of the history of litigation leading to *Goldberg v. Kelley* and a description of the oral arguments and justices' decision process, see Martha Davis, *Brutal Need: Lawyers and the Welfare Rights Movement, 1960–73* (Yale University Press, 1993), pp. 111–118.

7. Unless otherwise noted, all quotes from Jack Anderson are from the author's interview with Jack Anderson, September 9, 1992, Oakland, California. See, too, "Notice of Action Taken," from Welfare Division to Johnnie B. Woods, Plaintiff's Exhibit "A" in *Woods v. Miller.*

8. See *Johnnie B. Woods, For Herself and All Others Similarly Situated, Plaintiff, v. George Miller, State Welfare Administrator and the Nevada Welfare Board,* Civil LV-1505; author's interview with Jack Anderson, September 9, 1992.

9. *Las Vegas Sun,* October 2, 1970.

10. Author's interview with George Miller, December 4, 1994, Carson City, Nevada. See also Alexis Jetter's interview with Sondra Phillips, September 14, 1992, Washington, D.C., in possession of author.

11. *Las Vegas Sun,* April 8, 1970.

12. *The Black Panther,* April 3, 1971, p. 4. See also Theresa Traber, *The Impact of Operation Nevada: An Organizational Campaign of the National Welfare Rights Organization,* unpublished senior honors thesis, Department of History, University of Michigan, Ann Arbor (1980), pp. 61–62.

13. Author's interview with Father Louis Vitale, December 9, 1994, Las Vegas, Nevada.

14. Author's interview with Michael O'Callaghan, March 18, 1997, Las Vegas, Nevada.

15. Author's interview with George Miller; *Reno Evening Gazette,* January 8, 1971.

16. *Nevada Appeal,* November 9, 1970; *Reno Evening Gazette,* January 8, 9, 1971.

17. *Reno Evening Gazette,* February 25, 1971; *The Washington Post,* March 14, 1971.

18. Author's interview with Maya Miller, September 2, 1992, Carson City, Nevada; Frances Fox Piven and Richard Cloward, *Poor People's Movements* (New York: Vintage, 1979), p. 333.

19. *Nevada State Journal,* February 26, 1971.

20. Author's interview with Emma Stampley, March 21, 1997, Las Vegas, Nevada.

21. Author's interview with Ruby Duncan, September 5, 1992, Las Vegas, Nevada; Traber, *The Impact of Operation Nevada,* pp. 72–73.

22. "Now It's Operation Nevada," *NWRO Welfare Fighter* 2, no. 5 (February 1971); "Operation Nevada for Welfare Rights," *The Black Panther,* February 27, 1971, pp. 4–5; Hesselden quote from Traber, *The Impact of Operation Nevada,* p. 74; author's interview with Ruby Duncan, December 11, 1994, Las Vegas, Nevada.

23. Author's interview with Father Louis Vitale.

24. Interview with Edward Sparer, cited in Traber, *The Impact of Operation Nevada,* p. 75.

25. *LVV,* January 28, 1971.

26. Author's interview with Ruby Duncan, September 5, 1992; Traber, *The Impact of Operation Nevada,* cites a similar story about Tillmon on page 75.

27. Author's interview with Ruby Duncan, September 5, 1992.

28. Author's interview with Jack Anderson.

29. Author's interview with Mahlon Brown III, December 8, 1994; Piven and Cloward, *Poor People's Movements,* p. 333, n. 40. See also: Operation Nevada NWRO, "Points for Door-

knockers"; Clark County Welfare Rights Organization, "Amended Interview Form No. 3";
NWRO/Welfare Fighter, February 1971, p. 6. All documents from the National Welfare
Rights Organization Collection, Manuscript Division, Moorland-Spingarn Research Center, Howard University, Washington, D.C.

30. Author's interview with Jack Anderson.

31. Author's interview with Mahlon Brown III December 8, 1994; Traber, *The Impact of Operation Nevada,* p. 94.

32. Author's interview with Jack Anderson.

33. Author's interview with Maya Miller, September 18, 1999, Carson City, Nevada; *Progressive Leadership Alliance of Nevada,* Newsletter, February 2001.

34. Ruby Duncan to Elliot Richardson, December 18, 1970; John L. Costa to Ruby Duncan, January 21, 1971; John L. Costa to Alan Bible, January 22, 1971; John L. Costa to Howard Cannon, January 25, 1971; Howard Cannon to Ruby Duncan, January 22 and February 2, 1971; Alan Bible to Ruby Duncan, January 8, 29, 1971. All in RDP.

35. William J. LaBadie to Howard Cannon, January 15, 1971; W. J. LaBadie to George E. Miller, n.d., "Final Report, ADC Review" (all in George Miller Papers, Nevada State Archive).

36. *Las Vegas Sun,* February 18, 25, 1971; *Reno Evening Gazette,* February 12, 17, 24, 1971.

37. Author's interview with Marty Makower, September 2–3, 1992. Carson City, Nevada.

38. Ibid.; author's interview with Marty Makower, April 11, 1997, Oakland, California.

39. *Las Vegas Review-Journal,* March 2, 1971; author's interviews with Rosie Seals and Emma Stampley, September 5, 1992, Las Vegas, Nevada.

40. Author's interview with Ruby Duncan, September 14, 1999; author's interview with Marty Makower, September 2–3, 1992.

41. "Get It Together Welfare Moms," leaflet in the personal collection of Ruby Duncan; "Don't Be Cheated, Know Your Rights!" NWRO Collection, Manuscript Department, Moorland-Spingarn Research Center, Howard University, Washington D.C.

42. Author's interview with Mary Wesley, September 7, 1992, Las Vegas, Nevada.

43. *LVV,* February 11, 1971; Author's interview with Ruby Duncan, September 14–15, 1999, Las Vegas, Nevada; Earl W. White, Esq., Brief of Amicus Curiae, in the U.S. District Court for the District of Nevada in *Johnnie S. Woods v. George Miller,* Civil-LV 1505.

44. Author's interview with Vincent Fallon, December 12, 1994, Las Vegas, Nevada; author's interview with Jack Anderson.

45. *NWRO Welfare Fighter,* February 1971, p. 6.

46. Author's interview with Ruby Duncan, September 6, 1992; author's interview with Vincent Fallon.

47. *LVV,* February 18, 1971; *Las Vegas Review-Journal,* February 17, 1971; *NYT,* March 21, 1971.

48. *NWRO Welfare Fighter* 2, no. 5 (February 1971).

49. Interview with Ruby Duncan, Summer 1997, Traber, *The Impact of Operation Nevada,* p. 143.

50. *Nevada State Journal,* February 21, 1971; *Reno Evening Gazette,* February 22, 1971.

51. Robbins E. Cahill, *Recollections of Work in State Politics, Government, Taxation, Gaming Control, Clark County Administration, and the Nevada Resort Association* (Reno: Oral History Project, University of Nevada, 1977), pp. 1464–1469.

52. Author's interview with Harriet Trudell, April 20, 2003, Las Vegas, Nevada.

53. Sondra Phillips, interviewed by Alexis Jetter, September 14, 1992.

54. See Annelise Orleck, "Tradition Unbound: Radical Mothers in International Perspective," in Alexis Jetter, Annelise Orleck, and Diana Taylor, eds., *The Politics of Motherhood: Activist Voices from Left to Right* (Hanover, NH: University Press of New England, 1997), pp. 3–20.

55. Mrs. Ruby Duncan to The Honorable Mike O'Callaghan, February 19, 1971, in the private collection of Ruby Duncan.

56. Author's interview with Michael O'Callaghan, March 18, 1997, Las Vegas, Nevada.

57. Author's interview with Vincent Fallon; *Reno Evening Gazette*, February 22, 1971.

58. Author's interview with Leola Harris, September 7, 1992, Las Vegas, Nevada; Author's interviews with Emma Stampley and Mary Southern, September 5, 1992, Las Vegas, Nevada.

59. Author's interview with Maya Miller, September 18, 1999, Carson City, Nevada.

60. *Nevada State Journal*, February 28, 1971, and March 5, 1971; Assembly Joint Resolution 9, February 1, 1971, "Memorializing the Congress of the United States to permit the department of health, welfare and rehabilitation of the state of Nevada to establish its own method of determining welfare eligibility," MMP. See also *Reno Evening Gazette*, March 4, 1971.

61. Author's interview with Father Louis Vitale.

62. Author's interview with Alversa Beals; author's interview with Maya Miller.

63. Author's interview with Ruby Duncan, December 9, 1994; Robbins E. Cahill, *Recollections of Work in State Politics, Government, Taxation, Gaming Control, Clark County Administration, and the Nevada Resort Association*, pp. 1464–1469.

64. *Washington Post*, March 14, 1971.

65. Theresa Traber's interview with Rev. Jerry Furr, October 27, 1978, Las Vegas, Nevada, cited in Traber, *The Impact of Operation Nevada*. See also *The Washington Post*, March 7, 1971.

66. *Nevada State Journal*, March 5, 1971; *Las Vegas Review-Journal*, March 5, 1971; *Las Vegas Sun*, February 27, 1971; *Reno Evening Gazette*, March 6, 1971.

67. *Nevada State Journal*, March 5, 1971; author's interview with Ruby Duncan, September 5, 1992.

68. Author's interview with Ruby Duncan, September 5, 1992.

69. For information on earlier celebrity involvement in poor women's movements, see Annelise Orleck, *Common Sense and a Little Fire: Women and Working Class Politics in the United States, 1900–1965* (Chapel Hill: University of North Carolina Press, 1995), Chapters 3 and 4.

70. *Las Vegas Sun* and *Las Vegas Review-Journal*, March 7, 1971; author's interview with Eddie Jean Finks, September 11, 1999, Las Vegas, Nevada; Alexis Jetter, interview with Sondra Phillips, October 10, 1992; *Life*, June 1971.

71. Alexis Jetter, interview with Sondra Phillips; author's interview with Harriet Trudell; author's interview with Alversa Beals, March 22, 1997, Las Vegas, Nevada.

72. *Las Vegas Sun* and *Las Vegas Review-Journal*, March 7, 1971; author's interview with Harriet Trudell.

73. Author's interview with Ruby Duncan, September 5, 1992.

74. *Las Vegas Review-Journal*, March 7, 1971.

75. Author's interview with Ruby Duncan, September 5, 1992, Las Vegas, Nevada, Washington, D.C.; *NYT*, March 7, 1971; *Washington Post*, March 7, 1971.

76. Author's interview with Mahlon Brown, April 22, 2003, Las Vegas, Nevada.

77. Author's interview with Louis Vitale.

78. Author's interviews with David Phillips, September 7, 1992 and September 14, 1999, and

with Emma Stampley, September 2, 1992, Las Vegas, Nevada. See also: *Washington Post, Nevada State Journal, Las Vegas Sun, Las Vegas Review-Journal, Reno Evening Gazette,* and *LVV,* March 14, 1971; *Los Angeles Times,* March 19, 1971; *NYT,* March 21, 1971.

79. Author's interview with Mary Wesley, March 22, 1997, Las Vegas, Nevada.

80. Author's interview with Harriet Trudell; author's interview with Ruby Duncan, December 11, 1994, Las Vegas, Nevada.

81. Author's interview with Louis Vitale, December 11, 1994, Las Vegas, Nevada.

82. "Support Life and Decency Not Vice," Leaflet of the Washoe County Welfare Rights Organization, n.d., private collection of Maya Miller.

83. *Reno Evening Gazette,* March 16, 1971; *Nevada State Journal,* March 18, 20, 1971.

84. Author's interview with George Miller; *Reno Evening Gazette,* March 19, 1971.

85. Author's interview with Mary Wesley, March 22, 1997; "Nevada Craps Out," *Good Times* 4, no. 12 (March 26, 1971): 16.

86. Author's interview with Essie Henderson, December 8, 1994, Las Vegas, Nevada.

87. Author's interview with Rosie Seals, September 5, 1992, Las Vegas Nevada; "Come To A Meeting," leaflet of the Clark County Welfare Rights Organization, n.d., in the possession of Ruby Duncan.

88. Author's interviews with Mary Wesley; *The Black Panther,* March 1971.

89. Author's interview with Emma Stampley, *Las Vegas Review-Journal,* March 19, 1971.

90. Author's interview with Eddie Jean Finks and Betty Jean Clary, September 14, 1999, Las Vegas, Nevada; author's interview with Emma Stampley; author's interview with Mary Wesley; author's interviews with George Miller and Vincent Fallon.

91. Author's interview with David Phillips.

92. Author's interview with George Miller.

93. Author's interview with Mahlon Brown III, December 8, 1994; In the United States District Court for the District of Nevada, *Johnnie B. Woods v. George E. Miller,* March 19, 1971, Civil LV-1505.

94. *Las Vegas Sun,* March 20, 1971; *NYT,* March 21, 1971; author's interview with Jack Anderson; author's interview with George Miller, December 4, 1994, Carson City, Nevada.

95. *Reno Evening Gazette,* March 22, 27, 30, 1971, and April 1, 1971; Theresa Traber's interview with Harriet Trudell, cited in Traber, *The Impact of Operation Nevada,* pp. 136–137.

96. "HEW News," Office of Public Affairs, Press Release, April 14, 1971.

97. Ruby Duncan, "Ruby Duncan Says," *LVV,* April 27, 1971.

98. Piven and Cloward, *Regulating the Poor,* pp. 333–334, n. 40.

CHAPTER 6: DRAGGING NEVADA KICKING
AND SCREAMING INTO THE TWENTIETH CENTURY

1. Author's interview with David Phillips, Las Vegas, Nevada, September 7, 1992.

2. Theresa Traber, "Interview with George Miller, October 6, 1978," cited in Theresa Traber, *The Impact of Operation Nevada: An Organizational Campaign of the National Welfare Rights Organization,* unpublished senior honors thesis, Department of History, University of Michigan, Ann Arbor (1980), p. 146. "Is the State Robbing You, The Taxpayer?" Clark County Welfare Rights Organization brochure, fall 1971, CCWRO Food for All folder, personal collection of Maya Miller.

3. Author's interview with B. Mahlon Brown III, April 22, 2003, Las Vegas, Nevada; *Los Angeles Times* report syndicated in *Las Vegas Review-Journal,* February 21, 1972.

4. "Is The State Robbing You, The Taxpayer?" Leaflet of Coalition for Alternatives to Welfare, personal collection of Ruby Duncan.

5. Nick Kotz and Mary Lynn Kotz, *A Passion For Equality: George Wiley and the Movement* (New York: Norton, 1977), pp. 261–278; Guy Drake, an amateur songwriter, released "Welfare Cadillac" in 1970 on the Nashville label, Royal American records. It was covered by Travis Bell the following year for Imperial records in Los Angeles. The cover got even more radio play and greater sales than the original. That year, too, black blues artist Jerry McCain recorded a response: "Welfare Cadillac Blues," also for Royal American records. That single got airplay in black stations and sold well in cities with large African American communities. The story of Cash at the White House is recounted in Chet Flippo, *Nashville Skyline*: "Courtesy of the Red, White and Blue," June 20, 2002 on CMT.com (http://www.cmt.com/news/articles/1455341/06202002/keith_toby.jhtml).

6. Statistics on racialized news coverage and its effect on viewers' perceptions of welfare are from Martin Gilens, *Why Americans Hate Welfare* (Chicago: University of Chicago Press, 1999), p. 136. I am grateful to Rhonda Williams for a paper presented at the 2001 Organization of American Historians conference in Los Angeles, in which she argued that media coverage of welfare rights protests heightened stereotyping of poor black women in the U.S. and detracted from popular support for poverty programs.

7. Gilens, *Why Americans Hate Welfare,* p. 136; See also Kotz and Kotz, *A Passion For Equality,* p. 285.

8. Guida West interview with Johnnie Tillmon, 1974, cited on p. 84, Guida West, *The National Welfare Rights Movement* (New York: Praeger, 1981).

9. NWRO Papers, Flyers, n.d., Box 2122, Manuscripts Division, Moorland-Spingarn Research Center, Howard University Washington, D.C.

10. Kotz and Kotz, *A Passion For Equality,* p. 290.

11. Teresa Traber, *The Impact of Operation Nevada,* pp. 80–81.

12. Author's interviews with Ruby Duncan and Alversa Beals, September 5, 1992, Las Vegas, Nevada.

13. Teresa Traber, *The Impact of Operation Nevada,* p. 176. See also *Las Vegas Review-Journal,* October 15, 1971 and July 19, 1972; *Las Vegas Sun,* August 5, 1971. Author's interview with Louis Vitale, December 9, 1994, Las Vegas, Nevada.

14. Author's interview with Jack Anderson, September 9, 1992, Oakland, California.

15. Author's interview with Marty Makower, September 2–3, 1992, Carson City, Nevada.

16. Author's interview with Essie Henderson, December 11, 1994, Las Vegas, Nevada; author's interview with Jack Anderson.

17. U.S. Department of Agriculture, Food Nutrition Service, "History of WIC 1974–1999 25th Anniversary" (1999); "WIC: A Success Story" (Washington, DC: Food Research and Action Committee, 1983); Victor Oliveira et al., *The WIC Program: Background, Trends, and Issues* (USDA Economic Research Service Food Assistance and Nutrition Research Report Number 27, October 2002), Chapter II: "WIC History" online at http://www.ers.usda.gov/publications/fanrr27/fanrr27.pdf; J. Larry Brown, "Hunger in the U.S.: A Brief History," http://www.knowhunger.org; *The Ages of Hunger: From Pre-Natal to Elderly: A Report on the Operation of Federal Food Programs* (Phoenix, AZ: Food for All, 1972).

18. *The Ages of Hunger,* p. 67.

19. Author's interview with Mary Wesley, March 21, 1997, Las Vegas, Nevada; author's interview with Essie Henderson; Barbara McRae, secretary of CCWRO FFA, and Ruby Duncan, "Report of CCWRO Food for All Project to the Misseduc Foundation," February 29, 1972.

20. *The Ages of Hunger;* Rosie Seals's testimony is from "Minutes of People's Hearings on HR-1" (September 29–30, 1971, Clark County Heald Auditorium), MMP.

21. National Education Association study, cited in *Las Vegas Sun,* January 20, 1970.

22. Barbara McRae and Ruby Duncan, "Report of CCWRO Food for All Project to the Misseduc Foundation"; author's interview with Mahlon Brown, December 9, 1994, Las Vegas, Nevada; résumé of Jack F. Anderson, circa 1982, RDP; *The Ages of Hunger,* pp. 17, 30–32.

23. *Las Vegas Review-Journal,* March 25, 1971; *LVV,* April 12, 1973; Report of the Clark County WRO Food for All Project, February 29, 1972, MMP.

24. Brown is quoted in the film *Ruby Duncan: A Moving Spirit* (Los Angeles: Franciscan Communications Center, 1977).

25. George Miller interview from Traber, *The Impact of Operation Nevada,* p. 158; author's interview with Ruby Duncan, September 6, 1992, Las Vegas, Nevada; *Las Vegas Sun,* June 8, 1971; *LVV,* July 15, 1971 and October 21, 1971; United Press International feature, *Nevada State Journal,* December 10, 1971.

26. Author's interview with Mahlon Brown, December 9, 1994; *Nevada State Journal,* December 10, 1971; *LVV,* December 9, 1971.

27. "A Short History of the Food Stamp Program," U.S.D.A. Food and Nutrition Service, online at http://www.fns.usda.gov/fsp/rules/Legislation/history.htm.

28. *Las Vegas Sun,* January 12, 1972.

29. First Report of the Clark County WRO Food for All Project; Traber, *The Impact of Operation Nevada,* pp. 162–164.

30. Author's interview with Essie Henderson, December 9, 1994, Las Vegas, Nevada; author's interview with Mary Wesley, September 7, 1992, Las Vegas, Nevada; First Report of the CCWRO Food for All First Project.

31. Author's interview with Essie Henderson, December 9, 1994.

32. Author's interview with Maya Miller, September 2–3, 1992, Carson City, Nevada.

33. Author's interview with Harriet Trudell, April 20, 2003, Las Vegas, Nevada; author's interview with Ruby Duncan, December 11, 1994.

34. Author's interview with Jack Anderson.

35. Report of CCWRO Food for All Project, January 28, 1972, MMP; *LVV,* January 27, 1972.

36. *LVV,* January 20, 1972; author's interview with Ruby Duncan, December 11, 1994, Las Vegas, Nevada; author's interview with Maya Miller; author's interview with Vincent Fallon, December 11, 1994, Las Vegas, Nevada.

37. Author's interview with Michael O'Callaghan, March 18, 1997, Las Vegas, Nevada.

38. Author's interview with Maya Miller.

39. Author's interview with Mary Wesley, September 7, 1992; *LVV,* January 27, 1972.

40. "Memo To: State Legislators Re: Restrictions Placed on the Education of ADC Children From: Clark County Chapter, National Welfare Rights Organization and Clark County Legal Services," n.d., MMP, Nevada Discourages Education folder. See also the *Las Vegas Sun,* February 12, 1972.

41. First Report of the CCWRO Food for All Project, p. 5; *Las Vegas Review-Journal,* February 13, 1972.

42. Author's interview with Emma Stampley, March 22, 1997, Las Vegas, Nevada; author's interview with Mary Wesley, 1992; *Las Vegas Review-Journal,* February 11, 1972. See Annelise Orleck, "Tradition Unbound: Radical Mothers in International Perspective," in Alexis Jetter, Annelise Orleck, and Diana Taylor, eds., *The Politics of Motherhood: Activist Voices from Left to Right* (Hanover, NH: University Press of New England, 1997).

43. *Las Vegas Sun,* February 6, 1972; author's interviews with Jack Anderson, Ruby Duncan; author's interview with Mary Wesley, March 22, 1997.

44. *Las Vegas Sun,* February 6, 1972.

45. Alexis Jetter interview with Sondra Phillips, September 14, 1992; *Las Vegas Sun,* February 10, 1972.

46. *San Mateo Times,* February 9, 1972; author's interviews with Emma Stampley and Mary Wesley.

47. Author's interview with Jack Anderson; *Las Vegas Review-Journal,* February 8, 9, 1972; *LVV,* February 10, 1972; *San Mateo Times,* February 9, 1972.

48. *Las Vegas Sun,* February 10, 11, 1972.

49. Ibid.

50. See A. D. Hopkins, "Jay Sarno: He Came to Play" in Jack Sheehan, ed., *Players: The Men Who Made Las Vegas* (Reno: University of Nevada Press, 1997), pp. 92–103; *Las Vegas Sun,* February 10 and 11, 1972.

51. CCWRO Memo, "Eat In at Circus Circus, February 15, 1972," in CCWRO Food for All Files, in the possession of Maya Miller; *Las Vegas Sun,* February 16, 1972.

52. Author's interview with Jack Anderson; *LVV,* February 17, 1972; *Las Vegas Review-Journal,* February 11, 1972; author's interview with Mahlon Brown, April 22, 2003.

53. *LVV,* February 17, March 2, March 9, 1972; author's interview with Jack Anderson.

54. Author's interview with Jack Anderson; *Nevada State Journal,* March 11, 12, 1972.

55. Author's interview with David Phillips; author's interview with Mahlon Brown.

56. Ibid.

57. Author's interviews with Ruby Duncan and Harriet Trudell

58. *Las Vegas Sun,* February 20, 1972; author's interview with Harriet Trudell.

59. On the McGovern rules, see "Democratic Rules," http://www.cnn.com/allpolitics/1996/conventions/chicago/facts/rules/index.shtml.

60. Author's interviews with Ruby Duncan and Essie Henderson, December 11, 1994; "I am Harriet Trudell," MMP. See also "1972 State Democratic Party Policy Re: Welfare," RDP.

61. Beulah Sanders, "From the Chair," *The NWRO Welfare Fighter* (January–February 1972): 5; "Poor People's Election Year Campaign 1972," *National Welfare Rights Organization* (January 9–November 7, 1972); "NWRO Election Year Project Report," April 30, 1972, personal collection of Ruby Duncan.

62. Author's interview with Emma Stampley, March 19, 1997; *NYT,* June 29, 1972.

63. *The NWRO Welfare Fighter* (June 1972); author's interviews with Ruby Duncan and Essie Henderson, December 11, 1994; author's interview with Mary Wesley, September 7, 1992.

64. Guida West, *The National Welfare Rights Movement,* pp. 221–222.

65. *LVV,* August 3, 1972; author's interviews with Ruby Duncan, Alversa Beals, and Mary Southern, September 5, 1992.

66. Author's interview with Ruby Duncan and Essie Henderson, December 11, 1994.

67. *LVV*, August 24, 1972.

68. Author's interviews with Ruby Duncan, Essie Henderson (December 11, 1994) , Jack Anderson, and Mahlon Brown (April 22, 2003).

69. "Preliminary Proposal to Present Concept of Operation Life" prepared for General R. G. Taylor, Chairman of the Board, First Western Savings and Loan Association, April 1972, RDP.

70. "Preliminary Proposal to Present Concept of Operation Life," and "Clark County Welfare Rights Organization Report to the Campaign for Human Development," July 12, 1973, RDP; "Poverty USA—Catholic Campaign for Human Development—A hand up not a hand out," available online at http://www.usccb.org/cchd/povertyusa/about.htm.

71. "Preliminary Proposal to Present Concept of Operation Life," pp. 3–6; author's interviews with Mary Wesley (September 7, 1992), Alversa Beals (March 19, 1997), and Essie Henderson (December 9, 1994), Las Vegas, Nevada. .

72. "It Started a Simple Way," unpublished document (Operation Life Inc.), p. 3, cited in Edward Zuckerman, "Community Control and State Autonomy: A Study of Welfare Policy in Nevada," unpublished undergraduate thesis, The Evergreen State College (1977).

73. Author's interview with Glendora Washington, April 28, 2003, Las Vegas, Nevada; author's interview with Georgia Phillips, September 14, 1999, Las Vegas, Nevada; author's interview with Alversa Beals, April 21, 2003, Las Vegas, Nevada.

74. "From the Cottonfields Through CDC: Reminiscences of Mary Wesley and Alversa Beals," *Operation Life Community Press* (December 15, 1977), pp. 6–7; Bill Vincent, "Operation Life Has Brought Hope," *Las Vegas Review-Journal*, January 28, 1973.

75. *LVV*, August 24, 1972.

76. *Las Vegas Review-Journal*, August 20, 1973; author's interviews with Kenneth Phillips and Roy Duncan Jr., September 14, 1999.

77. *LVV*, November 16, 23, 1972; *Las Vegas Sun*, November 16, 1972.

78. *LVV*, July 20, August 3, 1972; author's interviews with Ruby Duncan and Maya Miller.

79. Author's interviews with Maya Miller, Ruby Duncan.

80. Author's interview with Jack Anderson. "I aimed at the public's heart and by accident I hit it in the stomach," author Upton Sinclair commented after publication of *The Jungle* (1906), his muckraking book on the meat-packing industry.

81. Author's telephone interview with Maya Miller, March 11, 1999; *Las Vegas Sun*, February 8, 1972; *Reno Gazette Journal*, March 31, 1973; *Nevada State Journal*, February 16, 1973 and March 31, 1973.

82. *Reno Evening Gazette*, March 15, 1973.

83. Author's interview with Maya Miller, September 2–3, 1992.

84. *Reno Evening Gazette*, March 31, 1973; *Los Angeles Times*, April 3, 1973; *NYT*, April 1, 4, 1973; *Boston Herald*, April 4, 1973; *Nevada State Journal*, April 1, 3, 1973; *Las Vegas Review-Journal*, April 11, 1973.

85. Author's interview with Maya Miller, September 2–3, 1992; *Nevada State Journal*, April 1, 1973 and April 3, 1973; "Maya Miller to Dear Friends of the Nevada Legislative Assembly," April 1, 1973, and "Ruby Duncan to Friends in the Legislature," April 2, 1973 (both in the personal collection of Maya Miller).

86. *Las Vegas Review-Journal,* April 3, 1973; "Early morning memo from Maya," transcript of radio broadcast and comments to UPI, n.d., personal collection of Maya Miller, Food Stamp file, Legislature 1973 file; *LVV,* March 22 and April 12, 1973.

87. *The Ages of Hunger,* p. 56.

88. Ibid.; author's interview with Ruby Duncan, September 5, 1992, Las Vegas, Nevada; author's interview with Jack Anderson.

89. Author's interviews with Ruby Duncan, September 5, 1992, and December 11, 1994.

90. Author's interview with Renee Diamond, September 5, 1992, Las Vegas, Nevada.

CHAPTER 7: "WE CAN DO IT AND DO IT BETTER":
RESHAPING A COMMUNITY FROM THE BOTTOM UP

1. Author's interview with Marty Makower, September 2–3, 1992, Carson City, Nevada.

2. Author's interview with Leola Harris, March 22, 1997, Las Vegas, Nevada.

3. Author's interview with Diane Guinn, March 19, 1997, Las Vegas, Nevada.

4. Author's interviews with Alversa Beals (March 22, 1997), Ruby Duncan (April 19, 2003), and Harriet Trudell (April 20, 2003), Las Vegas, Nevada.

5. *LVV,* November 23 and December 21, 1972; *Las Vegas Review-Journal,* January 28, 1973.

6. *Operation Life Community Press,* November 26, 1973, and December 21, 1973, MMP, Box 3.

7. *Las Vegas Review-Journal,* January 28, 1973.

8. 113th Congress, *Congressional Record* 2883 (February 8, 1967); U.S. Department of Health, Education, and Welfare, Office of Assistant Secretary for Program Coordination, *Report of the Program Analysis Group on Child Health* (1966).

9. Anne Marie Foltz, "The Development of Ambiguous Federal Policy: EPSDT," in *MMFQ/Health and Society* (Winter 1975), cited in Ed Zuckerman, *Community Control and State Autonomy: A Study of Welfare Policy in Nevada,*. unpublished senior thesis, The Evergreen State College (June 3, 1977).

10. Author's interview with Jack Anderson, September 10, 1992, Oakland, California; Ruby Duncan with John Dombrinck, "Welfare Mothers Push for Justice," *Operation Life Community Press,* January 29, 1974.

11. Author's interview with Jack Anderson; author's interview with George Miller, December 4, 1994, Carson City, Nevada.

12. The following description of how Operation Life was awarded state contracts both to open and to do outreach for an EPSDT clinic is based on the author's interviews with Jack Anderson (September 9, 1992, Oakland, California), Essie Henderson (December 9, 1994, Las Vegas, Nevada), and Alversa Beals (September 5, 1992, and March 19, 1997, Las Vegas, Nevada). I have also drawn on Ed Zuckerman, *Community Control and State Autonomy.*

13. Author's interview with Jack Anderson.

14. Ibid.

15. Author's interview with Jack Anderson; *EPSDT: Some Whys and Wherefores* (New York: United Church Board of Homeland Ministries, 1976).

16. *EPSDT: Some Whys and Wherefores,* pp. 7–8.

17. Ibid.; Jack Anderson, "Can Welfare Mothers Do Community Economic Development?" *Clearinghouse Review* (April 1980).

18. Anderson, "Can Welfare Mothers Do Community Economic Development?" See, too, the author's interview with Marty Makower, September 2–3, 1992, Carson City, Nevada; *Operation Life Community Health Center Annual Report*, 1975, RDP; *Operation Life Time Line of Programs, 1973–1986*, RDP; *Child Health Assurance Act of 1979, Report of the Commission on Interstate and Foreign Commerce to the Committee of the Whole House*, 96th Congress, 1st Session (October 1979) and *Child Health Assurance Act of 1979, Report of the Commission on Interstate and Foreign Commerce to the Senate*, 95th Congress, 2nd Session (August 1978).

19. Author's interview with Georgia Phillips, September 14, 1999, Las Vegas, Nevada.

20. *Operation Life Community Press*, January 17, 1974, MMP, Box 3; author's interview with Ruby Duncan, December 11, 1994.

21. *Operation Life Community Press*, January 17, 1974; author's interviews with Ruby Duncan and Essie Henderson, December 11, 1994, Las Vegas, Nevada.

22. *Operation Life Community Press*, November 26, 1973 and December 21, 1973, MMP, Box 3.

23. Interview with Aldine Weems, *Operation Life Community Press*, November 10, 1977.

24. See Grace Franklin and Randall Ripley, *C.E.T.A.: Politics and Policy, 1973–1982* (Knoxville: University of Tennessee Press, 1984); *Operation Life Community Press*, November 10 and December 15, 1977.

25. U.S. Department of Agriculture, Food Nutrition Service, "History of WIC 1974–1999 25th Anniversary" (1999); *WIC: A Success Story* (Washington, DC: Food Research and Action Center, 1983); author's interview with Diane Guinn; *LVV*, September 12, 1974.

26. U.S. Food and Nutrition Service, *Implementation and Status of the Special Supplemental Food Program for Women, Infants and Children* (Washington, DC: Government Printing Office, 1974).

27. Anderson, "Can Welfare Mothers Do Community Economic Development?" p. 931.

28. Author's interview with Ruby Duncan, December 11, 1994, Las Vegas, Nevada; Duncan, "Welfare Mothers Push for Justice"; *LVV*, January 31, 1974 and March 14, 1974; "Operation Life Case Study," Third Party Evaluation by Polaris Research and Development, commissioned by the U.S. Community Services Administration/Office of Economic Development, 1981, MMP, Box 6.

29. Author's interview with Glendora Washington, April 28, 2002, Las Vegas, Nevada.

30. *LVV*, January 31, 1974; see Sar Levitan and Clifford Johnson, "Did the Great Society and Subsequent Initiatives Work?" in Marshall Kaplan and Peggy L. Cuciti, eds., *The Great Society and Its Legacy: Twenty Years of U.S. Social Policy* (Durham, NC: Duke University Press, 1986)

31. *Operation Life Community Press*, December 15, 1977.

32. *Operation Life Time Line of Programs, 1973–1986*, RDP.

33. *Las Vegas Review-Journal*, June 30, 1974; author's interview with Alversa Beals, March 19, 1997, Las Vegas, Nevada.

34. *Reno Evening Gazette*, November 1, 1974; *LVV*, November 14, 1974.

35. Author's interview with Renia Glasper, April 29, 2003, Las Vegas, Nevada.

36. *LVV*, January 16, 1975.

37. *Operation Life Community Press*, January 29, 1974; author's interview with Ruby Duncan, April 29, 2003, Las Vegas, Nevada.

38. Author's interview with David Phillips, September 18, 1999, Las Vegas, Nevada.

39. Author's interview with Mary Wesley, September 7, 1992, Las Vegas, Nevada; *Operation Life*

Funding History, Polaris Research Third-Party Evaluation of Operation Life Community Development Corporation, August 1981, MMP; Nancy Lange, Operation Life Project Coordinator, to Reverend John Martinson, January 14, 1977, RDP.

40. *LVV,* March 20, March 27, and April 10, 1975.

41. *LVV,* February 13, 20, 27, and March 6, 1975.

42. Author's interview with Maya Miller, September 2–3, 1992, September 14, 1999, and April 25, 2003, Carson City, Nevada; author's interviews with Ruby Duncan, September 5, 1992, and April 19, 1997, Las Vegas, Nevada.

43. Full testimony of Maya Miller and Ruby Duncan at the National Democratic Platform Committee meeting, Atlanta Georgia, April 1976, MMP, Box 3.

44. *LVV,* April 29, May 20, and June 3, 1976.

45. For a nuanced discussion of the Humphrey-Hawkins bill set in the context of the history of federal employment policy, see Margaret Weir, *Politics and Jobs* (Princeton University Press, Princeton, NJ: 1992). See also Donald C. Baumer's review in *American Political Science Review* 87, no. 1 (March 1993) and Jody Lipford, "Twenty Years After Humphrey-Hawkins: An Assessment of Fiscal Policy" in *The Independent Review* 4, no 1 (Summer 1999): 41–62.

46. *LVV,* April 29, May 20, and June 3, 1976.

47. *LVV,* April 29, May 20, and June 3, 1976.

48. Author's interview with Ruby Duncan, September 6, 1992, Las Vegas, Nevada.

49. Ibid. See also author's interview with Maya Miller, September 2–3, 1997, Carson City, Nevada.

50. Ronald Reagan, "Remarks at a Dinner Honoring Senator Russell B. Long of Louisiana," October 16, 1985, text available online at www.reagan.utexas.edu/resource/speeches/1985/101685d.htm; for biographical information on Long, see Robert Mann, *Legacy to Power: Senator Russell Long of Louisiana* (New York: Paragon House, 1992).

51. The "ethnic purity" controversy is recounted in the PBS documentary *Jimmy Carter,* produced, written, and directed for the *American Experience* series by Adriana Bosch, and narrated by Linda Hunt (Alexandria, VA: PBS Video, 2002).

52. Author's interview with Ruby Duncan, April 29, 2003, Las Vegas, Nevada; *LVV,* October 27, 1976.

53. Author's interview with Essie Henderson, December 11, 1994, Las Vegas, Nevada; author's interview with Ruby Duncan, December 11, 1994, Las Vegas, Nevada; author's interview with Harriet Trudell, April 20, 2003, Las Vegas, Nevada.

54. Author's interview with Ruby Duncan, December 11, 1994; *Daily News* clipping, n.d., in possession of Sondra Phillips.

55. Author's interview with Alversa Beals, March 22, 1997. See, too, *LVV,* October 7, 14, 1976.

56. *LVV,* August 12, 1976.

57. Author's interview with Ruby Duncan, September 6, 1992, Las Vegas, Nevada; author's interview with George Miller, December 4, 1994, Carson City, Nevada.

58. Author's interview with Ruby Duncan, 1992; *LVV,* January 14, 1977.

59. Ray Marshall, *The Labor Department in the Carter Administration: A Summary Report - January 14, 1981,* "Employment and Training Administration (ETA)," U.S. Department of Labor, available online at http://www.dol.gov/asp/programs/history/carter-eta.htm.

60. Author's interview with Ruby Duncan, December 11, 1994.

61. Maya Miller, "What is the Significance of Operation Life and Ruby Duncan?" unpublished

typescript, MMP, Box 6. This was Miller's answer to a question from the Women's Bureau of the Department of Labor, January 1979.

62. *LVV,* October 7, 1976.

63. Ray Marshall, *The Labor Department in the Carter Administration; LVV,* October 6, 1976.

64. Maya Miller, "What is the Significance of Operation Life and Ruby Duncan?"

65. Jody Lipford, "Twenty Years After Humphrey-Hawkins." See Alice Kessler-Harris, *In Pursuit of Equity: Women, Men, and the Quest for Economic Citizenship in 20th Century America* (New York: Oxford University Press, 2001), Chapter 1, for a discussion of gender and the controversy surrounding the Full Employment Act of 1946. For an interesting discussion of econometric studies of Carter-era public employment programs, see Richard P. Nathan, "Social Science and the Great Society," in Marshall Kaplan and Peggy L. Cuciti, eds., *The Great Society and Its Legacy: Twenty Years of U.S. Social Policy* (Durham, NC: Duke University Press, 1986), pp. 163–178. On public employment policy, see Peter B. Edelman, "Creating Jobs for Americans: From MDTA to Industrial Policy," in Kaplan and Cuciti, pp. 91–105.

66. Author's interviews with Ruby Duncan, April 29, 2003, and December 11, 1994; Karen Tumulty, "Franklin Raines: The New Cutting Edge Budget Chief," online at http://www.cnn.com/ALLPOLITICS/1997/02/03/time/tumulty.html.

67. "Statement of Ruby Duncan, President Clark County Economic and Welfare Rights Organization," welfare reform testimony before the Senate Finance Committee, November 2, 1977, MMP, Box 2.

68. On feminists and Carter's welfare plan, see Marissa Chappel, "Rethinking Women's Politics in the 1970s: The League of Women Voters and the National Organization of Women Confront Poverty," *Journal of Women's History* 13, no. 4 (2002): 155–179; Maya Miller, "What is the Significance of Operation Life and Ruby Duncan?" p. 7. For Duncan's views, see *LVV,* April 14, 1974 and March 11, 1977, and "Statement of Ruby Duncan, President Clark County Economic and Welfare Rights Organization," November 2, 1977.

69. For a discussion of Nixon's bill, see Jill Quadagno, *The Color of Welfare* (New York: Oxford University Press, 1994). And, for comparisons of Nixon's and Carter's plans, see R. Kent Weaver, *Ending Welfare as We Know It* (Washington, D.C.: Brookings Press, 2000), pp. 54–101. Tillmon made these comments in "My Brother's Keeper," a segment of Terry Rockefeller and Henry Hampton's documentary *America's War on Poverty* (Alexandria, VA: PBS Video, 1995).

70. Johnnie Tillmon, "Welfare As a Women's Issue," *Ms.,* February 1972.

71. Author's interview with Mahlon Brown, April 22, 2003; *LVV,* April 17, 1974, and March 11, 1977.

72. Maya Miller, "What is the Significance of Operation Life and Ruby Duncan?"

73. Ibid.

74. Miller, "What is the Significance of Operation Life and Ruby Duncan?" p. 6; *LVV,* January 7, 1977.

CHAPTER 8: CAN WELFARE MOTHERS DO COMMUNITY ECONOMIC DEVELOPMENT?: THE TRIUMPHS AND TRIALS OF OPERATION LIFE

1. *Los Angeles Times,* March 11–14, 20, and 31, 1976.

2. Ibid.

3. See A. D. Hopkins, "The First 100 Persons Who Shaped Nevada—Al Bramlet: The Organizer," *Las Vegas Review-Journal,* available online at http:www.1st100.com/part3/bramlet. html.

4. *LVV,* November 12, 1976; "An Innovation in Job Development for Low Income Women," grant proposal submitted to the Campaign for Human Development, 1977, RDP.

5. Ibid.

6. *LVV,* August 19, 26, 1976.

7. *LVV,* September 3, 1976.

8. *LVV,* September 16, 1976.

9. "An Innovation in Job Development for Low Income Women," RDP.

10. *Operation Life Community Press,* November 10, 1977.

11. Ibid.

12. *Operation Life Community Press,* November 10, 1977; "An Innovation in Job Development," Minutes of the Coalition of Low Income Women, 1982–1987, RDP.

13. Author's interview with Mary Wesley, September 7, 1992, Las Vegas, Nevada.

14. Jack Anderson, "Can Welfare Mothers Do Economic Development?" *Clearinghouse Review* (April 1980); author's interview with Ruby Duncan, April 29, 2003, Las Vegas, Nevada.

15. I am grateful to Christina Greene and to Rhonda Williams for making me aware of how much this was a national trend. See Rhonda Williams, *The Politics of Public Housing: Black Women's Struggles Against Urban Inequality* (New York: Oxford University Press, 2004) and Christina Greene, *Our Separate Ways: Women and the Black Freedom Movement in Durham, North Carolina, 1940s–1970s* (Chapel Hill: University of North Carolina Press, forthcoming).

16. George Miller, Nevada Welfare Administrator, to Charles Goady, Commissioner, Department of Health, Education, and Welfare, February 27, 1976; Minor Kelso, Chief Nevada State Medical Care Services, to Ruby Duncan, Chair Operation Life, April 7, 1976; George Miller to Ruby Duncan, May 18, 1976. Nevada State Archives, State Capital Complex, Carson City, Nevada; Author's interview with George Miller, December 4, 1994, Carson City, Nevada.

17. *LVV,* August 12, 1976.

18. *LVV,* August 19 and September 9, 1976.

19. Ruby Duncan to Jay Carr, State Health Officer, Nevada, July 19, 1976; Jay Carr to Ruby Duncan, July 23, 1976. RDP; *LVV,* July 29, August 5, 1976.

20. *LVV,* December 3 and December 10, 1976.

21. Author's interview with Renee Diamond, September 13, 1999, Las Vegas, Nevada; *LVV,* December 3, 1976.

22. Author's interview with Renee Diamond, September 5, 1992, Las Vegas, Nevada; author's interview with Maya Miller, September 14, 1999, Carson City, Nevada; telephone message to author from Marilyn Romanelli, September 10, 1999.

23. *LVV,* December 3, 1976.

24. *LVV,* December 24, 1976; *Las Vegas Sun,* December 23, 1976.

25. *LVV,* December 24, 1976; Jack Anderson, "Can Welfare Mothers Do Community Economic Development?" *Clearinghouse Review* (April 1980): 929–934.

26. Author's interview with Maya Miller, September 2–3, 1992, Carson City, Nevada.

27. Nancy Lange, Operation Life Projects Coordinator, to Reverend John Martinson, January 14, 1977, fundraising letter, RDP.

28. Author's interviews with Alversa Beals, Renia Glasper, and Glendora Washington, April 28, 2003, Las Vegas, Nevada.
29. Author's interview with Alversa Beals, April 28, 2003.
30. Author's interview with Jack Anderson, September 10, 1992, Oakland, California.
31. *LVV,* November 27, 1975 and January 8, 15, 1976; *Operation Life Community Press,* November 15, 1977; *Operation Life CDC Annual Report,* Spring 1979, RDP.
32. Ibid.
33. Author's interview with Renee Diamond, September 13, 1999; Operation Life Day Care Center License Application, City Commission, City of Las Vegas, January 5, 1975, RDP.
    For insight into the history of urban public housing programs, see Rhonda Williams, *The Politics of Public Housing.* On race and public housing, see Ronald H. Bayor, "Urban Renewal, Public Housing and the Racial Shaping of Atlanta," *Journal of Policy History* 1 (1989): 419–439; John Bauman, Norman Hummon and Edward K. Muller, "Public Housing, Isolation and the Urban Underclass: Philadelphia's Richard Allen Homes, 1941–1965," *Journal of Urban History* (May 1991): 264–292; Robert Halpern, *Rebuilding the Inner City: A History of Neighborhood Initiatives to Address Poverty in the United States* (New York: Columbia University Press, 1995).
34. "Operation Life Funding History," in Proposal For Funding, from Ruby Duncan to Gehebre Mehreteab, Program Officer, Ford Foundation, April 22, 1982. Ford Foundation Archives, New York City. L82-197; author's interview with Marty Makower, September 3, 1992, Carson City, Nevada; author's interview with Diane Guinn, March 19, 1997, Las Vegas, Nevada. For a good overview of the history and effects of CETA see Grace A. Franklin and Randall Ripley, *C.E.T.A.: Politics and Policy, 1973–1982* (Knoxville: University of Tennessee Press, 1984).
35. *Operation Life Community Press,* interviews with Essie Henderson and Alversa Beals, December 15, 1977; author's interview with Mary Wesley.
36. See RDP for numerous letters of appointment to Las Vegas and Clark County posts.
37. Author's interview with Maya Miller, September 2–3, 1992, Carson City, Nevada; *Operation Life CDC Annual Report,* Spring 1979.
38. Author's interview with Diane Guinn ; author's interview with Maya Miller, September 15, 1999, Carson City, Nevada.
39. Author's interviews with Marty Makower, September 2–3, 1992, Carson City, Nevada, and April 11, 1997, Oakland, California.
40. Report of the Twentieth Century Fund Task Force on Community Development Corporations, *CDCs: New Hope for the Inner City* (New York, 1971), p. 42. See too Harry Edward Berndt, *New Rulers in the Ghetto: The Community Development Corporation and Urban Poverty* (Greenwich, CT: Greenwood, 1977), pp. 32–33; *Amendment to S2007, The Economic Opportunity Act, Title VII, Community Economic Development* (June 9, 1971) and *Economic and Community Partnership Act of 1974,* Bill S3789 (July 23, 1973); Robert Zdenek, "Community Development Corporations" in Severyn T. Bruyn and James Meehan, eds., *Beyond the Market and the State: New Directions in Community Development* (Philadelphia: Temple University Press, 1987), pp. 112–127.
41. Neal R. Peirce and Carol F. Steinbach, *Corrective Capitalism: The Rise of America's Community Development Corporations* (New York: Ford Foundation, 1987), pp. 57–59; Greg Squires,

ed., *Organizing Access to Capital: Advocacy and the Democratization of Financial Institutions* (Philadelphia: Temple University Press, 2003).

42. Author's interview with Maya Miller, September 2–3, 1992; *Operation Life CDC Annual Report,* Spring 1979, RDP.

43. *CDCs: New Hope for the Inner City,* p. 42.

44. Author's interview with Ruby Duncan, September 6, 1992, Las Vegas, Nevada.

45. Letters to Ruby Duncan and Ella Stackhouse, November 8, 1977, from Richard A. Pettigrew, Assistant to the President for Reorganization, the White House, in the Jimmy Carter Presidential Library, MC-3.

46. *Operation Life Community Press,* December 15, 1977.

47. Author's interviews with Mary Wesley, March 22, 1997, and Rosie Seals, March 20, 1997; interviews with Mary Wesley and Aldine Weems, *Operation Life Community Press,* December 15, 1977.

48. *Operation Life Community Press,* November 10, 1977 and December 15, 1977; *Operation Life CDC Annual Report,* Spring 1979.

49. Author's interview with Marty Makower, April 11, 1997.

50. *Operation Life Community Press,* December 15, 1977; *Operation Life CDC Annual Report,* Spring 1979, RDP.

51. *Operation Life CDC Annual Report,* Spring 1979; author's interview with Marty Makower, September 2–3, 1992.

52. Jack Anderson, "Can Welfare Mothers Do Economic Development?"

53. Paul Starr, "Health Care for the Poor," in Sheldon Danziger and Daniel Weinberg, eds., *Fighting Poverty: What Works and What Doesn't* (Cambridge: Harvard University Press, 1986), pp. 106–132

54. Jack Anderson, "Can Welfare Mothers Do Economic Development?"; "Welfare Mothers Are Doing Community Development," Operation Life leaflet, July–August 1980, MMP, Box 7.

55. *Operation Life Community Press,* November 10, 1977.

56. Ibid.

57. Jimmy Guy Tucker to Ruby Duncan, July 10, 1979, RDP; Arnie Miller, Memorandum for the President, September 18, 1979, Jimmy Carter Presidential Library, PB 10; *Las Vegas Sun,* July 24, 1979; *Washington Post,* July 27, 1979; *NYT,* July 20, 1979; author's interview with Ruby Duncan, April 14, 1997, Las Vegas, Nevada.

58. *LVV,* September 14 and 21, 1978.

59. *LVV,* February 24, 1978; *LVV,* September 7, 14, 19, 21, 1978.

60. Author's interview with Father Louis Vitale, December 9, 1994, Las Vegas, Nevada.

61. Author's interview with Kenneth Phillips, September 12, 1999, Las Vegas, Nevada.

62. Handwritten notes on August 18, 1980, meeting with Mukai, MMP, Box 6, OLCDC Mukai Folder.

63. Notes on phone conversations, August 20, 1980 (Maya Miller and Sylvia Brown) and August 22, 1980 (Maya Miller and Ruby Duncan); MMP, Box 6.

64. Handwritten notes on August 18, 1980, meeting with Mukai; notes on phone conversations, August 20, 1980 (Maya Miller and Sylvia Brown) and August 22, 1980 (Maya Miller and Ruby Duncan).

65. *Congressional Quarterly Almanac* (1981), pp. 32, 256, 490–491.

66. Ibid. See also R. Kent Weaver, *Ending Welfare as We Know It* (Washington, D.C.: Brookings Institution Press, 2000), pp. 68–69.

67. Weaver, *Ending Welfare as We Know It; Congressional Quarterly Almanac* (1981).

68. Center on Budget and Policy Priorities, "Falling Behind: A Report on How Blacks Have Fared Under Reagan," *Journal of Black Studies* 17, no. 2 (December 1986): 148–172.

69. See Timothy Conlan, "The Politics of Federal Block Grants: From Nixon to Reagan," from *Political Science Quarterly* 99, no. 2 (Summer 1984): 247–270.

70. David Cohen, Associate Director of OED, to CDC Directors, July 15, 1981, RDP; Randy Stoecker, "The CDC Model of Urban Redevelopment: A Critique and an Alternative," *Journal of Urban Affairs* 19, no. 1 (1997): 1–22.

71. Sylvia Brown and David Cohen, Community Services Administration/Office of Economic Development, to Ruby Duncan, June 1, 1981, RDP.

72. Ibid.; Operation Life Senior Staff Meeting Minutes, September 30, 1980, RDP.

73. Patricia Kelley to Maya Miller, Chair of the Board, Operation Life CDC, June 14, 1981, CC: Dick Ellis, Title VII Project Director, Case Study of Operation Life for Office of Economic Development/Community Services Administration, MMP, Box 6.

74. Ibid.

75. Numerous documents in RDP document Operation Life's relationship with federal authorities during the 1980s, and the positive impact of its good relations with local government. See, among others, Ruby Duncan to Eve Hillenberg, Office of Community Services (Health and Human Services), January 26, 1982; Thomas Coyle, Office of Community Services, to Ruby Duncan, July 23, 1982 and August 11, 1982, discussing funding from city and county block grant programs, and from private foundations, as support for receiving funds from the federal government.

Author's interview with George Miller.

76. *LVV,* May 14, 1981; *Las Vegas Sun,* August 1, 1983.

77. *Operation Life Community Press,* March 1978. *Operation Life Community Press* started printing a regular column from the Sagebrush Alliance about radiation exposure and cancer.

78. Author's interview with Father Louis Vitale.

79. See the large collection of grant proposals relating to the Cove, RDP.

80. *LVV,* September 11, 1982.

81. Franklin and Ripley, *C.E.T.A: Politics and Policy,* pp. 185–211; Burt Barnow, "Thirty Years of Changing Federal, State and Local Relationships in Employment and Training Programs," *Publius* 23, no. 3 (1993): 75–94.

82. John P. MacKenzie, "Capitalistic Poverty Law," *NYT,* November 27, 1983.

83. Ruby Duncan to Gehebre Mehreteab, Program Officer, Ford Foundation, April 22, 1982, and Ruby Duncan to Bernard McDonald, Ford Foundation, April 30, 1982, in the Operation Life Files at the Ford Foundation Archives, New York City.

84. Ruby Duncan proposed these projects to program officer Ghebre Mehreteab, in letters dated November 18 and 22, 1982. See also "Recommendation For Grant Action," August 9, 1984, Susan V. Berresford to Franklin A. Thomas, in the Operation Life Files at the Ford Foundation Archives, New York City, and "A Very Special Meeting," a leaflet promoting the Operation Life meeting with Ford officers in December 1982, RDP.

85. See CLIW files, RDP.

86. Teresita Arroyo to Ruby Duncan, August 24, 1981; CLIW Record of Activities, February 22–28, 1982, RDP.

87. Author's interview with Sharon Glover Wilson, September 14, 1999, Las Vegas, Nevada.

88. Ruby Duncan to Robert Curvin, Program Director, Ford Foundation, February 14, 1991, Ford Foundation Archives; Flyer, "Big Girls Bundle of Joy Fashion Show," personal collection of Ruby Duncan; CLIW Report of Activities, June 1982, RDP; Ruby Duncan Release, April 27, 1983, personal collection of Ruby Duncan.

89. Author's interview with Renee Diamond, September 5, 1992; author's interview with Ana Luna, September 14, 1999, Las Vegas, Nevada.

90. Ruby Duncan to Jean Ford, December 31, 1985; Operation Life Grant Proposal to the Nevada Office of Community Services; Ruby Duncan Grant Proposal to the Charles Bannerman Fellowship Program for 1987 to 1989, RDP.

91. Author's interview with Georgia Phillips, September 14, 1999, Las Vegas, Nevada; author's interviews with Ruby Duncan, September 6, 1992 and April 14, 1997.

92. *Las Vegas Sun,* April 6, 1987, and March 26, 1988.

93. Author's interviews with Harriet Trudell, by telephone, March 11, 1997, and April 22, 2003, Las Vegas, Nevada.

CHAPTER 9: MAYBE WE WERE FIGHTING HISTORY: THE LEGACY OF OPERATION LIFE

1. Operation Life CDC Board of Trustees Meeting, n.d., 1986, RDP.

2. Ruby Duncan to Jean Ford, Nevada Office of Community Services, Grant Application, December 31, 1985, RDP; Edward Davis, "Homelessness in Las Vegas, Nevada: An Empirical Assessment of Poverty Amongst Plenty," unpublished paper presented at the Biennial Regional Inter-University Consortium on Social Development, 1989; Martin Kuz, "Working but Homeless," *Las Vegas Sun,* March 21, 1999.

3. *Emperor Jones/Paul Robeson: Tribute to An Artist,* Eugene O'Neill's play directed by Dudley Murphy (1933), with a tribute to Paul Robeson narrated by Sidney Poitier. Available from Home Vision Entertainment (1994).

4. *Las Vegas Sun,* January 29, February 3 and 5, 1980; typescript of Albert Dunn Press Conference, February 2, 1980, MMP.

5. *Las Vegas Review-Journal,* July 9, 1986; *Las Vegas Sun,* July 9, 1986. See also Susan Berresford to Franklin A. Thomas, "Recommendation for Grant Action," August 9, 1984, in the Operation Life files, Ford Foundation Archives, New York City.

6. *Operation Life Press Release,* July 7, 1986, RDP; *Las Vegas Review-Journal,* July 9, 1986; *Las Vegas Sun,* July 9, 1986.

7. *Operation Life Press Release,* July 7, 1986, RDP, pp. 3, 6.

8. *Operation Life Press Release,* July 7, 1986, RDP; *Las Vegas Review-Journal,* July 11, 1986; *Las Vegas Sun,* July 15, 1986.

9. Ruby Duncan to Congressman Joe Kennedy, May 15, 1989. Part of a package of documentation of Operation Life's troubles dating back to the 1986 battle with the city and communications during that crisis, asking for help. RDP, Box 17, Folder 29.

10. *Las Vegas Sun*, September 25, 1986; Thalia Dondero, Chair, Clark County Board of Commissioners, to Ruby Duncan, October 29, 1986; David Kirker, Director, HHS Office of Community Services, to Aldine Weems, September 25, 1986, RDP, Box 16, Folder 21.

11. Author's interviews with Ruby Duncan, September 14, 1999, and April 19, 2003, Las Vegas, Nevada; author's interviews with Glendora Jackson and Renia Beals, April 28, 2003, Las Vegas, Nevada; author's interview with Harriet Trudell, April 20, 2003, Las Vegas, Nevada; author's interview with Diane Guinn, March 22, 1997, Las Vegas, Nevada.

12. Author's interview with Harriet Trudell, April 20, 2003, Las Vegas, Nevada; *Las Vegas Review-Journal*, May 8, 1987.

13. Paul Starr, "Health Care for the Poor: The Past Twenty Years," in Sheldon Danziger and Daniel H. Weinberg, eds., *Fighting Poverty: What Works and What Doesn't* (Cambridge: Harvard University Press, 1986), p. 112.

14. Author's interview with Renee Diamond, September 5, 1992, Las Vegas, Nevada.

15. Department of Health and Human Services Public Health Service Region IX Memo, April 5, 1983: From Kent Angerbauer, Director, Division of Health Services to Deliver, to Chairpersons, Board of Directors, Region IX Community Health Centers, RDP; Minutes of the Operation Life Medical Center Board of Trustees, July 1985, RDP. .

16. *Las Vegas Sun*, September 25, 1986.

17. Author's interview with Marty Makower, September 2–3, 1992, Carson City, Nevada.

18. *Las Vegas Review-Journal*, December 11, 1986.

19. Sheridan Weinstein, Region IX HHS Health Administrator, to Aileen O'Neill, Chair, Board of Directors Operation Life Medical Center, December 4, 1986, RDP; *Las Vegas Review-Journal*, December 19, 1986; *Las Vegas Sun*, December 11, 1986.

20. Author's interview with George Miller, December 4, 1994, Carson City, Nevada; "Summary" (of events surrounding the clinic defunding), sent as attachment in Ruby Duncan to Maya Miller, May 11, 1989, MMP.

21. Minutes, Operation Life Board CDC Board of Trustees Meeting, October 27, 1987, RDP.

22. Aileen O'Neill to Barbara Vucanovich, February 20, 1987; Barbara Vucanovich to Aileen O'Neill, February 24, 1987; James Tyree to Aileen O'Neill, February 20, 1987; Richard Coughlin to Aileen O'Neill, February 23, 1987; William Pearson to Aileen O'Neill, February 24, 1987. RDP, Box 16, Folder 22.

23. *Las Vegas Review-Journal*, January 9, February 14, and April 23, 1987; "OL Board of Trustees Meeting Minutes," October 27, 1987, RDP.

24. *Las Vegas Sun*, January 19, 1987; Jack Anderson to Jean Wiley, November 16, 1989, RDP; author's interview with Alversa Beals, April 19, 2003, Las Vegas, Nevada.

25. Neal R. Peirce and Carol F. Steinbach, *Corrective Capitalism: The Rise of America's Community Development Corporations* (New York: Ford Foundation, 1987), pp. 45–46; *Las Vegas Sun*, January 19, 1987; *Reno Gazette Journal*, January 19, 1988.

26. *Las Vegas Sun*, July 20, 1988.

27. Joseph Denny to Ruby Duncan, July 1, 1988; Kathryn Haag to Ruth Moore, July 1, 1988; Ruby Duncan to Ruth Moore, July 11, 1988; Ruth Moore to Ruby Duncan, July 12, 1988, RDP.

28. Operation Life Board of Trustees Meeting Minutes, October 27, 1987, RDP; Maya Miller to Ruby Duncan, April 23, 1989; Ruby Duncan to Maya Miller, May 11, 1989, MMP.

29. Maya Miller to Ruby Duncan, April 23, 1989, RDP.

30. *Las Vegas Review-Journal,* February 27 and April 19, 1989; *Las Vegas Sun,* April 6 and May 9, 1989; author's interview with Renee Diamond, September 5, 1992, Las Vegas, Nevada.

31. Author's interview with Mary Southern, September 5, 1992, Las Vegas, Nevada.

32. *Las Vegas Sun,* November 28, 1988. See also the various proposals for funding to transform the Cove during the 1980s, RDP.

33. Author's interview with Ruby Duncan, September 11 and 12, 1999, Las Vegas, Nevada; *Las Vegas Sun,* July 27, 1989.

34. *Las Vegas Review-Journal,* January 24 and July 28, 1989; author's interview with Father Louis Vitale, December 11, 1994, Las Vegas, Nevada.

35. *Las Vegas Sun,* January 25, 1990; *Las Vegas Review-Journal,* January 25, 1990; author's interviews with Maya Miller, April 19, 2003, Carson City, Nevada, and Ruby Duncan, April 21, 2003, Las Vegas, Nevada.

36. Ruby Duncan to Othello Poulard, September 15, 1989; Ruby Duncan to Jack Anderson, September 15, 1989; Ruby Duncan to Audrey Rowe, January 23, 1990, RDP.

37. Economic Opportunity Board of Clark County Memorandum from James Tyree, May 31, 1991, RDP; author's interview with Harriet Trudell, April 22, 2003, Las Vegas, Nevada.

38. Ruby Duncan to Robert Curvin and Diane Bermudez, Ford Foundation, February 14, 1991, Operation Life Collection. 84-723. Ford Foundation Archive. New York City.

39. Author's interview with Ana Luna, September 14, 1999, Las Vegas, Nevada. A letter from Nevada health official Martin Brown to Operation Life, dated January 6, 1992, states that Operation Life's WIC program was funded to run through September 30, 1992. RDP.

40. Author's interview with Louis Vitale, December 9, 1994.

41. Robert E. Parker, "Social Costs of Rapid Urbanization," in Hal Rothman and Mike Davis, eds., *The Grit Beneath the Glitter: Tales from the Real Las Vegas* (Berkeley, CA: University of California Press, 2002), pp. 126–144; author's interview with Alversa Beals.

42. Author's interview with Mary Wesley, by telephone, September 11, 1999; author's interview with Rosie Seals, by telephone, December 15, 2003.

43. Author's interview with Essie Henderson, April 29, 2003, Las Vegas, Nevada.

44. Author's interview with Essie Henderson, December 8, 1994, Las Vegas, Nevada; author's interviews with Georgia Phillips, Sharon Glover Wilson, and Ana Luna, September 15, 1999, Las Vegas, Nevada; author's interview with Georgia Phillips, April 21, 2003, Las Vegas, Nevada.

45. Author's interview with Rosie Seals, April 22, 2003, Las Vegas, Nevada.

46. Author's interviews with Roy Duncan Jr. and Kenneth Phillips, September 12, 1999, Las Vegas, Nevada; author's interview with Georgia Phillips, September 15, 1999, Las Vegas, Nevada.

47. "Key Provisions in TANF Reauthorization Bills Passed by the Senate Finance Committee and the House," September 22, 2003, available on the Center on Budget and Policy Priorities Web site, http://www.cbpp.org/9-22-03tanf.htm.

48. Ibid. See also Sharon Parrott, Heidi Goldberg, and Shawn Fremstad, "Recycling an Unwise Proposal: State Concerns and New State Fiscal Realities Ignored in House Republican Welfare Bill," February 12, 2003, Center on Budget and Policy Priorities Web site, http://www.cbpp.org/2-7-03tanf.htm.

49. *Washington Post,* September 16, 2003; Vicky Lovell, "40-hour Work Proposal Significantly

Raises Mothers' Employment Standard," Institute for Women's Policy Research Publication D4 57 (Washington, DC: Institute for Women's Policy Research, June 2003).

50. *NYT,* September 3, 2003; "Confronting Hunger," *Center for Community Change News,* Winter 2005 (Washington, DC: Center for Community Change).

51. Author's interview with Jack Anderson.

52. Pierce and Steinbach, *Corrective Capitalism,* p. 58; Patricia Kelley, Third Party CSA Evaluator, to Maya Miller, Chair of the Board, Operation Life, June 1981, MMP.

53. See the Women's Economic Agenda Project Web site, http://www.weap.org; the Kensington Welfare Rights Union Web site, http://www.kwru.org; Alexis Jetter, "Welfare Warriors," *Harper's Bazaar,* September 1997.

54. "Close to Home," Ford Foundation analysis of human rights work in the United States, available online at http://www.fordfound.org/publications/recent_articles/close_to_home .cfm.

INDEX